JESUS

A Heart Full of Grace

JESUS

A Heart Full of Grace

WILLIAM G. JOHNSSON

REVIEW AND HERALD® PUBLISHING ASSOCIATION
HAGERSTOWN, MD 21740

The Review and Herald Publishing Association publishes biblically based materials for
spiritual, physical, and mental growth and Christian discipleship.

The author assumes full responsibility for the accuracy of all facts and quotations as
cited in this book.

Texts credited to Message are from *The Message*. Copyright © 1993, 1994, 1995,
1996, 2000, 2001, 2002. Used by permission of NavPress Publishing Group.

Texts credited to NIV are from the *Holy Bible, New International Version*. Copyright
© 1973, 1978, 1984, International Bible Society. Used by permission of Zondervan
Bible Publishers.

Texts credited to NKJV are from the New King James Version. Copyright © 1979,
1980, 1982 by Thomas Nelson, Inc. Used by permission. All rights reserved.

Bible texts credited to RSV are from the Revised Standard Version of the Bible,
copyright © 1946, 1952, 1971, by the Division of Christian Education of the National
Council of the Churches of Christ in the U.S.A. Used by permission.

Bible texts credited to RV are from *The Holy Bible,* Revised Version, Oxford
University Press, 1911.

This book was
Edited by Jeannette R. Johnson
Copyedited by James Cavil
Designed by Trent Truman
Cover art © Jay Bryant Ward. By arrangement with Mill Pond Press, Inc., Venice, Florida
34285. For information on art prints by Jay Bryant Ward, please contact Mill Pond Press
at 1-800-535-0331.
Electronic makeup by Shirley M. Bolivar
Typeset: 11/13 Berkeley Book

PRINTED IN U.S.A.

10 09 08 07 06   5 4 3 2 1

R&H Cataloging Service
Johnsson, William George, 1934-
    Jesus: A heart full of grace.

    1. Jesus Christ.   2. Devotional calendars—Seventh-day Adventists.
3. Devotional literature.   I. Title.

                    242.2

ISBN 10: 0-8280-1988-6
ISBN 13: 978-0-8280-1988-0

To

MADELEINE MARGARET JOHNSSON

and

JACQUELINE FRANCES JOHNSSON,

Beloved Granddaughters,
Gifts of Grace

Preface

some years ago I wrote a book of daily devotional readings on
the life of Jesus Christ. Titled *Behold His Glory,* it was based on
John 1:14: "And the Word was made flesh, and dwelt among
us, (and we beheld his glory, the glory as of the only begotten
of the Father,) full of grace and truth." That book brought the largest ongoing response of anything I ever wrote.

Now, almost 20 years later, I have prepared a new book of daily med-
itations. And I have come back to John 1:14, but with a difference.
Whereas the earlier work focused on the first half of the passage, this one,
Jesus: A Heart Full of Grace, centers on its second half.

I have been blessed in writing these readings. New insights into the
marvel of grace have enriched my understanding and led me to a closer
walk with the Master. The manuscript itself is a work of grace—grace, and
grace alone, made it possible. Two weeks after I began work on it, I was
given the most challenging and demanding work assignment of my entire
life—a project that so filled my waking hours and troubled my nights that
it seemed impossible to contemplate completing the just-begun
manuscript. And yet here it is; I praise God for it.

Several people assisted me in preparing the manuscript. Chitra
Barnabas keyed in the first 100 or so readings. Then Rachel Child took
over, not only completing the mechanical work but encouraging me by
suggesting a number of ideas for readings. Finally, my life partner,
Noelene, prayed me through the task and shared Bible texts that impressed her. Several of them formed the foundation for readings. To each
of these wonderful people, my deep appreciation.

JANUARY

Jesus

Jesus did many other things as well. If every one of them were written down, I suppose that even the whole world would not have room for the books that would be written. John 21:25, NIV.

Of all the names given children since the dawn of time, one stands alone, solitary, immovable. Although many men and women now take that name in oath or jest, one day every knee in heaven and earth will bow before Him who bears it and declare that He is King of kings and Lord of lords. That name is the sweetest sound to come from infant lips; it sustains us through life; and it will be our security when we embark on our final journey.

Jesus.

All our hopes—for this world and the next—center in Him. Our best joys, our highest aspirations, our cleanest motivations, spring from Him. Every other name will pass away; His, never.

It took me a long time as a minister of the gospel to get it—that the only preaching that really matters is that in which Jesus comes first, last, and center. It took me a long time as a Christian writer to get it—that the only topic that really matters is Jesus, full of grace.

So for quite a while now I have tried to write and preach grace. Which is to preach Jesus, because He is grace embodied. My efforts have been weak and vastly inadequate for the grandeur of the topic. But this I have found, again and again: regardless of my failings, a blessing has always come with the message.

Always.

So there will be a blessing in these readings, of that I am totally confident. Not because of any skill in my hand, but because of the subject. Unless I get in the way, the grace of Jesus will flow through these pages, warming and changing hearts and lives.

We have a full year on this topic, and I am excited, can hardly wait to get into it. But at the end of the 365 days we will have just begun. We will have been like children trying to ladle out blessings with a teaspoon from the vast ocean of grace. All the books that could ever be written wouldn't be enough to drain this topic dry.

Jesus is wonderful. He is the Man of matchless charms. He is our Friend, our Savior, our Lord. He is full of grace.

Getting It

And Elisha prayed, "O Lord, open his eyes so he may see." Then the Lord opened the servant's eyes, and he looked and saw the hills full of horses and chariots of fire all around Elisha. 2 Kings 6:17, NIV.

She was an old woman—in her mid-80s, she told me as we visited together after the church service. I had been preaching about grace; now she stunned me by saying, "At last I get it. I grew up in the church, but only in the past few months do I get it!"

"Get what?" I asked.

"That I don't have to do anything to make God love me. That He accepts me just as I am because Jesus died for me. What a difference that makes!"

She was like the young man with Elisha. The king of Aram sent horses, chariots, and soldiers to capture Elisha, who had been alerting the king of Israel to the Arameans' battle plans. The Aramean army came and surrounded Dothan, where Elijah was staying.

Early the next morning Elisha's servant got up and saw the enemy forces encamped all around. "Oh, my lord, what shall we do?" he cried out (2 Kings 6:15, NIV).

But the prophet replied, "Don't be afraid. Those who are with us are more than those who are with them" (verse 16, NIV). And then, after Elisha prayed, the Lord opened the young man's eyes, and he saw the hosts of heaven all around. He got it.

Could we be like Elijah's servant? Could we grow up in the church, go through elementary school, academy, even college, and never get it? Could we sit in the pews, return the tithe, be active in service, and never see the grace that surrounds us like a cloud?

Yes. The old woman's experience tells us that it could happen to us.

Let me go one step further. Could I be a church employee, even a minister, and never get it?

The answer makes me tremble: Yes!

Grace is out of this world. Unless the Lord opens our eyes, we'll never get it.

Lord, open my eyes so that I may get it!

The Atmosphere of Grace

I have swept away your offenses like a cloud, your sins like the morning mist. Return to me, for I have redeemed you. Isa. 44:22, NIV.

I'm a morning person. Most days you'll find me up before dawn, spending a quiet time with the Word and the Lord of the Word, and then heading out to walk to a park near our home. Often Noelene goes with me, and we walk and talk together with the Lord.

In the cold winter months I make the three-mile circuit long before sunup. Even on a moonless morning the stars supply ample light. They sparkle through the clear sky.

It's a wonderful way to start the day. I love the quiet, the peace. I love the feel of rested muscles stretching. I love the sight of an occasional deer or bluebird. Above all, I love the cool, clean air.

On these walks Ellen White's words about grace often come into my thoughts: "In the matchless gift of His Son, God has encircled the whole world with an atmosphere of grace as real as the air which circulates around the globe. All who choose to breathe this life-giving atmosphere will live and grow up to the stature of men and women in Christ Jesus" (*Steps to Christ*, p. 68).

What a marvelous thought—the atmosphere of grace! God's love surrounds us, before and behind, front and back, and on the side. We don't have to try to find grace—we are *in* grace.

This grace sustains the world. Even those who don't know it's there, who may deny God or cuss His name, benefit from it. The atmosphere of grace keeps purifying this earth of the filth and stench of sin, blowing in hope and life and a fresh start.

God invites us to breathe in this life-giving atmosphere. He invites us to inhale deeply and relax in Him. To keep breathing in grace, living and growing to the stature of men and women in Jesus Christ.

So, dear friend, breathe it in! Take a deep, deep breath and know that God loves you, that He desires to give you fullness of life right here and now, and an eternal existence in His presence. Know that just as the air always surrounds you, you can never go beyond the atmosphere of grace. No boundaries, no limits. God is always there for you.

How can I be so sure? Because God gave us Jesus, His only Son. God gave Himself.

History can never be the same; this world never the same. We're surrounded by an atmosphere of grace.

Paul's Favorite Word

To all who are in Rome, beloved of God, called to be saints: Grace to you and peace from God our Father and the Lord Jesus Christ. Rom. 1:7, NKJV.

The apostle Paul loved that word "grace." Usually he commenced his letters in the same way he started the Epistle to the Romans: "Grace to you and peace from God our Father and the Lord Jesus Christ" (Rom. 1:7, NKJV). Almost always he closed in a similar fashion, as in his final words to the church in Corinth: "The grace of our Lord Jesus Christ be with you" (1 Cor. 16:23; cf. 2 Cor. 13:14; Gal. 6:18; Eph. 6:24; Phil. 4:23; Col. 4:18; 1 Thess. 5:28, etc.).

In fact, Paul refers to grace about 100 times, far more than any other writer of the New Testament.

Why is this? Surely because Paul was ever conscious of God's saving power in his experience. All sin is heinous, but Paul's had a quality that set him apart from the former experiences of the other Christians. Paul, first known as Saul, wreaked havoc on the early church. Consumed with misguided zeal, he poured his energies into rooting out the hated followers of the Way. He forced himself into their homes and dragged off men and women to prison.

Not content with crushing the movement in and around Jerusalem, he sought letters from the high priest so that he might extend the work in Damascus. Luke's language in Acts gives us the picture: "breathing threats and murder against the disciples of the Lord" (Acts 9:1, NKJV).

Saul's reputation had spread far and wide. Even the godly Ananias, whom God told to go to Saul, was reluctant to go to him in his blindness (verse 13).

Paul never forgot where he had come from, calling himself the chief of sinners (1 Tim. 1:15) and "the least of the apostles," one not worthy to be called an apostle because he had persecuted the church of God (1 Cor. 15:9, NKJV).

But he could also write, "But by the grace of God I am what I am, and his grace to me was not without effect. No, I worked harder than all of them—yet not I, but the grace of God that was with me" (verse 10, NIV).

Grace made the difference in Paul—in his life and in his work. No wonder it became his favorite word.

The Day I Did It Right

Very rarely will anyone die for a righteous man, though for a good man someone might possibly dare to die. But God demonstrates his own love for us in this: While we were still sinners, Christ died for us. Rom. 5:7, 8, NIV.

God didn't wait for us to clean up our act before He sent Jesus to die for us. *While we were still sinners,* God came to us to set us free. That's grace.

Now Christ calls us, as His followers, to carry on His work. To love the unlovely, to give without attaching strings—this makes for fine sermons, but it is so hard to live out each day.

My life and ministry have at best been mixed. At times they have manifested grace; too often they have demonstrated self.

But one time I got it right. (Remember, for this one time there are scores of experiences on the other side.)

This day happened a long way back, when Noelene and I had just married and were starting out our ministry. Our first posting was at Vincent Hill School, a boarding institution in India, some 7,000 feet up in the Himalayas. The 12-grade school catered mainly to missionaries' kids; I was dean of boys and taught some Bible and other classes.

I recall well two brothers whom I had in the boys' hostel. The older, David, was tall, worked hard, and never got into trouble. Leslie, his brother, was short and often in trouble.

One Sabbath Leslie was making toast in his room. Toasters were banned in the dorm. The dean's apartment was situated on the ground level, and the smell of toast wafted down to the dean's nose. Soon I was up the stairs and knocking at Leslie's door.

Leslie scrambled to hide the evidence, but the room smelled undeniably of toast. He tensed up. He told me many years later that I simply looked around and said, "Les, could I borrow a tie for church?" He gave me one, and I walked out.

I have but the faintest recollection of the incident; but not Leslie. His life turned around that Sabbath morning when he didn't receive the punishment he deserved. That day I did it right.

Leslie went on to become a Seventh-day Adventist minister and missionary. It all began with a grace moment.

The Man Who Won't Go Away

He began to call down curses on himself, and he swore to them, "I don't know this man you're talking about." Mark 14:71, NIV.

Jesus, who changed the course of history more than anyone else, still impacts vast multitudes today—even of those who don't confess His name.

His name is uttered millions of times every day. For most it is spoken as a swearword, usually expressing dismay or disgust.

Ever wondered why people say "Jesus!" when they're angry or unhappy? You don't hear "Buddha!" or "Muhammad!" or "Krishna!" Why is it always the name of the Man of Galilee?

Could it be that Jesus, whom they seek to reject, is never far from their thoughts? Might there be a question festering deep within them about who this person really was, whether He might just have been who He claimed to be—the Son of God?

Jesus is the man who won't go away.

It was like that from the beginning in Galilee.

They tried to cast scorn on His person by saying He was illegitimate. But the crowds flocked to hear Him, to touch Him, to be made whole.

They said He cast out demons by Beelzebub, the prince of demons. But the demons came out, crying aloud, "I know who you are—the Holy One of God!" (Mark 1:24, NIV).

They said He was going crazy—even His own family said that and tried to take Him away from the crowds and back home (Mark 3:21). But He kept right on with His mission.

They told Him that King Herod was out to get Him, that He'd better run away and hide. But He didn't cringe, didn't flinch.

They came by night and seized Him in the garden, a traitor leading them to Him. They bound and beat Him and put Him through a kangaroo court. But He didn't try to escape.

They nailed Him to a cross, and sat around until He died. They thought that He was finished and that His movement was over. But He rose again from the dead, leaving the tomb empty.

He wouldn't go away.

He won't go away—even when, like Peter, we deny Him and cuss Him out.

And if we only knew, the fact that He won't go away is our hope.

The Little Horse That Could

For a righteous man may fall seven times and rise again. But the wicked shall fall by calamity. Prov. 24:16, NKJV.

For the year 1938 the most column inches in American newspapers was not logged by President Franklin Delano Roosevelt. Nor did it concern German chancellor Adolf Hitler, already embarked on his conquests to build the Nazi empire. And certainly not Winston Churchill, still in the political wilderness.

No, it was a horse named Seabiscuit that dominated the news in 1938.

America was still gripped by the Great Depression. Although conditions had eased somewhat, millions were still out of work (only the onset of World War II would bring the country fully back). But the cloud of doom was broken by a remarkable champion, the unlikeliest hero.

Seabiscuit was born of fine stud but was small. With ungainly stride he was quickly written off. For three years he was beaten and badgered, overworked and mistreated. He became angry, hostile, unapproachable, dangerous.

This is the horse that, against all odds, became the champion in 1938. He won event after event, set new speed records, and, in a dramatic match on November 1, ran one on one against the acknowledged champion, and beat him.

Some 40 million Americans, one third of all the population, clustered around radios to follow the race. The president was one of them.

Seabiscuit's story resonated with a nation bowed down by the Depression, a nation longing for a second chance.

But there's more. Seabiscuit's jockey was considered a "loser," too. He was too big to ride. Seabiscuit's trainer was old and out of touch. And his owner was a Buick salesman whose life had fallen apart after the death of his only son.

So it's the story of a horse that's too small, a jockey that's too big, a trainer that's too old, and an owner who doesn't know what he's doing. But he won.

And that, my friends, is what God does for us. That is grace.

A Tale of Two Words

May the grace of the Lord Jesus Christ, and the love of God, and the fellowship of the Holy Spirit be with you all. 2 Cor. 13:14, NIV.

Grace isn't the same as love. In closing his Second Letter to the Corinthians, Paul distinguishes between the two—God's love, and the grace of the Lord Jesus Christ.

Grace has a sharper focus than love. Love is general; grace is love reaching down to the unlovely, giving freely, forgiving, and raising to new life.

Grace always connects to Jesus. He was "full of grace," grace embodied. He is the divine demonstration, showing us what God is like—all-powerful but taking the form of a servant, upholding the universe but going to the cross to free us from the guilt and power of sin and giving us endless life.

Love and grace—these words have had sharply different trajectories in history. One has become a catchall for a range of emotions and experiences; the other remains pure, unsullied. One has been debased, has taken on negative connotations; the other is still a positive, beautiful word.

Think of the way we use "love" today:

I love mangoes. I love my dog. I love the Dallas Cowboys. I love my friend. I love my spouse. I love God.

One word! But the way we relate to mangoes (or apple pie or tacos) is vastly different from the way we relate to our wife or husband, let alone to God.

Our generation has become sex-crazy. It exploits the human body, especially the female body, for crass commercial interest, manipulation, and pandering to lust. For many people, used and abused or turned off by the exploitation of sexuality, "love" is a four-letter word.

Meanwhile, grace abides. It hasn't worn out despite all the times "Amazing Grace" is sung. It hasn't become mired in cynicism. Remarkably, in a time when language is twisted, turned upside down and inside out, grace remains.

Could it be because grace always connects to Jesus? He is the one who is ever new, ever fresh, ever lovely.

Miracle on Everest

He went to him and bandaged his wounds, pouring on oil and wine. Then he put the man on his own donkey, took him to an inn and took care of him. Luke 10:34, NIV.

Mount Everest, the highest point on Planet Earth at 29,035 feet, reveals human nature in sharp relief. It brings out the best and the worst, the bravest and the basest, in those who attempt to reach the summit. Every year many try, and every year some die. Because of the extreme conditions, those who succumb near the top are simply left where they fall. Climbers step over corpses on the path to the summit.

On May 25, 2006, a 50-year-old mountaineer, Lincoln Hall, made it to the top. On the way back, however, disaster struck: Hall's body refused to go farther. For nine hours the two Sherpas with him tried to talk him down the mountain, but he would not move.

The Sherpas' lives were now in danger. Convinced that the man lying in the snow was dead, they poked him in the eye and got no response. They collected Hall's backpack, oxygen, food, and water and left him lying at 28,000 feet. Dense darkness and bitter, −20°F cold descended on Mount Everest. And back in Australia, Hall's wife and two teenage sons received the news that their husband and father had perished just below the summit.

The next morning guide Dan Mazur was approaching the ridge at 28,000 feet. The summit loomed only two hours away for him and his two clients. Then they came upon an extraordinary scene: a man sitting on the ridge—head, hands, and chest uncovered! The stranger said, "I imagine you're surprised to see me." It was Lincoln Hall. He had been left for dead, but against all odds he had survived. He was hallucinating, taking off his gloves and swaying on a ledge with sheer drops on either side.

Two more climbers approached. Dan hailed them, but they just looked away, mumbling, "We don't speak English," and kept going. At that moment three men's dreams of reaching the summit died so that Lincoln Hall might live. Dan and his clients stayed with Lincoln for four hours, watching over him until the rescue team arrived.

This story is biblical in its dimensions. It's the tale of the good Samaritan in a modern setting. And above all it's a case study in God's incredible, unexpected, saving grace.

Channels of Grace

What, after all, is Apollos? And what is Paul? Only servants, through whom you came to believe—as the Lord has assigned to each his task. 1 Cor. 3:5, NIV.

The church in Corinth had split into factions. Some members said, "I follow Paul"; others said, "I follow Apollos"; and still others declared, "I follow Peter." And some even said, "I follow Christ." They formed allegiance to leaders, setting them up as gurus.

That's still a human tendency. The big trend today is to follow celebrities. And in the church we can fall into the same worldly mode of thinking by exalting preachers, professors, doctors, or whoever catches our fancy for larger-than-life status, a status that only Jesus deserves.

No, says Paul, Apollos and I and all the other leaders are only servants, instruments through whom the Lord brings His message. That's something that both leaders and members must never forget.

Ellen White uses an interesting word in describing our role: we are to be "almoners of His grace," dispensing the gift of salvation to those in need who cannot help themselves (*Selected Messages,* book 1, p. 168).

Especially to the big cities, where most people live today, and where so many are lonely, tired, frustrated, and searching for meaning. But also to everyone everywhere, for the whole world desperately needs the hope and new life that only God can give.

Whether I stand before the people in the pulpit, before the children in the classroom, before the patient on the operating table, before my colleagues or workmates, God wants me to be a channel of grace.

But channels get blocked. Pipes corrode, fill with gunk so that hardly anything can get by. Or, in electronic terms, static messes up the signal, or the signal keeps breaking up.

I want to be a clear channel for God's grace. I don't want to go off on an ego trip. I want His grace to flow through me, free and unhindered. I want His signal to come through loud and clear.

A Wretch Like Me

Here is a trustworthy saying that deserves full acceptance: Christ Jesus came into the world to save sinners—of whom I am the worst. 1 Tim. 1:15, NIV.

> "Amazing grace! how sweet the sound,
> That saved a wretch like me!
> I once was lost, but now am found,
> Was blind, but now I see."

Sung by congregations and choirs, played on the bagpipes, or rendered as a solo without accompaniment, "Amazing Grace" is one of the most beloved hymns of all time. Simple in both words and melody, it reaches into our innermost being with power unsurpassed.

John Newton composed "Amazing Grace" probably between 1760 and 1770 in Olney, England. The origins of the hymn in Newton's own experience, however, stretches back much earlier.

Born in London on July 24, 1725, Newton was the son of the commander of a merchant ship that plied the waters of the Mediterranean. At age 11 John joined his father and made five voyages with him.

When he was 19, John joined the H.M.S. *Harwich,* a man-of-war. He deserted but was soon recaptured, publicly flogged, and demoted to common seaman. At his own request he entered into service on a slave ship, sailing to the coast of Sierra Leone. Eventually Newton became captain of his own ship, also a slave trader. An infidel and libertine, he had long since abandoned the religious convictions instilled in him by his mother.

Then on May 10, 1748, he experienced God's salvation—twice. His ship became caught up in a violent storm, and, fearing that all was lost, he cried out, "Lord, have mercy upon us!" God delivered him and the ship, and later in his cabin, as Newton reflected on what he had said, he began to believe that God had used the storm to reveal His grace.

For the rest of John Newton's life he observed the anniversary of May 10, 1748, as the day of his conversion. Grace had brought him to fear, and grace had wiped away his fears.

> "'Twas grace that taught my heart to fear,
> And grace my fears relieved."

The Rest of the Story

But by the grace of God I am what I am, and his grace to me was not without effect. No, I worked harder than all of them—yet not I, but the grace of God that was with me. 1 Cor. 15:10, NIV.

The story of how John Newton—libertine, infidel, and slave trader—became a Christian after he cried out to God when his ship seemed about to sink has often been told. But there is much more to the remarkable story.

When John was about 25, he married Mary Catlett, with whom he had been in love for many years. Four years later he gave up the seafaring life forever and became surveyor of tides at Liverpool. Here he came in contact with the great outdoor preacher George Whitefield, and also John Wesley, founder of Methodism.

John Newton decided to become a minister. He had a difficult time at first, but eventually he was ordained as a minister of the Church of England and assigned to the parish of Olney in Buckinghamshire. Crowds came to hear him preach; the church had to be enlarged. Soon Newton was preaching in other parts of the country.

After several years the poet William Cowper settled at Olney. His arrival, and the friendship he and Newton established, would lead to a new and larger ministry.

Cowper assisted Newton in his services at Olney and elsewhere. They began a series of weekly prayer meetings, with the goal of writing a new hymn for each one. Several editions of *Olney Hymns* resulted. The first, published in 1779, contained 68 hymns by Cowper and 280 by Newton.

While "Amazing Grace" is undoubtedly John Newton's most famous hymn, he wrote many others that we love and sing to this day: "How Sweet the Name of Jesus Sounds" and "Glorious Things of Thee Are Spoken."

In 1780 Newton left Olney for London. Here he drew large crowds and influenced many, including William Wilberforce, who became a leader in the campaign to abolish slavery. Newton continued to preach until the last year of his life, when he was 82 and blind.

What a story of grace! Grace that delivers. Grace that transforms! Amazing grace indeed!

Receiving Without Deserving

So you also, when you have done all that is commanded you, say, "We are unworthy servants; we have only done what was our duty." Luke 17:10, RSV.

I would see him making his way across the campus, slowly pushing his wheelchair along. Hat pulled low over his ears, feet bundled up, hands thrust deep in mittens, he would propel himself along through the Michigan winter as he made his way to class.

Multiple sclerosis had struck Dave several years earlier. First he had felt it in his feet, then in his ankles, then in his legs. When he studied in my classes, his hands were beginning to stiffen; he could write only in broad strokes and would take his exams by pecking at a typewriter from his wheelchair.

"How's it going, Dave?" I would call out to the bundled-up figure, battling his way along the walkway. "The Lord is good!" he invariably replied with a smile.

One day he gave me a quotation from one of his favorite authors, Ellen G. White: "To him who is content to receive without deserving, who feels that he can never recompense such love, who lays all doubt and unbelief aside, and comes as a little child to the feet of Jesus, all the treasures of eternal love are a free, everlasting gift" (*Signs of the Times,* Feb. 28, 1906).

"That's me," said Dave. "I have nothing to bring to God—look at me!—and so I deserve nothing. But I'm content to receive without deserving. Isn't it wonderful?"

During the two years that Dave was on campus I never heard him complain. Multiple sclerosis had ravaged his body and broken up his marriage, but he didn't whine, "Why me?" Always it was "The Lord is good!"

The Lord *is* good. If we could but see ourselves we would all realize that we have nothing to bring to Jesus. This is just as true after we become Christians as before. All our righteous deeds are but filthy rags before His holiness (Isa. 64:6); our works of service but the performance of our duty—no big deal, and certainly nothing to commend us to Him.

But grace means that we get what we don't deserve, and don't get what we do deserve. To the person who is content with grace, who doesn't look for their name among the credits at the end of the movie, heaven opens up its storehouse of treasures.

Am *I* content to receive without deserving?

The New Song

And they sang a new song before the throne and before the four living creatures and the elders. No one could learn the song except the 144,000 who had been redeemed from the earth. Rev. 14:3, NIV.

I sit four rows from the front of the great concert hall, transfixed by the sounds emanating from the soloist.

He is nothing to look at; he is everything to look at. Short and paunchy, he has hair that is graying; his face is lined. His legs, braced by metal clamps, hang uselessly as he drags himself onstage. The conductor walks behind, carrying his violin and bow. With a great effort (while the audience holds its breath), he pulls himself up to the raised platform and the chair placed there for him.

But his face is wonderful. He beams as he tips his head, acknowledging the applause that greets his appearance. This is a man of compassion, kindness, tenderness—and great courage. This face shows the power of grace to overcome huge odds.

Conductor Leonard Slatkin raises his baton, and the National Symphony Orchestra launches into the opening bars of Beethoven's violin concerto. The magnificent work, composed in 1806, is long and difficult, establishing a new benchmark. It is *the* violin concerto by Beethoven. After this masterpiece he attempted no other.

All eyes are riveted on the little man in the folding chair from whom heavenly music emanates—Itzhak Perlman. Gone are the thoughts of limp legs and crutches. A profound gift is being shared. He plays with eyes tight shut, his features continually changing as he lives the experience.

The work goes on and on. For minutes he is a lone voice, the orchestra silent, the violin's tones soaring to the skies. Then it is all over and the audience leaps to its feet with shouts of "Bravo!" He looks around, almost surprised to see the people, his face gray with fatigue, then takes his crutches and maneuvers down from the platform and off the stage. The audience, on its feet, calls him back again and again and again.

Every Christian has a song that only they can sing. You have *your* song; I have mine. In the larger context every person on earth plays music that only they can play.

We shall sing on that beautiful shore and tell the story, "Saved by grace!"

The Heavenly Camper

The Word became flesh and blood, and moved into the neighborhood. We saw the glory with our own eyes, the one-of-a-kind glory, like Father, like Son, generous inside and out, true from start to finish. John 1:14, Message.

The text reads literally: "And the Word became flesh and pitched His tent among us."

Jesus was the heavenly camper, coming down from heaven to stay with us for a while. He existed long before He was born as Mary's baby, and after His death on Calvary He resumed the role He had had from eternity. "No one has ascended to heaven but He who came down from heaven, that is, the Son of Man who is in heaven" (John 3:13, NKJV). As His death was approaching He told His friends, "I came forth from the Father and have come into the world. Again, I leave the world and go to the Father" (John 16:28, NKJV).

He left the glories of heaven, where myriads of angels do His bidding, and "roughed" it among us. He became the lowest of the low—born in a manger, preaching from a borrowed boat, riding on a borrowed donkey, buried in a borrowed tomb.

But He knew it was only for a little while. He hadn't come to stay— He was just camping here.

Just for a while, but how much He accomplished!

"God commanded Moses for Israel, 'Let them make me a sanctuary; that I may dwell among them' (Ex. 25:8), and He abode in the sanctuary, in the midst of His people. Through all their weary wandering in the desert, the symbol of His presence was with them. So Christ set up His tabernacle in the midst of our human encampment. He pitched His tent by the side of the tents of men, that He might dwell among us, and make us familiar with His divine character and life. 'The Word became flesh, and tabernacled among us (and we beheld his glory, glory as of the only begotten from the Father), full of grace and truth' (John 1:14, margin, RV).

"Since Jesus came to dwell with us, we know that God is acquainted with our trials, and sympathizes with our griefs. Every son and daughter of Adam may understand that our Creator is the friend of sinners. For in every doctrine of grace, every promise of joy, every deed of love, every divine attraction presented in the Savior's life on earth, we see 'God with us'" (*The Desire of Ages*, pp. 23, 24).

Celebrity

For to us a child is born, to us a son is given, and the government will be on his shoulders. And he will be called Wonderful Counselor, Mighty God, Everlasting Father, Prince of Peace. Isa. 9:6, NIV.

O ur age has gone crazy over celebrities. We take ordinary men and women who have skill (or not so much) in singing and playing and put them in the spotlight. We single out gifted athletes and turn them into demigods.

Multitudes bask in their reflected glory. They line up for hours to catch a glimpse (oh, joy and rapture!) or to get their signature scrawled on a piece of paper. A huge industry spins off from the celebrity craze: fan clubs, apparel, bobblehead dolls, and endorsements.

Ladies and gentlemen, I give you a true celebrity, a Man who never will be exposed as a cheat or deceiver, whose secret life belied the press releases. I give you Jesus of Nazareth.

Boris Pasternak in his classic, *Doctor Zhivago,* captured something of the profound impact of this Man who puts all other "celebrities" in the shade. "Rome was a flea market of borrowed gods and conquered peoples, a bargain basement on two floors, earth and heaven, a mass of filth convoluted in a triple knot as in an intestinal obstruction. Dacians, Herulians, Scythians, Samartians, Hyperboreans, heavy wheels without spokes, eyes sunk in fat, sodomy, double chins, illiterate emperors, fish fed on the flesh of learned slaves. There were more people in the world than there have ever been since, all crammed into the passages of the Coliseum, and all wretched.

"And then, into this tasteless heap of gold and marble, He came, light and clothed in an aura, emphatically human, deliberately provincial, Galilean, and at that moment gods and nations ceased to be and man came into being—man the carpenter, man the plowman, man the shepherd with his flock of sheep at sunset, man who does not sound in the least proud, man thankfully celebrated in all the cradle songs of mothers and in all the picture galleries the world over."

Jesus, Lord of heaven and earth, Creator and Savior, I take You as Lord of my life. Walk with me throughout this day and keep me in Your care.

Rescued by a Dimple

Can a woman forget the baby at her breast and have no compassion on the child she has borne? Though she may forget, I will not forget you! Isa. 49:15, NIV.

A mother knows. Even after many years, a mother still knows her child.

On January 24, 2004, Luz Cuevas attended a birthday party in Philadelphia. She took one look at a dark-haired 6-year-old girl, saw the dimple on her face, and knew.

"When I see her, I saw that she was my daughter," says Cuevas, who speaks in halting English. "I want to hug her. I want to run with her."

Luz Cuevas had never accepted what everyone else accepted: that 10-day-old Delimar Vera, her only daughter, had perished on December 15, 1997, in a fire at her family's home. The infant's body was never found. Although the blaze was put out in 10 minutes, Delimar's room was gutted, and investigators concluded that the intense heat and flames had consumed the body.

But the mother was suspicious. First, when she went into the room and looked in the crib, it was empty. Second, a window of the infant's second-floor room was open, even though it was a cold winter evening.

Then there was the behavior of a family acquaintance. This woman stopped in several times after the baby was born, saying she was pregnant. After the fire, however, the visits abruptly stopped.

Now, after six years, Luz Cuevas looks—and *knows*. "I said to my sister, 'Look; she's my daughter,'" she told a reporter.

But she needed a way to prove it. At the party she told the girl she had gum in her hair and pulled out five strands. She folded them into a napkin, placed them in a plastic bag, and locked them in a safe at home. Then she contacted authorities.

"Because of TV, I knew they needed hair for the DNA," Cuevas said.

The DNA tests confirmed that the 6-year-old girl with the dimple, who was being called Aliyah, was indeed Delimar Vera.

Just like God. Because He never forgets. He *knows*.

Out of the Silence

In the beginning was the Word, and the Word was with God, and the Word was God. He was in the beginning with God. John 1:1, 2, NKJV.

The foundation of Hinduism and Buddhism is "In the beginning was the deed." A whole religious structure and philosophy rise from that cornerstone.

The word *karma* means works or deeds, and according to the structure the universe runs on implacable justice—we get what we deserve. Are you born into a poor family? It's because of the accumulated weight of karma, your deeds over countless incarnations. Understandably, under this system the goal of the spiritual life is to break the cycle of death and rebirth, to accumulate enough good karma so that one can be free at last.

In radical contrast the Bible proclaims, "In the beginning was the Word." Before the world came into being, the Word was there. Before the universe was born, the Word was.

The Word was with God, and the Word was God.

John's statement, so simple in expression, blows my mind. It tells me that from the beginning of beginnings God does not remain silent. The Word was God. The Word is God. God breaks the silence; God speaks.

What a difference a word makes! A word to the person trapped in earthquake rubble: "Is anyone down there?" A word from the doctor's office: "Your tests all came out fine. You're going to be OK." A word from the dean: "You've been admitted."

And these words especially: "I love you." "I forgive you."

Out of the silence of eternity, out of the vast cavern of space, God speaks. He says, "I have loved you with an everlasting love" (Jer. 31:3, NIV). "Fear not, for I have redeemed you; I have called you by name; you are mine" (Isa. 43:1, NIV).

Listen! The Word still comes to us. Out of the silence that grips us when our heart is breaking, when our dreams collapse like a house of cards, when we cry out to God and our words bounce back from heavens of brass and we feel we cannot go on, Jesus speaks.

He still speaks. He always has. He always will.

He is the Word made flesh, full of grace and truth.

Hang on, dear friend. Trust Him, no matter what your feelings shout out. Believe, only believe. Cling to the Word.

God Cares

Cast all your anxiety on him because he cares for you. 1 Peter 5:7, NIV.

In the thirteenth century Frederick II, emperor of the Holy Roman Empire, performed an experiment to find out what kind of speech children would develop if left to themselves in their early years. He selected a few newborn babies and ordered that no one should speak to them. Although he arranged for the babies to be suckled and bathed, he strictly forbade anyone to sing or talk to them. But the experiment failed—all the babies died!

A "wild child" found in California provided an answer to Frederick II's question. Dubbed "Genie" by social workers to protect her privacy, she was a 13-year-old girl who had been kept apart in a small room and since infancy had not been spoken to by her parents.

Genie's father apparently hated children. From the age of 20 months until she was discovered 12 years later, Genie lived in almost total isolation. Naked, restrained by a harness her father had fashioned, she was left to sit on her potty seat day after day. At night he put her into a sort of straitjacket and caged her in a crib with wire-mesh sides. If she made any noise, he beat her. He never spoke to her.

Genie was found in November 1970 when her mother brought her to the welfare office. She was a pitiful, malformed, incontinent, unsocialized, undernourished adolescent. She couldn't straighten her legs. She couldn't stand erect. She didn't know how to chew. She weighed only 59 pounds. And she was silent; she could only whimper.

That Genie survived at all is remarkable. Through years of rehabilitation she learned to speak in garbled fashion. Although she apparently was born a normal child, her IQ tested at only 38 in 1971, and at 74 in 1977. Because she was denied opportunities some parts of her brain will never function as they might have.

We are all made for caring. No matter what our age, we are made to love and be loved. Without someone who cares, life is one sustained heartache.

The good news that Jesus, the heavenly camper, brought us is *God cares!* He cares infinitely. All that we know of compassion, kindness, and love is but the shadow cast from the God of infinite caring.

That's what Jesus taught. And that's what He lived. We are *special* to God.

Is My Name Written There?

Nothing impure will ever enter it, nor will anyone who does what is shameful or deceitful, but only those whose names are written in the Lamb's book of life. Rev. 21:27, NIV.

I quickly opened the package, nicely weighty, that had just arrived in the mail. Out tumbled a large book with a silver cover, and I wondered, "Whatever is this?"

Opening it, I remembered. A few months before, I'd received a telephone call from a person representing the alumni office of a university from which I had graduated. The young person explained that they were assembling a complete list of all the alumni of the university, with information about each graduate. He reeled off all the reasons I would want to own a copy and made his sales pitch. The price sounded a bit steep to me, but it would be handled by a credit card, so why not?

Here it was. The first thing I did was open up the volume and look under "J." It was there. My name was written there. I had four lines in small type.

I thumbed through the book, looking for names of people I knew, friends and former classmates. The book had been attractively assembled and contained a lot of information about the university and its history. But I began to have second thoughts. For *this* I put out $70? For four lines in small type?

Ever thought about how we want to see our name on the list? The new telephone directory arrives, and where do we turn first? We want to be sure our name got in.

And that they spelled it correctly. Some people have a name that, like mine, often gets messed up. There are a ton of Johnsons out there, but not many with a double *s*. You have to live in Chicago or Minneapolis to find a fair number in the directory. Some people get flummoxed. They remember that there are two of something or other in the spelling, and so my name comes out as Jonsson or Johansson.

But of all the lists on which we'd like to see our name, only one really matters—the Lamb's book of life. Getting printed in that book is worth all we have, but it cost more than we can ever give. It cost all of heaven.

And our name will be spelled just right.

Why I Believe

That which was from the beginning, which we have heard, which we have seen with our eyes, which we have looked at and our hands have touched—this we proclaim concerning the Word of life. 1 John 1:1, NIV.

In 1927 the famous atheist philosopher Bertrand Russell wrote a book titled *Why I Am Not a Christian*. It was but the latest of a long line of reasoned attacks on Jesus Christ and His followers. The efforts to discredit Christianity began in the very first century.

Over the years various Christian thinkers attempted counterarguments. They developed cases based on the design in nature, on cause and effect (every effect must have a cause sufficient to produce it), on the prevalence of moral values in all societies, and so on.

These efforts have a place; I do not discount them. However, for me the chief reason for faith belongs in a quite different realm. For every philosophical argument the believer brings forward, the atheist replies with a different argument. At the end of the day each feels satisfied with their respective position, and no one has "proved" the case, pro or con.

In fact, God is too big to be "proved" by human argument. He who is the author of reason is beyond reason; He who created the universe is greater than the universe.

That's why the basis for faith for me is altogether different from philosophical word games. More than any other reason, I believe because of the Man of Galilee, Jesus Christ. Instead of words, He is *the* Word made flesh.

In Acts 14 we read about Paul's and Barnabas' visit to Lystra in Asia Minor during their first missionary journey. There they saw a man crippled in his feet, lame from birth, who had never walked. The man listened intently to Paul, who felt impressed to call out, "Stand up on your feet!" (verse 10, NIV). And the man jumped up and began to walk.

When the crowd saw what had happened, they shouted out, "The gods have come down to us in human form!" (verse 11, NIV), and they called Paul Hermes and Barnabas Zeus.

But the one God, the only true God, did come down to us in human form. If we could stretch our minds and try to imagine what God would be like in human form, we can think of only one Person—Jesus. He is the essence of our hopes, the embodiment of our desires.

Jesus. That's why I believe.

Seventeen-Year Resurrection

Jesus said to her, "I am the resurrection and the life. He who believes in me will live, even though he dies; and whoever lives and believes in me will never die. Do you believe this?" John 11:25, 26, NIV.

The eastern half of the United States witnesses an amazing invasion every 17 years. Billions of insects with black bodies, red eyes, and delicate amber-veined wings come out of the ground and take over sidewalks, trees, porches, and streets. They fill the air with a buzzing, clicking, thrumming roar that is louder than any lawn mower.

They came in 2004, in 1987, in 1970. Indeed, in 1715, when a Swedish clergyman named Andreas Sandel wrote about them in Philadelphia: "In this month [May] some singular flies came out of the ground; the English call them locusts." But locusts they are not. They are cicadas. While some 3,000 kinds of cicadas populate the globe and most live conventional lives, these are the "periodical cicadas." They spend 17 years underground, then suddenly emerge into a frenzied and noisy adulthood. These cicadas burrow 18 to 24 inches deep in the soil, using their piercing mouthparts to feed on sap in tree roots.

During the months before their emergence, the mature nymphs dig tunnels to the surface. Here a mud turret, called a cicada hut, is sometimes formed. These huts, or half-inch-wide cicada holes at the bases of trees, become visible in April.

When the soil temperature reaches 64° F, the nymphs emerge en masse and climb onto nearby vegetation. They squeeze out of their nymphal skins, and voilà! A glistening winged creature of creamy color appears. After a few hours their bodies darken to blue-black. Four or five days into adulthood the males begin to play their internal kettledrums, called tymbals, trying to attract the interest of females. They mate; the females scratch incisions in thin tree branches, and lay their eggs. In August young cicada nymphs hatch out and each, smaller than a grain of rice, drop to the ground and work their way into the soil.

So learn the lesson of the periodical cicada. If the Creator watches over these creatures that lie buried for 17 years and emerge for but a month of life, will He not also bring His sleeping saints out of the dust? Be it 17 years, 170 years, or 1,700 years, will not Jesus, who is the resurrection and the life, waken His people to life everlasting?

When Grace Appeared

For the grace of God that brings salvation has appeared to all men. Titus 2:11, NIV.

The apostle Paul, writing to the young minister Titus, speaks of the "appearing" of grace on this earth, indicating a point in human history. His words are similar to John's in the famous introduction to his Gospel: "For the law was given through Moses; grace and truth came through Jesus Christ" (John 1:17, NIV). So when Paul writes that "the grace of God that brings salvation has appeared," we could substitute "Jesus appeared" and be true to his meaning. For Jesus, as John says, was "full of grace" (John 1:14).

Does this mean that the Old Testament is devoid of grace? Not at all. Grace runs like a golden thread from Genesis to Malachi, although the actual word is not used.

While the Old Testament is rich in the vocabulary of God's righteousness, justice, and mercy, its most wonderful word is *chesed*, which denotes Yahweh's compassion and mercy. *Chesed* is usually translated as "lovingkindness" in the King James Version, or as "steadfast love" in the Revised Standard Version. For example, "Shew thy marvellous lovingkindness, O thou that savest by the right hand them which put their trust in thee from those that rise up against them" (Ps. 17:7) and "Withhold not thou thy tender mercies from me, O Lord; let thy lovingkindness and thy truth continually preserve me" (Ps. 40:11).

This wonderful word especially ties in with the idea of covenant, which is a ruling concept of the Old Testament. Yahweh keeps His covenant. This means that His promises are absolutely sure. He is a faithful Lord, so we can trust in His *chesed*—His lovingkindness, or steadfast love—because it is as dependable as He is.

Oh, the richness of the revelation before Jesus came! But then He did come, and grace "appeared." Building on all that had gone before, summing it up and filling the cup to overflowing—that was Jesus, the Word made flesh. No longer through words alone, but through a *Life*—and a Death!

"We beheld his glory," wrote John, stammering to find words to express the One "full of grace and truth" (John 1:14).

Do *I* behold His glory even today?

In the Valley of the Kwai

The law was added so that the trespass might increase. But where sin increased, grace increased all the more. Rom. 5:20, NIV.

Many years ago a famous movie portrayed an eccentric British officer directing his troops, all prisoners of the Japanese, to build a railroad bridge in Thailand. Based on a book that had been published about the event, the movie was titled *The Bridge on the River Kwai.*

The book and the movie were based on fact but took great liberties with the truth. What actually happened in Chungkai, the prison camp on the Thailand border, is more gripping and more amazing than anything in the movie. Ernest Gordon, a Scottish officer who was there and survived against all odds, wrote up the true account in *Through the Valley of the Kwai.*

With the fall of Singapore in World War II, the Japanese armies had overrun Southeast Asia with lightning speed. Now they penetrated New Guinea and knocked on the doorstep of Australia. An even bigger prize beckoned in India, but the British Navy guarded the seas. A rail link ran north from Singapore to the Thai border, and another from Burma to India. If they could link Chungkai to Burma, they could attack India by land.

The prisoners of war were put to work to hack a route through the jungle. Barefoot and clad only in G-strings, they worked from 5:30 in the morning until late at night in 120° F heat. With guards shouting, "Speedo! Speedo!" their feet cut and bruised, gnats and insects crawling over their sweating bodies, they toiled to complete the work. Their rations were meager, and the men dropped and died like flies from thirst, exhaustion, disease, and starvation.

The railroad took one year to complete. Its 250 miles claimed more than 100,000 lives.

As prisoners became sick, they were sent back to Chungkai. The numbers continued to swell, until the camp contained nearly 8,000 starving, broken men. The camp became a hell on earth, where selfishness, hatred, and fear ruled; where the weak were trampled underfoot, the sick ignored, the dead forgotten. All self-respect vanished. The men fought for scraps of food, stole from each other, waited like human jackals to rob the dead.

If ever sin abounded, it abounded at Chungkai. But into this hellhole God's grace began to penetrate, slowly and imperceptibly but powerfully, until the place of abounding sin became the place of superabounding grace.

January 25

God Was There—In Hell

*If I go up to the heavens, you are there; if I make my bed in the depths, you are there.
Ps. 139:8, NIV.*

Ernest Gordon, who told the story of the miracle by the river
Kwai, made his bed in hell. Already suffering from dysentery,
malaria, blood infection, and beriberi, he came down with diph-
theria, which meant he could no longer work on the railroad.

Gordon was sent to the Death House, as the crude camp hospital was
dubbed. Located in a sea of mud at the lowest point of the camp, the "hospital" contained hundreds of dying men placed head to toe, with flies,
bedbugs, and lice crawling over everyone. It was a charnel house of vile
smells, rotting humanity, and hopelessness.

Some friends sought him out, found him among the rotting bodies,
and carried him on a stretcher to a small hut they had constructed. They
washed him, bathed the ulcers on his legs, dressed his sores. They prepared food for him and gave him massages. Gradually, sensation returned
to Gordon's limbs. Against all odds, he survived.

His turning away from death was but part of a much wider resurrection of the camp. What had happened in Chungkai?

Stories began to circulate of soldiers, believers in Jesus Christ, who
had given their lives in acts of self-sacrifice, heroism, faith, and love. Of a
big strong man who suddenly collapsed and died of starvation because he
gave his rations to a sick friend, who recovered. Of another soldier who
stepped forward and took the blame for a missing shovel and was beaten
to death. (That evening, when the tools were counted, none was missing.)
And others.

These acts of grace leavened the camp. The prisoners turned from the
law of the jungle to the law of Christ. They began to help one another.
They made artificial limbs and prepared medicines from jungle plants.
They gave the dead a funeral instead of burning the bodies in heaps. They
built a chapel, held services, conducted baptisms. They started a jungle
university and held classes. They formed an orchestra. They smiled,
laughed, and sang again.

Ernest Gordon became a believer. After the war he studied for
the ministry, and eventually became dean of the chapel at Princeton
University.

Great is sin's power, but grace is even stronger.

The Obedience of Grace

"This is the covenant I will make with the house of Israel after that time," declares the Lord. "I will put my law in their minds and write it on their hearts. I will be their God, and they will be my people." Jer. 31:33, NIV.

I once set out to write a book about grace (it emerged as *Glimpses of Grace*). When I mentioned the plan to a colleague, he responded, "Bill, we don't need another book about grace. You should write a book about obedience!"

Now, obedience is important. Throughout the Bible God calls us to it. But what sort of obedience? *That* is the question.

The only obedience that counts is the obedience of grace. When our hearts are won to God by His love, when we catch a glimpse of the glory of the Word made flesh who pitched His tent among us, showing us what God is like, and then went willingly to Calvary in our stead—when we fall at His feet and like Thomas cry out, "My Lord and my God" (John 20:28), then we want to serve and obey Him.

The obedience of grace means that God writes His law on our hearts and in our minds. No longer working as hirelings for reward, we live as sons and daughters in the household, part of the divine family. Casting our cares on Jesus, we take His yoke upon us and find that His yoke is easy, His burden light (Matt. 11:30).

An ancient poem attributed to Saint John of the Cross captures the essence of the obedience of grace, of the heart that has fallen in love with Jesus and wants nothing more than Him.

"I am not moved, my God, to love You
By the heaven You have promised me.
Nor does hell, so feared, move me
to keep me from offending You. . . .
It is Your love that moves me, and in such a way
that even though there were no heaven
I would love You;
And even though there were no hell,
I would fear You."

January 27

Blessed Enmity

And I will put enmity between you and the woman, and between your offspring and hers; he will crush your head, and you will strike his heel. Gen. 3:15, NIV.

The highway of life is littered with surprises. A young person, with the world at his feet, throws it all away and messes up his life. After 20 years of loving and working together to build home and family, a spouse abandons everything and runs off with someone else.

But there's the other side also. Kids who seemingly have the odds stacked against them; kids from broken, dysfunctional homes; kids with alcoholic parents; kids with no one close to them who even finished high school; kids who "ought" to die young from drugs, gang fights, or abuse but who somehow survive, who break the pattern, who maybe go on to achieve an education and make a contribution to society that is astonishing in view of their background.

We aren't alone in the battle that is life. If we were alone, all of us, regardless of our start in life, would be pawns of the devil. We'd be blown hither and yon, led captives in his train. What happened in the Garden of Eden—the Fall—bent our natures irresistibly toward sin. It's easier to lie than to tell the truth, to hate than to love, to fornicate than to keep faithful.

But we aren't alone. God didn't leave us in the pit we dug for ourselves. He put enmity between us and the serpent. We don't *have* to do Satan's bidding. We can turn to God.

What is this enmity, this antagonism against evil, that runs counter to our nature? It is grace.

"It is the grace that Christ implants in the soul which creates in man enmity against Satan. Without this converting grace and renewing power, man would continue the captive of Satan, a servant ever ready to do his bidding. But the new principle in the soul creates conflict where hitherto had been peace. The power which Christ imparts enables man to resist the tyrant and usurper. Whoever is seen to abhor sin instead of loving it, whoever resists and conquers those passions that have held sway within, displays the operation of a principle wholly from above" (*The Great Controversy*, p. 506).

Thank You, dear God, for the blessed enmity!

Miracle on the Freeway

Now by chance a certain priest came down that road. And when he saw him, he passed by on the other side. Luke 10:31, NKJV.

I don't believe in chance. Nor do I believe in luck. I believe in grace.

Grace means that good things happen, even in the midst of a bad world. Grace means that God is working to make good things happen. To the casual observer, it looks like chance or luck; but to the person who knows Jesus, full of grace, it's grace.

Ed Theisen, 46, lay on the concrete of the Gulf Freeway, just outside Houston, Texas. He had been driving in his car when another driver rear-ended his vehicle. Theisen got out to exchange insurance information with the other driver. Suddenly he felt weak. He grabbed a traffic barricade and slid to the ground. And disappeared from view.

The tow truck driver who hauled off his car didn't see him. The police who wrote up an accident report didn't see him. They figured he had walked away from the scene.

But Ed Theisen was still there, on the concrete. Paralyzed from a broken neck and a spinal cord injury, he lay on his side, staring at a concrete wall.

Theisen spent the whole night alone on the concrete. The hours stretched on until they reached 36. No one saw, no one heard.

Then, "by chance," someone riding in the back of a pickup truck spotted him and called the police. The officer poked Ed Theisen with a nightstick, thinking he was dead. But he was alive, covered in Houston pollution.

He wife, Debora, and relatives and friends were plastering their neighborhood with flyers when they got the word. Debora called the hospital and was told, "We have him here, and he is alive and is saying that he loves you."

Grace, not chance. Grace means that people who ought to die survive. Grace means that a good Samaritan comes along our way. Grace means that good things happen in the midst of pollution.

Even on a Houston freeway.

The Birth That Changed the World

But the angel said to them, "Do not be afraid. I bring you good news of great joy that will be for all the people. Today in the town of David a Savior has been born to you; he is Christ the Lord." Luke 2:10, 11, NIV.

From what towering event is all history reckoned?

Many years ago W. H. Fitchett gave the classic answer: "From the birth of a Jew, who . . . was a peasant in an obscure province in a far-off age; who wrote no book, made no discovery, invented no philosophy, built no temple; a peasant who died when, as men count years, He had scarcely reached His prime, and died the death of a criminal. . . . Yet civilized time is dated from the birth of this Jew! The centuries carry His signature, and years of the modern world are labeled by universal consent the 'years of our Lord.' . . .

"Every morning all the newspapers of the civilized world . . . readjust their date to His cradle. Each year, as it arrives, is baptized with His name. Calendars and acts of Parliament, business, and politics, and literature— the very dates on our checks and letters—all are thus unconsciously adjusted to the chronology of Christ's life. To write a human signature on Time itself, to put a human name on the brow of the hurrying centuries— this is a marvelous achievement: Caesar has not done it, nor Shakespeare, nor Newton. Genius is vain to accomplish such a task; the sword is vain; wealth is vain. But this Jew has done it. . . .

"No conqueror's sword has ever cut deeply enough on Time to leave an enduring mark. . . . Only one name survived; only one figure was visible across wide spaces of perished time.

"The incarnate Son of God, the Word made flesh who has come into the world's history to shape it to a new pattern—it is fitting that to Him all the years should pay the unconscious homage of bearing His name. The Christianized calendar represents the seal of Christ's kingship on Time itself. But to believe that a remote impostor, in a forgotten province of a perished empire, stamped Himself so deeply on Time as to compel all the centuries to bear His name is to believe that a child, with its box of colors, could change the tint of all the oceans!" (*The Unrealized Logic of Religion*, pp. 16-26).

Jesus, come into my life and change me today.

Beyond Words

For the law was given through Moses; grace and truth came through Jesus Christ. John 1:17, NIV.

I am a writer and editor, so words fascinate me. Words as they change in meaning from one culture to another or within the same culture.

Take the word "wrinkly," for example. When I grew up in Australia, it was an adjective referring to creases in the skin because of worry, age, or fatigue. These days, however, Aussies use it as a noun to designate a chronologically gifted person. That is, a wrinkly is someone who is old.

Which leads me to reflect on the first Christians and the challenge they faced in attempting to write about Someone who was beyond words. Although in many respects Jesus of Nazareth was just like any other human being, in other ways He was totally different. In the beauty and purity of His life, in His compassion and mercy, in the perfection of His character, Jesus was *sui generis*—one of a kind, unique.

How do you talk or write about a Man that outstrips the ability of language to express Him? Do you invent new words, a new vocabulary?

You could, but that wouldn't help. No one would know what you were talking about.

The other way (which is really the only way) is to take existing words and give them a new twist of meaning.

That's what the Christians did. In particular, they found an old, old Greek word, *charis,* and poured new content into it. This word, from which our English words such as "charisma" and "charismatic" are derived, originally had the sense of "favor." It was used in two main ways: first, to describe someone who was well-favored; second, to express appreciation.

The New Testament contains several examples of such uses, as when we read that Jesus increased in *favor* with God and man (Luke 2:52), or when Paul exclaims: *"Thanks* be to God!" (1 Cor. 15:57). In both cases the word is *charis.*

But the overwhelming use of *charis* in the New Testament is something new: "grace." No longer just favor but God's favor, shown to us in the gift of His Son. Favor without merit, favor totally undeserved.

Jesus, full of grace *(charis)* and truth, burst the boundaries of language. He did—and He still does. He is magnificent beyond words.

Encounter in Shanghai

Are not five sparrows sold for two pennies? Yet not one of them is forgotten by God. Luke 12:6, NIV.

Of all the interesting experiences I had during a visit to China, none was more fascinating than the encounter in a market in Shanghai.

"Good morning, sir!"

I whipped around, wondering where the perfect English was coming from. For the past hour I had wandered among stores large and small, and even in a department store I'd had a problem communicating with the shop assistants. In astonishment I saw that the voice belonged to a child, a pixie dressed in red, whose head barely reached my waist.

"Do you have a moment, sir?" she went on. "I am a student at an art college. We are holding an exhibition of our paintings. Would you like to see them?"

An art student? She looked as though she should have been in the fourth grade.

"May I ask you how old you are?" I said. "You look as though you are only 10."

"Oh, no; I'm 16," she replied with a smile.

I glanced at my watch—15 minutes until I was to meet up with my party. "OK," I said, and we set off through the market. She led me down the narrow street and up a flight of stairs. There, in a large room, I saw paintings on display. Another young woman, obviously older than the pixie, was there, and a man sat at a desk.

They welcomed me royally. "Is she really 16 years old?" I had to know.

"Yes. She has a baby face, doesn't she?"

I wandered around the room. The work varied in quality; some was very good. A series of four verticals depicting the seasons took my eye. I contemplated how I would get it home. My bags were already full.

Meanwhile they chatted about their art college. It was out in the country, they said. Everyone learned English as well as art. They had put on the exhibition for passersby, and any sales would benefit the college.

It was a magical encounter. I wished I could stay, but the time was up. Sadly I took my departure.

There are some 1.3 billion people in China. God knows every one by name: the pixie, her friend, the old man. Each one is precious, precious enough that Jesus died for them.

FEBRUARY

The Legion of the Losers

"Sir," the invalid replied, "I have no one to help me into the pool when the water is stirred. While I am trying to get in, someone else goes down ahead of me." John 5:7, NIV.

Broken in body and broken in spirit, he was a pathetic sight. Blind, lame, paralyzed . . . Among the crowd of disabled people, he was the most hopeless case. The disease that had crippled his body for 38 years had snuffed out hope. He lay, day after day, waiting for a miracle.

This story in the fifth chapter of John is one of the strangest in the Bible. Especially verse 4: "From time to time an angel of the Lord would come down and stir up the waters. The first one into the pool after such a disturbance would be cured of whatever disease he had" (margin, NIV).

Something doesn't ring true here. Is this the way God works, granting healing to the person who, elbowing others aside, gets to the water first? The whole idea runs directly counter to grace.

In fact, the oldest manuscripts don't have this verse, which is why you won't find it in most modern translations. Interestingly Ellen White, in commenting on the passage, remarks that it was "commonly believed" that an angel came down and stirred up the waters (*The Desire of Ages*, p. 201). That the waters moved from time to time was no doubt true, but the cause was probably from an underground spring.

When Jesus saw the invalid lying by the pool, He asked him, "Do you want to get well?" Instead of replying "Yes!" this quintessential loser could only respond, "I have no one to help me into the pool. . . . Someone else goes down ahead of me."

He didn't ask to be made well. He didn't have faith. He didn't even know Jesus' name.

But Jesus healed him nevertheless. "Get up! Pick up your mat and walk." And at once the man was cured. He picked up his mat and walked.

Jesus loves losers. Grace means that the most hopeless cases—people so down and out that they can't even ask for help—find new life.

Heaven will be filled with the legion of the losers. Like you and me.

The Gentleman Athlete

Do you not know that in a race all the runners run, but only one gets the prize? Run in such a way as to get the prize. 1 Cor. 9:24, NIV.

Looking back from the perspective of today's culture of highly paid athletes with coaches and publicity agents, the story seems almost unreal.

On the morning of May 6, 1954, medical intern Roger Bannister made his rounds at St. Mary's Hospital in London. Then he boarded the train for the hour's ride to Oxford. It was a Thursday afternoon, and about 1,000 spectators had gathered for an obscure track meet. One television camera was there, plus a handful of reporters who had been tipped off in advance.

Roger Bannister was studying to be a doctor. In his spare time he also trained, without fanfare, as a middle-distance runner. He ran during his lunch hour, at night, and on weekends. He had no coach, no trainer, no dietitian. He ran on second-rate cinder tracks, in parks, anywhere he could find.

Bannister had been selected to compete for his country in the 1952 Summer Olympics in Helsinki, Finland. But everything went wrong. Instead of a gold medal in the 1,500-meter race, he came in fourth. He was a failure; he had let down Oxford, proud of its tradition of runners, and England.

Time was running out for Bannister. He was 25, and a career in medicine was consuming more and more of his time. Rather than wait for another try at the 1956 Games, Bannister set his mind on an even greater goal. In modern athletics one barrier stood, seemingly impregnable. No one had run a mile in less than four minutes.

That afternoon in Oxford, on a windy, rainy day, Roger Bannister did it. On a heavy course he broke the tape at 3 minutes 59.4 seconds, collapsing into the arms of friends. Afterward, there was no multimillion contract from Nike. Instead Bannister went on to have a distinguished career as a neurologist.

We are all runners in the race of life. On earth, competition rules. But in the Christian race, the race made possible by grace, we help each other toward the finish line. In this contest everyone who completes the course gains the prize of eternal life.

February 3

Mastering the Art of Living

And whatever you do, whether in word or deed, do it all in the name of the Lord Jesus, giving thanks to God the Father through him. Col. 3:17, NIV.

One of the big mistakes many Christians make is dividing their time into "sacred" and "secular." In sacred time, they think, God is near, and our behavior should reflect His presence. But in secular time, somehow, God is removed, and our actions take on a different character.

But Paul tells us that *whatever* we do—whenever, wherever—is to be done in the name of the Lord Jesus Christ, to be done thankfully. That is, to be done in grace.

Worship is not a one-day-a-week affair. When by the Spirit we master the art of living in grace, all of life is worship. Our work is worship. If Jesus came to us again on earth and we wanted to take Him to our church, maybe He would say, "No; take Me to the place where you work."

A friend shared with me the following quotation. Although it doesn't mention God, it sets forth wisdom that I seek:

> "A master in the art of living
> Draws no sharp distinction between
> his work and his play,
> his labor and his leisure,
> his mind and his body,
> his education and his recreation.
> He barely knows which is which.
>
> He simply pursues his vision of excellence
> through whatever he is doing, and leaves
> others to determine
> if he is working or playing.
> To himself he always
> seems to be doing both."

How much more will this be true if God is at the center of our lives! When we live in grace, all living, whether work or play, is transformed.

Surprise in the Cul-de-sac

For we are to God the aroma of Christ among those who are being saved and those who are perishing. 2 Cor. 2:15, NIV.

For years Noelene and I were lousy neighbors, and it bothered us. When we moved to Silver Spring, Maryland, we bought in a cul-de-sac, the second house of seven. None of our neighbors were Adventists. We plunged into our work at world church headquarters. We both traveled; our home became our refuge. Our neighbors hardly ever saw us, and when they did it was merely a wave or a hello.

It didn't seem right to us. We were telling the world about Jesus but had no time for the people next door.

The neighborhood in general was changing; property values were falling. We thought maybe it was time to leave suburbia and move farther out. But it was as though the Lord said to us, *Stay right where you are but get to know your neighbors. I have a surprise for you.*

So we stayed put. And the Lord began to open our eyes.

The first neighbor who became our friend was Jimmy, who lived kitty-corner from us. He came over to admire the daffodils that bloom early and abundantly in front of our south-facing home. We talked gardening; he showed us his magnificent backyard and told us the secret—mulch.

We noticed Jimmy's health going down. He had to take time off, then eventually quit working altogether. He grew thin and gaunt. The last time we saw him alive was in bed, his large frame emaciated from the ravages of AIDS.

Meanwhile, next door to us, in the third house, time was taking its toll. One day as I was mowing the lawn I saw my neighbor suddenly fall. I ran over and helped him get up. Tests showed he was a very sick person: Lou Gehrig's disease had struck. By December he was in a wheelchair. Just before Christmas, when the *Adventist Review* staff and their families came for a party, we all went over and sang carols. His face had frozen. Unable to smile, only his eyes shone. Within two weeks he was no more.

There were four other homes in the cul-de-sac. Two of them held neighbors who became our friends; the other two seemed impenetrable.

But God, who had surprised us already, wasn't finished with the cul-de-sac.

Love Thy Neighbor

If you really keep the royal law found in Scripture, "Love your neighbor as yourself," you are doing right. James 2:8, NIV.

Until I began to work on this book, I hadn't realized how much the Bible has to say about relationships with our neighbors. In both Testaments the idea of "neighbor" occurs more than 150 times.

Noelene and I had a problem. Here we were, the second house in the cul-de-sac, and two neighbors seemed absolutely closed to us.

Bruce and Shirley lived right next door, in the first house on the cul-de-sac. It seemed as if we had absolutely nothing in common with them. Anytime we saw either of them, day or night, they had a cigarette in their hands.

Slowly we began to make conversation over the fence. Then we got an idea. When our son and his wife came for a visit with their new baby, we decided to invite the neighbors, along with friends, to an open house. And Bruce and Shirley came. For the first time ever we saw them without a cigarette.

Later that year we invited them to a relaxed summer meal on the patio. After nervously inquiring about our dietary preferences, they invited us back.

We became good friends. When they retired and moved away, they urged us to visit them for a meal. We did. With great pride they showed us their new home, which they were keeping smoke-free.

The other "impossible" family lived opposite us. They never seemed to be home; we didn't even know their names. Occasionally we'd notice a car pull into the driveway, but we didn't see any faces.

Then that terrible Tuesday happened: September 11. On the national day of prayer that Friday we decided to invite our neighbors to gather together at our home in the evening for a simple time of reflection, readings, and prayers, with light refreshments. And our neighbor came by to tell us that it was a great idea but was sorry he and his wife had a prior appointment.

That was the seventh and last neighbor we came to know on the cul-de-sac. Looking back, we wonder how we could have gone on so long in our own little cocoon.

It really is a beautiful day in the neighborhood.

The Fragrance of Grace

But thanks be to God, who always leads us in triumphal procession in Christ and through us spreads everywhere the fragrance of the knowledge of him. 2 Cor. 2:14, NIV.

The apostle Paul here likens the Christian life to the Roman "triumph," the huge procession through the streets of Rome given for a successful general. The parade—spoils of war, exotic animals, captives, and finally the conquering general himself—usually made its way through air that was perfumed with incense or vast quantities of rose petals.

And, says Paul, we are in Christ's triumphal procession. He is the conquering hero, we His willing captives, spreading as we go the fragrance of His grace.

Have you noticed how we associate aromas and places? We catch a whiff, a suggestion of a fragrance, and our mind races back to an event perhaps many years ago. We are back there, living again a welcome experience.

Likewise with people. We associate someone special to us with their individual fragrance. It may be a scent or a perfume. Whenever we smell that scent, we think of them.

When we lived in India, we came to love the lady-of-the-night, a small vine with tiny white flowers that give off their fragrance at night. We'd awaken in the wee hours and enjoy the sweet, soft scent drifting in through the open window. We'd go strolling on the campus of Spicer College in the evening and cross a small invisible stream of fragrance and track it to its source, perhaps many yards away in the tiny white flowers, blooming unobtrusively but transforming the night air.

I loved that little flower. If I could catch a whiff right now, I would be back on the campus.

I love flowers; I don't care for fake flowers. Some imitations look just like the real thing, but it's easy to expose what they really are—just smell them. Only living flowers have the fragrance.

Which leads me to search my heart. Am I real or fake? As I go through life, do men and women and boys and girls catch a sweet fragrance—the fragrance of Christ, the fragrance of grace?

The Triumph of the Light

The light shines in the darkness, but the darkness has not overcome it. John 1:5, NIV.

True or false: *The world is beautiful. This world is ugly.*
True, and true again.
True or false: This life is wonderful. This life is monstrous.
True, and true again.

We are in a conflict, the great controversy between good and evil, between the light and the darkness. The light shines in the darkness, and the darkness has not overcome it. Never has, never will. Praise God for that!

In his popular book *The Road Less Traveled* (Simon and Schuster, 1978), psychotherapist M. Scott Peck tells of a remarkably successful businessman who came to see him. Born illegitimate, he had passed through a series of foster homes with a total absence of affection. At age 17 he was jailed for a vicious assault, and after six months' confinement he found a job as a menial stockroom clerk in a nondescript company. To social workers his future looked grim. Within three years, however, he had become the youngest department head in the history of the company. Five more years, and he had married another executive and started his own company. By the time he met Peck he had become a loving and effective father, a self-educated intellectual, a community leader, and an accomplished artist.

This man's case is but one of a series of examples Peck explores. From his dealings with such people Peck concludes that "there is a force, the mechanism of which we do not fully understand," that operates routinely to promote our physical and mental health. The wonder, says Peck (who was not a Christian when he wrote the book), is not that we get sick but that we don't get sick more often, and that we recover when we should die.

The most amazing part of Peck's book comes in its concluding section, as he reflects on what his experiences as a psychotherapist suggest. As he struggles to understand the tilt of the universe in our favor, he falls back to the only word that seems to fit: *grace!*

Dr. Peck found it to be true. The light shines in the darkness, and the darkness has not overcome it. Has not, does not, will not!

Counting the Hairs

Indeed, the very hairs of your head are all numbered. Luke 12:7, NIV.

Jesus' words knock me over. God cares *so* much about me that He even knows how many hairs I have on my head?

No doubt someone, in this age of measuring everything under the sun, has done a count. No doubt somewhere you can find the average number of hairs on a woman's head or a man's head. But the figure would be just that—an average. Jesus wasn't talking about averages, however; He wanted us to know that a loving Father loves us intimately, individually, personally.

On a trip to China I gained an insight into Jesus' words. We had appointments in Shanghai, but they fell through, and we found ourselves with an hour to kill. The tour guide said, "I can take you to an exhibition nearby."

He took us to a large, ornate building with a very high ceiling and several floors. We walked by displays of exquisite jade carvings and artifacts assembled from China's past greatness. Then we entered a room with what I at first thought were paintings on display, but the paintings caught the light in a manner I had never seen before. Looking closer, I realized that these artworks were not composed with brush and oil but woven in silk.

A woman dressed in black sat at a desk, intent on the scene she was weaving, strands of varied colors falling from the frame. Through an interpreter she told me that she had learned this art as a child; now she was 62.

A photograph stood on her desk. That was the owner of the company, she said. Next to it was a replica (an uncanny likeness better than a photocopy), a three-dimensional imitation that caught the light and held the eye more than the original.

It was stunning. I enquired how long the work had taken her. "Eight months," she replied.

Thread by thread she had woven it, hair by hair. Had she cared to (and I'm sure she didn't), she could have counted each hair as she made it part of the new creation.

And our Creator wove us together thread by thread, hair by hair. Lovingly He pored over His work; and lovingly He still hovers over us. "You are precious to Me," He says. "I know all about you. I made you! You are Mine!"

A Song in the Night

By day the Lord directs his love, at night his song is with me—a prayer to the God of my life. Ps. 42:8, NIV.

O n October 13, 1944, a most unusual concert was performed in the Czech garrison town of Terezin. Located about midway between Prague and Dresden, the town of some 5,000 inhabitants was occupied under the Nazi invasion and was given its original German name of Theresienstadt.

Theresienstadt became the site of a gestapo prison. It served as a concentration camp through which nearly 74,000 Czech Jews passed on their way to the infamous Auschwitz. Some of the camp's inhabitants, however, stayed on at Theresienstadt for years. They included several musicians and composers, Viktor Ullmann being one of them. Conditions at the camp were far less harsh than elsewhere, and the musicians were able to continue their creative work and even organize an orchestra. Ullmann, in fact, wrote about 20 pieces between 1942 and 1944, including an opera. In the face of overwhelming odds he personified a spirit of creativity, resistance, and initiative.

For the Nazis, the activities at Theresienstadt provided a false front. They invited the International Red Cross to inspect the camp on a prearranged date to attend the concert, which included works composed in the camp. The Nazis brought in cameras and sent out the film as a propaganda piece. The players were lent black suits for the occasion; the podium for conductor Karel Ancerl was framed with potted plants to conceal the clogs he wore.

Three days later, however, all the camp's remaining inhabitants, about 2,500, were sent to Auschwitz. Their usefulness to the Nazis had run its course. Most were murdered upon arrival at Auschwitz, Viktor Ullmann among them.

Before Ullmann was shipped to Auschwitz, he was persuaded to leave his Theresienstadt compositions behind. Fragments have been preserved and are now entering the repertoire of orchestral music around the world.

It is impossible to judge this music independent of its biographical context. It is music, not as decoration or for profit, but as a power larger than life: music necessary for survival.

It is a song in the darkest night.

A Radical New Approach

Submit to one another out of reverence for Christ. Eph. 5:21, NIV.

G race isn't something merely for sermons and songs. God intends that grace will permeate every aspect of our being, transform every relationship, and make us Christlike in the totality of our lives.

Grace introduces a radical new approach to the family. No longer are we hung up about who's the boss. Instead of authority, the essence is servanthood. We aim to serve, not to command; to help, not to rule; to affirm, not to dominate. We're followers of the One who told His disciples, "Whoever wants to become great among you must be your servant, and whoever wants to be first must be your slave—just as the Son of Man did not come to be served, but to serve, and to give his life as a ransom for many" (Matt. 20:26-28, NIV).

Our kids—Adventist kids, Christian kids—have a difficult time grasping the plan of salvation because what we try to teach them after age 10 is out of sync with the way we brought them up. While they're babies, toddlers, and little ones we teach them reward and punishment (disapproval). Then suddenly they're supposed to learn that God deals with us on just the opposite basis, that He doesn't save us because we're good or punish us or turn from us when we're bad.

I have yet to find a child-rearing program that takes seriously the grace principle. I see various well-meaning Christian books and ideas based on a chain of command, authority structures, discipline, leadership, and so on. But in light of the biblical teaching of grace, the radical new approach to the family, I think they miss the mark, some woefully so.

Christians understandably take very seriously their role as parents. They understand that in the delicate task of shaping values and attitudes they stand in the place of God for little ones. The problem is this: we get in the way. We don't deal with them as God does. We can seem quick to punish and slow to forgive. Even the songs about Jesus that we teach them may convey subtly or directly that He doesn't like them when they do bad things. We may school them in a reward-and-punishment pattern that will stay with them for life, permanently distorting their concept of God and making the Holy Spirit's task much harder.

Raising children. Who is sufficient for these things? Somehow, in spite of us, good things happen. For God is great, and He loves our kids even more than we do.

Grace in the Family

Unless the Lord builds the house, its builders labor in vain. Unless the Lord watches over the city, the watchmen stand guard in vain. Ps. 127:1, NIV.

In our world of fractured relationships, no institution has suffered more than the family. Holy wedlock too often becomes unholy deadlock, as wedded bliss descends into wedded mess.

Here's a story making the rounds:

Three men were sitting together bragging about how they had set their new wives straight on their duties.

The first man had married a woman from South Dakota, and bragged that he had told his wife she was going to do all the dishes and housecleaning at their house. He said that it took a couple days but that on the third day he came home to a clean house and dishes.

The second man had married a woman from Minnesota. He bragged that he had given his wife orders that she was to do all the cleaning, dishes, and cooking. He reported that the first day he didn't see any results, but the next day was better. By the third day his house was clean, the dishes were done, and he had a huge dinner on the table.

The third man had married a Missouri woman. He boasted that he told her that her duties were to keep the house cleaned, dishes washed, lawn mowed, laundry washed, and hot meals on the table for every meal. He said the first day he didn't see anything, the second day he didn't see anything, but by the third day most of the swelling had gone down and he could see a little out of his left eye!

But Ellen White said it right: "The grace of Christ, and this alone, can make this institution [the family] what God designed it should be—an agent for the blessing and uplifting of humanity. And thus the families of earth, in their unity and peace and love, may represent the family of heaven" (*Thoughts From the Mount of Blessing,* p. 65).

Lord Jesus, rule in my family today!

The New Life of God's Grace

The same goes for you husbands: Be good husbands to your wives. Honor them, delight in them. As women they lack some of your advantages. But in the new life of God's grace, you're equals. Treat your wives, then, as equals so your prayers don't run aground. 1 Peter 3:7, Message.

Grace transforms the marriage relationship. It takes this most tender and intimate of human attachments and raises it to a new level. All that is beautiful and precious in the love of a man and a woman becomes ennobled and purified.

The wonderful thing about falling in love is that our world suddenly enlarges beyond the narrow focus on ourselves. We "lose" ourselves in the other: we think of them, notice details of appearance and mannerisms, study how to please them. We become a different and a better person.

But the initial attraction and fascination wears off. We naturally are selfish creatures, and a relationship that began with a high degree of self-lessness degenerates more and more into self-centeredness, demands, and unfulfilled expectations.

No marriage is perfect, because no man or woman is perfect. What starts out so grand diminishes to barely tolerating one another, staying together for the sake of the kids, or backbiting and abuse.

But grace, which transforms all our living, can transform the marriage relationship. Grace gives and forgives. As recipients of grace, we experience salvation as a free, undeserved gift, and forgiveness that sets us free from the burden of past failures, the oppressive weight of the present, and fear of the unknown.

Because we have been and are given so much and so freely, we want to give generously—beginning with our husband or wife. Because we have been forgiven our transgressions, we can more readily forgive the hurts and misunderstandings occasioned by our spouse.

In the new life of grace, says Peter, we are equals. Each family finds its own way in terms of who does what—balancing the checkbook, the vacuuming, shopping for supplies, etc. But in Christian marriage each carries out duties and chores, welcome or unwelcome, in a spirit of mutual helpfulness and desire to please. No one is the boss—only Jesus, who is the Lord of the home and the Lord of the relationship.

February 13

In The Lord

Children, obey your parents in the Lord: for this is right. Eph. 6:1.

A home where children honor, respect, and obey their parents—every Christian holds this ideal. But the issue is *why?* Why do the children do what's right? Why do they behave as their parents wish? Why do they speak respectfully to their parents?

They may do so because they're afraid to do otherwise. Afraid of what they'll suffer if they don't. Afraid of what will be withheld. Such isn't "obedience"—it's an external conformity, and its future is strictly limited. When the external restraints and motivations are withdrawn, it collapses like a house of cards. That's why "good" children from "good" Christian homes often cast off all restraints when they cut the family ties.

Another type of "goodness" arises out of respect for the Christian standards of the home. Children love and respect their parents and grow up as "good" children and "good" adults. They never sow wild oats, never bring disgrace on their parents' good name. But they also know that they're "good" and so feel no need of a Savior.

The only obedience that counts is the obedience that Paul identifies here, "in the Lord." The only goodness is the goodness that comes by His grace, as we realize our sinfulness, accept Jesus' death as our saving sacrifice, and yield ourselves to His love.

How can we help children find this obedience "in the Lord"? I wish I knew the answer.

Part of the answer surely lies in the modeling we provide as parents. Their concept of God will be shaped more by what we do—how we relate to them and to others—than by what we say.

If we're trustworthy, they'll learn trust and find it easier to trust God, whom they cannot see.

If we're generous, they'll find it easier to accept the incredible gift of salvation.

If we affirm them, they'll find it easier to grasp that God regards them as infinitely precious.

If we forgive them easily, they may be able to accept God's infinite forgiveness.

Who is sufficient for these things? None of us; but God promises to supply all that we lack.

If I Were Doing It Over

This is what the Lord says: "Restrain your voice from weeping and your eyes from tears, for your work will be rewarded," declares the Lord. "They will return from the land of the enemy. So there is hope for your future," declares the Lord. "Your children will return to their own land." Jer. 31:16, 17, NIV.

Parenting is maybe the most important work we'll ever be called upon to do, and also the most difficult.

Books there are, and manuals aplenty, by individuals who are sure they have all the answers—until they get children of their own!

Once, quite a few years back, Noelene and I were asked to conduct a seminar on how to have a happy family. We're not professionally trained in this area, but we agreed to do it. It must have been considered useful, because we received invitations to repeat it in other places. And so we did, but eventually we got out of that business. When our children entered their teen years, we discovered that our pat answers didn't work the way they were supposed to.

I think of the way Christians try to run their homes, to bring up their children. I think of the way Noelene and I established our home and raised our family. I look around and think back, and the words that ring in my mind are love (of course), respect, authority, obedience, reward, and punishment.

But not much of grace. Oh, grace was there, but not as the central, ruling principle. We weren't constantly acting out how Christ dealt, and deals, with us—certainly I was not. We often were too conscious of having a "good," a "correct," family because I was a pastor, Noelene a minister's wife, and Terry and Julie the children of a preacher. Noelene and I stayed faithful to each other, and our kids behaved well.

We had a happy family, but I wish I had the opportunity to do it over. I'd like to serve more, instead of being so concerned about my own needs. I'd be more generous so that the kids would have a better idea of how incredibly generous God is. I'd want to throw out forever the crazy self-centered feelings and words over who should be the first to say "I'm sorry" after a tiff. I'd try to help Terry and Julie know clearly, beyond a shadow of a doubt, that they can never do anything, go anywhere, that would lessen Noelene's and my love for them, that the welcome mat is always out, day and night. And that we're proud of them, and always will be.

Growing in Grace

But grow in the grace and knowledge of our Lord and Savior Jesus Christ. To him be glory both now and forever! Amen. 2 Peter 3:18, NIV.

I take off my hat to Uceba Babson of West Palm Beach, Florida. When she donned cap and gown for her high school graduation the audience gave her a standing ovation, and the governor of the state sent her a letter of congratulation.

Uceba Babson at her graduation was a few months past her ninetieth birthday!

When Uceba started school as a child, she used to walk for more than a mile to a one-room schoolhouse. In 1931 she gave up school and married a vegetable farmer.

Seventy years after her last high school class, Uceba decided to go back to school. She had 81 grandchildren and great-grandchildren, and had outlived three husbands, but still nursed the dream of finishing high school.

She rose at 4:00 a.m. each day and drove herself to the adult education center. And the many hours of study for math, English, science, and social studies courses paid off—she made it! "This is something I promised myself a long time ago," she said at her graduation. "It's been a challenge, but a wonderful challenge."

We who follow Jesus are students in His school of lifelong learning. The riches of His grace are so abundant that we can never exhaust them. God intends us to be ever learning, ever growing in Jesus, "in whom are hidden all the treasures of wisdom and knowledge" (Col. 2:3). Throughout eternity we will explore new depths of His inexhaustible grace.

"It is the Lord's desire that His followers shall grow in grace, that their love shall abound more and more, that they shall be filled with the fruits of righteousness, which are by Jesus Christ, unto the praise and glory of God" (Ellen G. White, in *Signs of the Times,* June 12, 1901). "Sanctification is not the work of a moment, an hour, or a day. It is a continual growth in grace" (Ellen G. White, in *Review and Herald,* May 6, 1862).

What a prospect—always learning, always growing!

What a future, now and eternally!

I take off my hat to Uceba Babson, who went back to school after 70 years and graduated at 90. That's the spirit the Lord of grace calls us to, whether we're 9 or 90.

The Divine Solar System

For it is by grace you have been saved, through faith—and this not from yourselves, it is the gift of God—not by works, so that no one can boast. For we are God's workmanship, created in Christ Jesus to do good works, which God prepared in advance for us to do. Eph. 2:8-10, NIV.

Grace, faith, and works. How many arguments have swirled, and still swirl, around these terms. Are we saved by grace *plus* works, or by grace alone? If by grace alone, then what is the place of works? And what about faith—is it something for which we can take credit?

It's tempting to think of grace, faith, and works as a triangle—a triangle with one long side (grace), but a triangle nonetheless.

Tempting, but wrong. In a triangle the sum of any two sides will be greater than the third. But that isn't true here. Faith and works combined don't begin to measure up to grace.

Rather, we might think of a divine solar system, with grace as the sun and faith and works separate planets revolving around it.

There can be only one sun, because there is only one Sun of righteousness (Mal. 4:2). The universe of salvation has no place for human glory; any glory apart from Jesus is glory reflected from Him. Only His grace—unlimited, immeasurable, all-encompassing, and free—gives us hope of eternal life. Salvation comes to us as a gift, not as our "just deserts." To change the analogy and pick up a beautiful statement from Ellen White: "This robe [the robe of Christ's righteousness], woven in the loom of heaven, has in it not one thread of human devising" (*Christ's Object Lessons,* p. 311).

Not one thread—not even one! Nothing, but nothing, in which we can boast.

Faith is a planet in the divine solar system. Faith doesn't come from within ourselves so that we might gain credit because of it. Faith itself is a gift of the God of grace, a gift that enables us to say yes to grace when all those around us choose to say no.

Further out in the divine solar system is another planet—works. Like faith, works come from the Sun of grace, Jesus. As we say yes to Him, His light shines upon us and into us, transforming us, renewing us, re-creating us in His image. He reflects the glory of the Lord; we grow more like Him.

The divine solar system always has these three elements—grace the sun, with faith and works as planets.

Breaking the Cycle of Abuse

When Jesus saw her, He called her forward and said to her, "Woman, you are set free from your infirmity." Then He put His hands on her, and immediately she straightened up and praised God. Luke 13:12, 13, NIV.

For 18 years she had been bent over, unable to straighten her back. For 18 years she had dragged her weary way through life, struggling to keep her balance, eyes always forced to the ground. She never lifted her gaze to see the sunrise, never followed the flight of a bird or the drift of a cloud, because she could not.

This Sabbath she struggled to the synagogue and found a place in the section set apart for women. With eyes downcast she listened as the wandering teacher from Nazareth began to expound the Scriptures. Entranced, she hung on every word; but interest turned to astonishment as Jesus abruptly called her out of the congregation.

"Woman, you are set free from your infirmity," He said, as He put His hands on her. Immediately healing power coursed through her body, freeing up joints and straightening bones. She stood up straight—for the first time in 18 years!

Many people today are crippled with an infirmity as real as the woman's. They go through life with their eyes downcast, gripped by an evil force that they cannot break. They know only a pattern of life that their parents—and their grandparents—knew; and that their own offspring are cursed to perpetuate.

I am referring to family abuse, which runs in satanic cycles. Children grow up abused by parents who were abused, and the children give the wheel another spin. Perhaps its most tragic aspect is that it wields its power over families that profess to be Christian. I have seen it—seen it at work among those who are brought up to attend church, who even have the opportunity of a Christian education. But despite all the sermons and classes, the cycle of abuse continues, and I want to weep.

I believe that Jesus can break the cycle of abuse. I believe that His grace is more powerful than the accumulated weight of the generations. I believe that people can change—we can change. We don't have to accept abuse with its degradation and loss of self-respect; we don't have to abuse our kids even though we were abused.

Jesus calls us forward. He calls us by name and says, "You are set free from your infirmity." And for the first time we can straighten up and praise God.

The Pool of Tears

When Esau heard his father's words, he burst out with a loud and bitter cry and said to his father, "Bless me—me too, my father!" Gen. 27:34, NIV.

Esau's bitter cry rings down through the ages. It is the plea of sons and daughters longing for parental approval.

On the face of it, we wouldn't expect Esau's cry. Superficially, he came from a family in which God was worshipped and love was manifested. His father, Isaac, a God-fearing man, loved Rebekah, his wife (Gen. 24:67). The couple waited a long time to have children, and eventually had just two—twins, Esau and Jacob. This was a home in which the children were wanted, gladly welcomed, and loved.

Further, the picture of Esau we get from the Bible is that of a strong, self-sufficient individual. He "became a skillful hunter, a man of the open country" (Gen. 25:27, NIV). We don't expect to see a man like this bursting into tears.

But the home was far from the model one it appeared to be. The parents had favorites. Isaac loved Esau, but Rebekah loved Jacob. And of course the sons knew it.

So Esau, for all his apparent boldness and indifference to emotion, felt deeply insecure. When Jacob tricked Isaac into giving him the blessing of the firstborn—a blessing Isaac thought he was giving to Esau—Esau wailed. Earlier he had treated the blessing in a cavalier fashion, letting it go for a plate of lentil stew; but now, seeing his brother get the gift, he cried out for his own blessing.

Bringing up kids is an education for the parents as well. As they learn, we continually learn more about ourselves. We're surprised how different one child is from another. And when they get older we're astonished how their perspectives on growing up in the family vary.

Within each of us a pool of tears begins to gather very early. Even the best of families are broken by sin, and kids detect (or think they detect) words and deeds that show that a sibling is preferred. The pool of tears continues to grow in secret. When it bursts into the open in adult years, it amazes parents and other family members.

But grace makes the difference. Grace assures parents that God loves and accepts us and helps us to demonstrate our approval. By words of commendation, by hugs, by little attentions, we pass on the blessing.

The Gentleness of Jesus

A bruised reed he will not break, and a smoldering wick he will not snuff out, till he leads justice to victory. Matt. 12:20, NIV.

One of the great characteristics of Jesus, full of grace, is gentleness. He dealt tenderly with every person who came His way, regarding each as precious, seeking to find an avenue to the soul so that the gospel might find lodging.

To the rich young ruler Jesus spoke about possessions. To the woman by the well, waterpot in hand, He spoke of water. To the lawyer He spoke about the greatest commandment in the law. To the woman caught in the act of adultery, her guilt plain to all and to herself, He spoke not a word.

After Matthew in his Gospel summarizes Jesus' ministry to the sick, he quotes Isaiah 42:1-4, a wonderful "servant" passage that describes the work of the Messiah. No harshness here. No sternness. No violence. Only kindness, compassion, sensitivity, and thoughtfulness.

That's Jesus. What a Savior! What a friend!

Gentleness isn't weakness. Jesus was gentle, not weak. When the occasion called for it, He could be strong and tough, upturning chairs and tables and putting to flight merchants and money changers before His flailing whip.

Most of the time, however, Jesus was the epitome of gentleness. With children. With mothers. With people cast out by society. With men and women broken in body and spirit.

The world applauds power; we applaud the gentle Jesus. The world applauds stratagems, cleverness, and "doing whatever it takes to win." We applaud the gentle Jesus.

His gentleness is more powerful and accomplishes more than any president, potentate, or politician. His gentleness makes people new.

His gentleness makes us gentle. "As apostles of Christ we could have been a burden to you, but we were gentle among you, like a mother caring for her little children," wrote Paul (1 Thess. 2:6, 7, NIV).

Gentle Jesus, make us like You today.

Are Your Ears Opened?

The Sovereign Lord has opened my ears, and I have not been rebellious; I have not drawn back. Isa. 50:5, NIV.

This wonderful prediction of Jesus' obedience to the divine will has its roots in the instructions God gave to Moses. When the Scripture says that Jesus' ears were *opened*—not *open*—it signifies more than a readiness to hear and follow God's leading. The twenty-first chapter of Exodus gives us the background to these words. Here we find first of all the Lord's gracious provision to help His people from falling into lifelong bondage: "If you buy a Hebrew servant, he shall serve six years; and in the seventh he shall go out free and pay nothing" (Ex. 21:2, NKJV). God loves freedom and wants His people to be free. Thus, if this law were followed, no Hebrew could have been kept in servitude for more than six years.

But there was an added provision: "But if the servant plainly says, 'I love my master, my wife, and my children; I will not go out free,' then his master shall bring him to the judges. He shall also bring him to the door, or to the doorpost, and his master shall pierce his ear with an awl; and he shall serve him forever'" (verses 5, 6, NKJV).

Here we find the person who had chosen freely to be a servant for life. His pierced ear bore witness to all that because he loved his master he would serve him forever. He was the man whose ear had been opened.

Even so, the Lord Jesus, Creator of heaven and earth, humbled Himself. He "made Himself of no reputation, taking the form of a bondservant, and coming in the likeness of men" (Phil. 2:7, NKJV). No external compulsion drove Him to do it, only the compulsion within Himself, the compulsion of love.

Through every stage of His journey, at every point of His mission, Jesus put God first. His ears weren't opened literally, but the ears of His heart were. As long as He lived, He served in perfect obedience.

So, dear friend, are your ears opened? Do you love your Lord so much that you are prepared to say, "I want to be Your bondservant for life. I want to be like Jesus, ready to go or to stay, to speak or to be silent, to be and do only what You plan for me."

May that be your prayer and mine for this new day.

The Inverted Pyramid

Here is my servant, whom I uphold, my chosen one in whom I delight; I will put my Spirit on him and he will bring justice to the nations. Isa. 42:1, NIV.

I sat in church marveling at the inspiration of the service. By most accounts it should have been a downer, since it was a funeral for a man, only 44 years old, who died suddenly and unexpectedly, leaving a grieving wife and two sons.

Yet the note was not of tragedy; rather, celebration of a life lived to the glory of God. Victoriano Orion won no worldly acclaim and was awarded no honors, but the testimonies of those who knew him and were blessed by him revealed that his was a life that counted for eternity and that his heavenly laurels are assured.

Devoted husband and father, Vic, as he was called by those who were close to him, found time to help others in need. A friend, surprised and honored that he had been invited to speak, related how because of poor health he was unable to care for home needs. But Vic, alone or with his sons, took care of everything. They painted the house, repaired the gutters, cared for the garden, fixed the car. In eight years or so, Vic came by "maybe a hundred times," usually staying two hours or more to help, and sometimes the whole day.

Former U.S. assistant secretary of the Navy James (Johnny) Johnson told how Vic dropped off an inspirational book at his office one day. A few days later he was back with another, and then another. Johnson and Vic became close friends. Vic at no point tried to persuade Johnson to come to his church; but the winsome influence of his faithful, loving life won over Johnson's heart.

Vic's life wasn't written up by *Time, Newsweek,* or the Washington *Post.* It's somewhere more important: in the Lamb's book of life.

Victoriano Orion's life reflected the One whom he loved and in whom he trusted. Jesus, in a series of striking scenes in the book of Isaiah, is called "my servant," and said of Himself, "The Son of Man did not come to be served, but to serve" (Matt. 20:28, NIV).

Most people view life as a pyramid, with the goal of getting to the top. But Jesus inverts life's pyramid. Instead of trampling on others, we, like Him, bear them on our shoulders.

The Abundance of Grace

Still other seed fell on good soil. It came up, grew and produced a crop, multiplying thirty, sixty, or even a hundred times. Mark 4:8, NIV.

In Jesus' famous parable the sower went out scattering seed. Some fell on the path, and the birds came and ate it up. Other seed fell on rocky places, where the soil was scant. The seed sprouted quickly, but dried up in the sun's heat. Still other seed feel among thorns, which grew up and choked the young plants. But some seed fell on good soil, which yielded a bountiful harvest.

I have long understood the parable as teaching the various hearers of the gospel. Although frequently designated as the parable of the sower, it is really the parable of the soils. This understanding of the parable no doubt points to truth but misses important aspects—and the most important one of all.

A study of ancient methods of agriculture helps us grasp the meaning behind Jesus' words. Unlike modern agriculture, where the soil is first plowed and then the seed planted in the furrows, the old way was to scatter the seed on unplowed ground and then dig it in. This is why the seed in the parable seems to go everywhere.

The seed that fell on the path, on rocky ground, or in the thorn bushes came there by accident, not deliberate placement. Most of the seed fell just where it was intended—in good ground. If we concentrate on the three unproductive soils we imply that the sower's work was largely (75 percent) wasted; but it was not.

To the contrary, the sower's work produced an abundant harvest. In fact, the harvest exceeded all expectations. "Studies of the yield in Palestinian grain fields where the agricultural methods were followed show that a tenfold harvest was a good yield and that the average was about seven and a half. This means that all three of the numbers in the harvest (30 times, 60 times, 100 times) are intended to depict not a normal harvest, but a miraculously abundant one" (Larry W. Hurtado, *Mark* [1983], p. 58).

From a human standpoint the harvest in the parable was impossible. But the gospel isn't about human power—it's about the kingdom of God, God's work.

Grace is abundant beyond our imagination.

Grace Is Like a Garden

You will be like a well-watered garden, like a spring whose waters never fail. Isa. 58:11, NIV.

The story of the Bible revolves around two gardens. In the first—a perfect garden, without weeds, pests, or bugs, where no invading deer or rabbits wrought havoc—our first parents fell. They turned away from God's plan of life and happiness and yielded to the blandishments of the tempter.

Night fell over the garden. Death and decay blew in with a moan. In sorrow they made their way out of the garden to face a life of toil and struggle.

But all that they lost was won back in another garden. On a Thursday night when the moon was at the full a Man struggled with His destiny. The weight of the world's accumulated woes from the fall in the first garden rolled upon Him. In anguish He three times prayed that the Father would spare Him from the ordeal: "My Father, if it is possible, may this cup be taken from me. Yet not as I will, but as you will" (Matt. 26:39, NIV). So intense was His agony that His sweat fell like large drops of blood on the ground (Luke 22:44). And His disciples slept.

That night in the Garden of Gethsemane love prevailed. Jesus took the bitter cup and drank it. And thereby planted a new garden, the garden of grace.

My mother had a "green thumb." Her garden was her favorite place. It was not a large plot, but it was beautiful, with a succession of annuals and perennials as the year ran its course; with a thick, manicured lawn; with shrubs and ferns and climbing things; with flowers that loved the light, and others that thrived in the shade.

After many years I began to receive the same blessing in my own garden. It was there all along, in the Scriptures as well as in Ellen White's counsel, but somehow I never took it seriously. To work the soil; to plant, water, and weed; to watch for seeds to sprout and bulbs to burst through the ground—what satisfaction! What therapy for muscles and mind! What return to simplicity!

Grace is like a garden. It is filled with beautiful blooms and fragrant scents, with enchanting colors that attract hummingbirds and butterflies. All this lavish display, just for our enjoyment. Endless variety, endless wonder.

Just like grace.

Grace Is a Kingdom

This Isaiah-prophesied sermon came to life in Galilee the moment Jesus started preaching. He picked up where John left off: "Change your life. God's kingdom is here." Matt. 4:17, Message.

Some people want God to set out a smorgasbord of choices for His followers. We select what we like, and pass by the others. But Jesus declared that a kingdom had come, not a smorgasbord.

Some people want God to follow majority rule. A democratic model suits them fine. But Jesus spoke of a kingdom, not a democracy.

Some people want God to govern by consensus. We'll all get together with Him, talk matters through, and decide what to do. But Jesus said, "Don't try to change God. Change your life. His kingdom is here."

According to the Gospels, Jesus spoke of "the kingdom" no fewer than 50 times. About half His references used "kingdom of heaven"; the rest, "kingdom of God." It seems impossible to make out any significant difference between the two—the expressions are interchangeable. The real point, however, is how often talk of "the kingdom" fell from the lips of Jesus.

Most people today, Christians included, don't care for the kingdom idea. After a couple centuries of democracy, they find it archaic and even distasteful. Even in those nations of the West where kings and queens still reign, they have no effective power. They are monarchs without a kingdom, mere figureheads.

Some of Jesus' most startling statements began, "The kingdom of heaven is like . . ." With this preface He told startling stories, stories that turned the social order on its head, stories that end with a surprising twist. Workers who toil for only one hour but who receive a full day's wages. A big party put on for a wayward son. The beggar who makes it into heaven ahead of the wealthy guy.

This isn't democracy, let alone a smorgasbord or government by consensus. This is something out of this world.

This is God's kingdom, where He, He alone, says what goes.

Instead of force, politics, scheming, and machinations, grace rules here. Grace is a kingdom.

Divine Blindness

He has not observed iniquity in Jacob, nor has He seen wickedness in Israel. The Lord his God is with him, and the shout of a King is among them. Num. 23:21, NKJV.

These words are remarkable on two counts: the person who uttered them, and their seemingly contradictory content.

The speaker is Balaam, son of Beor, the flawed prophet. He stands on Mount Pisgah and gazes over part of the tribes of Israel. The Moabite king, Balak, worried about the advancing Israelites, has hired Balaam to utter a curse on them. Balaam, greedy for the rewards proffered by Balak, is eager to get involved, but God tells him no! However, Balak keeps asking, and eventually God lets Balaam do what his heart is set on.

So now Balaam stands beside seven altars that Balak has built on the mountain. He has offered a bull and a ram on each altar; now he seeks a word from the Lord.

And the word comes. What a message it is! Instead of the curse that Balak seeks (the curse that will make Balaam rich), God puts words in the prophet's mouth that he would prefer not to utter. Thus, a majestic blessing comes upon Israel from the unlikeliest of sources.

God "has not observed iniquity in Jacob, nor has He seen wickedness in Israel," declares Balaam. Extraordinary! Is God blind? This factious, carping, whining bunch that has wandered about in the wilderness for 40 years because of their unbelief and disobedience—how can the Lord put such words in Balaam's mouth?

Because something was there blocking the divine eyesight: an apple! "He [God] kept him as the apple of his eye," wrote Moses of Israel (Deut. 32:12). In spite of all their faults and failings, God regarded Israel as precious. When He looked at Israel, He saw not their waywardness but His own image.

What a picture of grace! This is just how the Lord looks on you and me today, friend of mine. When He sees us, He doesn't behold our broken promises and messed-up lives. He sees Himself—He sees Jesus.

Believe it—you're the apple of His eye. And so am I. So go out into a new day with your head held high and a spring in your step. You are *someone.* Yes; a child of God!

The Tactful Christ

The Master, God, has given me a well-taught tongue, so I know how to encourage tired people. He wakes me up in the morning, wakes me up, opens my ears to listen as one ready to take orders. Isa. 50:4, Message.

How often our words get in the way of God's plan! The sharp retort, the clever quip that stings, the mean innuendo—we fall, and fall again. No wonder the apostle James tells us that if anyone doesn't stumble in words, that person is perfect (James 3:2).

"Boys flying kites haul in their white-winged birds. You can't do that when you're flying words," wrote Will Carleton. Our words go out from us and, as much as we would like to haul them in, they have passed out of our control. Even though we may say we're sorry, may apologize, may try to correct the harm, we've wounded someone—perhaps someone we love dearly—and the scars remain even after the wound heals.

Not so with Jesus. His words brought hope and healing. They pointed the hearer upward; they never strengthened fear. Encouraging words. Inspiring words. Motivating words.

"The Savior never suppressed the truth, but He uttered it always in love," wrote Ellen White. "In His intercourse with others, He exercised the greatest tact, and He was always kind and thoughtful. He was never rude, never needlessly spoke a severe word, never gave unnecessary pain to a sensitive soul. He did not censure human weakness. He fearlessly denounced hypocrisy, unbelief, and iniquity, but tears were in His voice as He uttered His scathing rebukes. He never made truth cruel, but ever manifested a deep tenderness for humanity. Every soul was precious in His sight. He bore Himself with divine dignity; yet He bowed with the tenderest compassion and regard to every member of the family of God. He saw in all, souls whom it was His mission to save" (*Gospel Workers,* p. 117).

How could Jesus maintain such tenderness and compassion in the midst of the terrible pressures of His mission? Isaiah tells us: Every morning Jesus woke up listening for His orders from the Father. He turned toward God and away from self. He went out to meet each day fortified with divine tact.

And what a difference that made!

When Life Turns to Lemons

See to it that no one misses the grace of God and that no bitter root grows up to cause trouble and to defile many. Heb. 12:15, NIV.

What do you do when your life turns to lemons? Do you become bitter, blaming your "luck" or blaming God? Or do you let the grace of God sustain you, no matter how tough the going becomes?

Some time ago the Associated Press carried a beautiful story of a little girl who refused to be beaten down by ill fortune. Just before her first birthday Alexandra Scott was diagnosed with neuroblastoma. This form of cancer, which strikes about 700 children in the United States each year, has a survival rate of 40 percent.

Alex was 8 when her story ran in the press. She had been receiving chemotherapy and radiation treatment for seven years. But Alex was one brave little girl who fought back, and worked with a plan to raise $1 million for cancer research.

When she was only 4, she set up a lemonade stand. She raised $2,000 in a single day. Each year thereafter, more "Alex's Lemonade Stands" sprang up, operated by friends and volunteers. So far her stands have brought in more than $2 million.

By 2004, when the story ran, all 50 states in America had stands open for business. A chain of grocery stores set up stands at their store, and in Minneapolis, Minnesota, a family whose son had the same type of cancer as Alex set up shop at the baseball stadium. A group of homeless people in Houston, Texas, sponsored a stand, as did an elementary school in Milwaukee, Wisconsin.

Tired and exhausted by the cancer treatment, Alex nevertheless refused to cut back on her activities. She insisted on appearing on the *Today Show* to publicize the fifth annual Alex's Lemonade Stand Day.

All the money raised by this wonderful child went to cancer research. She gave $150,000 to the Children's Hospital of Philadelphia, where she received treatment. The remainder went for research in other centers.

Life turned to lemons very early for Alexandra Scott. But she took the lemons and made lemonade.

Lord, keep me sweet today, no matter what comes down my life's pathway. Keep me in Your grace, secure and trusting in You.

The Form of the Fourth

He answered and said, Lo, I see four men loose, walking in the midst of the fire, and they have no hurt; and the form of the fourth is like the Son of God. Dan. 3:25.

Of all the ripping good yarns from the past century, none is more enthralling than Sir Ernest Shackleton's last expedition to Antarctica. But it's more than a story of extraordinary courage. A divine element caps it off.

A century ago Antarctica beckoned explorers. After Roald Amundsen won the race to the South Pole, one great goal remained: to cross the continent from sea to sea. In 1914, right at the outbreak of World War I, Shackleton set out to do it.

By early 1915 his ship, the *Endurance,* had come within 80 miles of the continent. Then the ice closed in around them, locking them in a vise. They drifted for nine months and, when the ship sank, made their way to a desolate sliver of land named Elephant Island.

Then Shackleton and five others set out for the whaling station of South Georgia, 800 miles away, in a 22½-foot-long open boat. More than two weeks later they staggered ashore. They had come through not only towering waves but a hurricane that sank a 500-ton steamer.

But they had landed on the opposite side of the island from the nearest whaling station. With 5,000- to 10,000-foot peaks, crevasses, and glaciers, South Georgia had never been crossed. Another first, another heroic effort: 36 terrible hours without rest, and Shackleton and two others staggered into Stromness station.

This wonderful story, however, is about more than courage. Shackleton later reflected: "When I look back at those days, I have no doubt that Providence guided us, not only across those snowfields, but across the storm-white sea that separated Elephant Island from our landing place in South Georgia. I know that during that long and racking march of 36 hours over the unnamed mountains and glaciers of South Georgia, it seemed to me often that we were four, not three."

Four, not three. Like the three Hebrew youths who were accompanied by a Fourth in the fiery furnace.

Have you also felt that presence? Do *you* know the form of the Fourth?

MARCH

Giving With Grace

But when you give a banquet, invite the poor, the crippled, the lame, the blind, and you will be blessed. Luke 14:13, NIV.

Christmas was always a big event in our home. My mother, though small in stature, overflowed with energy and activity that came to a climax at the Yuletide season. Beginning about July she would begin to prepare personal gifts, each made with her own hands. When December rolled in, she would begin food preparations: jams, jellies, pies, cakes, and breads. She had nine children of her own, then grandchildren, and finally great-grandchildren. The big Johnsson Christmas party grew to 40 and more, and everyone received a handmade gift.

But that wasn't all. Several days before Christmas Mother entertained a very different group of people. She brought home shut-ins and others who, left to themselves, would not get to enjoy the warmth of a family Christmas dinner. And each one who entered the modest home was made to feel welcome.

Mother, a giving person, gave with grace. She hadn't studied theology, but she lived the gospel.

Giving with grace is rare and becoming rarer, as the tide of selfishness sweeps across society. Most of us find it well-nigh impossible to simply give—to give without strings, without expecting something in return. At the very least we want Uncle Sam to give us a break on our taxes; at the most we seek to obligate the receiver. We want something back.

We also find it hard to keep quiet about our gift. Jesus told about the hypocrites who sounded a trumpet in the marketplace so that everyone would know how generous they were. They sought—and got—the reward of human praise; but that was the extent of their reward. But you, said Jesus, you My followers give your gifts without fanfare, and "your Father, who sees what is done in secret, will reward you" (Matt. 6:4, NIV).

I think of my mother's Christmas with its simple gifts of love and can't help contrasting it with the Christmas of many people who live in affluence. Christmas has become a high-stress event, with giving one of the chief stressors.

Oh, for simplicity in giving! That's the way God gives—with grace.

The Treasury of Snow

Have you entered the treasury of snow, or have you seen the treasury of hail . . . ? Job 38:22, NKJV.

No invention or technology of humanity can withstand a glacier. This moving river of ice will thrust aside any barrier we might try to throw in its pathway.

The snow from innumerable falls over hundreds of years packs down into ice so dense that all air bubbles are squeezed out. As the ice layer builds up and up into a wall hundreds of feet thick, it begins a slow descent to the valley, its huge weight carving a path through solid rock, scouring the earth's surface, picking up boulders and grinding them to dust.

A glacier is both beautiful and terrible. From a distance it looks silent and still, the sunlight reflecting blue from its crisscrossed surface. But up close the glacier shrieks and moans under fearsome stresses as it grinds on its inexorable course. And the glacier is dangerous. Snow bridges hide crevasses that plunge into impenetrable darkness.

I have seen glaciers in various lands, but only after we visited Alaska did I begin to grasp their amazing power. We flew from Denver to Anchorage, and the last two hours I looked down on range after range of jagged, snow-laden mountains with countless glaciers carving out count- less valleys. The scene was breathtaking in the scale of its wild wonder.

A few days later Noelene and I cruised in a small boat on Prince William Sound. We saw glaciers that plunged into the sea, that "calved" before our eyes as huge walls of ice cracked and collapsed into the water.

For many years it was thought that no life could exist on the glacier. But that's not so. A tiny worm, as small as a thread, lives near the surface among the ice crystals. When the shadows steal over the glacier, this tiny creature, related to the earthworm, rises to eat pollen that has lodged on the surface.

"Have you entered the treasury of snow?" the Lord asked Job. No doubt Job had heard of snow, and perhaps seen it; snow falls occasionally on Jerusalem and the surrounding area. But Job could have had no inkling of what a river of accumulated snow—the glacier—was like.

Even so, we have but a glimpse of the wonder of the world God has made—and of His grace.

No Night There

On no day will its gates ever be shut, for there will be no night there. Rev. 21:25, NIV.

Can you imagine living in a place where it never gets dark—ever? People who live in regions far to the north know something of what it would be like. As you go farther and farther north, the sun in summer sets later and later, until you reach the Arctic Circle. North of the circle there are days that it doesn't set at all.

I spent some days in Alaska in June, and it was a new experience. Although I stayed at Palmer, some 50 miles north of Anchorage and well below the Arctic Circle, sunset came only at 11:45 p.m. Even though the sun was gone, it stayed light. By 4:30 the next morning the sun was up, and so was I. But already others were going about their business for the day. A garbage truck was making stops, and newspapers were already lying in driveways.

Because it doesn't get dark, sleeping poses a problem. Even with shades pulled tight, the room is light; and when a shaft of sunlight finds a crack, it pierces your eyes.

With continuous light, the land bursts forth in prodigious abundance. I saw the most beautiful peony I had ever seen—deep red, with multiple layers, and nine inches across. People told me of cabbages that grow to weigh 100 pounds (that's a lot of coleslaw!), of carrots that weigh 30 pounds each, and still succulent because of the rapid growth.

No night there! But only for a while. After the glory of the summer the days begin to shorten, and night comes on with relentless step. By midwinter in Anchorage the sun appears for only a few hours. North of the Arctic Circle, hardly at all.

And with night come the curses of the night: alcoholism, divorce, suicide. On the purely natural level, we are creatures of the light. Endless night shatters us.

In the new heavens and the new earth God's people, who are children of the Light, will enter upon an existence that we cannot comprehend in this life. There, we will walk in the light of the Lamb, who came to our earth, pitched His tent among us for a little while, showed the glory of the Father, and died on Calvary to set us free to eternal life.

No night there.

Grace Is a Party

"We're going to feast! We're going to have a wonderful time! My son is here—given up for dead and now alive! Given up for lost and now found!" And they began to have a wonderful time. Luke 15:23, 24, Message.

Grace is a party. That seems startling, even surprising. But that is what Jesus taught.

It's like this. We are here. We might never have been, but we are because the party wouldn't have been complete without us. In this world beautiful and terrible things happen, but God says, "Don't be afraid. I am with you. Nothing can ever separate us. It's for you I created the universe. I love you."

These words seem too startling to be true, but in fact they are. Jesus' most famous parable, a story beloved around the world in all ages, tells the story of the loving father and his two sons.

Preachers usually refer to the story as "The Prodigal Son," but it is really about both sons. The younger one sowed wild oats, came back home in rags, and was accepted. But his brother had a different set of problems. At the end of the story he is outside the home, arguing with his father, while his young brother is safe inside.

Like so many of Jesus' parables, this one has a surprise ending. It reverses the scale of human values. One son, the "good" one, worked hard and never did anything to disgrace the family name. But he didn't "get it."

Grace is something you can never earn; you can only be given it. No way to deserve it or bring it about. It's a gift. But like any other gift, grace can be ours only if we reach out and accept it.

However, the chief person in the story isn't either of the sons but the father. He never gives up on his sons, never quits hoping and waiting. And when the prodigal shows up, he runs to meet him, stifles his protestations of regret, calls for the best robe and the ring.

And throws a party.

Wonderful but true. Grace is a party.

Receiving With Grace

Freely you have received, freely give. Matt. 10:8, NIV.

I don't know which is harder—to give with grace or to receive with grace. Human giving comes with strings attached; divine giving does not. And human receiving continually seeks to introduce an element of personal worth or merit; divine receiving is content to accept us just as we are.

It is very difficult for us to receive without deserving. When the credits roll at the end of the program, we want our name to appear, be the type size ever so small.

The Old Testament recounts a story familiar even to children and celebrated in gospel song—the healing of Naaman, general of the Syrian army. A captive Israelite girl tells about a great prophet in her country who is famous for miraculous deeds. Surely he could help her master! So Naaman goes off to Israel with a retinue of gift-bearing attendants. After a contentious encounter with the king of Israel and swallowing his pride, Naaman at last agrees to do just what Elisha, who has not appeared in person, prescribes for the healing: he bathes seven times in the Jordan. And, as the song emphasizes, on the seventh dip Naaman comes up restored.

But the story has a sequel that rarely receives mention. Elisha has a servant, Gehazi, who is a greedy person. After Naaman is healed, he wants to shower his gifts on Elisha. Elisha, however, refuses to accept a cent; the miracle wrought that day came from Yahweh, not from the prophet. God alone deserves the praise and the credit.

So Naaman sets off for his home country, all the gifts he has brought still with him. The servant Gehazi now takes matters into his own hands. He has been a silent bystander in the story, witnessing Naaman's healing and then his abortive efforts to reward Elisha. Gehazi reasons to himself, *This isn't right! Naaman received the gift of healing, so he ought to give something back. Elisha is stupid to have turned him down.*

Gehazi runs after Naaman's party. When he catches up, he lies and tells Naaman that Elisha has changed his mind and will receive a gift after all. Naaman gladly gives him money and garments, but the gift turns to a curse as Naaman's leprosy comes upon greedy Gehazi.

It's still hard to receive with grace. But that's the essence of the gospel. We bring nothing; we receive all.

The Appalling Christ

Just as there were many who were appalled at him—his appearance so disfigured beyond that of any man and his form marred beyond human likeness—so will many nations marvel at him, and kings will shut their mouths because of him. Isa. 52:14, 15, margin, NIV.

The *appalling* Christ? The idea seems impossible! We know the gentle Jesus, the kind Jesus, the resolute Jesus, the sacrificial Jesus—but not the appalling Jesus.

But that is precisely how Isaiah, the gospel prophet, sums up Jesus' ministry in this arresting passage.

Jesus, predicts the Scripture, appalls, and in two respects.

First, He appalls because of His appearance, which is so marred and disfigured that it no longer looks human. In these few words Isaiah paints a picture of the sufferings of Jesus that all four Gospel writers will record 700 years later. Matthew, Mark, Luke, and John will tell us that Jesus was beaten and spat upon, and that a crown of thorns was pressed onto His head. And especially they note that the Roman soldiers scourged Him, and this surely was the most excruciating of all the abuse heaped upon Him. "The Roman scourge (Gr. *phragellion* from Latin *flagellum*) was a cruel instrument of torture. To its leather lashes were attached pieces of metal or bone to increase the suffering. . . . The victim was stripped to the waist, usually bound to a post with his hands tied together, and the scourge applied to the back with lacerating blows. Eusebius (*Hist. Eccl.* iv. 15) tells us that martyrs of Smyrna, tortured about A.D. 155, were so unmercifully beaten that the veins, muscles, and sinews were exposed, and even the entrails became visible" (*Seventh-day Adventist Bible Dictionary* [1979], p. 988).

All this Jesus endured, and more. As intense as was the physical pain He bore, even worse was the hiding of the Father's face as the weight of humanity's sins rolled upon Him.

Seeing Jesus, good men and women were appalled. Am I also appalled?

But, says the Scripture, Jesus appalls in a different manner. Many nations will marvel at Him; kings fall silent before Him. "Nations all over the world will be in awe, taken aback, kings shocked into silence when they see him" (Isa. 52:15, Message).

For this Jesus of Calvary, who suffered such abuse, was God's Man, even the Son of God, who will return as King of kings and Lord of lords.

The Resolute Christ

Because the Sovereign Lord helps me, I will not be disgraced. Therefore I have set my face like flint, and I know I will not be put to shame. Isa. 50:7, NIV.

Jesus of the firmly set jaw. This is a picture we don't usually have of Him. We are used to the generals whose faces show resolute determination—the Pattons, the Napoleons, the Eisenhowers—but not Jesus of Nazareth. Too often we think of Him only as the gentle Shepherd, gathering the lambs in His arms.

But Isaiah's prediction came to fulfillment in a Gospel description that echoes Isaiah's words: "As the time approached for him to be taken up to heaven, Jesus resolutely set out for Jerusalem" (Luke 9:51, NIV). Mark fills in the details for us: "They were on their way up to Jerusalem, with Jesus leading the way, and the disciples were astonished, while those who followed were afraid" (Mark 10:32, NIV).

It is a powerful scene: Jesus strides ahead, perhaps wanting to be alone with His thoughts. The disciples follow apprehensively. The demeanor of Jesus, now so different, makes them anxious. His jaw is set firm, His eyes glow with intensity, His whole bearing bespeaks determination. He has reached a decision and is going forward with it no matter what the cost.

The conclusion seems inescapable: Jesus chose to go up to Jerusalem, knowing that rejection, scorn, betrayal, flogging, and death awaited Him there. His life wasn't scripted; He wasn't an actor, far less a puppet. He could have chosen not to go to Jerusalem and the cross. He could have failed in His mission. In coming to earth, He risked "failure and eternal loss" (*The Desire of Ages*, p. 49).

What a Savior! What a Lord! The resolute Christ won our salvation.

And we who would follow in His train today, should we expect to be "carried to the skies on flowery beds of ease," as the old hymn put it? Is our brand of Christianity a feel-good, warm and fuzzy following of Jesus? Or do we know what it means to set *our* face like a flint, to determine to stay loyal to Him, no matter what the cost?

Paul knew the need of the flinty jaw. Against all advice he too set out to Jerusalem, knowing that bonds and suffering awaited him there.

This is tough grace—grace of the resolute Christ.

Jesus Wasn't a Hollywood Star

He had no beauty or majesty to attract us to him, nothing in his appearance that we should desire him. Isa. 53:2, NIV.

I t is a startling fact that the Gospels, which cover the life and death of Jesus of Nazareth in four accounts, devote not one word to His actual appearance. They don't give us a clue as to His height, coloring, eyes, or mannerisms.

When Hollywood producers set out to portray Jesus, as they do from time to time, they select a good-looking actor. They, for whom appearances count so highly, can't imagine that the most influential Person in human history could be anything but striking in appearance.

And they are dead wrong. Nowhere in the Gospels, or elsewhere in Scripture, do we find that people were attracted to Jesus because of His appearance. Rather, the contrary. Isaiah prophesied that the Messiah wouldn't have any beauty or majesty to attract, no outer qualities to lead men and women to want to be with Him.

The prophet Samuel, sent by God to anoint a new king of Israel, had to learn this lesson. "Do not consider his appearance or his height, for I have rejected him. The Lord does not look at the things man looks at. Man looks at the outward appearance, but the Lord looks at the heart" (1 Sam. 16:7, NIV). And the Lord passed over all the older sons of Jesse, handsome as they were, and chose the youngest, David, a mere teenager.

Jesus wasn't a Hollywood star. All the evidence of the Bible points to the conclusion that in appearance He was ordinary. A comment from Ellen White, as reported by family members, lends support. She mentioned a painting of Jesus as being the closest representation to what she had seen in vision. And in that painting Jesus is no Hollywood star.

Jesus had no beauty of appearance, but what a life! *That* was full of beauty. He had no majestic proud bearing, but what character! No human being ever came close to His majestic righteousness, full of justice and mercy, full of grace and truth.

"The King of glory stooped low to take humanity. . . . His glory was veiled, that the majesty of His outward form might not become an object of attraction. He shunned all outward display. Riches, worldly honor, and human greatness can never save a soul from death; Jesus purposed that no attraction of an earthly nature should call men to His side. Only the beauty of heavenly truth must draw those who would follow Him" (*The Desire of Ages*, p. 43).

A Shoot Out of Dry Ground

He grew up before him like a tender shoot, and like a root out of dry ground. Isa. 53:2, NIV.

When Abraham Lincoln was campaigning for the United States presidency, his supporters sang a jingle:

"Old Abe Lincoln came out of the wilderness,
Out of the wilderness, out of the wilderness,
Old Abe Lincoln came out of the wilderness,
Down in Illinois."

This tall, melancholy figure seemed an unlikely candidate to lead the young nation as it faced its greatest test—a split across the center over the issue of slavery. Yet Honest Abe, straightforward and unassuming, continually denigrated even by members of his own cabinet, proved to be the man for the hour. His unswerving convictions held the North on course, his public addresses, thrust aside or belittled by contemporaries, rang with unfading compassion, justice, and wisdom.

Abraham Lincoln, arguably the greatest United States president, was a shoot out of dry ground.

But what shall we say of Jesus, Son of Mary? He came from Nazareth, and that hamlet, small as it was, had built up a bad reputation. "Nazareth! Can anything good come from there?" exclaimed the pious Nathanael (John 1:46, NIV). And the Gospels give us a glimpse of Jesus' neighbors. When He preached in their synagogue and the message wasn't to their liking, they became angry, drove Him out of town, and tried to throw Him over the cliff! (See Luke 4:28-30.)

We still fall prey to Nathanael's error. We quickly write off someone because they don't have the right family connections, the right education, the right skin color, or the right bank account. Without even seeing them, without giving them a chance, we jump to the conclusion based on preconceived notions and prejudices.

I find this a scary thought. Messiah came from Nazareth. God's shoot grows up out of dry ground. Today I want my eyes to be open to see God's shoot, regardless of the ground.

Beautiful Feet

How beautiful on the mountains are the feet of those who bring good news, who proclaim peace, who bring good tidings, who proclaim salvation, who say to Zion, "Your God reigns!" Isa. 52:7, NIV.

O thers may see it differently, but I have never thought of the foot as a beautiful part of the body. To me, the foot belongs in Paul's category of "less comely" members that are nevertheless essential to the whole.

I love to walk. For the past 30 years I have also run, although less frequently as the years move on. Noelene and I often begin the day with a walk and prayer time in the park; and sometimes we walk in the evenings. Over the course of the years I figure we have walked around the world, and then some. And with 17 marathons behind me, plus the miles of training for them, my feet have covered many more thousands of miles.

After the long runs my feet look pretty beaten up. Seeing the blackened nails, Noelene often says to me, "You have the ugliest feet in Washington!" She is probably right, but it always seems an insult to these faithful burden bearers, an unkind cut to my person.

After much urging from her (and, truth to tell, a recalcitrant callus on the ball of my left foot that made me hobble), I yielded and made an appointment to see her podiatrist. Apprehensive, I waited for him to say, "Wow! Your feet are really ugly!" But instead he spoke in almost admiring tones: "You have strong feet." ·

There! I knew it deep down. Maybe not beautiful, *definitely* not beautiful, but strong. What are feet for, anyway? Who wants beautiful feet if they aren't strong?

Not so fast. The Scripture tells of beautiful feet. Feet that go out on the mountains to bring good news. Feet that maybe get beaten up because they go far, and over rough roads, through rivers, across ice, and over deserts to proclaim salvation, even "Your God reigns!"

God calls these beaten-up feet beautiful feet. What they do is more important than running any marathon. These are like Jesus' feet, given for others in missions of mercy.

I can have beautiful feet.

Calvary

But he was pierced for our transgressions, he was crushed for our iniquities; the punishment that brought us peace was upon him, and by his wounds we are healed. Isa. 53:5, NIV.

The Romans did not invent the cross. But they took it over and employed it for centuries to effectively deter opposition to the empire.

The cross suited their purposes ideally. It was preeminently a means of *public* execution. The opponent of the Pax Romana was paraded through the streets, carrying his cross or one member of it. Passersby would see—and shudder. The place of execution itself was a public one. Let the crowds see the fate of anyone who dared to rise up against Rome! And death came slowly. The victim might linger for days, nailed or tied to his cross, until exposure and loss of body fluids brought merciful release.

The Romans employed the cross extensively, but never on their own citizens. When emperors occasionally ignored this restriction, widespread indignation and rioting resulted. The cross was a symbol of shame and humiliation, too horrendous for a citizen of Rome. The apostle Paul, for example, a Roman citizen, was not crucified. He was put to death with the sword.

But Jesus of Nazareth, lacking Roman citizenship, could be crucified, and He was.

"The spotless Son of God hung upon the cross, His flesh lacerated with stripes; those hands so often reached out in blessing, nailed to the wooden bars; those feet so tireless on ministries of love, spiked to the tree; that royal head pierced by the crown of thorns; those quivering lips shaped to the cry of woe.

"And all that He endured—the blood drops that flowed from His head, His hands, His feet, the agony that racked His frame, and the unutterable anguish that filled His soul at the hiding of His Father's face—speaks to each child of humanity, declaring, It is for thee that the Son of God consents to bear this burden of guilt; for thee He spoils the domain of death, and opens the gates of Paradise. He who stilled the angry waves and walked the foam-capped billows, who made devils tremble and disease flee, who opened blind eyes and called forth the dead to life—offers Himself upon the cross as a sacrifice, and this from love to thee. He, the Sin Bearer, endures the wrath of divine justice, and for thy sake becomes sin itself" (*The Desire of Ages*, pp. 755, 756).

Living Forever

Behold, I will create new heavens and a new earth. The former things will not be remembered, nor will they come to mind. Isa. 65:17, NIV.

Ever thought what it will be like to go on living forever? to reach 100 years, and you've only just begun? To turn 500, and you're still a babe, as it were, and then to pass Methuselah's 969 (the longest span recorded in the Bible) and reach 1,000? And still the future stretches out ahead, on and on without end!

I find it almost impossible to contemplate. We're so used to measuring in terms of days, months, and years. The threescore-and-ten or fourscore span is what we use as our yardstick. If someone goes beyond and attains his or her century, they get a letter from the president or the queen. And a few rare individuals keep on going long enough to make the news when they die at 118 or thereabouts.

But in God's new creation there will be no death. There was no death in Eden; there will be no death in Eden restored. Death is an enemy, and it will be the last enemy destroyed.

In terms of life as we now know it, living forever could seem boring. That's only because we fail to grasp God's ability to introduce a totally new order of society. Totally new and totally better.

A quotation from Ellen White (one of my favorites, one that I frequently find in my mind) states this of God's new order: "We shall ever feel the freshness of the morning and shall ever be far from its close" (*The Great Controversy*, p. 676).

What a prospect! I love the morning. I wake up and praise God for the new day the stretches out to greet me, bright with hope, radiant with anticipation. And in God's new creation we shall ever feel that freshness, that surge of energy and expectation. The years as they roll will not diminish it; millennia flying by will not dull it.

In this anticipation of the future we find the ultimate dividing line between believers and nonbelievers. For the latter, this life, the present social order, is all that enters into their thinking. Just this life, nothing more. So eat, drink, and be merry, for it will soon be over.

But for followers of Jesus, this life is *not* all there is. Our Savior and Lord offers us life to the full, here and now, and the promise of eternal existence, full of joy.

Hallelujah, what a Savior!

Love on a Lawn Mower

A friend loves at all times, and a brother is born for adversity. Prov. 17:17, NIV.

Some time ago the Washington *Post* ran a picture of an old man with a curly white beard sticking out from his chin. He wore a cowboy hat he had bought in Mexico about 15 years before, with a band of pesos circling the crown. And he was seated on a 1966 John Deere lawn mower.

The story that ran with the picture was titled "The Lawn and Winding Road." It was about Alvin Ray Straight, 73, who drove his mower all the way from Laurens, Iowa, to Blue River, Wisconsin, about 250 miles total, spluttering along at 5 miles per hour, pedal to the metal. It took him six weeks to do it.

Radio deejays and reporters had a field day with him, this grizzled old character, creeping along back roads, past cornfields and cow pastures, towing a makeshift trailer with foam rubber bedding, a couple of blankets, and some food.

But it wasn't a comedy. It was a love story.

Straight wanted to see his brother, Henry, who had had a stroke. But what does a man do when he lives 30 miles from the nearest bus station (and doesn't trust their driving anyway), when he can't see well enough to drive a car anymore, when his brother is 80 and time is running out?

Straight spent the winter "thinking on" how he could make the trip. He decided at last he'd go under his own power, with his own hand on the steering wheel.

His first mower lasted only 30 miles before the engine blew. He got a tow home, bought the John Deere mower, and started out again.

Four days into the trip he had to replace the starter and generator. Ninety miles later he ran out of money. His next Social Security check was two weeks away. He pulled over to the side of the road and waited.

Straight got within 30 miles of the Wisconsin border when heavy rains stopped him for another week. At last he arrived at his brother's trailer in Blue River. He had broken down and made the last few furlongs with a farmer pushing his crippled Deere.

What drew Alvin Straight across the long roads on his chugging mower? He said, "I knew I had to come when I heard about his trouble last year. I had to see my brother."

Reminds me of another Brother who couldn't stay home.

Starched Collars and Salvation

We do not dare to classify or compare ourselves with some who commend themselves. When they measure themselves by themselves and compare themselves with themselves, they are not wise. 2 Cor. 10:12, NIV.

The grace of Jesus motivates and empowers us to grow more like Him. Whenever the spirit of self-righteousness or judgmentalism rears its head we can be sure that self has thrust aside Jesus. That spirit is never far from God's people, as illustrated by a humorous incident related by Adventist pioneer James White.

During June 1844, 22-year-old James White attended an Adventist conference in Poland, Maine, where about 40 believers were meeting. The weather was hot, and White's clothes had become soiled from travel.

An astonished James heard a certain Elder H pray, "O Lord, have mercy on Brother White. He is proud, and will be damned unless he gets rid of his pride. Have mercy upon him, O Lord, and save him from pride. . . . Break him down, Lord, and make him humble. Have mercy upon him. Have mercy." The prayer continued for quite some time.

When Elder H finally finished, all sat in stunned silence. White finally said, "Brother H, I fear you have told the Lord a wrong story. You say I am proud. This, I think, is not true. But why tell this to the Lord? . . . Now, sir, if I am proud, . . . you can tell before these present in what I am proud. Is it my general appearance, or my manner of speaking, praying, or singing? . . . Please look me over. Is it my patched boots? my rusty coat? this nearly worn-out vest? these soiled pants? or that old hat I wear?"

Elder H assured White it was none of those things. Rather, he said that Brother White's symbol of pride was the starched linen collar he was wearing. White quickly explained that his own shirt was dirty, and a good sister had offered to wash it for him. In the meantime, she had lent him one of her husband's shirts that had a starched linen collar. In fact, White didn't own a shirt with a starched collar. Whereupon Elder H again dropped to his knees and prayed, "O Lord, I have prayed for Brother White, and he is displeased with me for it. Have mercy on him! Have mercy!"

This was White's first experience with fanatics. Writing about this incident years later, he commented, "To see a coarse, hardhearted man possessing in his very nature little more tenderness than a crocodile, and nearly as destitute of moral and religious training as a hyena, shedding hypocritical tears for effect is enough to stir the mirthfulness of the gravest saint."*

---

*Adapted from James White, *Life Incidents* (1868), pp. 112-117.

Mookie

Each of you should look not only to your own interests, but also to the interests of others. Phil. 2:4, NIV.

All around us, day by day, God is working out beautiful grace stories if only we open our eyes to see them. Sometimes these stories happen right next to us. For example, Mookie, in the *Adventist Review* office.

One day staff member Merle Poirier chanced upon an ad in a local newspaper inviting volunteers to commit to training a dog that will help a blind person to expand their world. The Guiding Eyes for the Blind organization breeds the puppies, but looks for people who will give 18 months of their time working with the dog, which they then turn back to the organization. And that is how Mookie, a male black Labrador retriever, came into the Poirier family.

First, Merle had to take a six-week course herself on how to train the puppy. Mookie would be always on a leash and would be taught not to bark, jump up on people, or eat his food until he was told to do so. Incredible as it seems, he would learn obedience at such a level that he would eventually sit before a bowl of food, saliva running from the corners of his mouth, but not touch it until Merle gave him the word.

Mookie gave up all things that dogs naturally do in order that one day he might guide a blind person to work, the grocery store, the bank, or the post office. And Merle gave herself to preparing Mookie for service.

But Mookie started serving long before his time was up, and in a manner totally unexpected. In a cruel turn of events, sickness struck the Poirier home. Husband Tim went through a series of surgeries and rehabilitation, and spent many hours in recuperation at home. During those trying months Mookie helped bind the family together, taking their thoughts away from the worry of the moment. And Tim, alone for long periods, found in Mookie a companion.

Mookie went on to receive a jacket from the Guiding Eyes Organization, identifying him as a guide dog in training. The next phase of his training oriented him to the inside of buildings, boosting his confidence and socializing him to new situations and sights. Then he was ready to guide a blind person.

This, I think, is a beautiful story all around, on the part of both Mookie and the Poirier family. It's a story of kindness, compassion, service, and grace.

Some Woman!

He who finds a wife finds what is good and receives favor from the Lord. Prov. 18:22, NIV.

A good marriage is a gift of God's grace. To find a spouse who will love you in spite of yourself (as God does), and who will stick by you through laughter and pain, toil and tears (as God does), is, my friend, a blessing of incalculable worth.

I'm on my way to Alaska for camp meeting, and my seatmate on the long flight from Denver is a retired businessman who is heading north to go fishing. We talk and talk, and he learns that Noelene and I married straight out of college and went to India as missionaries,

"She married you and went to India?" he exclaims. "Your wife must be some woman!"

Some woman she is. I could fill a book elaborating on that, but one incident jumps out above all others since Noelene's first bold "Yes" to me and to India.

It was the Sabbath just after Thanksgiving, and early the next morning we'd be flying out of Baltimore-Washington International Airport, on our way to Fort Lauderdale, where we'd board a cruise ship for a seven-day jaunt in the western Caribbean. We eagerly looked forward to leaving the cold and ice for the blue waters and warm days that lay ahead.

As we approached the door of the church, Noelene's heel caught in a slight irregularity on the pavement. Our daughter, visiting from Chicago, was next to her, and I was a step behind, but before we knew it she had crashed, face-first, onto the concrete. Blood poured from her nose and mouth and all over her heavy coat as she lay prostrate on the cold sidewalk.

Immediately friends rushed into action, calling a nurse who stabilized the bleeding. Next, a trip to the emergency room of Washington Adventist Hospital for a quick examination and X-rays of nose, mouth, face, arms, and wrists. When the X-rays showed that she had broken her nose but no other bones, her first question to the doctor was: "Will I be able to go on the cruise?"

But that wasn't all. We had invited guests for lunch. Friends called around to tell everyone the lunch was canceled. However, at 12:45, when she was discharged, Noelene told them to come anyway. She sat at the table, eyes swollen almost closed, lips bruised. And she went on the cruise, wearing large dark glasses to disguise the large dark patches.

Some woman!

The Saving Grace of Laughter

A merry heart doeth good like a medicine: but a broken spirit drieth the bones. Prov. 17:22.

Have you ever wondered just why we laugh? Only humans laugh, and it seems altogether unnecessary in terms of raw existence, although modern medical science has discovered that what the wise man said about laughter is true: laughter is therapeutic.

Our age has turned laughter into a business, with canned laughter brought in on cue to enhance TV sitcoms, and stand-up comedians who make a living telling jokes to people who pay to drink and listen, perhaps the modern equivalent of the court jester.

Life is funny. God put humor into our very makeup. When we laugh, we enter into something uniquely human. And in a world cursed by the fall of our first parents, humor comes as a saving grace. When we laugh, we affirm that no matter how dark the picture may seem, it isn't the final reality. Through laughter we rise up above, transcend it.

The Africans who were brought to America in chains knew this truth. Subjected to the brutality and degradation of slavery, they looked evil in the eye and beat it. Through their songs of faith and hope—and their humor—they beat it.

A couple years ago a British university set out to discover how humor works in different cultures. They sent a selection of funny stories to tens of thousands of people in different countries. Here's the winner:

Sherlock Holmes goes camping with Dr. Watson. They pitch their tent under the stars and turn in for the night. Several hours later Holmes wakes up Watson.

"Watson, look up and tell me what you deduce."

Watson looks up and sees the starry heavens and replies, "In the vast universe I deduce that there are other planets like ours, and that some of them have life on them."

"No, you idiot," says Holmes. "Someone has stolen our tent!"

Why do we laugh at that? Because we see ourselves in it, failing to see the woods for the trees, jumping to absurd conclusions.

This is us. This is life. And we laugh—a gift from the God of grace.

Legs

His pleasure is not in the strength of the horse, nor his delight in the legs of a man. Ps. 147:10, NIV.

My father loved to go to the seaside. He didn't own an automobile, so we'd take the trolley (tram, as we called it in Australia) into the city of Adelaide, then change to another one for the 30-minute ride to the beach.

Once there, we'd put on our swimsuits and plunge into the water. Sometimes we'd walk along the sand at the edge of the ocean, splashing barefoot through encroaching waves. Often we just sat on the sand, looking out at the sea. My dad must have recalled the days when he sailed the world; sometimes he would speak about ships and captains and places he visited.

Because he was approaching 50 when I was born, my most vivid memories of him are of an older person. I remember noticing his legs, crossed with blue lines and networks of small, blue capillaries and some dark, smudgy patches. My father had worked hard, worked with his hands, carried loads of brick and cement. His legs showed the toll.

To the child, however, those legs were interesting, not repulsive. They were my father's legs, he who had carried me on his shoulders in years that even then I couldn't recall; who had labored hard and honestly, through heat and dust and sweat, to put bread on the family table.

Dad has long since passed to his rest, but I still go to the seaside. Walking or running on the cold wet sand and splashing through the waves in the early light of the day with sea birds wheeling and calling is, perhaps, the closest I get to the joys of eternity in this life.

I sit on the sand and look out over the ocean. I notice my legs, now crossed with blue lines and networks of small, blue capillaries. I see dark smudgy patches near the ankles. I too have worked hard, but not in physical labor. These legs have carried my son and daughter (and now my granddaughters) in my arms and on my shoulders. These legs have carried me on long flights to many countries. They have sustained me through mountain hikes and marathons.

The psalmist says that the Lord doesn't delight in the legs of a man. Rather, He delights in those "who fear him, who put their hope in his unfailing love" (Ps. 147:11, NIV).

The Rejected Christ

He came unto his own, and his own received him not. John 1:11.

The story of Jesus of Nazareth is incredible in many ways, but none more than this: the Creator of the universe came to the world He had made, but we, His creatures, rejected Him.

How could it be? How could creatures of dust spurn the hands that fashioned them? How could men and women, bound by a life span of 70 or 80 years, turn their backs on the One who is eternal?

What condescension! What forbearance! What humility! Even to come as a human being, accepting the working of the laws of heredity, would be a massive step down. But to come knowing that rejection, suffering, and death awaited Him—the story boggles the mind.

Long before John penned the poignant words "He came unto his own, and his own received him not" Isaiah had foretold the rejection:

"He was despised and rejected by men, a man of sorrows, and familiar with suffering. Like one from whom men hide their faces he was despised, and we esteemed him not" (Isa. 53:3, NIV).

They rejected Him then; they still reject Him, Why? Because He is the Light that shines into the heart of every person. The Light reveals what we are like. In the Light we see ourselves as we truly are, and it's not a pretty sight. That's why, in Jesus' time and still today, most people respond with "Put out the Light!"

"This is the verdict: Light has come into the world, but men loved darkness instead of light because their deeds were evil" (John 3:19, NIV).

But the rejection wasn't total, praise God, and still isn't today. In the original Greek text the two words translated "own" in John 1:11 are different. He came to His *own world,* and His *own people* received Him not. He commanded the waves, and they obeyed Him; He broke the loaves and fishes, and they multiplied in His hands. And nature covered His face in darkness as He hung in agony on the cross.

And there *were* some people (not the majority, but some) who did not reject Him, who did not say "Put out the Light!" but who opened their hearts to receive Him.

Then, some. Today, some.

I want to be among them, today and every day.

I And Thou

God said, "It's not good for the Man to be alone. I'll make him a helper, a companion."
Gen. 2:18, Message.

J esus, full of grace, always had time—always *took* the time—for everyone He met. He was never too hurried, too busy, or too programmed to stop and talk.

How different from our lives today! We live in a communication age, but find it hard to communicate at the most basic level, which is one on one. Our technology—the telephone, e-mail, the Internet—enables us to send and receive messages to and from all over the world, but the more tools we invent, the more they seem to frustrate us or dry up the springs of the warm, personal networking that God put into our very beings when He said, "It's not good for the man to be alone."

We dial a number (speed dial, of course) and hear a voice say, "Press 1 if you want ____ , press 2 for ____ , press 3 for ____ ," and so on. We feel like shouting, "I don't want a machine; I want a person!" And to rub in the insult, the recording claims, "Your call is important to us." Oh, yeah? Not important enough to warrant personal service!

We receive an e-mail (along with a bunch of others that we don't want) that asks us about some item. If we don't drop what we're doing and get back to the party who sent the message, within hours we get a brusque follow-up: "At 8:57 this morning I sent you the following message. . . . I have not heard back from you."

And the Internet, which opens up a mine of information and a lot of other stuff right out of the devil's snake pit, can hook us into hours of solitary sitting before the computer screen, neglecting the one-on-one fellowship our spouse and kids crave from us.

A half century ago the philosopher Martin Buber wrote a small but influential book that, translated from the German, was titled *I and Thou*. In it he analyzed relationships, drawing the distinction between those of an "I-it" character and those of an "I-thou" nature. In the former we relate to the other as a thing, an object; in the latter, as a person. And it's this latter we crave, especially as relationships become more and more impersonal.

Loving Someone We Cannot See

You never saw him, yet you love him. You still don't see him, yet you trust him—with laughter and singing. 1 Peter 1:8, Message.

Ever heard critics of Christianity say, "You people talk about loving God, but that's nonsense. It's hard enough to love someone you can see; how do you expect me to love someone I can't see?"

It sounds like a convincing argument, but it isn't, really. The best answer I ever heard came from Jennifer, who used to sit, week by week, in the Sabbath school class I taught occasionally. Jennifer has been blind since she was a young child.

One morning I brought up the old question about loving someone we cannot see. "Why, that's not a problem at all," said Jennifer. "I have never seen you, Pastor Johnsson, but I know you. I hear your voice; you speak to me, and I speak to you. Anytime I hear you, I know it's you, even if you aren't speaking to me. You don't have to be able to see someone in order to know them or to love them. And it's the same with God."

What an answer! We can't see God, but we can speak to Him. We call that prayer. And God speaks to us in a myriad ways, but especially through His Word. That's why taking time to study the Bible (not rushing through it or delving into it willy-nilly) is so important.

We get to know a person by taking time to talk with them. Real conversation is always a two-way street: speaking and listening. The more we share with each other, the better acquainted we become.

It's just the same with the Christian life. God is real, not a figment of the imagination. Jesus Christ rose from the dead and is alive forevermore. We may know Him as well as we know a friend. In fact, He can become our best and truest friend—if we will let Him.

The Bible uses the word "know" hundreds of times in both the Old Testament and the New Testament. While the word sometimes denotes intellectual knowledge, getting the facts straight, overwhelming usage points to personal, experiential knowing, the knowing of relationship. Sometimes "to know" means intimate closeness, as in Adam "knowing" Eve.

That personal, private knowing—the knowing of love—is what God offers us today. We may *know* Him, even though we cannot see Him.

A Cruise With a Difference

Then those whose lives honored God got together and talked it over. God saw what they were doing and listened in. A book was opened in God's presence and minutes were taken of the meeting, with the names of the God-fearers written down, all the names of those who honored God's name. Mal. 3:16, Message.

Carnival Cruise Line had never seen a group like this one. They came from across the United States, from Canada, India, and even New Zealand; 121 strong, they ranged in age from early teens to the 80s. Every evening their section of the restaurant rang with laughter and animated conversation, without alcohol as a lubricant. On ship's talent night three of their number entertained the packed house with class performances. While others on the cruise were getting drunk or playing the casinos, these people got together to look at old pictures, share stories—and to sing and pray.

The sign on their hospitality desk read "VHS Reunion," and a lot of the passengers wanted to know what it was all about and who these people were who seemed to have so much fun. When they learned that VHS stood for Vincent Hill School, a small Adventist boarding school in India that closed in 1969, they were even more bewildered. It didn't make sense that alumni, teachers, and friends would want to get together after so long a time.

Vincent Hill School has a mystique. Carved out of the first ridge of the Himalayas at 6,500 feet, for most of its existence it could be reached only by foot or donkey or in a kandi, a large basket carried by a coolie. The location was wild, grand, and magnificent. Leopards roamed the mountains and sometimes came on the campus. Everything was either up or down, and the slopes were all steep.

But there was more to it. The school's motto, "Educate for Eternity," proclaimed its values. Here young people came from India and many other lands to study and learn the art of living, now and forever. They went out from the school and changed the Adventist Church and the world for the better.

God was honored at Vincent Hill School. God was honored as its alumni, faculty, and friends met together to talk it over, reliving good times and bad.

And just maybe a book was opened in God's presence and a heavenly secretary took minutes of the meeting, writing down the names of the God-fearers.

Beyond Imagination

Now to him who is able to do immeasurably more than all we ask or imagine, according to his power that is at work within us. Eph. 3:20, NIV.

The God of grace is infinite in wisdom. He knows the end from the beginning: He sees a problem or difficulty long before we become aware of it, and knows the best way to tackle it. Eons before evil reared its ugly head in a perfect universe, millennia before our first parents yielded to the tempter's seductions and brought the Fall, God saw it all and made provision to save the lost world and all creation.

And God not only *knows;* He can *do.* He is infinite in power. As the Scripture notes again and again, "He is able." He has a thousand ways to deal with a situation that we can't even see.

Life inevitably brings us into circumstances that cause us stress. We can't see any way over, under, or through a financial problem, a work situation, a family falling apart, a health worry. If we can only believe it, only trust Him, God can do way beyond what we can ask.

We pray, but maybe we don't know what we really should be praying for. God can give us an answer far better than what we ask Him for with our limited perspective. We sit and dream about what it would be like to have events turn out in what we think would be the perfect pattern, but God's future for us is way beyond anything we can imagine,

For many years I had the great privilege of guiding the ministry of the *Adventist Review,* the church paper of the world Seventh-day Adventist Church. It was a challenging assignment, one far beyond my natural abilities or strength. It drove me to my knees in a manner that no other work had ever done. I gradually learned the lesson of waiting on God in every situation. He had the answer, and my job was to draw close enough to Him so that He could reveal it to me.

The biggest concern I had over those 24 years was the slowly declining circulation. I set my heart on building it to 100,000 and, ably assisted by colleagues, tried many and varied ways to attain it. But nothing worked. We'd see a jump for a while; then it would taper off again. I slowly resigned myself to the reality. But then, right at the close of my tenure as editor, the church leadership asked us to develop a global church paper. Its circulation was more than 1 million per month, 10 times beyond my shortsighted goal!

Beyond imagination indeed!

When the Skin Sags

You're all I want in heaven! You're all I want on earth! When my skin sags and my bones get brittle, God is rock-firm and faithful. Ps. 73:25, 26, Message.

On a flight from Denver to Anchorage, Alaska, I happened to sit next to a retired businessman. I was on my way to speak at a camp meeting; Ed was going fishing. From Anchorage he would catch another plane, and then another small one after that. In the Far North he would spend several days with five others on a boat, with cook provided.

We talked and talked. Ed had bought a business that supplied medical equipment, built it up to the national level, and then gone international. Eventually he was spending the majority of his life in airplanes, traveling from one city to another and from one country to another. He had flown more than 2 million miles on United Airlines, and during the flight the flight attendant kept dropping by to thank him and to bring more free drinks. He kept talking until at last he lapsed into an alcohol-induced slumber.

Ed lived for fishing. He fished in the United States and in Canada. He fished in Europe. He fished in Brazil. Twice he had gone to Australia to fish. He was full of fish stories, eager to hear of any exotic fishing sites I might know about.

"And when I get too old to fish," he said, "I guess I'll just sit at home and remember all the fishing I did."

As he drifted off to sleep, I stayed awake reflecting on his words. Oh, he seemed a pretty decent sort of fellow, and I have nothing against fishing (I did some of that myself long, long ago). But fishing as the center of one's life? Is that all there is to it? Weren't we made for something, for Someone, far greater?

Indeed we were! God made us for Himself. As Augustine said long ago: "Thou hast formed us for Thyself, and our hearts are restless until they find their rest in Thee."

God is all I want in heaven!

God is all I want on earth!

He is the first, the last, and the best. His grace purifies and channels the restless energies of youth, His grace sustains and guides our middle years, and when the skin sags and our bones get brittle, His grace is still there—rock-firm, faithful.

God only gets better.

Greening of Grace

A green Shoot will sprout from Jesse's stump, from his roots a budding Branch. Isa. 11:1, Message.

Recently after I addressed a meeting of ministers one stayed back to put a personal question to me. "How is it," he asked, "that you have been able to stay fresh and optimistic after so many years in the ministry?"

It's true; I have enjoyed a long ministry—47 years, as I write this. And "enjoyed" it the accurate term of use. My life and work have been, and continue to be, richly blessed.

I don't understand why I have been, as many people today would say, "so lucky." I don't believe in luck; I believe in grace. And all that has come my way or gone out through me is because of grace.

It's been many years now (I can't tell you just when) since I began to be aware of the marvel of grace. It was after I accepted Jesus as Savior and Lord, after I answered His call to ministry. Yes, I appreciated God's forgiving love and felt His transforming presence in my life. Grace was at work, and it was wonderful.

But somehow—not suddenly, not through any book or sermon or event that I can pinpoint—I began to *live* in grace. Began to experience Jesus, sung continually in my heart, and His praise on my lips. Began to accept the incredible truth that He loved me unconditionally, just as I am, even as He continues to call me up higher.

Maybe it was when I began to try to treat others with grace—that is, as God treats me—that its full force hit home. Only then did I start to grasp how selfish, mean, prejudiced, and, yes, even racist, I am.

However it happened, I have been graced. I am graced. Jesus has given me new life, taking me into His family as His child. This is all that matters now and eternally.

Grace means the greening. Grace means hope, hope that a flower will bloom in the desert, that out of the dried-up, apparently lifeless stump a green shoot will sprout. And not just a shoot, but a Shoot, even Jesus, who brings light out of darkness and life out of death.

When I feel down (for who does not at times?), I remind myself of this life-changing, universe-changing truth. And with it comes the greening of grace.

The Message of Chronicles

David, together with the commanders of the army, set apart some of the sons of Asaph, Heman and Jeduthun for the ministry of prophesying, accompanied by harps, lyres, and cymbals. Here is the list of the men who performed this service. 1 Chron. 25:1, NIV.

How many earnest Christians set out to read through the Bible, from Genesis to Revelation, only to see their aspirations founder on the shoals of Chronicles? The seemingly endless genealogies and interminable lists of names, with scant narrative interspersed, makes for dry reading indeed. One might say that, like the telephone directory, the cast is terrific but the plot is weak.

The Bible has one Author—the Holy Spirit—but many writers. It isn't so much one book as a library of 66 different volumes that differ widely in content and genre. All 66 parts, however, have a single purpose: to reveal God's will and plan for us. All tell us what God is like, how great, how powerful, how wonderful, and above all, how gracious.

Eugene H. Peterson has captured the essence of the two writings that make up First and Second Chronicles. In *The Message,* his attempt to put the Bible in contemporary language, he includes an introductory essay to these works (as he does for all the writings of the Bible) and notes in part:

"Names launch this story, hundreds and hundreds of names, lists of names, page after page of names, *personal* names. There is no true story-telling without names, and this immersion in names calls attention to the individual, the unique, the personal, which is inherent all spirituality. . . . Holy history is not constructed from impersonal forces or abstract ideas; it is woven from names—persons, each one unique. Chronicles erects a solid defense against depersonalized religion.

"And Chronicles provides a witness to the essential and primary place of accurate worship in human life. . . . In the way this story of Israel's past is told, nothing takes precedence over worship in nurturing and protecting our identity as a people of God—not politics, not economics, not family life, not art. And nothing in the preparation for and conduct of worship is too small to be left to whim or chance—nothing in architecture, personnel, music, or theology."

To which I can only respond, Amen! The God of the universe, who made us and redeemed us; the God of matchless grace, who knows us each by name, knows all about us and loves us just the same. To this God we have nothing to give but ourselves. We can only fall down and worship Him.

Suffused With Grace

God is good to one and all; everything he does is suffused with grace. Ps. 145:9, Message.

There are various ways to look at the world. One way is to see everything that happens as shaped wholly by natural causes. All that we see around us, all that has been, is, and will be has a rational explanation that can be found if we search long enough for it.

More and more people, especially in developed societies, have moved toward this view. For them, God effectively died with the onset of the modern scientific age and its accompanying technology. We are alone in a vast, cold universe; we have no prospect of existence after this little life is over.

Several years back someone very dear to me unexpectedly passed to his rest. I wrestled with the prospect of making a flight halfway around the world to be at his funeral, then for several reasons decided simply to send a message to be read to those assembled.

Later I received an audiotape of the funeral, and it made me sick inside. Throughout the entire event there was no prayer, no hymn, no scripture, and no mention of God. Led by a "eulogist," the bereaved family members simply gave personal recollections of the deceased. At the close the eulogist played a selection from the favorite music of the departed one, "The Three Tenors." What a way to live! What a way to die!

Other people look at the world through eyes blurred by superstition. They posit forces for good or evil, unseen powers that can strike and do us in. These forces must be handled with care and the proper ritual. Possibly many professed Christians fall under this category.

The way I see the world is vastly different from either of the above. It is the biblical way, the way that affirms that there is a God, that He communicates with us, and that He is love. This Being, who is all-powerful, "is good to one and all." All that He does—everything—is suffused with grace.

So I am not alone in a vast cold universe. I am not subject to the capriciousness of malevolent forces. I am a child of the King of heaven, known and loved personally by Him as though I were the only person on the planet.

How do I know this isn't just wishful thinking? Because He sent Jesus, and He was "full of grace" (John 1:14).

When Life Swings Low

When I tried to understand all this, it was oppressive to me till I entered the sanctuary of God; then I understood their final destiny. Ps. 73:16, 17, NIV.

One of the features of the psalms that attracts me is their brutal honesty. Here we find David, Asaph, and others crying out to God through the full range of human experiences: joy, delight, despair, pain, anger, frustration. The psalms are prayers that were originally intended to be sung, but they are more direct and confrontational than any prayer you will hear in church today.

In Psalm 73 we find Asaph wrestling with an old, old question: Why do bad people have it so good, and good people have it so bad? That concern is as modern as this morning.

"As for me, my feet had almost slipped; I had nearly lost my foothold," confesses Asaph (verse 2, NIV). He had fallen into the trap of envy (always a self-destructive fault) as he saw the arrogance and prosperity of the wicked. From Asaph's perspective those who ignored God didn't have struggles, were healthy and strong, and went through life without burdens. They felt no restraint on the pride, violence, callousness, scoffing, and oppression that marked their lives. They thought that God either didn't know or didn't care, because He never intervened in their folly,

Ever felt like Asaph? Ever felt like saying, "God, where are You? Why don't You do something to put an end to the mess evil people have made of Your world?"

So Asaph concluded, "My efforts to follow God and live a life according to His will are all useless. I might as well quit, because it's the righteous, not the God-scoffers, who have a hard time."

By focusing on negatives, we talk ourselves into a blue funk. That's what happened to Asaph. It was all oppressive to him. But then he took a walk. He went into the sanctuary—the Temple—and the clouds lifted. He had been focusing on the short view; the sanctuary lifted his eyes to the long view.

"Then I understood their final destiny" (Ps. 73:17, NIV). The wicked may appear to be cruising on Easy Street, not a care in the world, but they're actually on Slippery Slope. Suddenly they crash to ruin, to oblivion. Their house, which seemed so secure, was made of cards.

Jesus always took the long view, and so must we. As we live by His grace and for His glory, He bids us to keep looking up, even to Him—in the heavenly sanctuary.

The Reluctant Clematis

So he said to the man who took care of the vineyard, "For three years I've been coming to look for fruit on this fig tree and haven't found any. Cut it down! Why should it use up the soil?" Luke 13:7, NIV.

I didn't plant a fig tree, but I felt just like the man in the parable. My beef was with a clematis plant that defied all my efforts to get it to bloom, that seemed to taunt me to try a new line of attack.

For years I had admired the clematis on my neighbor's fence that came to life each spring and bloomed so luxuriantly and gorgeously. I wanted a clematis for my yard, and I had just the spot for it by the mailbox next to the curb. I imagined a clematis wrapping itself around the post that supported the box and festooning it with purple or deep-pink flowers.

Problem: the soil around the mailbox was hard and rocky. I had tried to start a small flowerbed there once before, but it failed dismally under summer's drought and heat. So each spring I'd entertain thoughts of a clematis, but each summer I'd put off the plan for another year.

Then came the spring when I happened upon boxed clematis plants in a large store. Through the clear plastic on the front of the box I could see pale-green tendrils. This clematis was ready! So I bought the box (it contained two plantings), took it home, and began to figure out how to get it into the ground.

A couple weeks went by before I could work up a bed for the clematis plants, but at last I had them planted. I waited. And waited. Finally one reluctant shoot appeared, then another. They seemed to struggle for life and only reached a couple of inches all summer.

The next year I tried again. Another box. More planting, watering, fertilizing. The result was worse. By August the stunted plants were withering away. Soon they were dead.

But not quite. I noticed some green low on the stems of the dried-up plants. I hesitated, then decided to keep watering. New growth appeared. More fertilizer and water.

And the next spring—voilà! I could hardly believe my eyes. The clematis plants emerged from hibernation healthy and vigorous. They grew, climbed—and bloomed in luxurious profusion.

I'm glad that like the man in the parable I gave the clematis another chance. That's how God treats us.

Modern Heroes

They defeated him through the blood of the Lamb and the bold word of their witness. They weren't in love with themselves; they were willing to die for Christ. Rev. 12:11, Message.

One of the great stories of 2006 was the amazing feat of Mark Inglis, who climbed Mount Everest on artificial legs. Inglis, a mountain guide, had been caught in a severe blizzard on Mount Cook in New Zeeland in 1982. Forced to take shelter in an ice cave for two weeks, he suffered severe cold; both legs had to be amputated below the knee.

But Inglis didn't sit around and mope. Rather than feel sorry for himself, he went back to school and became a research biochemist. And he continued to climb mountains, eventually scaling Mount Cook on artificial legs in 2002. Then, in May 2006, he achieved the ultimate: he stood atop Everest!

I salute Mark Inglis. He is a modern hero.

I salute every age who overcomes misfortune, who refuses to give in, whose determination and pluck keep driving them on until they accomplish what others call impossible.

The Bible is a book of heroes. The men and women whose lives light up its pages—Moses and David, Esther and Deborah, Peter and Paul—did amazing things. They were bold in vision and in act. They cast scorn on the word "impossible." Because *God* was with them—motivating them, inspiring them, empowering them—they pressed on and up until they reached God's top.

Standing at the head of the line, towering above all others, is the Leader. Jesus is the greatest hero of the Bible. "Because he never lost sight of where he was headed—that exhilarating fihish in and with God—he could put up with anything along the way: cross, shame, whatever" (Heb. 12:2, Message).

God is looking for modern heroes. For young men and women who, inspired by a divine dream, will do amazing things for the glory of His name and uplifting of humanity. Yes, heroic acts that surpass even the conquest of Everest.

Many people want to look like heroes. But God's heroes aren't in love with themselves; they love Jesus, the Lamb whose blood has set them free to new live and new purpose. They aren't ashamed to be called His followers, for they love Him more than life itself.

Who will be a hero for Jesus today?

The Gift and the Claim

Then the master called the servant in. "You wicked servant," he said, "I canceled all that debt of yours because you begged me to. Shouldn't you have had mercy on your fellow servant just as I had on you?" Matt. 18:32, 33, NIV.

A longstanding discussion among Christians centers on the respective roles of the divine and the human in our salvation. Some Christians put all the weight on the divine side, reducing the human to the vanishing point. At the other extreme is theology that makes the human will so strong that of itself it can bring about obedience to God's law in the life of the converted person.

These ongoing debates frequently feature the writings of the apostle Paul. Paul teaches unequivocally that salvation comes by grace alone through faith alone (e.g., Eph. 2:9), but judgment is according to works (e.g., Rom. 14:10-12). How can these seemingly contradictory ideas be reconciled? For me, the answer comes not from theological argument but in Jesus' parables. And of these His story of the unmerciful servant (Matt. 18:21-35) provides the clearest explanation of all.

Remember the parable? Here's a man who owes the king a fabulous amount—10,000 talents. We can hardly grasp the size of the debt; 10,000 is the largest number in the book, and a talent is the largest unit of money. Today we'd speak of maybe $50 million or $1 billion to gain a sense of the figure. The servant begs for time to pay off the debt. How many lifetimes did he hope to have? He could *never* pay it off. But surprise—the king forgives him everything. Just like that. Go free; I cancel the debt.

Now, the man who has been forgiven so much encounters a fellow servant who owes him 100 denarii (a few thousand dollars). This man also begs for time to pay off his debt, but instead the first man throws him into jail. Eventually word gets back to the king, and he is angry. Summoning the servant for whom he had canceled the huge debt, he tells him that because of his actions the deal is off.

This is a parable of the kingdom of heaven, a story about grace. We could sum it up in two words: gift and claim. Salvation is a gift, an incredible gift; but that gift brings with it a claim on our lives. The grace that forgives transforms us into God's likeness.

APRIL

Karen's Song

But I am a worm and not a man, scorned by men and despised by the people. Ps. 22:6, NIV.

Alas! and did my Savior bleed? And did my Sovereign die? Would He devote that sacred head for such a worm as I?" wrote Isaac Watts in a famous hymn. Ever since, some people have choked over the last line.

In these days of feel-good psychology and self-realization the old "worm" theology is out. A generation that denies that sin exists certainly doesn't want to be put down with expressions like that.

But from a biblical standpoint, Isaac Watts was correct. The good news about God begins with the bad news about us. Before Him all our professed righteousness hangs in filthy rags. We have nothing in ourselves to commend ourselves to Him. Nothing. We are indeed worms. Until we admit our great need, the Word cannot supply His grace.

There's another side to feeling like a worm, however, and this aspect has an ominous, terrifying quality.

On a long flight to another country, when I tired of reading I put on the headset and tried out the musical offerings. A voice from a generation past—pleasant, nostalgic, with an edge of sadness—came through the sound system. I looked up the entertainment guide and read that the featured program was selections from the songs of Karen and Richard Carpenter.

Karen Carpenter—her story came back to one as I heard again the plaintive voice. Karen, accompanied by her brother, Richard, achieved great success as a recording artist in the 1970s, selling more than 100 million albums by the 1990s. Glamorous and loved, she was the idol of young girls. Despite the fame she achieved, however, Karen had a low image of herself. When she looked in the mirror, this attractive young woman could think only of how ugly she was. In 1983 Karen, only 32, died from cardiac arrest brought on by anorexia nervosa. For several years she had starved herself. At the time, the explanation seemed almost impossible to accept, but since her tragic death the condition has become well recognized from the struggles of other young women.

The other side of the "worm" theology is the one that I wish Karen Carpenter could have found. In God's eyes we are not worms. We are loved, we are precious, we are special, we are beautiful. We are princesses and princes of the King of heaven,

The Quest for Perfection

Be ye therefore perfect, even as your Father which is in heaven is perfect. Matt. 5:48.

These words of Jesus have challenged and crushed, motivated and mortified sincere souls in every century since He uttered them. They cry out still in our day, and we must take them seriously.

Some people have taken, and still take, them to be a demand for absolute sinlessness. And understood this way, these people find within themselves something that rises up and says, "I will be that person! I will do whatever it takes to weed out all flaws from my life so that I can stand without fault before God!"

These earnest souls fall into a deep pit, the pit of self-delusion. Their lives become focused on themselves and turn inward, whereas the life Jesus calls us to always turns outward to bless others. If they continue on this course they inevitably either end up proud of their supposed righteousness or come to throw out religion altogether.

What did Jesus mean by these haunting words? As always in Scripture, the context sheds light on the meaning. We need to go back to verse 43, in which Jesus quotes from the Old Testament: "You have heard that it was said, 'Love your neighbor [Lev. 19:18] and hate your enemy.' But I tell you: Love your enemies and pray for those who persecute you, that you may be sons of your Father in heaven" (verses 43-45, NIV).

So Jesus is telling us that we should relate to people—all people, not just our friends—in the way that God relates to them. He is kind to all, generous to all, without distinction or partiality. Then comes verse 48, which is the conclusion of the argument: We should be complete and mature (this is the meaning of the original), just like our heavenly Father, in all our dealings.

Eugene Peterson expresses Matthew 5:48 this way: "In a word, what I'm saying is, *Grow up*. You're kingdom subjects. Now live like it. Live out your God-created identity. Live generously and graciously toward others, the way God lives toward you" (Message).

And Ellen White says: "We are to be centers of light and blessing to our little circle, even as He is to the universe. We have nothing of ourselves, but the light of His love shines upon us, and we are to reflect its brightness. 'In His borrowed goodness' we may be perfect in our sphere, even as God is perfect in His" (*Thoughts From the Mount of Blessing*, p. 77).

And Peter

But go, tell his disciples and Peter, "He is going ahead of you into Galilee. There you will see him, just as he told you." Mark 16:7, NIV.

Oh, the gentleness of Jesus! On that Easter morning, just risen from the dead, He sends an angel to speak to Mary Magdalene and the other women who have come to the tomb. And as the angel tells them the good news of the resurrection, he singles out Peter. Tell the disciples, he said, and make sure you tell Peter, also.

On the fateful Friday morning when Jesus stood in the judgment hall, Peter failed the test. He capitulated before the words of a servant girl; he shrank in the face of questions about his relationship to the Master. With oaths and coarse language Peter denied his Lord. He forfeited his right to a place among the apostles, let alone his accustomed role as leader.

But Jesus turned and looked at Peter. He looked not in condemnation but in sorrow, not in anger but in love. That look melted Peter's heart. He rushed from the high priest's courtyard and into the night with bitter tears.

The Sabbath that followed must have been the bleakest of Peter's life. Jesus was dead. His hopes for an earthly kingdom lay in ruins. His self-confidence was shattered. The other disciples mistrusted him.

We are Peter. We have abandoned Jesus in His hour of need. We have capitulated before the mocking crowd. We have denied the Lord we profess.

But Jesus looks at us in sorrow and love. That love melts our heart, and we want to run out into the night. We wonder what lies ahead, search for a glimmer of hope.

Then Jesus sends the word to us. He calls us by name, includes us in the good news He gives other humanity. "Tell Peter," He says.

"Tell Tom, Dick, and Harry; tell Mary, Martha, and Jane. Tell them that I am alive forevermore and do not hold their sins against them. Tell them that I am the Lord of new hope and new starts. Tell them that they can have a second chance—that although they abandoned Me, I will never abandon them."

Gently, lovingly Jesus calls us back to Himself. Gently, lovingly He leads us over the same ground so that we may learn to lean on His mighty arm, and, leaning, overcome.

Jesus, call my name today!

April 4

Each Light-filled Hour

Oh, how sweet the light of day, and how wonderful to live in the sunshine! Even if you live a long time, don't take a single day for granted. Take delight in each light-filled hour. Eccl. 11:7, 8, Message.

Taken alone, anyone could utter these words from Ecclesiastes. Even a pagan might give praise to the gods and goddesses of nature.

But these words do not stand alone. They come in the context of the writer's "Honor and enjoy your Creator while you're still young" (Eccl. 12:1, Message) and his closing words: "The last and final word is this: Fear God. Do what he tells you" (verse 13, Message).

God makes all the difference. When we know Him as Creator and Redeemer, as our personal Friend and Lord, we look out on His creation through grace-filled eyes.

And how rapturously beautiful is that creation! Marred and defaced by the effects of sin, it nevertheless bears the stamp of a beneficent Maker.

I love the light. I love the dawn's first gleaming; the early rays reflecting off lake and mountain and surf; the full-throttled power of midday; the soft light of the gloaming.

I love the gentle coolness of the moon, the silent wonder of the stars. On an island in the antipodes, far from city lights, I lay on my back and gazed amazed at the startling clarity of the Milky Way and the Southern Cross.

If the sun or the moon or the stars rose only once a year, everyone would turn out to witness the event. So as the wise man said: "Don't take a single day for granted."

This world is incredibly beautiful, this life incredibly wonderful. I want to take delight in each light-filled hour.

On a morning walk in the park, Noelene and I saw a bluebird sitting on a pole only feet away. This shy little chap didn't move as we stood and watched. Then another bluebird flew by, and another, and another. Then two males went by in tandem, their majestic colors brilliant in the light. For an enchanted moment it seemed as if we were surrounded by bluebirds.

"A moment of grace," whispered Noelene. What a way to start the day!

Lord, may I look out on Your world today through grace-filled eyes. Show me the wonder of Your world and the beauty of Your people.

God of the Lost Years

I will restore to you the years which the swarming locust has eaten, the hopper, the destroyer, and the cutter, my great army, which I sent among you. Joel 2:25, RSV.

I glanced at my appointment calendar and froze. Scheduled to see me in a short while was a man who had attacked me fiercely by words and by video. Years before he had started out with the goal of serving as an Adventist minister, but he had very soon gone down an independent road from which he leveled criticisms at the church and its leaders. I wondered what he could want with me.

He arrived at my office, accompanied by his wife. Within moments he was begging my forgiveness with earnest pleas and tears. I told him that I forgave him, and he proceeded to recount how the Lord had intervened in his life to radically change his attitude.

Gradually he shared the story of his life, how he started out to be a minister, how he went off on a detour, how he built up a large private ministry with strong financial support. Now he had lost it all. His decision to cease criticizing others had resulted in the loss of his following and their money. Approaching middle age, he found his life in ruins, his hopes shattered.

Could there yet be a place of service for him? he wanted to know. I assured him that God gives us a second chance, that He is able to bring good out of a seemingly hopeless situation. I advised him to be content with a low profile and to accept whatever responsibility was offered him, no matter how small, without thought of monetary compensation.

During the course of that wonderful, tearful conversation, I pointed him to words found in the book of Joel: "I will restore to you the years which the swarming locust has eaten" (Joel 2:25, RSV). I told him to claim this promise of a new start; that although lost opportunities had gone forever, God could bring new opportunities. God could still make something beautiful out of the years ahead.

The words of the text resonated in his soul, and he and his wife went away with hope. For many months he indeed ate "humble pie," but the day came when he received an invitation to pastor two small churches. What joy! What fulfillment of the word of the God who sets aside our lost years and gives us a new start!

The Training of Timothy

For this reason I am sending to you Timothy, my son whom I love, who is faithful in the Lord. He will remind you of my way of life in Christ Jesus, which agrees with what I teach everywhere in every church. 1 Cor. 4:17, NIV.

Timothy seems to have had an unusual problem: He was perpetually young. This traveling companion of, and assistant to, the apostle Paul was a young man when he heard the good news from Paul, and many years later Paul still related to him as a young person.

We find many references to Timothy in Acts and in Paul's letters, and together they enable us to piece together a fairly complete portrait of his personality and work. Timothy came from the city of Lystra (in modern-day Turkey); he was half Jewish, his mother being a Jewess and his father a "Greek" (that is, a non-Jew [Acts 16:1]). His godly mother, Eunice, and devout grandmother Lois taught him the Old Testament Scriptures from childhood (2 Tim. 1:5; 3:15). As a young man, now a Christian, Timothy was viewed by the believers as someone of great promise (Acts 16:3). Paul saw his potential and took him under his wing first, however, circumcising him to avoid unnecessary controversy with the Jews.

Paul and his young intern traveled and labored together for the Lord. They became very close. While writing to the Corinthians, Paul called him "my son whom I love" (1 Cor. 4:17, NIV). To the Philippians he wrote, "I have no one else like him. . . . As a son with his father he has served with me in the work of the gospel" (Phil. 2:20-22, NIV). And in his letter to Timothy he calls him "my dear son" (2 Tim. 1:2, NIV).

Perhaps it was natural for Paul always to think of Timothy as being young. But more likely Timothy had a quiet, even diffident, personality that made him seem younger than he was. We find Paul counseling the Corinthians: "If Timothy comes, see to it that he has nothing to fear while he is with you" (1 Cor. 16:10, NIV). And then some 10 years later, when Timothy had to have been in his 30s, to Timothy himself: "Don't let anyone look down on you because you are young" (1 Tim. 4:12, NIV). In Paul's final letter several years later, written as he faced imminent death, he counseled, "God did not give us a spirit of timidity. . . . So do not be ashamed to testify about our Lord, or ashamed of me his prisoner" (2 Tim. 1:7, 8, NIV).

Paul had no son of his own. In God's kindness He gave him Timothy.

Iron Man

Even to your old age, I am He, and even to gray hairs I will carry you! I have made, and I will bear; even I will carry, and will deliver you. Isa. 46:4, NKJV.

Of all the extreme sporting contests few can match the Ironman triathlon. Participants must swim 2.4 miles, then cycle 112 miles, and top it off with a marathon run—the full 26.2 miles. As if this weren't enough, each leg must be completed within a designated time frame or the person is disqualified.

Very few people ever attempt the Ironman, and of those who do, only about seven out of 100 complete the event. It is the ultimate in its demands on body and will. To finish is to be a hero.

Rick Hoyt completed the Ironman. He is the unlikeliest hero and perhaps the toughest of all. Rick was born with cerebral palsy and suffers from spasticity and quadriplegia. Physicians told his parents that he would never amount to anything; that he'd be a vegetable if he survived, and that they should put him in an institution.

But the parents could not bring themselves to put away their first-born. Rick's dad saw in his son's eyes *something*—something struggling to express itself, the light of a person within.

Rick "spoke" his first words when he was 12—not by voice, but through a computer. He went on to finish public high school, then college, graduating from Boston University.

One day Rick read about a charity event, a five-mile run. He wanted to help raise funds, so his dad registered and ran, pushing Rick all the way in a little cart. Rick was delighted. "When I'm running I don't feel handicapped," he said.

It was the start of a remarkable father-son sporting career. Rick has competed in more than 200 events. He has run right across the United States.

And yes, he has completed the Ironman contest. With his father towing him in a rubber raft, he "swam" the 2.4 miles. Perched on the handlebars, he "cycled" 112 miles. And at last he ran the marathon, pushed by the same devoted father.

What a triumph of the human spirit! What a love story! And what a picture of grace.

We are Ricks. We are nothing to look at, ready to be tossed aside. But a loving Father carries us—carries us all the way—to the finish line.

Kidnapped!

But none of these things move me; nor do I count my life dear to myself, so that I may finish my race with joy, and the ministry which I received from the Lord Jesus, to testify to the gospel of the grace of God. Acts 20:24, NKJV.

As Pastor Paul Ratsara, a Seventh-day Adventist minister from Madagascar working in Kinshasa, stepped onto the curb of a thoroughfare, a man approached him. A feeling of fear and dread overtook him when, just a few yards farther along, the back door of a parked car was flung open. "Get in!" demanded the man.

Pastor Ratsara thought to resist, but quickly changed his mind when he saw the gun in the kidnapper's hand. Despite his fears, he climbed into the back seat. The man with the handgun followed him and shut the door. The bandits demanded everything the pastor was carrying. He emptied his pockets. Once they had relieved him of his possessions, the driver threw the car into gear and quickly made his way through the suburban shanties in the direction of the Congo River a few miles away. "We are going to kill you and dump your body into the river," the leader informed him.

Please, Lord, if You want me to die, I'm ready—I'm in Your hands. But if You want me to live, please rescue me.

His short, desperate prayer complete, he began to talk to his captors with confidence. "I'm a missionary," he explained. "I come from Madagascar. I came here to serve God and humanity, including you men."

The car began to slow. The gang began to argue among themselves in their own dialect. Finally the leader said to the others, "No, we are not going to take this man. He is a man of God. We will let him go. We aren't going to keep him." The driver turned the car around, then accelerated back down the lonely road toward the city. As they approached the city limits, the thieves piled all they'd taken from the pastor into his lap. Finally they stopped, and Pastor Ratsara stepped into the fresh air of freedom.

"I reflected a lot on what happened," Pastor Ratsara says. "I've learned that in order to live, you have to be ready to die; in order to be free, you have to be free from the fear of death; and when you no longer hold your life dear, then you are truly free. My prayer every day is to be in tune with God, to know that His angels are with me. I pray all the while."

The Rehabilitation of Richard Nixon

Don't insist on getting even; that's not for you to do. "I'll do the judging," says God. "I'll take care of it." Rom 12:19, Message.

We all know the story of Richard Nixon's fall from the United States presidency, but who knows about his rehabilitation?

It was the Christmas season of 1977, and Senator Hubert H. Humphrey had returned to his home near Minneapolis, Minnesota. His remarkable political life was almost over, and, emaciated by cancer, Humphrey was dying. In the lane at the back of the house a cluster of reporters were already forming a death watch.

Minnesota's Happy Warrior began to call old friends and associates around the nation and the world. He ostensibly called to give them season's greetings, but everyone knew he was taking his leave of them.

He reached his old adversary, Richard Nixon, on Christmas Eve, only to learn that the Nixons were both ill, depressed, and alone. Something troubled Humphrey deeply about this conversation with Nixon, and the next morning he again called the former president, the man who in 1968 had given Humphrey his most bitter defeat. He told Nixon that he had a farewell gift to give him.

He said that he knew he had only days to live and that he had made the arrangements for the events that would follow his death: his lying in state in the Capitol in Washington, his funeral and interment in Minnesota. Humphrey told Nixon that he was inviting him to attend the ceremony that would conclude the lying in state in Washington and that he wanted him to be present and to stand in the place of honor of a former president.

Nixon had resigned from the presidency in disgrace only three years before and had not returned to Washington. Sensing Nixon's profound depression, Humphrey spontaneously fashioned an excuse enabling his old rival to return to the capital.

Three weeks later Humphrey was dead. At the close of the ceremony in Washington the crowd gasped as Richard Nixon was escorted to the place of honor with the others, near the flag-draped casket.

That began Nixon's rehabilitation. A gift of grace from a dying man.

The Elder and the Egg

For if the willingness is there, the gift is acceptable according to what one has, not according to what he does not have. 2 Cor. 8:12, NIV.

Justus Devadas, president of Spicer Memorial College in India, told the following story, which I find full of grace.

Several years ago Justus had helped establish several new congregations in villages in south India, and he decided to pay them a visit. At one church he found just a small group with the pastor gathered for worship. But the elder was conspicuously absent.

"He is so faithful," said the pastor. "He never misses church." So they waited and waited to begin the worship service. No elder. So they went ahead without him.

Toward the close of the service, Devadas saw an old man enter the church, a simple man of the village, dressed in very modest clothing. "I am sorry to be late," he told the pastor. "I so much wanted to be present on time, but when I looked I discovered I had no money to give as an offering. I could think of only one way I could bring an offering—my chicken. So I waited for the chicken to lay an egg. I wanted to hurry the chicken up, but the chicken took its time!" Then the elder reached into the folds of his clothing and brought out his offering—a carefully wrapped egg.

I think of the abundance of material goods that I possess—all I need, and so much more—and am moved by the loving devotion of this dear man. Men and women who willingly give back to the Giver, not out of desire to win approval, but from hearts overflowing with gratitude—of such is the kingdom of heaven.

In the Old Testament we read about a mistake made by King David. A plague broke out. People died from Dan to Beersheba, from north to south. As the destroying angel was about to strike Jerusalem, the prophet Gad told the king to build an altar on the threshing floor of Araunah the Jebusite, where the angel had paused. When David approached Araunah, he offered to give his threshing floor, plus oxen, for an offering without charge. But David said, "No, I insist on paying you for it. I will not sacrifice to the Lord my God burnt offerings that cost me nothing" (2 Sam. 24:24, NIV).

The king and the elder. Three thousand years apart, but the same spirit.

Cottage Cheese by Mail

Dead flies putrefy the perfumer's ointment, and cause it to give off a foul odor; so does a little folly to one respected for wisdom and honor. Eccl. 10:1, NKJV.

When we worked at Spicer Memorial College in India, a missionary couple arrived on campus to manage the college farm. They weren't young; in fact, they were not many years from retirement. It was a courageous step for these dear people to take to leave their homeland after never having served abroad and try to adjust to a vastly different climate and culture. But they stuck it out and gave good service.

One of the many things from home they missed was cottage cheese. It was the farm manager's favorite, and how he longed for a taste of it again! None was available in India.

One day when I went to the college post office to pick up our mail, I detected a foul odor. It came from a grease-stained package swarming with flies, addressed to the farm manager. You guessed it—cottage cheese! Someone back home had heard of his craving for his favorite food and thought they'd send him a surprise. With more goodwill than understanding, they went to the supermarket, bought a carton of cottage cheese, wrapped it up, and mailed it to India. Somehow they never stopped to think that you don't attempt to send cottage cheese by mail even in Canada or the United States, let alone to the burning heat of India.

College cheese is wonderful—if it's fresh. And if it's fresh, it's cold. I like it a lot. But I also know how repulsive it can become if left too long in the refrigerator or if the refrigerator isn't cooling sufficiently.

Christians are like cottage cheese. When we keep close to Jesus and live by His grace, we will be a delight to everyone who "tastes" us. But when we let ourselves become separated from Him, we stink up the neighborhood.

Over the course of the centuries Christianity got a bad name because the followers of Jesus, who professed so much, lived lives so unlike Jesus'. The stink started at the top, with popes, prelates, and priests who lived in luxury with their mistresses while the common people groveled in poverty and ignorance.

Before we rush to judgment, let's point the finger at ourselves. Let's search our hearts and today, *this* day, go forth clothed with the grace of Jesus. Only then will our lives be as delicious as fresh cottage cheese.

Joshua and the Angel

Then He answered and spoke to those who stood before Him, saying, "Take away the filthy garments from him." And to him He said, "See, I have removed your iniquity from you, and I will clothe you with rich robes." Zech. 3:4, NJKV.

In the book of Zechariah (a largely neglected portion of the Scriptures) we find one of the loveliest portrayals of grace in all the Bible. The central character is Joshua, high priest of the band of Jews who have recently returned from exile in Babylon and who are attempting to re-build Jerusalem and the Temple.

Joshua has a problem: he is clothed in filthy garments. While the high priest's garments should be spotless and beautiful, his are anything but. And Joshua represents the entire fragment of a nation—they all are clothed in filthy rags, utterly unclean before a holy God.

That's us, every one of us. Even the good things we do (and we do plenty of the other variety) are like an unclean thing before God (Isa. 64:6).

In the scene in Zechariah 3, Satan stands at Joshua's right hand to op-pose him. The old serpent, "the accuser of our brethren" (Rev. 12:10), specializes in that work. He points out Joshua's faults—his filthy gar-ments; he points out the faults of the little band of Jews; and he points out our faults.

And he is right.

But there's more to the story. Another character steps forward: the Angel of the Lord. The Angel is the divine Mediator, the Intercessor, even our Lord Jesus Christ. The Lord says to Satan, "The Lord rebuke you, Satan! The Lord who has chosen Jerusalem rebuke you! Is this not a brand plucked from the fire?" (verse 2, NKJV).

Praise God, Jesus stands up for us to plead our case. He has chosen us. We are a brand plucked from the fire. And before His mighty presence the enemy of our souls, who specializes in pointing out our failings and shortcomings, has to slink away.

The order went out to Joshua, and it goes to us: " 'Take away the filthy garments from him.' . . . 'See, I have removed your iniquity from you, and I will clothe you with rich robes.' . . . 'Put a clean turban on his head' " (verses 4, 5, NKJV).

In ourselves we are nothing. With Jesus we are everything. Our righ-teousness is filthy rags. His righteousness is a rich robe that covers us and cleanses us.

The Refinement of Grace

The man's name was Nabal (Fool), a Calebite, and his wife's name was Abigail. The woman was intelligent and good-looking, the man brutish and mean. 1 Sam. 25:3, Message.

I t bothers me when those who take the name of Jesus set a low goal for themselves; indeed, seem to take pride in a low goal. "I'm rough and ready," they say. Why not refined and ready? Seems to me the religion of Jesus lifts our sights, motivating us to improve every excellence, to seek the noble and the best in every aspect of life.

I'm not talking about putting on airs to impress others, a veneer of refinement, but the real thing—like Jesus. He was, says Ellen White, the embodiment of refinement (*Testimonies for the Church*, vol. 2, p. 467). And she was bothered by Christians who lacked the graces that grace should bring. Writing to ministers, she noted, "There are some who, becoming wearied by the superficial gloss that the world calls refinement, have gone to the other extreme, and one fully as harmful. They refuse to receive the polish and refinement that Christ desires His children to possess. The minister should remember that he is an educator, and that if in manner and speech he is coarse and unrefined, those who have less knowledge and experience will follow in his steps" (*Gospel Workers,* p. 93).

Among the stories associated with David, who became Israel's greatest king, we find a classic that you might call "The Lady and the Oaf." Out of the blue we read about Abigail. She was both beautiful and smart (thus giving the kibosh to the myth that a woman, especially if blond, can't be both).

In a classic marriage of opposites, this outstanding woman was linked to a rich but hopeless fellow. Nabal was his name, which means Fool; and he was well-named. David, on the run from crazy King Saul, had a run-in with mean-spirited Nabal. David's men had provided protection for Nabal's shepherds, but when David sent for a little return, Nabal blew up. "Who is this David? Who is this son of Jesse?" he retorted (1 Sam. 25:10, Message).

In a towering rage David gathered his men to finish off Nabal. However, the wise and beautiful Abigail heard about it and, taking a gift, intercepted the future king with a message of grace. And David turned around.

The story even has a classic ending. The next morning when Nabal heard about it, he had a heart attack and died. And Abigail became David's wife.

Building by Grace

Who are you, O great mountain? Before Zerubbabel you shall become a plain! And he shall bring forth the capstone with shouts of "Grace, grace to it!" Zech. 4:7, NKJV.

As followers of Jesus we are all builders. We each are building a life, and we are building up His temple on earth, the church. How shall we build? The answer for both is the same: by grace, and grace alone.

No discussion about building would be complete without looking at the work of the Jews who returned from exile in Babylon to rebuild Jerusalem and the Temple. In fact, four books of the Bible deal with the project: Ezra, Nehemiah, Haggai, and Zechariah. We can learn a lot about building from these books. Ezra and Nehemiah tell the story.

The little band of optimists quit Babylon and embark on the task. The odds against them are huge. Their numbers are few, the task is huge, and adversaries seek to block their work. And the opposition comes from within their own rank. Some Jews are secretly in league with their foes.

The work goes slowly, eventually grinding to a halt. The people, dispirited, forget about rebuilding the Temple and care for their own concerns. The project has failed.

But no! God raises up two prophets. One, an old man named Haggai, bears a simple, straightforward message from the Lord: "Rise and build—now!" The other, a young man named Zechariah, also encourages the people to go forward with the work, but by telling them a series of striking visions that the Lord has given him.

One of Zechariah's visions, the lampstand and the olive trees, candidly faces the enormity of the task that the Jews, led by the governor Zerubbabel, face. It is indeed a "great mountain." But the word from the Lord of hosts is "'Not by might nor by power, but by My Spirit.' . . . 'Who are you, O great mountain? . . . You shall become a plain!'"

And the work went forward. Through blood, sweat, and tears it went forward until it was finished with shouts of "Grace, grace to it!"

That's the way the building today gets done, in our lives and in the church. Blood, sweat and tears—with grace over all.

True Grace

With the help of Silas, whom I regard as a faithful brother, I have written to you briefly, encouraging you and testifying that this is the true grace of God. Stand fast in it. 1 Peter 5:12, NIV.

Peter's expression "true grace," which occurs only here, startles us. Could he be suggesting that there is a false grace, something other than grace masquerading as grace? Elsewhere Peter notes that some people distorted the meaning of Paul's letters (2 Peter 3:16). Paul was the preeminent exponent of grace; I wonder if the distortion that Peter refers to might have been a twisting of the Pauline message of grace?

Whatever the background, Peter wasn't scared of grace. He begins his first letter with a greeting similar to Paul's, "Grace and peace be yours in abundance" (1 Peter 1:2, NIV), and closes his second one with "Grow in the grace and knowledge of our Lord and Savior Jesus Christ" (2 Peter 3:18, NIV).

In Peter's first letter, where the expression "true grace" occurs, the idea of grace runs like a golden thread throughout. Peter was writing to Christians who had suffered for their faith and who faced the threat of new trials, as passages such as the following verses make clear: "If you suffer for doing good and you endure it, this is commendable before God" (1 Peter 2:20, NIV). "But even if you should suffer for what is right, you are blessed" (1 Peter 3:14, NIV). "Do not be surprised at the painful trial you are suffering. . . . Rejoice that you participate in the suffering of Christ. . . . If you suffer as a Christian, do not be ashamed" (1 Peter 4:12-16, NIV).

True grace isn't a shallow flight of feeling. It's grace that enables a man or woman to stand tall for God, however hard the winds blow. True grace puts iron in the will, a firm set to the jaw, a fire in the eye.

To all who would preach a watered-down gospel, the German pastor Dietrich Bonhoeffer, who died at Hitler's hand, gave the decisive response: "Cheap grace is the preaching of forgiveness without requiring repentance, baptism without church discipline, Communion without confession, absolution without personal confession. Cheap grace is grace without discipleship, grace without the cross, grace without Jesus Christ, living and incarnate."

Which is not grace at all.

The Gate of Heaven

He was afraid and said, "How awesome is this place! This is none other than the house of God; this is the gate of heaven." Gen. 28:17, NIV.

Here is Jacob, too clever by half, caught in his own snare. He's on the run from his brother, Esau, whose blessing of the birthright he obtained by deceiving their father. Esau is angry and waits for the day when he can do away with his brother. But not just yet, not until their aged father, Isaac, has passed to his rest.

So Jacob flees. He heads north to Haran, where his uncle Laban lives. All Jacob's scheming doesn't seem so clever now. Night comes on, and he is alone. No meal with the family tonight. No familiar bed on which to lay his weary body. He will have to make do as best he can; his life has become a matter of brute survival.

He looks for a place to stretch out, and settles down for the night. No covers under or over him on this night, and no pillow. He pulls a stone to him and rests his head on it.

Have you tried to sleep with a stone pillow? I have, and I can tell you it isn't fun. If you are tired enough, you'll eventually drop off, but not for long. And when you wake up, your neck feels as if it's broken.

So here is Jacob, lying alone in the wilds, his head resting on a stone. Never did he feel so far from home, never so far from the God of Isaac and Abraham.

At last he falls into a fitful sleep. And then something wonderful happens. God gives him a beautiful dream. In that terrible place he could maybe expect to have nightmares, but instead he sees a stairway resting on the earth with the top reaching to heaven, and the angels of God ascending and descending on it. And above the stairway stands the Lord proclaiming, "I am the Lord, the God of your father Abraham and the God of Isaac. . . . I am with you and will watch over you wherever you go, and I will bring you back to this land" (Gen. 28:13-15, NIV).

When Jacob wakes up, he thinks, "Surely the Lord is in this place, and I was not aware of it. . . . This is none other than the house of God; this is the gate of heaven" (verses 16, 17, NIV).

It's still true. The Lord is in this place. No matter how lonely it seems, however God-forsaken, He hasn't forsaken it, or us. Angels of God ascend and descend on the heavenly stairway by our rock pillow as He says to us, "I am with you and will watch over you wherever you go."

The Heavenly Wrestler

Then the man said, "Your name will no longer be Jacob, but Israel, because you have struggled with God and with men and have overcome." Gen. 32:28, NIV.

Did you ever notice a peculiar feature of the way the Bible designates God's chosen people, the Jews, in the Old Testament? Their famous ancestor was Abraham, man of towering faith (plus very human weaknesses). We would expect the chosen people to be called "the children of Abraham," but instead they are everywhere called "the children of Israel."

Israel? That's another name for Jacob, the quintessential cheat of the Old Testament. He cheated his old, blind father; he cheated his brother, Esau; he cheated his uncle Laban. How could God pass by Abraham and choose the name of this dubious character for His people?

The answer is grace! God did for Jacob what He has done for cheats and rascals down through the ages, and what He still does today: He gives them a second chance, and a third chance and a fourth chance. And God keeps on loving them, keeps on calling them back, takes them over the same ground where they have fallen and fallen again, keeps them learning until they wise up and let Him be Lord of their lives. Then they become different, changed, new men and women. Jacob becomes Israel.

God had been working on Jacob a long, long time. Maybe Jacob was beginning to wise up, but it all came to a head one night. He was returning to Canaan, coming back a wealthy man with two wives, 11 sons and a daughter, and large flocks and herds. But then he received a message that terrified him: Esau was coming to meet him with 400 men! He sent the women, children, and animals across the ford in the brook Jabbok and planned to spend the night in desperate prayer.

Suddenly he was attacked. A man seized him and grappled with him. Jacob fought for his life; but as the struggle went on and on, he began to realize that this was no ordinary man with whom he was contending. Indeed it was not! It was Jesus, who still comes to us, who strives to bring us to the new life He offers.

Jacob found that new life, and with it a new name, Israel, which means "he struggles with God."

Buying Favor

But Esau said, "I already have plenty, my brother. Keep what you have for yourself."
Gen. 33:9, NIV.

Jacob, coming back home after 20 years in Haran, was still scared
of his twin brother. Hearing that Esau was on the way to meet him
with 400 men, Jacob sent on ahead droves of animals: 200 female
goats and 20 male goats; 200 ewes and 20 rams; 30 female camels
and their young; 40 cows and 10 bulls; and 20 female donkeys and 10
male donkeys. He made sure that some distance separated each herd. He
also instructed his servant to tell Esau that the animals were a gift from
Jacob, who was coming behind (Gen. 32:13-18).

Quite a gift! If Esau had any question about his brother's attitude
toward him, this was the answer. Jacob was scared and anxious to do
whatever it took to please him. He sought to buy Esau's favor.

That approach to others fit the pattern of Jacob's life. Scheming and
manipulative, he thought he could figure a way out of any situation. It's
still the same today. We all have a lot of Jacob in us, some of us more than
others. For many people, money will buy anything; every person has a
price. But God is looking for men and women "who will not be bought or
sold, . . . who in their inmost souls are true and honest, . . . who do not
fear to call sin by its right name, . . . whose conscience is as true to duty
as the needle to the pole, . . . who will stand for the right though the heavens fall" (*Education,* p. 57).

Jacob even tried to buy God's favor. After he awoke from the marvelous dream of the stairway reaching to heaven, he made a vow. If God
would watch over him and bring him safely home again, he would return
to God a tenth of all that the Lord gave him (Gen. 28:20-22).

Before we judge Jacob harshly, let's look at our own hearts. How often
do I seek to manipulate God? When I return the tithe (which is His) and
give offerings, do I expect Him to do me a favor because I have (in my
mind) done Him a favor?

God's favor isn't for sale. It's free—absolutely without price. We call
it grace.

Even Esau could have helped Jacob to see that. The succession of
herds didn't matter to him. He forgave and accepted his brother without them.

The Grace of Home Cooking

*The Son of Man came eating and drinking, and they say, "Look, a glutton and a winebib-
ber, a friend of tax collectors and sinners!" But wisdom is justified by her children. Matt.
11:19, NKJV.*

Jesus wasn't a glutton, but neither was He an ascetic. The fact that
His enemies could accuse Him of overeating shows that He liked
to eat. And in the Gospel accounts we often find Him in a social
setting, sometimes conveying important truths.

I think His favorite place to dine wasn't in the large dining room of
some Pharisee who had invited a crowd of wealthy friends and associates
to meet Him. Rather, it was a little home in Bethany, where He could be
with His friends Lazarus, Martha, and Mary. No catered banquet here, just
home cooking (which is better).

If Jesus lived on earth today, I think He would still prefer the grace of
a well-cooked meal in a setting of interesting conversation, laughter, and
caring that friends provide. Such a setting is a gift from the Father's hand,
the Father who made mangoes and nectarines, blueberries and pineap-
ples, autumn squash and Idaho potatoes, and grains that bake into fragrant breads.

Grace is a table of home cooking in the company of friends.

Noelene and I are beach people (indeed, our whole family is).
Whenever we can we get away, across the Chesapeake Bay, and to the
coast. On the way we always pass through the little town of Bridgeville,
where stately old houses sleep peacefully, and a wide-awake policeman
sits in his patrol car, radar gun in hand. Just beyond the edge of town you
see a sign that says "Jimmy's," and the parking lot is full of cars, no matter what the day or the hour.

One day curiosity got the better of us, and we pulled into the parking
lot. Jimmy's seats maybe 150 people in very basic decor, and chances are
you have to wait to get a table. The printed menu is straightforward, but
attached you find two handwritten pages, offering scores of other choices,
plus a third handwritten page with today's "specials." Everything is home
cooked here. *Real* mashed potatoes, delicious lima beans, stewed toma-
toes, and a range of incredible pies and cakes. And when the server brings
the check, you get a shock—it seems way too little.

I think Jesus would enjoy eating out at Jimmy's.

The Man Who Walked With God

Enoch walked with God; then he was no more, because God took him away. Gen. 5:24, NIV.

Death and taxes are the two great certainties of human existence, and before there were taxes, there was death.

The fifth chapter of Genesis records the earliest generations of human life on earth. It reads like a dirge, repeating "then he died" again and again. "Adam lived 930 years, and then he died"; "Seth lived 912 years, and then he died"; "Enosh lived 905 years, and then he died"; "Kenan lived 910 years, and then he died"; "Mahalalel lived 895 years, and then he died"; "Jared lived 962 years, and then he died" (verses 5, 8, 11, 14, 17, 20, NIV).

Suddenly the pattern breaks. Enoch, the seventh generation from Adam and father of Methuselah, doesn't die. God simply takes him away. After this startling break the dirge comes back: "Methuselah lived 969 years, and then he died"; "Lamech lived 777 years, and then he died" (verses 27, 31, NIV).

Who was this man who walked with God and after 365 years on this earth was translated to unending life? What sort of life was his to give humanity hope that the dread curse of death, the grim reaper, would not forever hold us all in its cold grip?

We know so little about him. Apart from the bare-bones account in Genesis, we find him mentioned, briefly, in only two other places in Scripture. Hebrews tells us that "he did not experience death. . . . For before he was taken, he was commended as one who pleased God" (Heb. 11:5, NIV). In Jude we read that Enoch prophesied of the Lord's coming in judgment upon all the ungodly (Jude 14, 15).

The most intriguing characteristic of Enoch, however, is what we find in the earliest record. "Enoch walked with God." These were the days before the Flood, when men and women of mighty intellect plunged headlong into lives of violence and dissipation, using their creative powers to invent ever new expressions of evil. In such a generation one man stood apart. He chose God; God became His best friend. And at last God gave him the supreme acknowledgment of His grace. He took Enoch to be with Him.

Dear God, let me walk with You today.

Cutting Off Your Right Hand

And if your right hand causes you to sin, cut it off and throw it away. It is better for you to lose one part of your body than for your whole body to go into hell. Matt. 5:30, NIV.

These are strange words, and they come from Jesus. Whatever could He mean by them?

During the course of the centuries some Christians have taken them literally. Early in the third century the scholar Origen, struggling to control his sexual urges, castrated himself. And occasionally others, thinking they were following Jesus, mutilated their bodies.

But that thinking was all wrong. Jesus was the *Healer,* not a mutilator; He made men and women *whole* in body, mind, and spirit. True religion expands our experience, not diminishes it.

The context helps us understand what Jesus meant. He is delivering the famous Sermon on the Mount, and six times He says, "You have heard that it was said. . . . But I tell you." In every case He takes a regulation out of the Old Testament law and raises the bar higher.

In Matthew 5:27-30 He quotes the seventh commandment of the Decalogue, which forbids adultery. He extends the scope of the command, showing that to look on a woman lustfully breaks its intent. Then He says, "If your right eye causes you to sin, gouge it out and throw it away. . . . If your right hand causes you to sin, cut it off and throw it away." That is, anything that leads us to sin, no matter how much we like it, must be banned from our lives.

Radical stuff? Yes, but it's a matter of life and death. A fox or a wolf caught in a trap will gnaw off its paw in order to save its life. And Aron Ralston, climbing solo in Utah's Canyonlands National Park in April 2003, faced a similarly bone-chilling choice. He accidentally set loose an 800-pound, medicine-ball-sized boulder that crushed him inside a narrow slot canyon. On the sixth day of the ordeal and becoming delirious, Ralston took the only way out—he severed his forearm with a dull Leatherman pocket knife.

Radical; but he chose life over death.

We too must make a radical break with any darling habit that would pin us to death. Are you hooked on Internet pornography? Cut if off—cut off the Internet. Take the computer out of your bedroom, out of your home. Whatever habit gets in the way of salvation, cut it off—cut off your right hand.

Grace calls us to take radical measures.

As in the Days of Noah

But Noah found grace in the eyes of the Lord. Gen. 6:8, NKJV.

Sunrise, sunset. Marriages, births, and deaths. Feasting and festivals; parties and pleasure. Buying and building; work and play. Life went on and on, like a CD stuck on "repeat."

It had always been like this. It would always be like this.

So they thought. But God said, "No! No more of this." He saw that every imagination of the thoughts of the heart was only evil continually, that all flesh had corrupted their way upon the earth. And He said, "I have determined to make an end of all flesh; for the earth is filled with violence through them; behold, I will destroy them with the earth" (Gen. 6:13, RSV).

In the midst of the prevailing evil, one man stood out. Noah found grace (that is, favor) in the eyes of the Lord. And to him the Lord gave a message of warning to a doomed generation and a mission to build an ark for the saving of those who heeded.

The book of Hebrews tells us that this man, "being warned by God concerning events as yet unseen, took heed and constructed an ark for the saving of his household" (Heb. 11:7, RSV). Faith indeed—building a boat with no water to sail it in, preaching doom on a world basking in sunshine. This man looked beyond what his eyes saw and his reason told him, looked to God, the Creator of heaven and earth, who said He would (and who could) destroy it all.

And, said Jesus, as it was in the days of Noah, so will be the coming of the Son of man. Life will appear to go on and on, as though nothing can break the unerring cycle. *"They did not know* until the flood came and swept them all away"; "so will be the coming of the Son of man" (Matt. 24:39).

They did not know, so the Flood took them by utter surprise.

They did not know, but they might have known. One man—a man of faith, a man of God's favor—preached by word and by deed for 120 years.

It's been a while since Jesus promised, "I will come again" (John 14:3). Most people think that the promise is dead. But to their surprise, He will come.

In these days, so like those before the Flood, God is looking for Noahs.

Father Abraham

Abram believed the Lord, and he credited it to him as righteousness. Gen. 15:6, NIV.

I n Abraham, the father of the faithful, we see ourselves. We see faith not as something that he had as a solid, immovable trait from the beginning, but as a growing experience of trusting God.

From one point of view Abraham was a poor example of faith. When he took his household to Egypt for a while because of the famine in Canaan, he cooked up a plan that he thought would protect him and his wife, Sarai. Sarai was beautiful, and Abraham was afraid that the Egyptians would kill him in order to take her. "Say you are my sister," he told her (Gen. 12:13, NIV).

God had already brought him a long way, from Ur of the Chaldees to Haran in northwest Mesopotamia and down to Canaan. He had gone out in faith, heeding the call of God, not knowing where he would end up, but trusting Yahweh.

But in Egypt his faith faltered. Could not—would not—the One who had watched over him these many miles and many years in a variety of circumstances still protect him? Of course. But Abraham took his eyes off the Lord, allowed the immediate circumstances—a foreign land, a people seemingly ignorant of God—to shake his trust.

It was a shortsighted, foolish plan he devised. In fact, it seems remarkably self-centered. Abraham was concerned most of all for his own skin.

Yet we find this man making the same stupid mistake years later with Abimelech, king of Gera (Gen. 20). Does that sound familiar? God brings us over the same ground, trying to teach us to trust Him. God doesn't give up on us.

"Abraham believed the Lord, and he credited it to him as righteousness." Our text for the day is the classic statement of righteousness by faith instead of by human endeavor. Even after this ringing affirmation, however, we find Father Abraham, frustrated at Sarai's childlessness, taking the servant Hagar to be his concubine.

Slowly, gradually, Abraham learned to trust God. Slowly his faith grew and matured into rock-solid loyalty.

What about us?

Uncle Abraham

Is not the whole land before you? Let's part company. If you go to the left, I'll go to the right; if you go to the right, I'll go to the left. Gen. 13:9, NIV.

As father of the faithful, Abraham had an inconsistent and sometimes shaky record; but as uncle to Lot, he was a model. He invariably acted with kindness, helpfulness, and, above all, generosity. The grace that he had experienced flowed out toward his dead brother's son.

Lot's life, however, was a different story. A weak, dependent individual with few positive characteristics, Lot was the son of Haran, the third son of Terah. The family lived in Ur, a prominent city in those times. Haran died young, while his father was still alive.

Ur was a pagan city, but the Lord was there. He revealed Himself to Abram, who was a willing listener, telling him to leave Ur. And so the whole family moved, stopping first in Haran, where they settled for a while, until Terah died. Then Abram moved on to Canaan, and Lot went with him. Lot stayed with Abram in his journeyings, but eventually a problem arose. Both Abram and Lot by now had large flocks and herds. There simply wasn't land for both. When the herdsmen of each began to quarrel, Abram big-heartedly gave Lot the choice of land. "Take whichever you want," he offered.

Lot chose what looked the best—the well-watered plain of the Jordan River. Forgetting that Abram had been his protector and benefactor all the way from Ur, Lot thought only of his own interests. He lacked common respect and gratitude.

It was a disastrous decision. Soon the cities of the plain were attacked by a coalition of kings from the north, and Lot was carried off captive. But who came to his rescue? Good old Uncle Abe. Later the Lord determined to destroy Sodom and Gomorrah because of their great sin. Who pleaded that they be spared (thinking of Lot, of course)? Uncle Abe again!

God did destroy the cities. Lot was saved, though the angels had to pull him away from the impending doom. The last picture of Lot is even more pathetic: living in a cave, scared, drunk, and fathering children by his own daughters (Gen. 19:30-38).

Abram and Lot. Two stories, two ways. One gave and gained all; the other grasped and lost all.

Grace Abounding

And God is able to make all grace abound to you, so that in all things at all times, having all that you need, you will abound in every good work. 2 Cor. 9:8, NIV.

Opening the nineteenth season of her show, daytime talk TV queen Oprah Winfrey promised a "big announcement." Her program, *The Oprah Winfrey Show,* is seen in 109 countries and reaches nearly 30 million viewers every week. She averages an audience of 7.2 million per show.

At first she called 11 people onstage from the audience, each of whom needed a car. To each Oprah awarded a brand-new Pontiac G6 sedan, worth $28,400. Then she said, "But I have one car left—and someone in this audience still has a chance to go home with a new, fully loaded G6." As young women circulated through the audience, distributing little boxes to the crowd, Oprah instructed them not to open or shake the package until she told them to do so. Then she explained that the key to the remaining car was in one of the boxes. Calling for a drum roll, Oprah called on them to open the boxes.

She pointed, one by one, at different people in the studio. "You win a car! You win a car! You win a car!" she said. Then, "Everybody gets a car! Everybody gets a car! Everybody gets a car!"

The audience members leaped up and down. Some screamed, some wept. All the 276 people selected had been carefully screened to make sure that each was in need of a car. Some had heartrending tales to tell.

Oprah led them out to the parking lot of her studio, where new Pontiacs gleamed for each one. But that wasn't all. During the same show she also helped a homeless woman with a new wardrobe and a college scholarship, while a foster mom, who was about to be evicted, received a $100,000 check to buy the house, plus $30,000 for repairs and furniture.

Oprah Winfrey has amassed a $1 billion fortune, so she won't miss what she gave. "It's one of my favorite gifts to give to other people," she says.

God is far, far more generous. His grace overflows to everyone. You don't have to be one of the fortunate few selected. His grace abounds.

The Supreme Test

Abraham answered, "God himself will provide the lamb for the burnt offering, my son."
And the two of them went on together. Gen. 22:8, NIV.

After 4,000 years the story plunges into our heart a dagger as real as the knife in the old man's hand. If this were a tale cut out of pagan literature or some lurid tabloid-style account out of the modern media, we could toss it aside, from sight and from mind.

But we cannot toss it aside. It comes in Holy Scripture, as the climax of the saga of Abraham, father of the faithful. We *have* to read it, *have* to try to understand it.

The questions swirl. How could Yahweh, who proclaimed Himself to Moses to be the All-compassionate One, call on a father to kill his own son? How could the God who through the prophets thunders against the abomination of human sacrifice command Abraham, "Take your son, your only son, Isaac, whom you love, and go to the region of Moriah. Sacrifice him there as a burnt offering on one of the mountains I will tell you about" (Gen. 22:2, NIV).

Friend of mine, how would *you* react to such a word from the Lord? To plunge a knife into the heart of your child? To light a fire and burn your beloved offspring to charcoal and ashes? I doubt very much that I could do it. I think I would likely convince myself that this was not God's voice that I heard but the devil's.

Only if I lived so close to the Lord that I *knew* it was His voice would the barbaric deed come within the orbit of consideration. Only if my trust in Him was that strong and that clear could I perhaps go forward.

And that was Abraham. An old man now, he knew his God intimately. After all the zigs and zags of his past, after all the missteps of faith, he had matured to the point that the Lord could bring him to the supreme test— a test even greater than laying down his own life.

We must not overlook Isaac's part in the drama. The boy could have run away. Instead he allowed himself to be bound on the altar and await the end.

Only in the mystery of Calvary does the mystery of this strange story come to resolution. There we see Father and willing Son, going together to the place of death for the sins of the world.

And no angel forestalled the executioner's thrust.

A Viper in the House

In the end it bites like a snake and poisons like a viper. Prov. 23:32, NIV.

The daily news brings a strange story. A woman dies after being bitten by a pit viper. She drove herself to the emergency room (to the amazement of medical personnel), but succumbed after battling the deadly poison for several days.

Police went to the house to catch the viper, taking precautions to protect themselves. Inside they found not only the viper but other snakes in cages, plus an array of exotic animals.

Bizarre? Yes—and no. Before we rush to pronounce judgment, maybe we should ask ourselves whether a pit viper and other exotic creatures find shelter within the confines of our lives.

Warning against the seductive power of wine, the wise man spoke of its sparkling in the cup, its smoothness. But, he reminded us, "in the end it bites like a snake and poisons like a viper" (Prov. 23:32, NIV).

I can only wonder what attracted the woman to the deadly viper. Perhaps it was its appearance: I have seen vipers, such as the Russell's viper of India, with intricate patterns on their skin. Perhaps it was the thrill of keeping an animal that in one swift stroke could bring you to an early grave. One slip and you're done for.

Sin is like a viper. A darling sin is like a pet viper. We know it's deadly. Lack of knowledge isn't the problem. But we keep it in our house. No one else knows it's there, knows how attractive we find it. Maybe a motley crew of other foul and dangerous creatures also find a home within our lives.

It might be just what Solomon warned against—alcohol. It could be a drug habit. It could be pornography. Whatever it is, it bites like a snake and poisons our eternal life.

God's grace is overcoming grace. He wants us to walk in the fullness of His new life. But we have a part to play. "What we do not overcome will overcome us and work out our destruction. . . . Even one wrong trait of character, one sinful desire, *persistently cherished,* will eventually neutralize all the power of the gospel" (*Steps to Christ,* pp. 33, 34; italics supplied).

Get rid of that viper before it kills you!

The Covenant of Grace

Then God said to Noah and to his sons with him, "I now establish my covenant with you and with your descendants after you." Gen. 9:8, NIV.

With this verse we find the first mention of one of the great ideas of the Bible—the covenant. The term runs through both Testaments like a golden thread, occurring more than 200 times. And it draws us into the orbit of grace.

After the Flood God makes a covenant with Noah and his descendants. Later He makes a covenant with Abram, and still later with the 12 tribes who recently escaped from Egypt. After the wilderness wanderings, Joshua, who is approaching death, calls the people together to renew the covenant. When Israel becomes a monarchy, good kings like Hezekiah and Josiah do the same thing. The prophets point to days ahead when the Lord will make "a new covenant" with His people. And when Jesus sits down with His friends on that final Thursday night, He gives the cup to them, saying, "Drink from it, all of you. This is my blood of the covenant, which is poured out for many for the forgiveness of sins" (Matt. 26:27, 28, NIV).

The word "covenant" still finds wide use, especially in legal matters. People who purchase a condominium, for instance, frequently have to sign a covenant that spells out rights and responsibilities to other owners in the complex. At its heart a covenant signifies a mutual agreement, a contract. It is as old as human relationships; as old as buying and selling.

In gracious condescension to our sphere, God takes the deeply rooted idea and uses it to help us to understand and serve Him. It's as though He says, "Let's sit down at the table and talk things over. Do I have a deal for you!"

God's covenant always comes with promises, ultimately the promise of eternal life. Like a human contract, it also specifies responsibilities and obligations. But in one respect it differs greatly from the covenants we enter into in our business transactions. We make contracts between equal parties, but not so with God's covenant. We don't bargain with Him; He sets the terms.

Another way of thinking of covenant is the plan of salvation. God set it up; He offers us life as a free, everlasting gift, through the blood of Jesus. The covenant is absolutely sure, because He swears to it.

Our part is to say yes, and by that same grace to live as His sons and daughters.

Our Unsparing God

He who did not spare His own Son, but delivered Him up for us all, how shall He not with Him also freely give us all things? Rom. 8:32, NKJV.

The biblical God never stops with half measures. He is unsparing in character and action. Most of all He is unsparing of Himself. He is unsparing with sin. The infinite holiness and purity of God makes no compromise, no concession to evil. He created the universe perfect, but gave to all the power of choice because He wanted, and still wants, the free response from hearts of love to His love. With that freedom, however, comes the ability to say no to God. When that happened, when sin arose, God was unsparing.

"God did not spare the angels who sinned, but cast them down to hell and delivered them into chains of darkness, to be reserved for judgment" (2 Peter 2:4, NKJV). Once-perfect angels who went their own way had to leave. Our unsparing God, as much as He loved them, had to remove them.

Nor did God spare sin on earth. He "did not spare the ancient world, but saved Noah, one of eight people, a preacher of righteousness, bringing in the flood on the world of the ungodly" (verse 5, NKJV). The race of humans before the Flood was one of long life and towering intellect. But they turned their powers of creativity and huge energy to the pursuit of evil, until "every intent of the thoughts" was corrupt and "the earth was filled with violence" (Gen. 6:5, 11). And the One who is long-suffering and patient stepped in as the Unsparing, destroying the earth by the great Flood.

Further, God did not spare the cities of Sodom and Gomorrah, but turned them to ashes, "making them an example to those who afterward would live ungodly" (2 Peter 2:6, NKJV). The filthy conduct of the inhabitants of those cities, steeped in perversity, brought on the judgment of the unsparing God.

But that isn't all! The God who does not spare His wrath on sin took that wrath upon Himself. He so loved us that He gave His one and only, His best, His dear Son.

With such a gift, the ultimate gift, "how shall He not with Him also freely give us all things?" All things—*all* things—now and forever.

What a God!

Dead Man Walking

Therefore, there is now no condemnation for those who are in Christ Jesus. Rom. 8:1, NIV.

In those states of America that still enforce the death penalty, a chilling expression has come into vogue: "Dead man walking!"

The condemned person, usually a male, has exhausted all avenues of appeal. Chances are he has been on death row for many years, waiting, waiting as the court processes grind slowly on, as attorneys argue and plead for a way to spare his life. Perhaps the very last hope, an appeal to the governor for clemency, has been tried and has failed. Now no hope remains. The end has come. This is *it!*

The prisoner eats his last meal. He meets with the chaplain for the last time. He sends his last messages, says his last farewells. Then he is led from his cell. Manacled and fettered, he clanks down the corridor to the execution chamber. And the cry rings out as he proceeds to his death, "Dead man walking!"

We are all dead men walking. No, we're probably not murderers or rapists or kidnappers, waiting on death row for the fateful day to dawn, but we all stand condemned before the tribunal of the universe. We have sinned, we have broken God's law, we have rebelled against Him in heart and in deed—and we deserve to die. "The wages of sin is death" (Rom. 6:23), and those wages are ours.

But grace means that God doesn't treat us as we deserve. He treats us as Jesus deserves. We *were* dead men walking, but now we walk as sons and daughters of God, in the fullness of forgiveness and His new life. Yes, "the wages of sin is death," and those are our wages, but hear the second part: "The gift of God is eternal life through Jesus Christ our Lord."

Not wages, but gift. Not what we deserve, but what we don't deserve. Praise God!

"Christ was treated as we deserve, that we might be treated as He deserves. He was condemned for our sins, in which He had no share, that we might be justified by His righteousness, in which we had no share. He suffered the death which was ours, that we might receive the life which was His. 'With his stripes we are healed'" (*The Desire of Ages,* p. 25).

Dear Lord, may Your grace overflow in my life today, and may it flow out to others.

MAY

No Separation

Who shall separate us from the love of Christ? Shall tribulation, or distress, or persecu-tion, or famine, or nakedness, or peril, or sword? Rom. 8:35, NKJV.

The glorious eighth chapter of Romans moves from "no con-demnation" to "no separation." "There is therefore now no condemnation to those who are in Christ Jesus," writes Paul at the chapter's outset (verse 1, NKJV). *Therefore* no condemna-tion because of all that has gone before this chapter: universal sin, univer-sal guilt, but universal salvation provided. So those who are "in" Christ Jesus (meaning who have chosen to enter His orbit of saving grace) have been freed from condemnation.

Paul races on. With rapid strokes he sketches the new life in Christ, which is one in which the Spirit of God rules (verses 2-17), then touches on the sufferings of this life that the Christian endures, but endures in the hope of the ultimate restoration made certain by Christ's victory (verses 18-30).

Then, his words tumbling out in rising crescendo, Paul proclaims, "What then shall we say to these things? If God is for us, who can be against us?" (verse 31, NKJV). And the answer is No one and no thing. Not accuser, not devil, not angel; not trouble, not distress, not persecu-tion; not nakedness, not famine, not peril, not sword.

No one. No thing. No agency, no force in heaven or on earth.

Nothing can separate us from the love of Christ. He holds us by a hand that will never let go, the hand that was nailed to the cross for us.

Friend of mine, do you feel weak? Do you wonder if you can ever make it to the pearly gates? Do you feel overwhelmed by the mess that surrounds you?

Listen again to Paul's words. Remember, the one who speaks knew what he was writing about. When he refers to tough times, he'd been there. Trouble? Yes. Hard times? Yes again. Hated? He knew it. Hunger? Even that. The whole ball of wax—been there, done that. And still he could say, "Do you think anyone is going to be able to drive a wedge between us and Christ's love for us? There is no way! Not trouble, not hard times, not hatred, not hunger, not homelessness, not bullying threats, not backstabbing. . . . None of this fazes us because Jesus loves us" (Rom. 8:35-37, Message).

The God Who Sees Me

She gave this name to the Lord who spoke to her: "You are the God who sees me," for she said, "I have now seen the One who sees me." Gen. 16:13, NIV.

Here is Hagar, Egyptian maidservant to Sarai, wife of Abram. Hagar is pregnant with Abram's child, the child Sarai desperately wanted but could not have. And Hagar is wandering in the desert, alone.

The Lord had promised Abram that he would father a son and that his descendants would become as numerous as the stars. But no son came. The years marched on, and still no son. Hope failed. Sarai gave up hoping; so did Abram. And the only prospect of a son they both could think of was for Hagar to sleep with Abram. Which was a recipe for domestic disaster.

After Hagar got pregnant, relations between the two women took a 180-degree turn. Hagar gloated over the child in her womb, and Sarai's frustration now mingled with envy. Savagely she turned on her husband and blamed him for the whole mess. Abram, caught in the middle of two women fighting like cats, could only respond, "Do with her whatever you think best" (Gen. 16:6, NIV).

So Sarai mistreated Hagar. She made her life so miserable that Hagar, pregnant though she was, ran away. Out into the desert she ran. The desert was better than a tent near Sarai.

But God was in the desert. God is in our desert. God sent an angel with a message for Hagar. He sends His angels with a message for us. The angel told Hagar to go back and submit to Sarai. And although it wouldn't be easy for her, she would bear a son and become the mother of a vast multitude.

Hagar, shocked that God would take note of her, a humble maidservant on the run, said, "You are the God who sees me." The God who saw Abram and spoke to him in the desert also saw and spoke to her.

God sees us. How does that make you feel? Nervous, because Someone sees everything you do? Like the kids' song: "Be careful, little hands, what you do . . . little feet, where you go . . . for the Father up above is looking down in love."

For Hagar, God's seeing her was something wonderful. He looked down on her not to catch her in some fault, but help her. He saw her as a parent looks upon a cherished child—compassionately, protectively.

Dear Lord, in the midst of today's cares, remind me that You see me.

The Tattletale Who Made Good

The Lord was with Joseph and he prospered. Gen. 39:2, NIV.

Sometimes "good" people are mighty hard to live with. It has been said that "to live with the saints in heaven—that will be glory; but to live with the saints on earth—that's another story!"

Joseph, one of the most famous characters of the Old Testament, was a good boy. But he so riled his 11 brothers that they hated him and could hardly think of a kind word to say to him.

The problem was that Joseph, son of his father Jacob's old age, was Jacob's favorite. Jacob made no secret of his preference; he gave to Joseph a special gift, a richly ornamented robe. Which was a foolish thing to do, bound to sow discord and envy in the family circle.

For his part, Joseph only compounded the problem. He paraded the fancy robe that set him apart from his brothers. Even when Jacob sent him on a long walk to check up on his brothers, Joseph put on that robe. I expect he imagined himself to be on a tier above his brothers.

But that wasn't all: he was a tattletale. "He brought their father a bad report about them [his brothers]" (Gen. 37:2, NIV).

And then there were those dreams that he recited so smugly: his brothers' sheaves in the field bowing down to his sheaf; the sun, moon, and 11 stars bowing down to him. That one was over the top even for Jacob, who rebuked him for it.

The jealousy simmered; the hatred smoldered. When the opportunity arose, the brothers struck. They seized the tattletale, stripped him of the fancy robe, and threw him into a dry cistern. Then they sold him to a merchant caravan that happened to pass by.

In one day Joseph went from favorite son to slave on his way to a foreign land. But he also went from tattletale to servant of God, as he determined that, come what may, he would be true to his father's God. "His soul thrilled with the high resolve to prove himself true to God—under all circumstances to act as became a subject of the King of heaven. . . . One day's experience had been the turning point in Joseph's life. Its terrible calamity has transformed him from a petted child to a man, thoughtful, courageous, and self-possessed" (*Patriarchs and Prophets*, p. 214).

Many more struggles lay ahead, but he prospered in everything. He had chosen God, and God did not forsake him.

The Angel by Our Side

And your ears shall hear a word behind you, saying, "This is the way, walk in it," when you turn to the right or when you turn to the left. Isa. 30:21, RSV.

I t's so much easier to preach about Christianity than to live it. It is way easier to write a book about grace than to put what we know into practice.

Most of us don't have the problem of insufficient knowledge. Our problem is that what we know runs far ahead of our doing it. In fact, we use knowledge to try to avoid the doing—hence, so many theological arguments, as if knowledge is our means of salvation.

It isn't.

We are broken and needy. Unfortunately, we don't want to acknowledge it—even to ourselves. Only as we realize and admit that we can't make it by ourselves, only as we cast off our self-sufficiency and flee to Jesus, can we get the help that we need.

But when we *do* lay self aside and look to Jesus, what a difference! The Good Book is filled with promises, promises for us, and every one is "Yes!" and "Amen!" in Christ Jesus (2 Cor. 1:20, NIV). Like this good word from the Lord in today's text, assuring us of divine guidance as we go out into every new day.

Take this promise to heart, dear friend, and apply it to yourself: "When you rise in the morning, do you feel your helplessness and your need of strength from God? and do you humbly, heartily make known your wants to your heavenly Father? If so, angels mark your prayers, and if these prayers have not gone forth out of feigned lips, when you are in danger of unconsciously doing wrong and exerting an influence which will lead others to do wrong, your guardian angel will be by your side, prompting you to a better course, choosing your words for you, and influencing your actions" (*Testimonies for the Church*, vol. 3, pp. 363, 364).

Look at the threefold promise: the angel by our side:

(1) prompts us to a better course

(2) chooses our words for us

(3) influences our actions for good

I crave every one of these blessings. I want to choose the high road; I want my words to heal and encourage; I want my actions to serve a high and noble purpose.

Lord, grant me these blessings today.

Holy Pots

On that day HOLY TO THE LORD will be inscribed on the bells of the horses, and the cooking pots in the Lord's house will be like the sacred bowls in front of the altar. Zech. 14:20, NIV.

What could be more common than pots and pans? How might saucepans and skillets ever be considered holy—as well as the bells on horses?

The answer is: Anything dedicated to the Lord, no matter how seemingly ordinary or mundane, takes on a new character. It is set apart; it is His.

This way of looking at the world seems strange to most people today. We've grown used to explaining what happens through natural causes: earthquakes and hurricanes, plagues and pestilences. "Acts of God" have given way to the findings of science.

We live in a secular age. Even people who go to church tend to live six days as secular people and only on one day a week let the holy impact their lives. And Seventh-day Adventists, who regard the Sabbath as holy time, easily fall into the same trap, for instance, when they speak of the transition from the Sabbath to Saturday night as going from "sacred time" to "secular time."

This loss of a sense of the holy in daily life is the root of the shallow religion that passes for Christianity. If God is Lord of all (and He is), nothing is outside His sphere of influence. If He is Lord of time (and He is), all time—all seven days—belong to Him.

Those who walked with God through the centuries knew and lived by this truth. Out of the Middle Ages arose the simple writing that became a classic: *The Practice of the Presence of God.* For Brother Lawrence, working at the menial tasks assigned to him, every moment was sacred, every pot or pan that he washed hallowed by the presence of the Lord. He understood the truth enshrined in the text for today, understood how HOLY TO THE LORD could be inscribed on the bells of horses, how cooking pots become like the sacred vessels used in the sanctuary.

My friend, you and I are about to go out into another day. Chances are our day will take us into the world, the world that does not acknowledge God or give Him the time of day.

But we can; we *must.* Let's put our hand in His. He will sanctify every moment and every task.

The Depths of Grace

You make God tired with all your talk. "How do we tire him out?" you ask. By saying, "God loves sinners and sin alike. God loves all." And also by saying, "Judgment? God's too nice to judge." Mal. 2:17, Message.

Every now and then you hear someone say, "I couldn't believe in a God who would do such and such," or "God is too loving to care that about such a little fault," or make assertions along the same lines.

All such statements tell us nothing at all about God. They simply reveal what a particular person thinks about God.

It's dangerous to speak for God. When we attempt to do so, we put Him in a box—the box we have made. And God is way too big to be contained in any box. "'For my thoughts are not your thoughts, neither are your ways my ways,' declares the Lord. 'As the heavens are higher than the earth, so are my ways higher than your ways and my thoughts than your thoughts?'" (Isa. 55:8, 9, NIV).

The only way we can know God's thoughts and ways is through His revealing of Himself to us; that is, through His Word. Here alone we get it straight; here, and nowhere else.

Most people don't like that. They never have. As far back as Malachi's time, 400 years before Jesus, they thought they had God figured out. "God loves sinners and sin alike," they reasoned. "God's too nice to judge."

Sound familiar? This idea is God as Grandfather rather than Father. The indulgent God. The God who just has to save everyone. For too many people, this is their concept of the God of grace. It is a deficient view, a shallow view, a view that sells God short and diminishes grace.

We begin to catch glimpses of the depths of grace only when we begin to grasp the holiness of God. The One infinite in grace is the One infinite in holiness. Holiness means dazzling purity, righteousness, justice, and integrity from which sin and sinners flee away. Only in light of the Holy One do we begin to see how far we have fallen from His ideal for us.

But that same One is He who accepts us just as we are, calls us home to Himself, forgives us freely, and gives us a new start as His sons and daughters.

Which is grace abounding.

Excuses, Excuses

But Moses said to God, "Who am I, that I should go to Pharaoh and bring the Israelites out of Egypt?" Ex. 3:11, NIV.

Moses is the towering figure of the Old Testament. He overshadows even giants like Elijah, Daniel, and David. He is the leader par excellence God uses to bring the Israelites out of Egyptian bondage to the borders of the Promised Land.

The New Testament singles out Moses. He appears with Elijah on the Mount of Transfiguration, encouraging Jesus before He makes His way to Jerusalem and death (Matt. 17:3). And in the Apocalypse the redeemed from the earth join in singing the Song of Moses and the Lamb (Rev. 15:3). Moses is a Christlike figure, prefiguring the One far greater who leads His people out of the bondage of sin to the heavenly Canaan.

In view of the exalted place Moses holds in the Sacred Canon, it seems almost inconceivable that he made such a poor start when God called him to the task. Judged by his miserable response to the divine call, we would think that this man was doomed to fail.

Moses had been away from Egypt for 40 years. He left on the lam, fleeing for his life from Pharaoh's wrath. He found a new start in the stillness of the desert of Midian, working as a shepherd for Jethro and marrying his daughter. The years rolled by, reaching the fourscore mark; he long since had abandoned youthful dreams of delivering his native people.

Then God appeared to him in the burning bush, startling him with the announcement that he, Moses, was to go back to Egypt and bring His people out of bondage. Moses, flabbergasted, could only pile one excuse on top of another: Who am I to do this? (Ex. 3:11). Who shall I say has sent me? (verse 13). What if the people won't believe me or listen to me? (Ex. 4:1). I can't speak, so I can't possibly pull off this assignment (verse 10). And finally, after God had answered every objection, Moses simply said, "O Lord, please send someone else to do it" (verse 13, NIV).

This person who became the greatest leader in the Old Testament began as the most reluctant one. He felt utterly unworthy, incapable of doing the job. Once, long before, he had tried and failed wretchedly. Now he had no confidence in his abilities.

But therein lies the secret of what became Moses' great strength. Because Moses was more humble than anyone else on the face of the earth, God could use him in remarkable ways.

That's what grace can do—for us, also.

Learning and Unlearning

By faith Moses, when he had grown up, refused to be known as the son of Pharaoh's daughter. Heb. 11:24, NIV.

Moses, whom God had chosen to lead His people out of Egyptian bondage, had much to learn and much to unlearn before he could be ready for the task. Plucked from the Nile by Pharaoh's daughter, he grew up in the royal court. Learned in the wisdom of the age and trained for battle, he seemed to have all the characteristics desired for a mighty king of Egypt. But the very preparation that qualified him to lead Egypt disqualified him from leading Israel.

One day Moses reached a critical decision: he would throw in his lot with the people of God. He chose a band of slaves over the throne of Egypt; he would be their leader. A noble, even a breathtaking, decision—but Moses had much to learn and much to unlearn. Seeing an Egyptian ill-treating an Israelite, he took matters into his own hands. He killed the Egyptian and buried the body in the sand. But the matter became known, and very soon Moses was fleeing for his life from the wrath of Pharaoh.

He fled to Midian. He was 40, and his life had collapsed around him. He joined up with Jethro, and became a shepherd. He gave up plans of leading the Israelites to the Promised Land. His life was a failure. But God had a plan. In the solitude of the desert Moses would learn new lessons: to rely on God; to live simply and to deny self; to keep calm, regardless of the circumstances.

Further, "Moses had been learning much that he must unlearn. The influences that had surrounded him in Egypt . . . all had left deep impressions upon his developing mind and had molded, to some extent, his habits and character. Time, change of surroundings, and communion with God could remove these impressions" (*Patriarchs and Prophets*, p. 248).

No two lives are alike; God must work with us individually as He seeks to prepare us for the tasks He sees for us. And that means unlearning as well as learning. Sometimes I hear young people, who were brought up in Christian homes, lamenting their lack of "experience" of the pleasures of the world. They suggest that people who come to Christ later in life have an advantage. Not so: the longer we wait to accept Jesus, the more there is to unlearn. Snatches of worldly songs, impure jokes, and bad habits cling to the mind like cobwebs. Only communion with God can remove them. How much better to give Jesus our *whole* lives!

The Grace of Forgiveness

So they sent a message to Joseph, saying, "Your father gave this command before he died, 'Say to Joseph, Forgive, I pray you, the transgression of your brothers and their sin, because they did evil to you.' And now, we pray you, forgive the transgression of the servants of the God of your father." Joseph wept when they spoke to him. Gen. 50:17, RSV.

Forgiveness is like the rain: it washes away guilt and shame, making us clean again.

Forgiveness is like the wind: it blows away dirt and filth.

Forgiveness is like the snow: it covers our hurts and our flaws, and we become whole.

Forgiveness is like the ocean: it hides us in the boundless depths of love.

But forgiveness is difficult. When someone has wronged us, our natural inclination is to demand a tooth for a tooth, an eye for an eye. To forgive can seem soft, easy on sin and sinner.

We can only truly forgive (the forgiveness that doesn't keep a score of wrongs) when we have experienced the incredible forgiveness that grace provides. When we grasp how great is God's mercy toward us, then any wrong we have suffered from someone else pales by comparison. God's forgiveness sets us free to forgive others. "Be kind to one another, tenderhearted, forgiving one another, as God in Christ forgave you" (Eph. 4:32, RSV).

Some time ago I sat in my office and listened in amazement to the man who was visiting. Pastor Amon Rugelinyange, president of the Seventh-day Adventist Church in Rwanda, quietly recounted events in his country during the genocide of 1994, when 800,000 people were butchered during 100 days of mayhem. Among them were Pastor Rugelinyange's wife, three children, and nine grandchildren.

The story, gruesome as it was, wasn't the item that held me spellbound. This humble, sincere man of God spoke about forgiveness. How he had struggled to forgive the murderers of his wife and other dear ones. How the fact of God's forgiveness enabled him to extend forgiveness. How the church he leads has become an agent of reconciliation, targeting the prisoners, most of whom are murderers, and leading large numbers to the grace of Christ. And of one Christian in particular who saw her husband slashed to death and was herself left for dead but who survived and later extended forgiveness to the killer, taking him into her home and "adopting" him as her son.

Joseph wept when his brothers pleaded for forgiveness, telling a phony story about their father's request. Joseph wept—he already had forgiven them.

The Angel's Voice

Now an angel of the Lord spoke to Philip, saying, "Arise and go toward the south along the road which goes down from Jerusalem to Gaza." Acts 8:26, NKJV.

On a Saturday night Laura Hatch, 17, of Redmond, a suburb of Seattle, went to a teenage party and didn't return home. The next day her family filed a missing person's report with the police, and began to fear the worst.

Monday came; then Tuesday, and Wednesday. No sign of Laura or her Toyota Camry. Police were pretty sure she had run away. It was a parent's worst nightmare. The family began to adjust to the likelihood that she was dead.

Saturday, one week after Laura had disappeared, the parents organized a volunteer search party, but came up empty. That night, however, Sha Nohr, the mother of Laura's friend, had several vivid dreams of a wooded area and heard a message: "Keep going, keep going."

On Sunday morning Nohr and her daughter drove along the route Laura would have taken on her way home from the party. They prayed as they drove, asking that they might be led to wherever Laura was. Something drew Nohr to stop the car. Leaving her daughter in the car, she clambered over a concrete barrier and more than 100 feet down a steep, deeply vegetated embankment. As she peered down the ravine, she caught a glimpse of something much farther down—a car caught in the trees!

It was Laura's crumpled Toyota, and Laura was in the back seat. Her leg was broken, as were several ribs and bones around her eyes, and she had a blood clot in her brain. But she was alive and conscious, despite her injuries and eight days without food or water.

The neurosurgeon who treated Laura said that she may have been saved by her own dehydration—the lack of fluids kept the blood clot from growing and proving fatal.

That Sunday night a group of more than 100 people had gathered for a vigil. But when they heard the news of Laura's amazing rescue, they sang and cheered.

How to account for the miraculous finding of Laura Hatch? Only by supernatural agencies. Only a voice, a message outside natural processes, could have led Sha Nohr to stop the car right above the site where Laura Hatch lay in her wrecked car 200 feet below.

The God of grace—He who directed Philip to take the road south to Gaza—still speaks in our day.

May 11

Watching in Wonder

And the man, wondering at her, remained silent so as to know whether the Lord had made his journey prosperous or not. Gen. 24:21, NKJV.

Have you ever felt like the man in this story—tingling with excitement, hardly daring to breathe as you watch an answer to your earnest prayers unfold like a water lily before your eyes?

He had come a long way, this most trusted servant of Abraham. All the way from Canaan to northwest Mesopotomia, and by camel, not the fastest or most comfortable means of travel but the best the times had to offer. His master had laid a heavy burden on him: "Go to my country and my own relatives and get a wife for my son Isaac" (Gen. 24:4, NIV).

How would you feel about an assignment like that: Go far away and get a wife for my son, or a husband for my daughter? Where would you start in a strange land?

And if you found a young woman prepared to take seriously an offer from afar borne by a stranger, how would you convince her to sever ties to home and dear ones and venture forth to unite with the unseen bridegroom? The whole endeavor seems to our eyes full of risks and uncertainties, a long shot indeed. And the servant, realizing it, asked his master: "What if the woman is unwilling to come back with me to this land? Shall I then take your son back to the country you came from?" (verse 5, NIV). To which the answer was a resounding no.

So the servant sets out, taking 10 camels laden with gifts. After weeks of travel he arrives at the town of Nahor, probably named after Abraham's brother. It's evening; the camels are tired and thirsty, and he is tired and thirsty. He has the camels kneel down, and he prays.

He asks that God will give him success on this very day. He's standing beside a spring, and he prays that among the women from the town who will come to draw water will be *the* one. His mind frames a simple, daring request: "May it be that when I say to a girl, 'Please let down your jar that I may have a drink,' and she says, 'Drink, and I'll water your camels too' [going beyond expected hospitality]—let her be the one you have chosen for your servant Isaac" (verse 14, NIV).

The words are hardly out of his mouth when Rebekah appears, jar on shoulder. The servant gazes in the wonder at the beautiful young woman, then blurts out his request. She brings him water, then waters the camels, as the servant watches in wonder.

Dear Lord, teach me to wait in wonder on You today.

Shiloh

The scepter will not depart from Judah, nor the ruler's staff from between his feet, until Shiloh comes. Gen. 49:10, margin, NIV.

J udah was not the oldest son of Jacob. By the law of descent, the role of leadership should not have been his. Reuben, the firstborn, was entitled to that position. But God does not abide by those human rules and categories that we set up to assign some people as superior and others as inferior. God breaks through the human-made roadblocks of caste, color, sex, and status to accomplish His purposes. So He passed over the weak-kneed Reuben, "unstable as water" (Gen. 49:4), and designated Judah as the chief of the tribes of Israel.

When Israel wanted a king, Saul, a Benjamite, emerged as the nation's first monarch. Saul's reign soon fell into disobedience and failure, however; and God turned to a man after His own heart (1 Sam. 13:14). He chose a shepherd boy, a Judahite fresh from the hills of Bethlehem, tanned by the wind and the sun, a poet, and filled with unpretentious courage. Like his ancestor who received the promise of our text, David was not the oldest son in the family.

This shepherd boy rose to become Israel's most famous king. Mighty in war, strong in peace, the sweet singer of his people, he was a king admired and loved by the nation, despite his personal failures. Ever after, Israel looked back on the Davidic era in their history as the zenith of their fortunes.

And they looked forward to the new Davidic King. Though the nation went into captivity, they hoped for the tree, hacked down by enemies, to sprout again; for a shoot to grow out of Jesse, a Branch out of his roots (Isa. 11:1). They lived in hope, because the ancient promise foretold of such a King. Out of Judah at last would arise the supreme ruler, Shiloh—"he . . . whose right it is" (Eze. 21:27). Not an usurper, not a political hack, not a grasping general—but Shiloh. Israel's true King would appear, "and unto him shall the gathering of the people be" (Gen. 49:10).

After more than 2,000 years of waiting, a voice was heard: "Lo, I come . . . to do thy will, O God" (Heb. 10:7). A new son of David, a new Judahite, had come. In a Bethlehem stable a baby's cry broke the stillness of night. Shiloh, Israel's true King and He who would gather the nations to God by Himself, had come!

I Am

God said to Moses, "I am whom I am. This is what you are to say to the Israelites: 'I AM has sent me to you.'" Ex. 3:14, NIV.

In a world of many gods, the God of the Old Testament stood apart. Not many, just one: "Hear, O Israel: The Lord our God, the Lord is one" (Deut. 6:4, NIV). One, ever and only; one before all things; one now; one eternally. And so the Decalogue, written by the hand of the one God, gives as its first precept: "You shall have no other gods before me" (Ex. 20:3, NIV).

This one God called the shepherd Moses and commissioned him to go back to Egypt and set His people free. Back to Egypt with its multitude of deities—Ra, Amen, Isis, Osiris, Ptah, and so on; and so Moses asked, "Suppose . . . they ask me, 'What is his name?' Then what shall I tell them?" (Ex. 3:13, NIV).

The answer: I AM. The eternal, self-existent One, with a name that is beyond a name because it describes who and what God is.

Before all else: I AM. Beyond all else: I AM.

Everything and everyone grows old, but not the I AM. Everything else passes into nothingness, but not the I AM. The I AM is the Ancient of Days, because God existed before time began. But the I AM is the Eternally Young, as fresh as the dew on the morning grass, because endless existence stretches before Him.

From this verse, Exodus 3:14, comes the name of God used by believers today—Jehovah, or, probably more correctly, Yahweh. No one knows the exact name, because ancient Hebrew was written only in consonants (for this name YHWH), and the name was considered so holy that the Israelites never spoke it aloud.

But 1,500 years after Moses a Man appeared on earth and boldly claimed this most sacred name for Himself. "Before Abraham was born," Jesus of Nazareth claimed, "I am!" (John 8:58, NIV).

What presumption! What blasphemy! No wonder His hearers tried to stone Him.

But—what if? What if Jesus really was God in the flesh, that "in Him was life, original, unborrowed, underived" (*Selected Messages,* book 1, p. 296)? Then the One who had appeared to Moses at the burning bush, the Eternal One, had once again invaded time and space.

And He is the one who invites us today: "I will . . . be your God, and you shall be My people" (Lev. 26:12, NKJV).

The Blood on the Doorpost

For the Lord will pass through to slay the Egyptians; and when he sees the blood on the lintel and on the two doorposts, the Lord will pass over the door, and will not allow the destroyer to enter your houses to slay you. Ex. 12:23, RSV.

Egypt: the children of Israel stand on the knife edge of time, awaiting the moment of their deliverance. After 430 years in bondage they are about to walk away free. For years history has moved toward this climax. The hand of the oppressor has grown heavier, the cries of the oppressed more pitiful. Yahweh has heard them, and He has prepared a man in the desert of Midian who will match the demands of the hour.

Moses has confronted Pharaoh, warning of plague after plague. But Pharaoh, torn between reason and desire, has equivocated, promising but each time refusing to let the people go. Now the land lies in ruins; even Pharaoh's advisers plead with him to give up stubbornness and get rid the people who lie at the root of Egypt's calamities.

Still Pharaoh hardens his heart. And now Moses, at God's behest, warns of a tenth and final stroke: "Thus says the Lord: About midnight I will go forth in the midst of Egypt; and all the first-born in the land of Egypt shall die, from the first-born of Pharaoh who sits upon his throne, even to the first-born of the maidservant who is behind the mill; and all the first-born of the cattle" (Ex. 11:4, 5, RSV).

For the Israelites, however, God provided a way to escape the deadly plague. Each family was to select a lamb "without blemish" (Ex. 12:5), kill it, and apply its blood to the lintel and the doorposts with a bunch of hyssop (verses 21, 22). No one was to go outside the house until morning; while they stayed inside, the blood on the doorposts would protect them from the destroyer.

The apostle tells us, "Christ, our Passover, was sacrificed for us" (1 Cor. 5:7, NKJV). His blood on the doorposts of our lives protects us from eternal death. But is the blood on the doorposts of *my* life? Is the blood on the doorposts of my family? Are those precious to me safe inside, protected from the destroyer?

Chances are, dear friend, that your heart is heavy because of a child, grandchild, or dear one who isn't inside. Then just now commit them by name to the One abundant in mercy who loves them even more than you do.

Moses and Jesus

They sing the song of Moses, the servant of God, and the song of the Lamb, saying, "Great and marvelous are Your works, Lord God Almighty! Just and true are Your ways, O King of saints!" Rev. 15:3, NKJV.

Moses is the towering figure of the Old Testament, Jesus of the New. And they are similar in mission—Moses is a type of Christ.

Preeminently, both were deliverers of God's people. As Moses led the tribes out of Egyptian bondage and to the borders of the Promised Land, so Jesus leads spiritual Israel, people from every tribe and race who choose to accept His salvation, out of spiritual Egypt with its slavery to sin, and onward to our eternal home, the heavenly Canaan.

Moses, trained in the martial arts of Egypt, had to learn God's way of leadership, not by force of arms, not by violence, but by the gentle hand of a shepherd. In this Moses prefigured the work of the greater Leader: "He will feed His flock like a shepherd; He will gather the lambs with His arm, and carry them in His bosom, and gently lead those who are with young" (Isa. 40:11, NKJV).

For both Moses and Jesus, death was crossed with a tragic element. Moses, having led the people through 40 years of hardship and difficulties, died within sight of the goal—so near and yet so far! And Jesus' life came to a close in violent fashion. Rejected by the Jewish authorities, forsaken by His own followers, He was beaten, abused, spat upon, and executed between two thieves.

But death wasn't the end for either leader. God buried Moses in a valley in the land of Moab (Deut. 34:6), but He did not leave him in the grave. In God's good purpose He subsequently raised Moses from death, an act challenged by the devil (Jude 9). And when Jesus faced the climax of His work, the last journey to Jerusalem with its betrayal and death, Moses came with Elijah to encourage the Savior on the Mount of Transfiguration.

We don't know how long Moses lay in the lonely unmarked grave in Moab. But we know that the One greater than Moses—Moses' Savior and Lord—burst the bonds of death on Sunday morning, the third day after He died.

The Song of Moses and the Lamb—it's a song of deliverance and victory. I want to be there to sing it; do you?

The Day Moses Lost His Cool

And Moses and Aaron gathered the assembly together before the rock; and he said to them, "Hear now, you rebels! Must we bring water for you out of this rock?" Num. 20:10, NKJV.

oses was a humble, patient leader of God's people. They were a difficult bunch, complaining, whining, fickle. Granted that the desert didn't offer the comforts of civilization; but they were free, and surrounded daily with evidences of God's presence and leading.

Through the years of wandering, of hopes and disappointments, Moses kept his cool. When his leadership was challenged—first by Aaron and Miriam (Num. 12:1, 2); later by Korah, Dathan, and Abiram (Num. 16:1, 2)—he simply turned the matter over to God, trusting his vindication to the One who judges fairly. When Israel committed the gross sin of making and worshipping the golden calf, he offered to give his own life to spare the people (Ex. 32:31, 32).

Here was a truly unselfish leader, one in whom ego had been set to the side, who cared only for the well-being of those he led. But even this most exemplary of leaders suffered from the frailties of humanity. One day he lost his cool, and the result was catastrophic.

The twentieth chapter of Numbers gives us the setting. The 12 tribes arrived in the wilderness of Zin, and there Miriam died. The loss of his sister grieved Moses. The three siblings, Moses, Aaron, and Miriam, had battled together in the flight from Egypt and the years of wandering. Her death would have underscored the disappointment that so long after leaving Egypt they still hadn't made it to Canaan.

Compounding Moses' stress, the people once again began to complain, this time over the lack of water. They whined that they had been better off in Egypt, that the whole mission was a failure. They blamed Moses and Aaron for all their troubles.

God told Moses to gather the people before the rock and simply speak to it. But Moses, worn down by grief and the burdens of leadership, struck the rock twice with his rod. Water flowed out abundantly, but Moses had failed.

Once before, following the Lord's instruction, he had struck the rock and brought out water (Ex. 17:5, 6). That act symbolized Christ, the "spiritual Rock that followed them" (1 Cor. 10:4). This Rock was smitten once for us all. He was never to suffer again to bring us the life-giving water of His salvation. He died once—one for all.

Numbering Our Days

So teach us to number our days, that we may gain a heart of wisdom. Ps. 90:12, NKJV.

P salm 90, which carries the subscript "A Prayer of Moses the man of God," contrasts the brevity of human life with God's eternity. Its magnificent, rolling cadences stretch our minds, bidding us to look beyond the temporal and the transient to values that matter, now and forever.

"Lord, You have been our dwelling place in all generations" (verse 1, NKJV). What a magnificent concept! God, the Changeless One, our dwelling place. What more could time or eternity offer than this?

Is God *my* dwelling place? Can I sing along with the hymn writer:

> "Hiding in Thee, Hiding in Thee,
> Thou blest 'Rock of Ages,' I'm hiding in Thee"?

The psalm goes on to underscore how fleeting is this human existence. It is like a sleep (verse 5), like the grass that springs up and flourishes in the morning, but by evening is no more—cut down, withered (verse 6). Our years pass away like a sigh (verse 9); the best we can hope for is 70 or (if we are fortunate) 80 years (verse 10). Whether short or seemingly longer, our lives are "soon cut off, and we fly away" (verse 10, NKJV).

Then comes the admonition, as up-to-date as breaking news on the Internet: "So teach us to number our days, that we may gain a heart of wisdom" (verse 12, NKJV). What does it mean to number our days? To realize the supreme value of every new morning, of every flying moment. To realize that we do not know how many more mornings we may be granted—indeed, if any more—and determine to live life to the full, dedicating every task to the glory of the Creator and the uplifting of our fellow humans.

Life is precious. Time is very precious. Eternity tells us how precious. We have a heaven to gain and a hell to shun. Life tingles with meaning, with purpose.

This glorious prayer closes with grace. "Have compassion on Your servants. Oh, satisfy us early with Your mercy, that we may rejoice and be glad all our days!" (verses 13, 14, NKJV).

And it ends thus: "Let the beauty of the Lord our God be upon us, and establish the work of our hands for us" (verse 17, NKJV).

Amen! Do it today, Lord!

How God Leads

In all the travels of the Israelites, whenever the cloud lifted from above the tabernacle, they would set out; but if the cloud did not lift, they did not set out—until the day it lifted. Ex. 40:36, 37, NIV.

The book of Numbers supplies more details. Whenever the cloud lifted, whether by day or by night, the Israelites broke camp and resumed their journey. And no matter how long the cloud stayed over the tabernacle—for two days or a month or a year—they stayed put (Num. 9:15-23).

In this experience of God's people long ago we see two aspects of His leading: the divine side and the human side. God made His will known in dramatic fashion, by a sign before their very eyes. And the people watched and obeyed; they followed where God led, setting out whenever He indicated they should depart, and waiting on His evidence no matter how long it took.

Throughout the Bible God leads His followers, individually as well as collectively. He does so because He lovingly cares for them. He is the Good Shepherd; they are His people (John 10:1-18). I believe that God is still the same today. He wants to, delights to, lead us as individual Christians. He wants to, delights to, lead us as a church.

But we don't have a cloud over the tabernacle. We don't have a Urim and Thummim. How can we know His will? God has given us the Holy Spirit, His very own presence. By earnestly seeking to know the divine will, by determining to do only what will please God, and by being ready to obey, He reveals His plan as surely as the cloud pointed the way for the Israelites.

"Those who decide to do nothing in any line that will displease God, will know, after presenting their case before Him, just what course to pursue. And they will receive not only wisdom, but strength. Power for obedience, for service, will be imparted to them, as Christ has promised" (*The Desire of Ages,* p. 668).

They *"will know."* How? God has a thousand ways to reveal Himself: through a word of Scripture, through a friend, a strong impression, a providential event, and on and on. We may have to wait awhile, but we *will know.* God's people have always known.

The Last Words of Moses

The eternal God is your refuge, and underneath are the everlasting arms. He will drive out your enemy before you, saying, "Destroy him!" Deut. 33:27, NIV.

These are uncertain times. Everywhere we turn the news seems to be bad, whether it's internationally with war and mayhem, or nationally with fears of terrorist attacks and biological weapons. The world is at the end of its tether. Leaders struggle with huge, complex problems that defy human solution.

Time magazine ran a cover story titled "America the Anxious" and began the article inside with "A Nation on Edge." *Newsweek,* for its part, put on the cover: "Anxiety and Your Brain: How Living With Fear Affects the Mind and Body." In the United States stress mints are selling big, and antidepressants such as Prozac and Xanax register sales in the billions.

Where can we find security in times like these? Only in the Bible. Where shall we go to find a place of refuge? In Christ Jesus, the Solid Rock. The eternal God, He who is beyond time and space and our little woe-filled world, promises to be our refuge. Though all else fails, He will never fail; though all else crumbles, He changes not. In God and God alone is the one certain place of refuge in these uncertain times.

He further promises, "Underneath are the everlasting arms." As we place our arms under our children's arms, supporting their first wobbly steps, so the Lord puts His arms under us, keeping us safe, protecting us from harm.

God wants to sustain our every moment. In the midst of fear and doubt, when life crashes upon us, He wants to give us a deep calm, a sense of peace in His presence. That calm opens us to receive His grace, love, and strength.

And that's not all. The third promise in this marvelous passage assures us: "He will drive out your enemy before you, saying, 'Destroy him!'" Whatever that enemy be, dear friend—be it fear itself, worry, anxiety, unbelief, criticism—God can and will take care of it if we turn it over to Him.

God our Refuge! God our Sustainer! God our Victory! What a trilogy of hope.

These were Moses' last words, and he couldn't have said it better.

Sleeping Sweet

When you lie down, you will not be afraid; when you lie down, your sleep will be sweet.
. . . For the Lord will be your confidence and will keep your foot from being snared. Prov.
3:24-26, NIV.

The terrorist attacks on New York and Washington, D.C., struck fear into people's hearts. They wondered, *What does the future hold? Will it ever be safe to fly again?*

The United States government grounded all commercial flights for several days as it sought to ensure that the skies would be protected from further attacks. Even so, when flights resumed many people were slow to board an airplane. Businesspeople canceled trips; travel by train or car was suddenly the preferred mode for shorter journeys. The airlines took a huge hit, suffering staggering losses because of people's reluctance to fly.

My wife, Noelene, found herself in a dilemma. She had made arrangements to attend a conference near Denver, Colorado, that would be held one month after September 11, but she was afraid of getting on the airplane. As the date of the conference drew closer, she became increasingly apprehensive.

One night she woke up in a cold sweat, seeing herself aboard a flight hurtling to the ground, just like the ill-fated hijacked jet that crashed in Pennsylvania. Terrified, she contemplated changing her plans for Denver.

She got up and began to read her Bible. Her schedule for reading through the Scriptures called for her to be past Proverbs by this date, but she had fallen behind. As she read that early morning, the words of Proverbs 3:24-26 leaped from the page: "Have no fear of sudden disaster. . . . The Lord will be your confidence" (verses 25, 26, NIV). "When you lie down, your sleep will be sweet" (verse 24, NIV).

It was a word from the Lord, just right for the time, as God's words always are. Peace and trust flowed over her. She finished her reading, went back to bed, and fell into sweet sleep.

The conference in Denver, although it had been advertised for people of all denominations, garnered only a small number of brave souls. Noelene happened to eat breakfast with the convener early on, and mentioned how the Lord had calmed her fears. Impressed, he asked her to share the experience with the whole group, and she did. They were amazed at her story.

That's our God—full of grace, always looking out for us.

The Comfort of the Psalms

This poor man called, and the Lord heard him; he saved him out of all his troubles.
Ps. 34:6, NIV.

I love the psalms! They span the centuries and speak to me as clearly as some preacher I can see in person. Sometimes more clearly. Whether it's David, Asaph, the sons of Korah, or some unnamed person, their struggles are my struggles, their joys my joys, their hopes my hopes. And I also want their faith to be my faith.

No doubt the psalms are the best loved and most read portion of the Old Testament—indeed, of the whole Bible. Whenever selections of Scripture are put together—for instance, when a new translation is in preparation—you find the Gospels and the Psalms put under one cover, and often nothing else.

What is the ageless appeal of the psalms? Doubtless, their humanity. They speak honestly and frankly. They show us what real prayer is like, not clichés and pat formulas, not beautifully contrived expressions, but blood-and-guts wrestling with God. When the psalmist finds himself fallen on hard times, he tells God about it. When enemies surround him and malicious tongues wag, he tells God about it. When he is badly treated—falsely accused, betrayed by friends—and feels like punching out his foes, he tells God about it. And when, hardest of all to bear, he feels that God has let him down, he tells God about it.

Some of the prayers are of such a confrontational, questioning, challenging character that we would be shocked to hear them spoken aloud when we gather together for worship. The good elders would ensure that *that* person wouldn't be asked to lead the congregation in prayer again! He or she doesn't know what is appropriate for worship!

This poor man called. This poor woman called. Called, because they were in trouble.

We still call. We are still in trouble. We are weak, frail, broken. We are human.

But the psalms go further. A huge body of literature, music, and artwork portrays our weakness, our fragility, our brokenness, our humanity, but stops right there. The psalms don't.

The Lord heard. The Lord saved. There's the difference, and what a difference!

We aren't alone. There is a God, and He cares. He hears and He helps. Even today.

The Greening

For just as the Father raises the dead and gives them life, even so the Son gives life to whom he is pleased to give it. John 5:21, NIV.

Some time ago I heard a profoundly moving sermon by beloved church leader Walter Wright. The message, based on the Acts 3 story of the lame man leaping, was powerful in its own right; but it came with even greater force because of the occasion. Some five months earlier Pastor Wright had been diagnosed with a cancerous tumor in his right thigh, and this was his first public presentation since his recovery. He spoke with the penetrating clarity of one who has been to the edge of the valley of the shadow of death and returned to tell about it.

Pastor Wright and his wife received the grim news on June 9. The prognosis suggested the likelihood of surgery to remove his right leg, followed by an uncertain chance of survival. He told us how the forecast brought him to the brink of discouragement, but how the prayers of a large number of people, known and unknown, sustained him.

He likes to garden and, some days after hearing the prognosis, he and his wife were in their yard, admiring two young apple trees they had planted—a golden Delicious and a red Delicious. The trees bore 14 apples. Observing Japanese beetles on the leaves, he brought out insecticide and sprayed the trees thoroughly.

But the next day the leaves turned brown. Soon they withered and dropped off. The apples fell off also—all but two.

It seemed almost the last straw. He and his wife were surrounded by death.

Then something wonderful happened: the trees began to bud! They came to life in a second spring, and before long were covered in an abundance of fresh green foliage. To the Wrights, they were a sign of hope from a loving God.

Right into November the trees stayed green, long after everything else around them was stark and bare in the face of the onset of a Michigan winter. And the two apples were still there, except that now they had grown plump and full. Pastor and Mrs. Wright picked them and bit into them. They were the sweetest, juiciest applies they had ever tasted! With each bite, he said, he and his wife were saying and thinking, "Hallelujah!"

The surgeons removed the cancer—and they spared his leg.

The Lord Planted a Garden

The Lord God took the man and put him in the Garden of Eden to work it and take care of it. Gen. 2:15, NIV.

More and more, I am convinced that what we need to get our lives together in these hectic, uncertain times is basic stuff. Instead of being ruled by cell phones, e-mails, and the rat race, we should go back to the fundamental principles of living that we find in the Bible.

So I recommend that we take a look at a very old idea, one that began with God Himself at the Creation. The Lord planted a garden, the Scripture tells us (Gen. 2:8), and put the newly created humans in it to work it and to take care of it. Very few of us make our living off the land anymore, but we will find relaxation and peace of mind by planting a garden, be it big or small.When we moved to the Washington, D.C., area we bought a home that had a nice but unkempt lot. It had a wonderful stand of trees out back, some of them tall oaks 150 years old or more. The previous owner had planted some quality azaleas and other shrubs; however, the family had seven children, and the yard became a neighborhood playing field.

When we moved in, we faced a lot of work to get the lot into shape, but slowly it came around, little by little, year by year. The neighborhood kids ceased to treat it as common property, and slowly we developed a large green lawn. I dreamed of planting a flower bed across the front, but a large maple, growing ever bigger year by year, stood in the way.

After more than 20 years in the home, we made the decision: it was time for the maple to go. We had it cut down, and paid another service to grind up the stump. I set to work to fashion a garden. It took many hours of backbreaking labor to convert untilled soil intertwined with a network of roots, some as thick as my arm, into a bed suitable for planting.

Noelene and I bought books on perennials. We decided on phlox, with spiccata for contrast, a border of evergreen bushes alternating with pinks, asters for late blooming, a butterfly bush, daylilies, and a slow-growing Red Dragon Japanese maple. As an afterthought, we added a dahlia.

Our garden, so carefully crafted by the sweat of our brows, produced in abundant and spectacular fashion. Every major item exceeded our expectations. The dahlia grew to be five feet wide with hundreds of velvet purple blooms.

And we felt like Adam and Eve—deeply satisfied, happy, and closer to God.

The Road Less Traveled

For the Lord watches over the way of the righteous, but the way of the wicked will perish. Ps. 1:6, NIV.

T wo roads diverged in a wood, and I—I took the road less traveled by, and that has made all the difference" (Robert Frost). The road less traveled is still the way for followers of the Lord Jesus Christ. He told us, "Wide is the gate and broad is the road that leads to destruction, and many enter through it. But small is the gate and narrow the road that leads to life, and only a few find it" (Matt. 7:13, 14, NIV).

Psalm 1 sets forth the two ways. One is the way of the righteous person, who "does not walk in the counsel of the wicked or stand in the way of sinners or sit in the seat of mockers" (verse 1, NIV). Today we might put it this way: someone who refuses to go down the path of secular, materialistic values; who doesn't follow the crowd simply because it's the easiest course to pursue; who stays free of the corrosive influence of cynicism.

Instead, those who follow the road less traveled—God's way—"delight . . . in the law of the Lord," meditating on it day and night (verse 2, NIV). For the Hebrews, God's law encompassed more than the Ten Commandments, although this was the law's high point. Rather, the Torah (law) embraced all the revelation of the divine will that was available to humanity. For us today that means primarily the Bible, which the Lord has given to show us how to live. But to delight in the Bible requires that we spend *time*—alone, still, reverently, and prayerfully.

For those who follow the road less traveled, life flows out in abundance. They are "like a tree planted by streams of water" that bears a crop of delicious fruit and whose leaf doesn't wither (verse 3, NIV). Everything they do "prospers"—not that they get rich or are spared heartache and hard times, but that God is with them, come what may.

Not so those who follow the broad way. They're like chaff blown away by the wind—here today, apparently prospering and living it up, but tomorrow gone and forgotten (verse 4). And beyond this life they face the prospect of the judgment, when every human being has to give account to God of how they used the gift of life that He gave them.

The road less traveled is the best way. It's the way of fullness of life here and now—the opportunity to be fully alive—and the way that leads to eternal bliss. Best of all, it's His way, the way of Jesus, full of grace

Grace Upon Grace

And from his fulness have we all received, grace upon grace. John 1:16, RSV.

W e beheld his glory . . . full of grace and truth," wrote John the Beloved (John 1:14). And then he went on, "And of His fullness we have all received" (verse 16, NKJV). Jesus embodies grace; He is grace in its fullness, and that fullness overflows to us.

Eugene H. Peterson translates the passage like this: "We all live off his generous bounty, gift after gift after gift." I like that rendering. Since the essence of grace is God's favor, given freely, given without our deserving; "grace upon grace" (the literal translation) suggests gift upon gift. And Peterson's "gift after gift after gift" very aptly underscores the lavishness of grace. Our God is a God of abundance; "stingy" is not in His vocabulary. He is generous to a faulty prodigal in His mercy and compassion for sinners.

Here's an exercise to warm your heart: Look up "abundant," "abundantly," and "abundance" in a concordance. You will find these words occurring often in the King James Version, as well as in modern translations. When Moses asked to see God's glory, the Lord passed by and proclaimed His character, "abundant in goodness and truth" (Ex. 34:6, 7). And Paul states that God "is able to do exceeding abundantly above all that we ask or think" (Eph. 3:20).

An interesting expression, that. If we were editing Paul, we'd drop out "exceeding" as being redundant. But Paul knew what he was about; he piled on the adverbs because he was attempting to put into words something that cannot be reduced to words: the incredible ability of our God to supply all our needs, to do far more than we can request or imagine.

Jesus—in Him we see embodied the nature of our unstingy God. The Father, abundant in love, emptied heaven of its choicest Treasure, giving His only Son that we might have eternal life (John 3:16)—life more abundant now (John 10:10) and forever (1 John 5:11, 12).

No sin is too big for our unstingy God to forgive. Where sin abounds, grace superabounds. No situation is too desperate for the God of abundance to provide a solution. Not famine, peril, sickness, weakness, or fierce temptation. Not even death itself. In Ellen White's last written message we read: "So strong is His love that it controls all His powers, and employs the vast resources of heaven in doing His people good" (*Testimonies to Ministers*, p. 519).

Life Without Cell Phones

Be still, and know that I am God; I will be exalted among the nations, I will be exalted in the earth. Ps. 46:10, NIV.

Some time ago I took a business trip to a country where I had no computer and no cell phone. When I returned home after nearly two weeks away, I was at first surprised at how much I had missed—and then how little.

The gadgets that we think are so necessary have taken control of our lives. The technology that is supposed to save time for us ends up making our lives more pressured.

Look at e-mail. It's wonderful: I can send a message to someone on the other side of the world and get a reply within minutes, and all at minimum cost. The down side is that a lot of people who send me e-mails expect me to drop anything else I'm doing and fire off a reply. If they don't hear from me soon, their tone becomes angry, even rude and hostile.

Then there's the ubiquitous cell phone. Wonderful indeed! I dial in some numbers, put it to my ear, and hear someone thousands of miles away as clearly as if they were sitting by my side. But cell phones have a down side also, a big downside. In a word, it's pollution.

The air is getting more and more polluted with the noise of people jabbering into cell phones. You see a guy walking down the street, waving his hands and speaking loudly to himself. Not many years ago you'd have called for someone to take him to a hospital for insane people. No longer—he's just talking on his cell phone!

Why is it that people have to speak so loudly into their cell phones, no matter where they are—in airport lounges, on buses, in restaurants, waiting for planes to take off? And why do so many of us think that if a call comes in it's so important that we have to cut off any conversation in midsentence? E-mails and cell phones have taken control of our lives.

It's time to wrest control away from them. There are very few messages and very few calls that can't wait for a day, or a week, or longer.

Our big need today it just what the text tells us: Slow down! Stop! Be still!

That's the only way we can know God.

What Grace Is All About

Anyone who sets himself up as "religious" by talking a good game is self-deceived. This kind of religion is hot air and only hot air. Real religion, the kind that passes muster before God the Father, is this: Reach out to the homeless and loveless in their plight, and guard against corruption from the godless world. James 1:26, 27, Message.

I f James were writing today, maybe he'd add people in nursing homes to his list of those we should reach out to.

A friend sent the following from Australia: "When visiting with Mum and Dad in a nursing home, I noticed that people were rostered to come and personally feed some of the patients whose brains would not allow them to feed themselves. I noticed grace in action.

"It wasn't the usual thank-You-for-the-world-so-sweet-thank-You-for-the-food-we-eat stuff, but rather someone taking their personal time to come in regularly and spoon-feed people whose brain-grace had dropped out. The volunteer would come in bright and cheery (to number 18 on their list), prop the recipient up nicely on puffed-up pillows while they stood for what seemed ages as they coaxed down the nourishment, all the while chatting pleasant nothings to what appeared to be themselves.

"It seems elderly taste buds don't work anymore, and what looks so nice on the tray is received like something akin to cardboard. Even dessert isn't relished. However, the grace of the volunteer goes on its way to number 19 with the same cheer and bubbliness, and not a murmur is made.

"I got to thinking about all the people who are involved with this type of work—nurses in ICU wards, hospital nurseries, people on drips where nourishment is force-fed—and the grace they share seemingly without any reward at all.

"I guess that is what grace is all about. When I say my table grace, I often now include these volunteers and ask the Lord to provide them with integrity and patience as they take time to share grace."

I agree. Grace is about changing the world. Grace is about making someone's lot a little easier. Grace is about new life that, experienced, flows out to others like a fountain.

Grace is about Jesus, who was filled with it. And who lived just the way James describes.

Human Shield

This is my command: Love one another the way I loved you. This is the very best way to love. Put your life on the line for your friends. John 15:12, 13, Message.

On November 15, 2004, Rafael Peralta put his life on the line for his friends.

A sergeant in the United States Marines, Peralta and his buddies were in the thick of a firefight in Iraq, as American and Iraqi forces tried to wrest the city of Fallujah from insurgent control.

Peralta, 25, a platoon scout for the 1st Battalion, was assigned to the assault team that entered the insurgent safe house that day. He was one of the first marines to enter the house. Rifle fire rang out; Peralta, wounded, fell to the floor.

Moments later an insurgent rolled a fragmentation grenade into the area where Peralta and the other marines were seeking cover. The marines scrambled to escape and pounded on a locked door. But Rafael Peralta, still conscious, grabbed the grenade and cradled it to his body.

Although one marine was badly wounded by shrapnel from the blast, many more lives would have been lost if not for Peralta's selfless act of using his body as a human shield. "He saved half my fire team," said the corporal in charge.

Peralta had built a reputation for putting his buddies' interests ahead of his own. He showed that again, and for the last time, when he made the ultimate sacrifice.

I take off my hat to men and women like Rafael Peralta. In their own way they exemplify the spirit and sacrifice of One far greater, Jesus Christ.

We all were trapped under the enemy's deadly crossfire. Bloodied, our lives were leaking away on the hard floor of an alien land. Then the enemy rolled the grenade in our direction, and the end of it all was certain. We would die here, die without hope, die alone.

But One threw His body over the instrument of death. Cradling it to His bosom, He took the full force of its annihilating power. In shielding us, He died; we lived. He died so that we might live.

Now, and forever.

A Threefold Love Story

But Ruth replied, "Don't urge me to leave you or to turn back from you. Where you go I will go, and where you stay I will stay. Your people will be my people and your God my God. Where you die I will die, and there I will be buried." Ruth 1:16, 17, NIV.

The book of Ruth is a jewel. Sandwiched between the blood-thirsty tales of the Judges and the saga of Samuel, Saul, and David in 1 Samuel, Ruth is a literary and spiritual masterpiece. It is also a threefold love story.

The first love story is highly unusual: the deep love a young woman has for her mother-in-law. Naomi, bereft of her husband and sons in a foreign land, decides to go home. "Naomi" means "pleasant," but she was going back as "Mara," that is, "bitter." She had nothing to offer her widowed daughters-in-law, Orpah and Ruth—no abode, no wealth, no marriage prospect. Naomi was destitute and alone.

"Go back to your own people," she told Orpah and Ruth, and Orpah took her advice. But Ruth refused to leave her—she loved Naomi too much to let go of her. She would follow Naomi wherever life's pathway might lead, follow her until death.

This is true, pure love; love unselfish and faithful; love without thought of material benefit; love extraordinary. Such love originates from heaven.

The second love story also has an unusual twist. It involves a man and a woman. Nothing unusual in that except that they come from vastly different backgrounds. Boaz is much older, wealthy, and an Israelite. Ruth is young, a widow, poor, and a Moabite. Sometimes opposites attract; they did in this case.

But there was more to the story. Boaz was a near relative of Elimelech, the dead husband of Naomi, and under the Mosaic law he had the right and responsibility to buy back Elimelech's property and also to marry the childless widow (in this case, Ruth). Boaz became not only her lover and husband, but her protector and deliverer.

Which leads us to the third love story. The Hebrew word translated "kinsman" comes from the root that means "to redeem." Boaz, by his position and his actions, pointed forward to Jesus, our near kinsman who redeemed us. We had nothing to offer—only our deep need. But He took us in, joined us to Himself, to live with Him forever.

The Chosen

The Lord did not set his affection on you and choose you because you were more numerous than other peoples, for you were the fewest of all peoples. Deut. 7:7, NIV.

I n the verse immediately preceding our text for the day the Lord calls Israel "a people holy to the Lord your God." Of all the nations on the face of the earth, He chose the 12 tribes to be "his people, his treasured possession" (Deut. 7:6, NIV).

The sense of being God's chosen is a two-edged sword. It gives confidence and a sense of incredible self-worth; it can also lead to pride, superiority, and arrogance.

In designating Israel as His chosen, however, God through Moses made abundantly clear that they brought nothing of their own worth to commend them to the Lord. They weren't more numerous, more powerful, or more obedient than other peoples. In fact, they were less numerous than others and often stubborn, disobedient, and rebellious.

But God chose them. Why? Out of His own free will, He simply took unlikely material and said, "You are Mine, a special people that I set apart for My purposes."

God's choosing was an act of pure grace.

It still is. As followers of Jesus Christ, we today are God's chosen. "You did not choose me, but I chose you and appointed you to go and bear fruit—fruit that will last," He says (John 15:16, NIV). Peter tells us, "But you are a chosen people, a royal priesthood, a holy nation, a people belonging to God" (1 Peter 2:9, NIV).

Chosen. What a concept! We are special to God! Let us go out into this day with head held high and shoulders back, with a spring in our step and His praises on our lips.

But let's pray the Lord to keep us from pride and exclusiveness. He didn't choose us because we are better or more attractive or more useful to Him. We have nothing—nothing!—to recommend us to Him. But He chose us because He loves to give freely, to take the unlikeliest material and use it for His purposes. That is grace.

There's the catch: He chose us to "bear fruit," to do His will, to fulfill His plan. Which is to tell the world that the Savior has come, and will come again.

Tell the world: God wants everyone to join the ranks of the chosen.

Cards After Christmas

But while they were on their way to buy the oil, the bridegroom arrived. The virgins who were ready went in with him to the wedding banquet. And the door was shut. Matt. 25:10, NIV.

Every year we get Christmas cards that arrive late. Some miss it by just a day, some later, and some are *mailed* after Christmas Day! I have mixed feelings about these cards after Christmas. It's always nice to hear from a friend long removed, but these cards just don't seem to fit. The others arrived in good time (we have a relative overseas who makes sure we get hers and has it to us sometimes two months before December 25) and were hung or placed in a carefully planned pattern. The spaces are all filled, and then these latecomers show up. They usually don't make it next to the others on display; they're set aside in a pile.

I don't put store by Christmas Day, as though the date has particular significance attached to it. Most certainly it was not the date of the Savior's birth, because the shepherds were still outside with their flocks all night, something that renders December 25 out of the question because of the cold. No, it isn't that the late cards missed a day crucial in its own right. That day, however, represents the season that calls forth cards of goodwill and remembrance.

It's not a big deal to be late with your Christmas cards, but it is to be late with the Lord. Just before He went to the cross Jesus told the parable of the 10 girls who were invited to the wedding. Five made preparation and took along a vessel of extra oil for their lamps; five didn't. The bridegroom seemed to be delayed; everybody fell asleep. But at midnight the cry rang out, "Here's the bridegroom! Come out to meet him!" (Matt. 25:6, NIV). The five wise girls trimmed their lamps and went out to play their part in the festivities. But the other five had to hurry away and search for a store still open. By the time they got back, the door was shut, and they were shut out.

The text is one of the saddest in Scripture: "And the door was shut." So near, and yet so far. Almost there, but not quite.

Almost isn't good enough. Every day, *this* day, you and I must be sure that we are right with Jesus. We dare not go out into a new day without His sheltering protection and guidance. We must have Him right now and throughout the day.

Dear Lord, come fill my being with Your own sweet self. Come now, and stay with me throughout this day.

JUNE

The Elijah Blues

But he himself went a day's journey into the wilderness, and came and sat down under a broom tree. And he prayed that he might die, and said, "It is enough! Now, Lord, take my life, for I am no better than my fathers!" 1 Kings 19:4, NKJV.

Elijah was in a funk. Only a couple of days before, he was riding high, seemingly on top of the world. Alone, he had stood for Yahweh on Mount Carmel, challenging the prophets of Baal to show that their god could bring down fire from heaven. Before the assembled crowd—royalty, religious leaders, and common people—Elijah had demonstrated the awesome power of the living God. It had been a spectacular day for Yahweh and for Elijah.

It closed out with added fireworks. After Elijah prayed earnestly for rain to break the severe drought, the sky grew dark with clouds. The wind rushed in, and with it heavy rain. Fired with energy, adrenalin coursing, Elijah hitched up his garments and ran ahead of King Ahab, all the way to Jezreel.

So high, and now he was so low. Alone again, but now in the desert of Beersheba, way down south. He's been running, but in fear of his life. Jezebel, wife of Ahab, angry that her hired prophets had been killed on Mount Carmel, sent Elijah a message that she was going to kill him. And Elijah? He who had stood alone on Mount Carmel caved in and ran for his life.

Now he wants to die. He prays to die. He feels his life has been a failure.

Ever felt like Elijah? Of course. His story is our story. We get worn out doing good things and lose our perspective. We get focused on ourselves, come to think that we are the only one doing God's work, that without us everything will grind to a halt—and become discouraged.

Lows follow highs in the rhythms of nature. When we get pumped up with "success" and feel as if we are unstoppable, as sure as night follows day we're headed for a downturn.

The great thing about the story of Elijah is the way the Lord demonstrated grace when he was in the funk. God provided food and helped him to sleep; then God opened his eyes to the broader perspective—he wasn't alone, he wasn't indispensable. God was in control of events.

He still is.

God didn't answer his prayer out of the funk. Elijah didn't die—then, or ever!

The Story of Fred Hale

Honor your father and your mother, that your days may be long upon the land which the Lord your God is giving you. Ex. 20:12, NKJV.

A news report tells of the death of Fred Hale, Sr., documented as the world's oldest man. He died in his sleep in Syracuse, New York, while trying to recover from a bout of pneumonia. Hale was 12 days shy of his one hundred fourteenth birthday.

Fred Hale retired 50 years ago as a railroad worker and beekeeper. According to his grandson, Fred Hale III, he enjoyed gardening, canning fruits and vegetables, and making homemade applesauce. "He didn't need a lot to be happy."

Incredible. A life that spans three centuries, totally enfolding the twentieth. The two great wars—Fred Hale lived through them both. The rise and fall of Communism. The decline of the British Empire. The nuclear age. The cold war. When Hale was born, there were only 43 stars on the American flag.

The years kept on coming; Hale kept on doing new things. At age 95 he flew to Japan to visit a grandson who was in the United States Navy. En route back to America, he stopped off at Hawaii and gave boogie boarding a try. At 103, Hale was still living on his own—and shoveling the snow off his rooftop! He lived in his native Maine until he was 109, when he moved to be near his son, Fred, now in his 80s. And here's the bit I found the scariest in Hale's story: he held the Guinness world record for being the oldest driver. At age 108 he found slow drivers annoying!

Fred outlived his wife and three of his five children. He had nine grandchildren, nine great-grandchildren, and 11 great-great-grandchildren.

I would like to have met the old chap. The newspaper gives the bare facts; what was his life like? What wisdom, what perspective, might he offer to our generation? The bare facts suggest that he lived simply and apparently happily. He kept active. He tried new things as long as he lived. He was a strong individual. He had strong family connections.

In one area of life Hale's story is silent: Fred Hale's relation to God. That's something reporters studiously avoid today. Without Jesus as Savior and Lord, all else in Hale's long life would be only second-rate.

Belonging and Serving

For there stood by me this night an angel of the God to whom I belong and whom I serve. Acts 27:23, NKJV.

Paul was the speaker, and he addressed a band of desperate souls. They numbered 276 in all, and for 14 terrible days and nights they seemed about to go down to a watery grave, as the ship they were traveling in was blown about, beaten, and buffeted by a violent storm.

The voyage had been risky from the outset. Paul had warned them that it was too late in the year to attempt to press on farther across the Mediterranean. But the one in charge had followed the advice of the pilot and the owner of the ship over Paul's, and disaster had overtaken them.

For 14 days they'd been at their wits' end. All hope of making it to safety seemed lost. But then Paul rallied them. He told them that an angel had come to him in the night, assuring him that God would spare the lives of all on board, although the vessel itself would be lost. Demonstrating his confidence, Paul took food (struggling to survive, they hadn't eaten during the whole time), and urged them to do likewise.

I like the way Paul describes his relationship to God: "to whom I belong and whom I serve." Therein lay his assurance that all would be well in the end; therein we find the source of his strength in the midst of uncertainty, his calm though the storm raged all around.

It's still a good and accurate summary of the Christian's life: I belong to God, and I serve Him. We might tweak it to read: I belong to God; therefore, I serve Him.

Years before, the same apostle Paul had written to the Corinthians, urging them to abstain from sexual immorality: "Do you not know that . . . you are not your own? For you were bought at a price: therefore glorify God in your body and in your spirit, which are God's" (1 Cor. 6:19, 20, NKJV). And what about us today—do we get it? We aren't our own, aren't free to "do our own thing." We belong to God! We were bought at a price, a great price, even the life of Jesus Christ.

Paul often uses the term *doulos* to describe this relationship. It means slave or servant, as in Romans 1:1: "Paul, a bondservant of Jesus Christ" (NKJV). Jesus is Lord; we His servants. We live for Him; we serve Him.

Not grudgingly but willingly. He is the Lord of love; gladly we yield, joyfully we serve.

Lying to the Holy Spirit

Then Peter said, "Ananias, how is it that Satan has so filled your heart that you have lied to the Holy Spirit and have kept for yourself some of the money you received for the land?" Acts 5:3, NIV.

In one of Jesus' parables He likened the kingdom of heaven to a drag-net cast into the lake, which, as it is pulled to the shore, gathers a multitude of creatures both good and bad (Matt. 13:47-50).

   Thus it has ever been with the church. One of Jesus' inner circle turned out to be a traitor. In the early church we find "bad fish" among those gathered in by the gospel net, such as Simon the Sorcerer (Acts 8:9-13), and the husband-and-wife team of Ananias and Sapphira.

Up to this point in the book of Acts (chapter 5), all we read about the followers of Jesus is positive. God has poured out His Spirit upon them; they witness powerfully to the inhabitants of Jerusalem; they are united in prayer, teaching, and fellowship. No one lacks—those who are more prosperous sell their possessions and share with others in need. A notable miracle takes place: a man crippled from birth leaps and walks and jumps. The religious establishment warns, threatens, and imprisons the apostles, but they cannot be silenced.

Then—Ananias and Sapphira. They decide to sell a property they own to be part of the general practice. But when they bring the proceeds of the sale to the apostles, they lie. They say they are presenting the full return from the property, but in fact they have put aside part for themselves. No one directed them to sell the property. No one told them they had to give the full amount to the church treasury. But they wanted to look good—to the apostles and to the other members. They didn't want to appear stingy or materialistic, which is what they were.

How stupid! With the Holy Spirit's presence so abundantly manifested among the believers, did they think they could pull off a stunt like this one?

Love of money will do that to you. Even in the church. Love of money will deceive you into thinking that you can fool even the Lord. True then, true today.

God calls us to unswerving honesty. Honesty isn't the best policy, for it isn't a policy at all. Honesty is a principle. And it begins with God. When we are honest with the Holy Spirit, we will be honest with everyone else.

Managers of the Mystery

This is how one should regard us, as servants of Christ and stewards of the mysteries of God. Moreover it is required of stewards that they be found trustworthy. 1 Cor. 4:1, 2, RSV.

Paul's words strike home to everyone called to responsibility in the work of the church, whether a lay leader or an employee. We are not business executives, nor can the work of God ever be reduced to a worldly organization.

When I taught at the seminary, one day the president called me into his office and asked if I would take the spring Week of Prayer for the university. It turned out to be a good week, blessed by the Lord, but one aspect troubled me. I thought I should make myself available for students who wanted to talk, and met separately with the men's and women's deans to work out a schedule. The reception I received in one dorm was hardly friendly—in fact, it was icy. I got the distinct impression that this was their territory, and they didn't want anyone else horning in. I have no idea what lay behind the dean's attitude. Was it that the dorm was perceived as the dean's domain, to be managed by the dean alone?

But Paul tells us we aren't just managers; we are involved with something that goes beyond a business. There is a transcendent element. The nature of our work is such that we never fully control it; it has an elusive quality. God, not humanity, is at its center.

When Paul refers to Christianity as a mystery, he means God's plan, held close in His heart, to save the world. It was secret, but now in Christ Jesus He has made it known. It centers in Jesus, the God-man, the mysterious blending of eternal God with humanity. It involves a personal knowledge of God, so that Christ lives in us, the hope of glory. And it brings an invitation to the entire world, so that the Gentiles may be included among God's people.

At the heart of our religion lies a mystery, God's mystery. How God became man, how God saves us, how God turns the sinner to Himself. The heart of our religion eludes precise definition and explanation. But we want to define, to explain. And so, individually and corporately, we tend to gradually lose sight of the transcendent dimension.

In the work of the church we need to work together, share our plans, and coordinate our efforts. But let us ever remember that God is very big, bigger than our best plans, bigger than our boldest vision. God can, and does, work through our plans, but He also works outside our plans. God is God; we do not dictate His actions.

Fit for Heaven

We love because he first loved us. 1 John 4:19, NIV.

When are we fit for heaven?
Is it when we have lived a long life of discipleship and no longer yield to temptation? Or is it from the moment we accept Jesus as Savior and Lord, like the thief on the cross?

In her classic treatment of the life of Christ, *The Desire of Ages,* Ellen White offers an arresting answer: "Love to man is the earthward manifestation of the love of God. It was to implant this love, to make us children of one family, that the King of glory became one with us. And when His parting words are fulfilled, 'Love one another, as I have loved you' (John 15:12); when we love the world as He has loved it, then for us His mission is accomplished. We are fitted for heaven; for we have heaven in our hearts" (p. 641).

Her insights here are profound. They challenge us to a life in the grit and guts of the city, where people struggle to make it through the night and then through another day, where apprehension and fear of the future hold hearts in icy grip.

But I hear someone asking, "Doesn't the Bible tell us not to love the world?" Indeed. "Love not the world, neither the things that are in the world. If any man love the world, the love of the Father is not in him" (1 John 2:15). That same Bible, however, tells us, "For God so loved the world, that he gave his only begotten Son, that whosoever believeth in him should not perish, but have everlasting life" (John 3:16). So there are two ways to love the world: as sinful humans do, or as a holy God does.

John tells us what the former is like—"the lust of the flesh, and the lust of the eyes, and the pride of life" (1 John 2:16). But God's love of the world is a passionate, giving love that puts supreme value on every person, no matter how low on society's totem pole or how messed up.

And Jesus tells us how: "A new command I give you: Love one another. As I have loved you, so you must love one another" (John 13:34, NIV). The original text allows us to translate His words: "Love one another, as I have loved you, *so that* you may love one another." John makes the point clear: "We love [not just God or His people, but everyone] because he first loved us" (1 John 4:19, NIV).

As we meditate on amazing grace, as His divine love floods over our being, we begin to be changed into His likeness. And as God loves the world, so do we.

Jesus in a Slouch Hat

Since the children have flesh and blood, he too shared in their humanity so that by his death he might destroy him who has the power of death—this is, the devil. Heb. 2:14, NIV.

What are the odds in a secular society that a book on the story of Jesus would sell like hotcakes? Astronomically long. Yet Australian journalist, author, and broadcaster Kel Richards has written such a best seller. His *Aussie Bible,* released in 2003, was reprinted in one month.

The Aussie Bible isn't a paraphrase, much less a translation. Rather, it selects incidents and teachings from the Gospels and weaves them together into a seamless narrative, placed squarely in an Australian setting. Appropriately, the book carries the designation "Retold by Kel Richards."

Here's the story of the shepherds: "There were some drovers, camped out in a paddock nearby, keeping an eye on their mob of sheep that night. Their eyes shot out on stalks when an angel of the Lord zapped into view, and the glory of the Lord filled the air like a thousand volts of electricity. The angel said: 'Stop looking like a bunch of stunned mullets.[1] Let me give you the drum,[2] the good oil.[3] It's top news for the whole crew—everyone, everywhere. Today . . . a rescuer has been born. He is the Promised One, the King, the Lord. And here's how you'll find him: the little nipper[4] is wrapped up in a bunny rug, and lying in a food trough.'

"And before you could say, 'Well, I'll be blowed!' the whole sky was filled with more angels than you could count, all singing away at the top of their lungs (if angels have got lungs, that is), 'God is great! God is bonzer![5] And to everyone on this planet who's on God's side, peace and goodwill. And by the way, Happy Christmas.' (Which rather confused the drovers, because they'd never heard of Christmas before.)"

This same Jesus, who died on a Roman cross outside Jerusalem, lives today. He is the Second Adam and, in that sense, the Universal Person. We should search the Scriptures to learn more and more about Him. But we also should visualize Him as by our side at the computer, in the kitchen, in the classroom. Because He is.

In a slouch hat. Or in a baseball cap.

---

[1]surprised
[2]news
[3]reliable news
[4]child
[5]good

The Incredible Shrinking Soul

Because I live, you also will live. John 14:19, NIV.

As scientists probe ever deeper into the biochemical reactions within our brain, the notion of the soul as a separate entity becomes increasingly suspect. And those people, Christians or other, who believe in the soul as the guarantee of immortal life, find their hope threatened.

Francis Crick, who with James Watson discovered the double helix of DNA, spent many years researching into consciousness, partly with the goal of disproving the soul. Crick claimed that he and other researchers found the group of cells responsible for generating consciousness and one's sense of the self. He said that one day all humanity will come to accept that the concept of souls and the promise of eternal life were a deception, just as they now accept that the earth is not flat.

Crick was part right and part wrong.

Right: the concept of souls is a deception. It has no biblical basis. The Scriptures teach that we are *whole* beings, with body, mind, and breath inseparably linked. The Creation account establishes the reality: "The Lord God formed the man from the dust of the ground and breathed into his nostrils the breath of life, and the man became a living being" (Gen. 2:7, NIV; "a living soul" [KJV]).

In this account the Creator does not put within the body a separate entity eternal in its essence, a "soul." Adam does not *receive* a soul; he *becomes* a soul as he receives life-breath from God. And when that life-breath ceases—when he dies—his existence ceases.

Wrong: the promise of eternal life is not a deception. It springs from Jesus Christ, the conqueror of sin and the grave, He who died on Calvary but who is alive forevermore and who assures us: "Because I live, you also will live" (John 14:19, NIV).

Resurrection is a notion beyond human reasoning. Nothing—nothing—continues beyond the grave. But in God's memory nothing is lost. We "sleep," safe in Him. And at our Lord's return we rise from the dead as new beings, with new bodies but with the old "us" keyed in by the fingers of a loving Father.

The idea stretches our minds. It would stretch our faith also, except for one fact: *Jesus did it! He died and rose again!*

And so shall we.

Men as Trees Walking

And he looked up and said, "I see men; but they look like trees, walking." Then again he laid his hands upon his eyes; and he looked intently and was restored, and saw everything clearly. Mark 8:24, 25, RSV.

I t is, no doubt, the strangest passage in the Gospels. Whatever was going on here? Did Jesus' divine power fall short at His first attempt? Or could there be a deeper meaning to the passage—for the disciples and for us?

As always, the setting of Scripture helps us to understand it. Mark alone records this miracle and, immediately before, notes that Jesus strongly rebuked the disciples because of their lack of understanding. "Do you have eyes but fail to see, and ears but fail to hear?" He said (Mark 8:18, NIV).

The disciples recognized Jesus as the Messiah, but the Messiah of popular expectation, not God's Sacrifice for sins.

Many people today see men as trees walking. They are happy with a political Jesus, but not the Jesus of Calvary. They want a comfortable Jesus, a Jesus who reinforces the status quo, but they'll have no part in the Jesus of the Via Dolorosa.

Many Adventists see men as trees walking. They grew up in the church, got passing grades in Bible classes, live respectable Christian lives. But they don't know Jesus as the living Lord of their lives.

Many live on the edges of the church, repeating, generation by generation, cycles of abuse and debilitating habit. They have never experienced the power of Jesus to break old patterns and set them free to a new and better life, have never thrilled at the prospect of "higher than the highest human thought can reach is God's ideal for His children. Godliness—god-likeness—is the goal to be reached" (*Education,* p. 18).

Many see the church as a familiar institution, feeble and flawed. They don't see the glorious future that Jesus intends for it.

I believe passionately that we can change. Jesus is still the healer. He can touch our blind eyes, or our myopic eyes, so that we can see.

He can touch us today!

A Believer's Questions

Behold the proud, his soul is not upright in him; but the just shall live by his faith." Hab. 2:4, NKJV.

One of the most appealing features of the Bible is the honesty with which it addresses the human condition. It doesn't water down, much less cover up, the failures of heroic figures like David in the Old Testament and Peter in the New. This is one reason for the timeless power of the Scriptures: they speak to you and me today just as though they were written for us, which, in fact, they were.

In the Bible we often find people who know God well dialoguing with Him, sometimes with surprising directness. But no book of the Bible is quite as blunt as the little book of Habakkuk.

"O Lord, how long shall I cry, and You will not hear? Even cry out to You, 'Violence!' And You will not save" (Hab. 1:2, NKJV), he cries out to God. All around him the prophet saw plundering, strife, contention, and wickedness, and what was God doing? Apparently nothing.

That is a very modern question: "God, why don't You do something?" It was the question asked by the Jews at Auschwitz, the question we ask when our loved one struggles with a life-threatening disease.

God answered Habakkuk, telling him that He was about to bring the Babylonians down on the land. They would be His instruments of His judgment on the sinful nation.

The Babylonians! That was too much for Habakkuk to handle. Israel might be at fault, but the idolatrous, pagan Babylonians—they were 10 times worse! "Why do you look on those who deal treacherously, and hold Your tongue when the wicked devours a person more righteous than he?" (verse 13, NKJV).

That is also a modern question. "God, why did You do that to me? Why do You make me suffer like this?"

But God gave the prophet the answer, the answer for us also: "The just shall live by his faith" (Hab. 2:4, NKJV). God told Habakkuk, and He tells us, to trust Him. We see only the picture near at hand; He sees the big picture. He loves us, and if we let Him, He will resolve it all so that our story has a happy ending.

A Prayer for Revival

Lord, I have heard of your fame; I stand in awe of your deeds, O Lord. Renew them in our day, in our time make them known; in wrath remember mercy. Hab. 3:2, NIV.

Remembering is an important part of the believer's life. Throughout the Old Testament we find psalmists and prophets taking the people back to the mighty acts of Yahweh in Israel's history: the plagues of Egypt, the passing through the Red Sea, the 40 years in the wilderness, the conquest of Canaan. Jesus also instructed us concerning the Lord's Supper: "Do this in remembrance of Me" (1 Cor. 11:24, NKJV). For the people of God and individuals, the statement stands true: "We have nothing to fear for the future except as we shall forget the way the Lord has led us" (*Testimonies to Ministers*, p. 31).

For none of us is spiritual life a steady, unwavering line pointing steadily upward. We have ups and downs; at times our work seems "hard and dry," as the old hymn says. At times we become weary in well-doing, mentally and spiritually exhausted with the cares of trying to serve the Lord and build up His church.

We should do what Habakkuk did—go back in our minds to a time when God's presence was manifested in a marked way in our lives. When the tempter comes in like a flood, go back to the mighty acts of God in your life. When your heart burned within you and you turned your life over to Jesus as Savior and Lord. When you experienced a dramatic answer to prayer or an extraordinary intervention, a gift of grace.

On a visit to Korea I visited a wonderful spiritual retreat center secluded in the mountains. Christians of all ages come here for several days or a week; laypeople and clergy come; many come back year by year. In this center almost total silence is maintained—no conversations, and certainly no telephones or radio. Operated by the Seventh-day Adventist Church, the center features a separate area comprised of small individual prayer rooms, with mats and heating for those who wish to spend the entire night in communion with God.

Friend, do you feel flat in your spiritual experience? Go back to where you met God in the past. He's still the same, mighty to save and mighty to renew.

The God of grace will revive you.

Too Busy to Turn Back

Therefore, my dear brothers, stand firm. Let nothing move you. Always give yourself fully to the work of the Lord, because you know that your labor in the Lord is not in vain. 1 Cor. 15:58, NIV.

If Christianity could succeed in Corinth, it could make it anywhere. Corinth, strategically located in the narrow strip of land connecting northern Greece and the Peloponnesus, and with port cities close by, was a roistering, cosmopolitan hub. Greeks, Romans, Jews, and Asians gathered here.

They came for business, and they came for a "good time." To the south of the city a mountain rose steeply about 1,800 feet above the lowland, and on its summit stood a citadel and temple of Aphrodite. This temple had some 1,000 slave girls who served as sacred prostitutes. The city was universally known for its immorality. The term *Corinthian girl* was synonymous with prostitute, and "to Corinthianize" meant to cast off moral restraints.

Paul came to this wild, licentious place and preached and founded a church (Acts 18:1-18). One of his converts was Erastus, mentioned in Romans 16:23 as the city treasurer (NKJV), possibly a commissioner of streets and buildings at Corinth. Interestingly, archaeologists turned up an inscription with his name and identifying him as a public official.

To be a Christian in Corinth wasn't easy. (Is it easy anywhere?) Even in our times port cities aren't noted for their churches! The congregation of new believers met in a house, or houses, and the members were raw recruits to the gospel army. Paul greets them as "saints" (1 Cor. 1:2), and then goes on to address a host of problems—factions, incest, lawsuits, cohabitating with prostitutes, disorder in the worship service, doubts about the Resurrection, and so on.

There was plenty in Corinth, in the city and in the church, to cause Erastus, or anyone else, to lose their faith. But Paul says, "Stand firm. Let nothing move you." Don't let anything, *anything,* shake your confidence in Christ or turn you from the path of following Jesus. And what's the best way to keep on the straight and narrow? "Always give yourself fully to the work of the Lord."

It's still good advice for the followers of Jesus. Today let's give ourselves fully to the work of the Lord so that Satan can't get a foothold in our lives.

Half Full, or Half Empty?

To the pure, all things are pure, but to those who are corrupted and do not believe, nothing is pure. Titus 1:15, NIV.

The way we look at life makes all the difference. Is the glass half full, or half empty?

Two men looked out from prison bars. One saw mud; the other saw stars.

When we allow Jesus to rule our lives, His new life gives us heavenly vision. Grace opens our eyes to His working; we become alert to evidences of His providence and leading. It bothers me to hear believers continually whining and grumbling because they focus on the glass as half empty instead of half full.

A reader of the *Adventist Review* shared the following thought:

"This morning I looked out my third-story window (facing east) and saw a sunrise that was more beautiful than any artist could ever paint. The spectrum of rose and purple and gold, with the background of a blue sky, was so stunning that I kept saying, 'Thank You, God, for this wonderful sight.'

"As I reflected on this sight and on the wonders of nature that I see either from my apartment or when I travel a mile away to a nature center, the thought occurred to me that God must have had a wonderful time during Creation week. I think of all the interesting (what word should I use?) creatures He made: elephants, zebras, buffalo, squirrels, chipmunks, purple martins, bobolinks (remember the poem 'Bobolink, bobolink, spink spank spink'). And then all the beautiful flowers He made (roses, chrysanthemums, peonies, pansies, gladiolas, sunflowers that revolve with the fun—facing east in the morning and gradually turning toward the west as the sun moves through the sky). I think of the song 'How Great Thou Art.'

"Finally, when I remember the fertilized human egg, about one hundredth of a pinhead in size but containing the blueprint for the unbelievably complicated human body, I wonder why anyone should be an atheist. If any one of the major parts of the human body were missing—the brain, mouth, throat, heart, lungs, kidneys, liver, large and small intestines—human life could not exist. So did all the parts of the human body suddenly evolve into homo sapiens? How blind can some scientists be?"

Why?

About the ninth hour Jesus cried out in a loud voice, "Eloi, Eloi, lama sabachthani?"—which means, "My God, my God, why have you forsaken me?" Matt. 27:46, NIV.

Here is the best and noblest Man who ever lived, and He utters the universal question: Why?

"There is only one question that really matters: Why do bad things happen to good people?" writes Rabbi Harold S. Kushner. "All other theological conversation is intellectually diverting; somewhat like doing the crossword puzzle in the Sunday paper and feeling very satisfied when you have made the words fit; but ultimately without the capacity to reach people where they really care. . . .

"The misfortunes of good people are not only a problem to the people who suffer and their families. They are a problem to everyone who wants to believe in a just and fair and livable world. They inevitably raise questions about the goodness, the kindness, even the existence of God" (*Why Bad Things Happen to Good People,* pp. 6, 7).

Ever hear the story about the farmer and the horse? I won't vouch for its authenticity, so treat it like a parable, which it is (sort of). There once was a farmer who owned a horse. And one day the horse ran away. All the people in the town came to console him because of the loss. "Oh, I don't know," said the farmer, "Maybe it's a bad thing, and maybe it's not."

A few days later the horse returned to the farm, accompanied by 20 other horses. All the townspeople came to congratulate him on having a stableful of horses. "Oh, I don't know," said the farmer. "Maybe it's a good thing, and maybe it's not."

A few days later the farmer's son was out riding one of the new horses. The horse got wild and threw him off, breaking his leg. Again the people came to console the farmer because of the accident. "Oh, I don't know," he said. "Maybe it's a bad thing, and maybe it's not."

A few days later the government declared war and instituted a draft of all able-bodied young men. They carted off hundreds of young men, except for the farmer's son, who had a broken leg. "Now I know," said the farmer, "that it was a good thing my horse ran away."

And from the perspective of eternity we will look back and acknowledge that God did it all just right. Until then, let's keep trusting the One who uttered the despairing "Why?" on Calvary.

Perfect Peace

Peace I leave with you; my peace I give you. I do not give to you as the world gives. Do not let your hearts be troubled and do not be afraid. John 14:27, NIV.

Paul's customary salutation in his letters ("Grace and peace to you from God our Father and the Lord Jesus Christ") links grace and peace. Grace is the source, peace the result. Because of grace we have peace.

Peace originates with Jesus, full of grace, who, in His departing blessing, bestowed the gift of peace on the disciples. That is still true—the only true peace today is found in Jesus. You can seek personal peace by running to "experts," who will gladly take your money, invite you to open up your past, and try to help you get beyond it. Don't get me wrong: Counselors and counseling have their place. But until you let Jesus into your life you will always have a void, an unfulfilled longing deep within.

"Peace, perfect peace, in this dark world of sin?
The blood of Jesus whispers peace within."
—Edward H. Bickersteth

Here's how a deeply devoted Christian writer describes Jesus' inner life: "In the heart of Christ, where reigned perfect harmony with God, there was perfect peace. He was never elated by applause, nor dejected by censure or disappointment. Amid the greatest and the most cruel treatment, He was still of good courage" (*The Desire of Ages,* p. 330).

What a wonderful way to live. And how different from the way most people today go through life, including those who profess the name of Jesus!

The whole tenor of the age runs in the opposite direction. Instead of Christ's gift of perfect peace, the age seeks nonstop excitement. Faster and faster. Louder and louder. Scarier and scarier. More and more thrilling. Get the adrenaline pumping and keep it pumping.

But we can't sustain it. The higher we fly, the deeper will be our inevitable crash.

Do we *really* desire the peace Christ offers us? We need to start by laying aside the coffee and the pills that get us up and help us to come down. We need to build order into lives: get enough sleep, forget about *The Late Show.* We need to be quiet every day, quiet enough to talk to God and to listen, to feed on His Word.

Serious about perfect peace? Give God a chance.

Our Father

With a God like this loving you, you can pray very simply. Like this: Our Father in heaven, reveal who you are. Matt. 6:9, Message.

One of the saddest commentaries on our age is that for many young people "father" is a painful word. Kids with deadbeat dads, kids who never knew who their father was (maybe their mother didn't know either), kids whose dad beat them and abused them—how can they think of "father" in positive terms?

A great need today is for fathers to find their rightful place in the home and in society. Not just to exercise authority (although there is a sad lack of that), but to model the love of the heavenly Father. Without human examples, flawed though they be, children have a difficult job to love a God whom they cannot see.

The Bible predicts that such a work of reformation will take place before Jesus' return. We find it in the very last words of the Old Testament: "See, I will send you the prophet Elijah before that great and dreadful day of the Lord comes. He will turn the hearts of the fathers to their children, and the hearts of the children to their fathers; or else I will come and strike the land with a curse" (Mal. 4:5, 6, NIV).

Many troubled children, like many troubled adults, are looking for someone to love them. If they never knew a dad, they live with the nagging question Why? Why didn't he stay with my mother? Why has he never visited me? Why did he walk out on us? And with that, the terribly sad self-examination: What did I do to make him not want to stay, not want to love me?

Oh, the breaking hearts of our times. How to find ways to help these breaking hearts to become aware that they are loved, are precious to the heavenly Father! Oh, to be able to help them to grasp this truth:

"All the paternal love which has come down from generation to generation through the channel of human hearts, all the springs of tenderness which have opened in the souls of men, are but as a tiny rill to the boundless ocean when compared with the infinite, exhaustless love of God" (*Testimonies for the Church*, vol. 5, p. 740).

What is our Father like? Just like Jesus, full of grace and truth.

Starters and Finishers

Being confident of this very thing, that He who has begun a good work in you will complete it until the day of Jesus Christ. Phil. 1:6, NKJV.

Most of my life I've been thin. It's not something I take credit for; I have one of those bodies that stays at constant weight year after year. During my doctoral studies, however, something began to happen. Perhaps it was the many hours sitting in research and deep thought as I worked on the dissertation, maybe a change related to age, but I slowly began to put on the pounds. And I was hardly aware of it—that's the way weight gain creeps up on you. But I was jolted into awareness by a former student who met me and said, "You must have put on 30 pounds! You've ballooned!"

Hardly a diplomatic greeting, but it certainly got my attention. Which led me to make some lifestyle changes, among them putting in place regular patterns of exercise, which have become part of my life now for more than 30 years and have brought benefits of many kinds. This was when I began running—very short distances at first, then farther and farther, until I could compete in and complete the Marine Corps Marathon each year.

Running opened up a new world (and by the way, I ran—and run—slowly; I'm no great athlete). A world of clear-eyed, lean men and women; a world without cigarette smoke; a world of intensity, power, and determination; a world of self-discipline and espirit de corps.

Also a world of starters and finishers. At the start of the Marine Corps Marathon 20,000 (or more) runners, 70 percent of them competing for the first time, jog back and forth in nervous apprehension, burning up energy they will sorely need before the day is over. Crowds of well-wishers. Bands. Thousands of marines, men and women, busy with a host of tasks. The air pulses with music, is electric with energy and anticipation.

Three, four, five, six, seven hours later, the sound and the fury have ebbed away. Weary but triumphant figures limp to cars, medals hanging from necks and silver wraps over shoulders. They made it! But a couple thousand others slink away, disappointed—the dropouts.

We all are runners in the race of life. We aren't competing against each other; everyone who finishes is a winner. In this race also a great many start, but many drop out. But with Jesus we can make it! He who began His work in us promises to finish it!

So run your race this day, claiming that promise.

The Will to Believe

Let's see how inventive we can be in encouraging love and helping out, not avoiding worshiping together as some do but spurring each other on, especially as we see the big Day approaching. Heb. 10:24, 25, Message.

J esus indicated that faith would be in short supply when He comes back. Today doubt, skepticism, and unbelief flourish; even many professed followers of Jesus are weak and faltering in their faith.

At a time like this let's light a candle instead of cursing the dark. Let's lean into the wind, reminding ourselves that the Christian life grows stronger by conflict; that it's a battle and a march; that soft chairs and easy times make us flabby and flaccid.

I believe strongly in exercising the will to believe. That is, seizing every opportunity to nurture faith, and spurning every opportunity to nurture unbelief. We need to think, to wrestle, with difficult issues (there's no future for a church that buries its head in the sand), but always in the context of faith. We are followers of Jesus Christ, our Lord and Savior; we have examined His claims and made our decision; there's no turning back. We start on this foundation and never move from it.

One simple but important way in which we exercise the will to believe is by getting up on Sabbath morning and going to worship services. Attendance at church is not simply an option for the Christian. We are members of the body of Christ. We are not alone. Just as the hand, eye, or foot cannot exist apart from the other members, so we cannot "go it alone."

So we refuse to drift along with the common crowd, floating in the lake of doubt. We rise up to hear the preaching of the Word, to share the fellowship of the saints, to strengthen and to be strengthened.

Yes, it is possible to worship out in nature. It is possible to go aside quietly on one's own for study and prayer. But such times should be exceptions. As Christians, because we are Christians, we belong in church on Sabbath morning. Church is the fellowship of grace. And absenting oneself from church is clear evidence that the spiritual life has started on a toboggan slide.

The big Day is approaching. Soon the One who came the first time to reveal the Father's love and to rescue us from sin and death will come back. Then the fellowship of grace will stretch from pole to pole and from sea to sea.

Keep a Song in the Heart

Let the word of Christ dwell in you richly, teach and admonish one another in all wisdom, and sing psalms and hymns and spiritual songs with thankfulness in your hearts to God. Col. 3:16, RSV.

Jesus sets the heart singing. His grace liberates us to new life and new song. The Protestant Reformation brought in congregational singing, Martin Luther himself composing many hymns. And whenever a church or a person today experiences revival, singing breaks forth.

One of the best ways to meet temptation or to banish spiritual blues is to keep a song in the heart. Simply humming a few bars, or even thinking of the words and tune, gives a lift to the spirit. "How often to the soul hard-pressed and ready to despair, memory recalls some word of God's—the long-forgotten burden of a childhood song—and temptations lose their power, life takes on new meaning and new purpose, and courage and gladness are imparted to other souls!" (*Education,* p. 168).

In one of the early annual sessions of the Seventh-day Adventist Church, held in the old Battle Creek church, the meeting bogged down. As the members struggled with a depressing situation, pioneer leader James White stood up and called to his wife, "Come, Ellen, let us sing for them." Standing on the platform, they lifted their voices in an old hymn of courage:

> "When faint and weary toiling,
>   The sweat drops on my brow,
> I long to rest from labor,
>   To drop the burden now—
> Then comes a gentle chiding,
>   To quell each mourning sigh:
> 'Work while the day is shining,
>   There's resting by and by.'"

By the time James and Ellen finished the first stanza, the spirit of the song was moving among the whole audience, who joined together in the chorus:

> "Resting by and by,
> There's resting by and by . . ."

And renewed, the session moved ahead.

Cousin Fred

We were not idle when we were with you, nor did we eat anyone's food without paying for it. 2 Thess. 3:7, 8, NIV.

In his letters the apostle Paul always starts with the "what" of grace, the source of our salvation. But he invariably ends with the "so what"—how we are to live as children of the Lord of grace.

One of Paul's rules for believers was "If a man will not work, he shall not eat" (2 Thess. 3:10). And Paul himself set the example. Although he might have claimed his right as an apostle to be supported by the church, he chose to make his own way so as not to burden anyone.

Today many people seek to do as little as they can to get as much as they can. If possible, they want a free ride altogether. They dream of striking it rich, living on easy street, never having to work again. And so they play the lottery.

Jack Whittaker, of Charleston, West Virginia, took home the richest undivided jackpot in United States history—a cool $314 million. Whittaker settled for a lump sun of $113 million after taxes, and settled back to enjoy a life of leisure.

Two years later his wife, Jewel, told a reporter, "I wish all of this never would have happened. I wish I would have torn the ticket up." Since winning the lottery Jack Whittaker had been arrested twice for drunken driving and been ordered into rehab. He was charged with attacking a bar manager, and accused in two lawsuits of making trouble.

He reminds me of Cousin Fred. When I was growing up in Australia, my cousin Fred, much older, was an average Joe with a steady job and a wife and kids. Then one day he won the lottery. He quit his job on the spot and never worked another day of his life. He began to drink heavily, becoming an alcoholic. Before long his wife couldn't take any more and filed for divorce. Cousin Fred ended his days a miserable failure of a man.

The gambling industry dangles its hollow baubles before the poor and the desperate. It preys on the element in society least able to lose still more of this world's goods. It creates losers all around.

The answer to the poor and the desperate—and to all of us—is grace, not gambling. Grace lifts us up to live and work with the dignity of a child of God.

People Are Wonderful

What is man that you are mindful of him, the son of man that you care for him? Ps. 8:4, NIV.

Of all the vast scope of God's creation, magnificent in complexity and variety, people are the most wonderful. Psalm 8 tells us that, but in a manner that surprises us. The first half of the psalm seems to show the *smallness* of humanity, as the psalmist considers the glory of the heavens, with moon and stars the work of God's fingers. Indeed, as we look up at the Milky Way on a clear night we feel so puny. With David we want to say, "What is man that you are mindful of him, the son of man that you care for him?"

But the psalm suddenly reverses itself. Humanity isn't puny after all. We have exalted status because God made us only a little lower than the angels. He crowned us with glory and honor, and put in subjection to us all the creatures that walk, roam, fly, or swim (verses 5-8). Seeing the glory of humanity, the psalmist exclaims again:

"O Lord, our Lord, how majestic is your name in all the earth!" (verse 9, NIV).

What a place heaven will be! We'll get to meet an endless array of fascinating people from all races and all generations! I'm looking forward to it. And even now I find great enjoyment from the folks who come my way (or is it that the Lord sends them my way?).

Like a surprising doctor I met this week. For months my good wife, put off by my running-battered feet, had urged me to visit her podiatrist. Only after I developed a sore spot on the flat of my left foot did I grudgingly consent to making an appointment. I was in for a surprise.

The doctor's waiting room was the tiniest I'd ever seen—only three chairs. And I went in to see him to the minute of my appointed time. When I commended him for it, he replied, "I space out patients so they won't have to wait. That's why I have only a small waiting room." We began to talk, and he told me he was writing a book, a story for children. He sometimes gets up in the middle of the night and writes for three hours. He was eager to learn how to find an editor, how to get published. He also shared his philosophy of life: "A lot of people feel discouraged when they have a birthday because they're getting old. I look back on the past year and think of the hundreds of people who are walking around without pain because of me."

What a man! What a visit! I left feeling better from head to sole.

Living Deliberately

Then Jesus was led up by the Spirit into the wilderness to be tempted by the devil. Matt. 4:1, NKJV.

Henry David Thoreau was just a few days short of his twenty-eighth birthday when he left society on July 4, 1845. He moved into a cabin he had built on the shore of Walden Pond, and lived alone for two years, caring for his needs. Apparently he didn't intend to write a book when he went to Walden, but nine years later his *Walden; or, Life in the Woods* came off the press. Although it sold slowly at first, it eventually became an American classic.

In *Walden* Thoreau tells why he embarked on his famous experiment at living alone. "I went to the woods because I wished to live deliberately, . . . and not, when I came to die, discover I had not lived." Living in monkish simplicity, he studied the minutiae of nature around him cycling through the seasons. The long periods of silence afforded the opportunity to think and reflect on who he was and what he wanted his life to be.

Long before Thoreau went into the woods, Jesus of Nazareth went into the desert. He too went to think and reflect on who He was and His purpose in life. Unlike Thoreau, Jesus was about to embark on a mission of supreme magnitude, one on whose success or failure the destiny of humanity—indeed, of the entire universe—hung. Because of this mission He had come to earth, leaving His heavenly glory, veiling His majesty, setting aside His divine prerogatives where "thousands at his bidding speed, and post o'er land and ocean without rest" (Milton).

The Spirit led Jesus into the wilderness. The same Spirit had directed Him to leave Nazareth and make His way south to the Jordan, near Jericho, where the Baptist was proclaiming the dawning of the kingdom of God. Jesus joined the throng around John and asked John to baptize Him, not because He had unconfessed sin but as an affirmation of John's message and as a public declaration of the start of His mission.

Now He struggled in the desert. Unlike Thoreau, Jesus faced the heat of Satan's temptations. Every test sought to sabotage His mission; but for every test Jesus leaned on God and His Word.

We can learn much from Thoreau. We need to learn how to live life deliberately. We can learn more from Jesus. His example shows us the way to power in the deliberate life.

Saul Among the Prophets

When all who had formerly known him saw him prophesying with the prophets, they asked each other, "What is this that has happened to the son of Kish? Is Saul also among the prophets?" 1 Sam. 10:11, NIV.

The Bible goes on to tell us that the words "Is Saul also among the prophets?" became a saying among the children of Israel (verse 12). It obviously was an expression of the seemingly incredible, something apparently too way out to believe, such as "Has hell frozen over?"

The saying tells us volumes about the man who became Israel's first king. Apparently no one considered him to be a spiritual leader, whatever other qualities he possessed that commended him to the popular imagination. How sad that Saul should be so regarded as he took over the reins of authority.

Yet the saying as it was initially uttered was true. Although Saul had led a life careless of the Lord and His will, after Samuel anointed him leader of Israel he changed. Samuel told him that on his way back to this father's house he would meet a procession of prophets. "The Spirit of the Lord will come upon you in power, and you will prophesy with them; and you will be changed into a different person" (verse 6, NIV). And it happened. "God changed Saul's heart" (verse 9, NIV), and when he came upon the procession of prophets, he joined them in prophesying.

True then, true today: we can find Saul among the prophets. And we can be a Saul among the prophets. No matter what our past may have been, how careless or indifferent to God, He can give us a new heart. If we are willing, He can bring down His Spirit upon us in power, and we can join with the most spiritual people in the church.

Unfortunately, Saul's story didn't end there. He started out well as king; the end of his reign was another matter. Late in the day we find him obsessed with envy of David, whom he fears is the one the Lord has chosen to succeed him. David flees for his life to Samuel at Ramah; Saul sends a band of soldiers to capture him. But the Spirit of God comes upon the soldiers, and they start to prophesy. Saul sends more men; the same thing happens. Then he sends a third company, with the same result. Last of all, Saul goes in person, but the Spirit of God comes even upon him. And so the saying once again is heard: "Is Saul also among the prophets?" (1 Sam. 19:24).

Yes, Saul was again among the prophets, but not willingly so. He who had started so well now had murder in his heart. What a fearful warning to each of us!

The Odds of Grace

Very rarely will anyone die for a righteous man, though for a good man someone might possibly dare to die. Rom. 5:7, NIV.

A news report brings the fascinating story of two sisters who gave birth about an hour apart at Northside Hospital in Atlanta, Georgia. Ashlee Spinks, of Indianapolis, and Andrea Springer found out when they were six months pregnant that they were due to deliver on the same day, so Spinks came to Georgia several weeks early to be with her sister.

Each delivered sets of twin boys by scheduled cesarean sections.

And the sisters themselves are twins.

The couples did not use fertility drugs to conceive the babies, but twins run in the families of all four parents.

The news report quotes a physician, who specializes in high-risk pregnancies, as saying that the chances of twin sisters being pregnant with twin boys due on the same date are probably one in a million.

In our world people have become used to talk about chance. The study of statistics enables one to state accurately the odds for or against a certain event occurring. Such calculations serve us well in making decisions; they help us to bring order into our lives.

Let's always remember, however, that chance and odds need to be seen against a much larger backdrop. For instance, scientists have calculated the odds against all the variables needed to bring the universe together just happening, and the figure is so large as to be mind-boggling. Yes, it is feasible that the astronomically remote possibility did just come about, but it's far more reasonable that a colossal Mind brought everything together. For this reason many astrophysicists and astronomers today, unlike those of a previous generation, acknowledge some sort of divine Being as the source of the universe.

What are the odds of salvation? Now and then someone dies for a friend or a good person, as Paul notes; but what are the odds of the Maker of heaven and earth dying for a lost world? What are the odds of the Eternal One entering time and space, condescending to be born as a baby? What are the odds of the Sinless One taking upon Himself our guilt and shame?

What are the odds? The odds of grace, which knows no limit and shatters all expectations.

Who Is My Enemy?

When a man finds his enemy, does he let him get away unharmed? May the Lord reward you well for the way you treated me today. 1 Sam. 24:19, NIV.

David had just spared Saul's life. The king, crazed with jealousy, was pursuing his young general with 3,000 handpicked men. He had tracked him to the wilderness of En-gedi, that dry, rugged area that rises above the Dead Sea, where the famous scrolls were found.

The king had gone into a cave to relieve himself, totally unaware that back in its recesses David and his men lay hidden. "This is your chance!" they whispered to David. "God has given Saul into your hand!" But David resisted the temptation to strike down the king in cold blood. Instead he crept up behind him and cut off a piece of his robe.

After the king had left, David came out of the cave and called out after him. Holding up the piece of clothing, he told the king how he had spared his life. And Saul was shocked: his entire being had become consumed with eliminating the person he saw as his rival. If David had fallen into his hands, the result would have been swift and final.

Saul regarded David as his enemy, but David did not regard Saul as his enemy, even though Saul was trying to kill him. David exhibited the spirit of Jesus, who said, "Love your enemies and pray for those who persecute you, that you may be sons of your Father in heaven" (Matt. 5:44, 45, NIV). And Jesus did just that: "When they hurled their insults at him, he did not retaliate; when he suffered, he made no threats. Instead, he entrusted himself to him who judges justly" (1 Peter 2:23, NIV).

God has no enemies, and neither should we. Whatever others may think about us, say against us, or do to us, they are still sons and daughters of God—our brothers and sisters, people whom God loves and for whom Jesus died. Only grace can bring about this shift in our attitudes, but it can, and does, as we allow God's Spirit to transform us into the likeness of Jesus.

Many people go through life constantly looking over their shoulder to see who is trying to do them ill. They spend hours of negative energy imagining plots, schemes, and bad scenarios. God is calling us to a better life. Let's leave the shadows of doubt and suspicion and go out into the sunlight. Let's walk today in the spirit of Jesus, in grace and with love to all people.

Formula for Revival

If my people, who are called by my name, will humble themselves and pray and seek my face and turn from their wicked ways, then I will hear from heaven and will forgive their sin and will heal their land. 2 Chron. 7:14, NIV.

Solomon had just finished dedicating the Temple he had built for Yahweh's glory. He had prayed an earnest, public prayer, the essence of which was a petition that, no matter what sin the people might commit or what calamity overtake them, God would hear and grant their desires if they directed their prayer to the Temple.

Shortly after, God appeared to him at night with an answer. The divine response made clear that while the Temple was the focal point of worship, it had no power in itself to ensure that the Lord would grant their requests. What was more important was the manner in which the people approached God, humbling themselves, praying, seeking God's face, and turning from their wicked ways.

This fourfold formula for successful prayer still speaks to us. It provides a prescription for revival that we should take to heart and follow, both individually and corporately.

Revival begins with humility. It is the hungry person whom God feeds, not the one who feels satisfied; the thirsty who receives the living water. So long as we are filled with pride and self-sufficiency we have no room for God. "I live in a high and holy place," says the Lord, "but also with him who is contrite and lowly in spirit, to revive the spirit of the lowly and to revive the heart of the contrite" (Isa. 57:15, NIV).

Humility leads to prayer with a difference, prayer that works, prayer that God answers. When we realize our great need, God can hear us. Jesus told about two men who went into the Temple to pray. One, full of himself, went away no different; but the other could only cry out, "God, be merciful to me a sinner!" (Luke 18:13, NKJV), and he went home right with God.

To seek God's face is to seek His favor, which means to be at peace with Him. When God means more to us then all else, when we are prepared to lay aside cherished sin as the Spirit convicts us, God can do great things for us.

The last step, turning from our wicked ways, describes repentance. Indeed, all four do. Repentance begins with a change of heart, but it results in a change of life.

My Redeemer Lives!

I know that my Redeemer lives, and that in the end he will stand upon the earth. Job 19:25, NIV.

T he book of Job, a classic of literature, plumbs the depths of human experience as it wrestles with the age-old problem of suffering. Here we find our questions to God, especially the huge "Why?" Here we find the clichés and pat answers given by the comfortable, the "comforters" of the despairing Job. But in the end God manifests Himself, and when He does so He commends the questioning Job and rebukes his know-it-all friends.

In the midst of this remarkable book, suddenly we come upon one of the most precious treasures in all the Bible. It is all the more wonderful because it totally breaks the pattern of all that has gone before.

Job has been lamenting his fate, cursing the day of his birth, feeling unjustly treated by God, and pleading for a chance to make his case before his Maker. And the three "comforters," Eliphaz, Bildad, and Zophar, have been telling him that he really deserves the suffering that has befallen him—he is a bad man, and he needs to confess his sin and repent.

The nineteenth chapter presents Job's sufferings in pitiable light. He laments that his friends only make him feel worse (verse 1-5) and that God gives him no opportunity to get the justice he deserves (verses 7, 8). Job has been stripped of honor and dignity; his hope is gone; all his relatives and acquaintances have abandoned him (verse 9-16). He has become an object of loathing, scorn, and ridicule, even to those he loves. He is nothing but skin and bones (verse 17-20). "Have pity on me, my friends, have pity, for the hand of God has struck me," he cries out, and our hearts go out to him (verse 21, NIV).

Then, seemingly out of the blue, comes the remarkable, wonderful outburst of trust and assurance: "I know that my Redeemer lives, and that in the end he will stand upon the earth. And after my skin has been destroyed, yet in my flesh I will see God; I myself will see him with my own eyes—I, and not another" (verse 25-27, NIV).

"I know!" This is the assurance that grace brings. I know Jesus, my Redeemer. I *know* that He is alive. I know that He will come again and raise the dead. And so I know that, because He lives, I too will live.

Free to Swing

So if the Son sets you free, you will be free indeed. John 8:36, NIV.

G irls and swings were made for each other. I didn't realize it until Noelene and I entered into the blessed estate of grandparenting. After waiting forever, we got a granddaughter and, a bit later (double blessing), a second one. And we began to notice something: the girls ran straight for any swing they saw in sight.

Actually, it started earlier, before they could run, or even walk. They loved to be put in a little support seat and swung back and forth. As they grew—and how they still grow—their love for swings and swinging seems only to grow stronger. They pump themselves higher and higher, so high that at times my heart is in my mouth; or they just swing lazily back and forth, back and forth.

I wonder: Is this the image that more than another captures the lightness, the joy, of a girl's childhood and youth—hair flying in the wind, not a care in the world, just swinging, swinging, swinging the hours away?

Seems to me that this image captures the essence of grace in the life of the Christian—every Christian. Jesus sets us free! Jesus brings a lightness of being, the joy of living as a child of God.

"The mass of men lead lives of quiet desperation," wrote Henry David Thoreau. They never experience the lightness of grace. Sin lies heavy upon us. Sin enslaves us. But Jesus promises, "Everyone who sins is a slave to sin. . . . So if the Son sets you free, you will be free indeed" (John 8:34-36, NIV).

The sins of our past—what we did, what we failed to do—weigh us down, bend our backs. Jesus offers us release. The sins of the present— our bad habits, our ingrained ugly behavior that seems impossible to overcome—drag us down. Jesus offers us the freedom of His forgiveness and new life.

Our worries—the cares that press in upon us, the uncertainties, the apprehensions—strangle our energies. Jesus offers us the joy and lightness of an 8-year-old girl on a swing.

He also said, "You will know the truth, and the truth will set you free" (verse 32, NIV). But He is the truth (John 14:6). That's the secret: to know Jesus. Every day. Today.

Integrity

Finally these men said, "We will never find any basis for charges against this man Daniel unless it has something to do with the law of his God." Dan. 6:5, NIV.

Ever since Watergate, the discovery of dirty tricks in American politics, journalists have been on the trail of dirt. Watergate catapulted "investigative journalism" to a new intensity; and it presupposes that if you probe deep enough, you'll find dirt.

In the Bible long, long ago we find a pack of men looking for dirt. Not journalists—these are administrators of King Darius the Mede. They hold responsible positions in the kingdom, but they aren't happy. The king is planning to set a foreigner, Daniel by name, over the whole realm. Although an older man, Daniel has exceptional qualities that distinguish him from all the other government servants. He's a standout, which makes the others jealous.

So they go looking for dirt. Surely there's a taint of corruption in his past. If they turn over enough stones, surely they'll find something under one that they can use to embarrass Daniel and keep him from getting the promotion. They search hard, but they come up empty. No trace of crookedness with this man, not a speck of anything shady or underhanded.

At last they conclude that there's only one way to get at him—through his religion. "We'll never find any basis for charges against this man Daniel unless it has something to do with the law of his God," they conclude. He's a Jew, and worships Yahweh, a strange God in that land.

So they cook up a scheme, and the king unwittingly goes along. He issues a decree that no one is to pray to any god or man for 30 days—only to Darius. The king seals the order, then Daniel's enemies watch, and strike. Daniel, unfazed by the decree, prays as usual, his windows open for any to see him. Before long he is arrested and thrown into the lions' den. But he has the last word. The lions don't touch him. Instead they maul his opponents, who become the objects of the king's wrath.

What a testimony to Daniel's life! No charges against this person except with regard to his walk with God! This is integrity indeed. Inner life matching outer appearance, solid gold.

Dear Lord, make me such a person of integrity.

The Threefold Christ

Grace and peace to you from him who is, and who was, and who is to come, and from the seven spirits before his throne, and from Jesus Christ, who is the faithful witness, the firstborn from the dead, and the ruler of the kings of the earth. Rev. 1:4, 5, NIV.

The book of Revelation gives us a glimpse into the future. God, for whom past, present, and future are all known, provides this writing "to show his servants what must soon take place" (verse 1, NIV).

But the Apocalypse is far more. As "the revelation of Jesus Christ" (verse 1, NIV), it not only conveys His message about what lies ahead; preeminently it is the revelation about Him. In this book we see Jesus first and foremost, and to concentrate on events and nations without discerning the One who is leading history to its glorious climax is to miss the ultimate message of Revelation.

Throughout this book we find glorious descriptions of Jesus and His work—who He is, and what He has done, is doing, and will yet do. Periodically the action breaks as the inhabitants of heaven—the four living creatures, the 24 elders, and myriads of angels—break out in hymns of worship and praise.

At the outset we meet a threefold description of Jesus. He is the faithful witness, the firstborn from the dead, and the ruler of the kings of the earth. Each of these characteristics will come to the fore in the book, and each speaks to us today.

As the faithful witness, Jesus looks both into the future and into our lives with unerring discernment. When He tells us that good will triumph over evil in the long run, we can take that to the bank. And when He looks into our lives and says, "I know your deeds, that you are neither cold nor hot" (Rev. 3:14, 15, NIV), we have to confess that His diagnosis is correct.

The faithful witness is also the firstborn from the dead. He has been there, done that. He is the first to break death's chains, and now we follow the Leader. Though our body perish, we too will live again.

And He is the ruler of the kings of the earth. Presidents, prime ministers, monarchs, the big shots, the power brokers—He is more powerful than all. He is King of kings and Lord of lords, and one day they too will acknowledge Him as such (Rev. 19:16).

Hallelujah! What a Savior!

JULY

A Wildly Wonderful World

What a wildly wonderful world, God! You made it all, with Wisdom at your side, made earth overflow with your wonderful creations. Ps. 104:24, Message.

From the minutest subatomic particle to whirling galaxies, the universe is incredible beyond our imagination. What a wildly wonderful world God made!

What sort of Mind breathed such complexity into the simplest forms of life? Simple? Nothing is simple—not the earthworm, not the human cell. Complexity and interdependence meet us at every level of the creation.

Sometimes men, caught up in their little sphere of knowledge, speak as though they can create life, as though gaining an understanding of *how* a biochemical process takes place means that they have mastered the process itself. How shortsighted! What sort of Mind conceived such a universe? A Mind wonderful in its ability to bring and hold together seemingly infinite bits of information. No computer on earth can approach this Mind.

Once it was believed and taught that no life can exist totally devoid of sunlight, that the deep ocean floors could support no form of existence. Now we know that the conventional wisdom was wrong; in the darkness of deepest ocean depths strange plant creatures find life.

What sort of Mind spoke and it was, who snapped His fingers and galaxies sprang into being, whose universe stretches into infinity, seemingly without end? A Mind that loves variety, infinite variety, and that loves to create.

Once, most scientists of the starry heavens were unbelievers or agnostics, holding that nature alone was sufficient to account for the universe. No more. The studies of cosmologists and astrophysicists have revealed such an intricate *balance* in the universe that the probability of it all "just happening" defies reason. Although they may not understand God as the Bible portrays Him, more and more they acknowledge that an incredible, marvelous, infinite Mind was and is behind it all.

What sort of Mind keeps track of every man and woman, boy and girl among the more than 6 billion on Planet Earth? A Mind that loves and cares infinitely, a Mind infinite in grace.

How to Be Number One

Sitting down, Jesus called the Twelve and said, "If anyone wants to be first, he must be the very last, and the servant of all." Mark 9:35, NIV.

A small pearl-fishing settlement clustered along a tidal inlet on the Persian Gulf. For centuries it barely survived, but everything changed in the 1960s. Black gold—oil—was discovered, and Dubai began to grow.

A short distance away even greater reserves of oil were found at Abu Dhabi. Today its sands make it the fourth-largest oil producer in the world. In Dubai the oil began to run out years ago, but before it did the rulers had embarked on an ambitious scheme of development: to transform the city into the Hong Kong of the Middle East. They would encourage business, eliminate taxes, welcome tourists. And in only a few years they have wrought something like a modern miracle, albeit a secular one.

An ultramodern city rises from the desert. Everything is new—and big. The dazzling airport will see 40 million passengers pass through it in 2010. The climate is warm, with four months of oppressive heat (110° F-120° F) and stifling humidity. But Dubai has constructed the largest indoor ski run (1,300 feet), with 6,600 pounds of fresh snow manufactured in the desert and dumped on the slopes each night.

And that's not all. Dubai has the world's tallest—and most expensive—hotel. The largest shopping mall outside North America. And soon to be completed: the world's first underwater hotel and the largest human-made islands (in the shape of a palm tree and visible from outer space).

Rainfall averages about three inches per year, but Dubai has golf courses, racetracks, boulevards lined with trees and hedges, lakes and parks. Water makes the desert bloom—and the water comes from massive desalinization plants (largest in the world, of course!).

Dubai, mind-boggling, is a tribute to human ingenuity. But Jesus, full of grace, teaches us to walk a different way. He tells us that the meaning of life isn't found in the newest, the biggest, the costliest. Only in service.

Do you want to find a life fulfilling and satisfying? Cast yourself into the furrow of the world's need. Help someone. Give hope. Give good news—the good news.

Today.

The Threefold Gift

To him who loves us and has freed us from our sins by his blood, and has made us to be a kingdom and priests to serve his God and Father—to him be glory and power for ever and ever! Amen. Rev. 1:5, 6, NIV.

The threefold Christ—faithful witness, firstborn from the dead, ruler of the kings of the earth—bestows on us a threefold gift. Do you want a lift as you start out into a new day? Listen to His blessing. He loves us. He loves you. He loves me. "I have loved you with an everlasting love," He tells us (Jer. 31:3, NIV). Even though we don't deserve it. Even though we messed up. Even though we're too often stubborn and rebellious, too often proud and self-sufficient.

When the late theologian Karl Barth, already famous in Europe, visited America, reporters asked him to sum up his work. Barth, who wrote massive volumes as he developed his theological system, replied thus:

> "Jesus loves me,
> This I know;
> For the Bible tells me so."

Loved—loved by God! It seems too good to be true. But it's the faithful witness who pronounces it, and He *does* not lie. He really does love us. He showed us how much He loves us by dying to set us free from sin. Sin is a terrible weight, a heavy chain that drags us down in this life and down into eternal ruin. But Jesus set us free. Just as He set free demon-possessed men and women, just as He freed the lepers from their disease and separation, just as He unloosed the woman bent over and bowed, so He set us free.

Free to *live*. Free to sing. Free to laugh. Free to be. Free to do.

And all by His blood. Our freedom came at a high price, even His life.

Now we are a kingdom of priests. Whenever a person lets Jesus be Lord of his or her life, there He rules, there His kingdom is established on earth. We are that kingdom—the kingdom of those who confess Jesus Christ as supreme above all governments and gods.

And we are priests. We don't need a priest to represent us before the throne of God. We come boldly there ourselves, because He is our great high priest (Heb. 4:14-16). Loved, set free, direct access to God—what a gift from the threefold Christ!

Christ Towers Over All

From beginning to end he's there, towering above everything, everyone. Col. 1:18,
Message.

Jesus, Husband of the bride,	Matt. 1:21; Eph. 5:25
Prince of Peace of valor tried,	Isa. 9:6
Captain of the ransomed host,	Heb. 2:10
Blessed Savior of the lost,	Luke 2:11
Fruitful Vine, bright Morning Star	John 15:1; Rev. 22:16
Sun whose Light is seen afar,	Mal. 4:2; John 8:12
Advocate before God's throne,	1 John 2:1
True and Faithful, Corner Stone.	Rev. 19:11; 1 Peter 2:6
Bread, our starving souls to feed,	John 6:48
Fountain to supply our need,	Jer. 2:13; John 7:37
Paschal Lamb, Beloved of God,	John 1:29; Eph. 1:6
David's Branch, and Jesse's Rod.	Zech. 3; Isa. 11:1
Shepherd of thy fleecy fold,	John 10:11
Judah's Lion, noble, bold,	Rev. 5:5
Faithful Brother, Constant Friend,	Heb. 2:11; Matt. 11:19
The Beginning and the End.	Rev. 22:13
The High Priest whose name we plead,	Heb. 4:14
Judge, Redeemer, promised Seed,	Acts 10:42; Job 19:25; Gen. 3:15
Kind Physician in our woes,	Jer. 8:22
Gilead's Balm, and Sharon's Rose.	Jer. 8:22; S. of Sol. 2:1
Prophet of Thine Israel,	Acts 7:37
Messenger, Immanuel,	Mal. 3:1; Isa. 7:14
"Rock of Ages, cleft for me,"	Isa. 26:4, margin
Father of eternity.	Isa. 9:6
Son of God, and Son of man,	Matt. 16:13, 16
Wonderful, the great I AM,	Isa. 9:6; John 8:58
Christ, the Lord our Righteousness,	Matt. 16:16; Jer. 23:6
Timely Refuge in distress.	Heb. 6:18

Broken People, Broken Pieces

Not only that, but all the broken and dislocated pieces of the universe—people and things, animals and atoms—get properly fixed and fit together in vibrant harmonies, all because of his death, his blood that poured down from the Cross. Col. 1:19, 20, Message.

This marvelous passage, so well put into contemporary language by Eugene Peterson, tells us two great facts. Almost everyone will assent to the first; far fewer know and experience the reality of the second.

First fact: the universe is broken. Lives are broken—my life is broken. Nature is broken. Everything is broken.

Does anyone question this fact? Not anymore. It's scarcely fathomable, but only a century ago a great many people thought just the opposite. Motivated by the dawning of the Enlightenment in the eighteenth century, spurred on by Darwin's theory, they embraced a robust optimism about the future. The world was getting better and better, on track toward Utopia. Human nature could be perfected; the spread of knowledge through education would bring on a golden age free of war, social problems, ignorance and superstition.

The dawning of the twentieth century saw the launch of a new journal. Imbued with the prevailing optimism, its founders, looking ahead, dubbed it *The Christian Century*.

A hundred years later the name seems incongruous. This period of two terrible world wars, of Adolf Hitler and Idi Amin, of the Berlin Wall and the gulags, of Hiroshima and Nagasaki—*this* was the Christian century? What a farce. We saw evil unmasked as perhaps never before in human history. We experienced the reality of the demonic in human conduct.

But now the second fact: Christ is the one who fixes broken lives and broken pieces. He is the Healer, the Great Physician. He makes people whole. He puts together the broken and dislocated pieces of the universe. Out of chaos He brings order, just as He did at the Creation. Out of discord He makes vibrant harmony.

By and large, the Jews reject Jesus as Messiah. Their reason? The kingdom didn't come. If He had been the Messiah, God's kingdom would have spread on earth.

But it did. Wherever and whenever a broken life finds healing and wholeness in Jesus, the kingdom has come. It happened during His time on earth. It still happens.

Let it happen in your life today!

J u l y   6

Tsunami

He reached down from on high and took hold of me; he drew me out of deep waters.
2 Sam. 22:17, NIV.

On December 26, 2004, a massive earthquake shook the seabed off the coast of Sumatra. It created a tsunami that rolled out in concentric circles to strike Indonesia, Thailand, Sri Lanka, India, Bangladesh, and even parts of Africa. The devastation left in its wake beggared description. At least 150,000 people dead; millions of others homeless, displaced, or without food and safe water.

Among the images that came before us with ever-increasing horror as reports came in during the next week, a series of three photographs were particularly gripping. The first shows confused vacationers on the Rai Leh Beach in Krabi, Thailand, looking at the water receding prior to the tsunami. Another shot shows swimmers running to the shore as they see the tower of water approaching. But in the third we see a woman running toward the gigantic wave, which is engulfing boats just beyond those still in the water.

Who was this woman? Why did she run toward the wall of death? And what happened to her? Several days later the answers became known. Her name: Karin Svaerd, 37, from Sweden. Her sons Anton, 14; Filip, 11; and Viktor, 10; plus her brother and brother-in-law were snorkeling, oblivious to the disaster about to strike them. Karin yelled at them to run, but they could not hear her. In desperation she sprinted into the waves in an effort to save them.

The family, caught in the tsunami, was tossed around under water. But amazingly, wonderfully, each managed to get to their feet and make it to higher ground. Anton and little brother Filip were hurled among the beach bungalows; Karin somehow managed to grasp a tree trunk; another family member landed in a swimming pool. All survived.

Karin became a hero to her fellow Swedes and to others as the media around the world carried the pictures. "I did not care. I was looking at my children. I wanted to hold them and care for them," she said.

I did not care. I was looking at my children. I wanted to hold them and care for them. Just like the One who, disregarding His own fate, saw us and, wanting to hold us and care for us, plunged into the tsunami of sin.

Grace Is a Many-splendored Thing

As each one has received a gift, minister it to one another, as good stewards of the manifold grace of God. 1 Peter 4:10, NKJV.

The word translated "manifold" is the Greek *poikilos*, which means "many-colored, spotted, or dappled; hence worked in various colors, variegated, elaborate, inlaid."

Grace is a many-splendored thing. It is a tapestry of colors, intricate and artful, wrought by the Master Weaver. Grace is always beautiful, always surprising in its complexity, always encompassing every aspect of our existence.

One day, I visited the Blue Souk (literally, the blue market) in Sharja, one of the entities that make up the United Arab Emirates. In the West the nearest thing to the market is the shopping mall, but the comparison isn't close at all. The only resemblance is the parking area with parallel lines outside the Blue Souk, which is a stately building in Moroccan style, built of white marble and decorated, of course, in blue.

Inside on three levels you find store after store filled with treasures of the Middle East. Shawls from Kashmir. Carpets from Persia and Afghanistan. Silks and woolens. Brassware. A dazzling array, and much of it individually wrought.

A Yemeni shopkeeper rolled out an exquisite rug from Persia. "All by hand," he said. "Three years in the making." Every thread in place, every line straight, every color blending. Just like grace. The Divine Weaver designs that it will motivate, energize, and beautify everything that happens in our lives and in the church. So, says Peter, "if anyone speaks, let him speak as the oracles of God. If anyone ministers, let him do it as with the ability which God supplies" (1 Peter 4:11, NKJV).

And the result? "That in all things God may be glorified through Jesus Christ, to whom belong the glory and the dominion forever and ever. Amen."

I confess that too often my life and witness displays a blotchy, broken pattern instead of a tapestry of grace. So does the church, because it is the sum total of people like me. But the marvel of this many-splendored thing called grace is that it accepts this messed-up pattern, this brokenness. Grace waves a wand over my life and over the church, and we become beautiful and whole in the eyes of God.

O Master Weaver, work out in my life today the tapestry of Your grace.

His Hand Is on the Wheel

You will guide me with Your counsel, and afterward receive me to glory. Ps. 73:24, NKJV.

Have you seen the painting by Harry Anderson of Jesus guiding the ship? The wind is blowing, the spray flying, and the vessel rocking, but all on board are secure, confident. A calm, serene look marks Jesus' countenance as He pilots the ship through the storm. His hand is on the wheel.

With each passing year the times seem to grow ever more perilous. The problems confronting leaders of society become more complex and more intractable. But His hand is on the wheel.

At times the church plunges and tosses in the midst of angry seas. Gigantic waves threaten to engulf the good ship, Zion, sending her to a watery end. But His hand is on the wheel.

Each one of us will sail into violent seas, if we have not already. Tossed to and fro and up and down, we wonder if we can survive. But His hand is on the wheel.

"Fearful perils are before those who bear responsibilities in the cause of God," writes a devoted Christian woman, "perils the thought of which make me tremble. But the word comes, 'My hand is upon the wheel, and I will not allow men to control My work for these last days. My hand is turning the wheel, and My providence will continue to work out the divine plans, irrespective of human inventions.'. . .

"In the great closing work we shall meet with perplexities that we know not how to deal with, but let us not forget that the three great powers of heaven are working, that a divine hand is on the wheel, and that God will bring His purposes to pass" (*Evangelism*, p. 65).

Friend of mine, go calmly into this day. Just now lay every burden and every care at the feet of Jesus. Nothing is too large or too small for Him. If something is bothering you—waking you up in the wee hours of the night, hanging like an albatross around your neck—take it to Him. He wants to give you peace. He wants you to keep secure and confident, no matter how hard the wind blows, how keenly the salt spray stings your face.

His hand is on the wheel. He's waiting for you to let Him take over the wheel of your life. Just ask Him to do so right now.

Song of a Heart Set Free

For the Lord God is a sun and shield; the Lord will give grace and glory; no good thing will He withhold from those who walk uprightly. Ps. 84:11, NKJV.

salm 84 overflows with rejoicing in God's grace. Like the other psalms, it was set to music. In modern times the words have become a lovely solo in English.

"How lovely is Your tabernacle, O Lord of hosts!" cries out the psalmist. "My soul longs, yes, even faints for the courts of the Lord; my heart and my flesh cry out for the living God" (verses 1, 2, NKJV).

What a contrast with the way we often approach worship! We drag ourselves out of bed, look for a seat at the back of the church, and grumble if the preacher goes past noon.

But when the grace of Jesus floods our heart, when we know He has set us free, and we love Him with all our being, we will look forward to every opportunity for worship or prayer. Religion won't be a burden, a drag; it will spring from within.

It's time to worship God in spirit and in truth, as Jesus told us (John 4:24). It's time to quit playing games, time to stop straddling the fence with the world and let God be Lord in our lives.

"Even the sparrow has found a home, and the swallow a nest for herself, where she may lay her young—even your altars, O Lord of hosts," the psalmist goes on (verse 3, NKJV). He would like to be a bird resting in the Temple, always close to the presence of God.

"For a day in Your courts is better than a thousand. I would rather be a doorkeeper in the house of my God than dwell in the tents of wickedness" (verse 10, NKJV). Can we say that? What's our favorite place, our favorite activity? Is Jesus our favorite person, His name the most precious word to fall from our lips, His worship what we long for more than any other activity?

He still is our sun and shield, could we but know it. In His light we see light and walk in light; in His warmth spiritual life grows green and sturdy. And as our shield He guards us, lovingly protecting us because we are His own. "I am your shield," He said to Abram (Gen. 15:1, NKJV), and He says it to us, also.

Today He offers us grace and glory—grace for every situation and the glory of His presence. And no good thing will He withhold from us.

The Man Who Became an Iron Pillar

For behold, I have made you this day a fortified city and an iron pillar, and bronze walls against the whole land. Jer. 1:18, NKJV.

The story of Jeremiah highlights the enabling power of grace. It shows how God took a reluctant, shy young man and made of him an iron pillar standing for truth in an age of lies, for sanity at a time of craziness.

Jeremiah tells us more about himself than does any other prophet. With beguiling honesty and frankness he shares his doubts and his fears, his pain and his joys. He lets us in on his arguments with the Lord Himself. So his book is as much the story of a person and God as it is the story of God and a wayward nation.

God called Jeremiah to be His messenger while he was still young. Jeremiah sought to refuse the divine commission because he could not handle public speaking, but the Lord replied, "Do not say, 'I am a youth,' for you shall go to all to whom I send you, and whatever I command you, you shall speak. . . . Behold, I have put My words in your mouth" (Jer. 1:7-9, NKJV).

The times were dangerous and uncertain. Already the northern kingdom of Israel had fallen captive to Assyria. Now only little Judah was left, and the Babylonian army under King Nebuchadnezzar was threatening. During Jeremiah's ministry the Babylonians twice attacked and twice carried away captives, leaving Judah a weak, diminished kingdom. But even so, its king, Zedekiah, enamored of Egypt's power, rebelled, bringing down the wrath of Babylon in a final assault that destroyed both Temple and city.

Throughout this tumultuous period Jeremiah's messages consistently were the opposite of what the people wanted to hear. False prophets proclaimed that all would be well: Jerusalem would not fall, and the captive exiles in Babylon would soon come back. But Jeremiah said no! This city will fall. Don't fight the Babylonians, because you will lose.

He sounded like a traitor and was tried and punished as a traitor. But he was right, no matter that his message was unpopular. He was God's man with God's message for the hour; he was a true patriot. The loneliness of office and the harshness of the message he was commissioned to give weighed on Jeremiah. He wanted to quit, wished he'd never been born. But God's grace sustained him, enabled him to surmount huge obstacles. God make him an iron pillar.

Grace Is an Anointing

You are fairer than the sons of men; grace is poured upon Your lips; therefore God has blessed you forever. Ps. 45:2, NKJV.

P salm 45 has intrigued and inspired the followers of Jesus Christ for centuries. Although in its original setting it is a song of praise to the king and his bride, Christians have seen, and see, a second meaning—a hymn to the King greater than David, Israel's true Messiah.

So exalted is the description that no monarch of Israel could fulfill the ideal. In verse 6 we read, "Your throne, O God, is forever and ever" (NKJV), and in the New Testament the writer of the book of Hebrews quotes these words as part of his argument that Jesus, God's Son, is greater than any angel (Heb. 1:4-14).

Meditation on the psalm has led to gospel songs. "Gird Your sword upon Your thigh, O Mighty One, with Your glory and Your majesty. And in Your majesty ride prosperously" (Ps. 45:3, 4, NKJV) resulted in the spirited "Ride On, King Jesus." And later in the psalm, from "All Your garments are scented with myrrh and aloes and cassia, out of the ivory palaces, by which they have made You glad" (verse 8, NKJV) came the solo "Out of the Ivory Palaces."

And the psalmist cries out, "You are fairer than the sons of men; grace is poured upon Your lips" (verse 2, NKJV). Here grace is an anointing, like the fragrant oil on Aaron's head that ran down his beard and over his garments (Ps. 133:2).

When Jesus came to His hometown of Nazareth and stood up to preach in the synagogue, He selected Isaiah's prediction of the Messiah: "The Spirit of the Lord is upon Me, because He has anointed Me to preach the gospel to the poor" (Luke 4:18, NKJV; Isa. 61:1, 2, NKJV). As He spoke, "all bore witness to Him, and marveled at the gracious words which proceeded out of His mouth" (Luke 4:22, NKJV).

Anointed lips indeed! Lips that spoke words of hope, of encouragement. Lips that smiled on little children. Lips that cried out to the heavenly Father in all-night seasons of prayer. Lips that agonized in Gethsemane in the shadow of the cross. This was Jesus, Messiah, the Anointed One, full of grace and truth. This was—is—our Savior, Lord, and Friend.

Although we can never attain to the perfection of His experience, He calls us to walk in His steps. We too may know the anointing of grace—on our lips and everywhere.

Yes, today. Now. Just ask Him for it.

The Spirit of Grace and Supplication

And I will pour on the house of David and on the inhabitants of Jerusalem the Spirit of grace and supplication; then they will look on Me whom they pierced. Zech. 12:10, NKJV.

The latter chapters of the book of Zechariah prophesy a time of religious revival for the people of Israel. As they turn back to God, He will intervene to defeat their enemies and give them peace and prosperity.

So far as we are aware, this predicted time was never realized, not because God failed to keep His word but because all His promises are conditional on our response to Him. By failing to walk in His will, we frustrate the divine plan.

These chapters speak to Christians with special power because they embody several passages that apply to Jesus. We read of Israel's king riding into Jerusalem in triumph, as Jesus did on Palm Sunday before the Crucifixion (Zech. 9:9, 10; Matt. 21:1-11), of the 30 pieces of silver (Zech. 11:12), and of wounds in the hands (Zech. 13:6). And in the text for today we see another messianic reference: "They will look on Me whom they pierced" (see also Rev. 1:7).

While it is difficult to be sure of the precise interpretation of the details of these final chapters of Zechariah., the overall thrust is clear, and we gain precious insights for Christian living today. I find the expression "the Spirit of grace and supplication" especially worth contemplating.

It was originally a promise meant for Israel, but we may claim it too. It is a promise of the Holy Spirit's work in the life: He brings grace and supplication. That is, He not only assures us of God's favor—His acceptance and forgiveness, in spite of our unworthiness—but also puts within us a deep desire to commune with God in prayer.

The old spiritual asks, "Were you there when they crucified my Lord?" and the answer of the heart, touched by the Spirit of grace and supplication, is "Yes! I was there. My sins put the Son of God on Calvary's tree. I pierced His hands and His side."

We will never turn to the Lord in earnest supplication if left to ourselves. We'll spend all our time justifying ourselves to others and to ourselves. But the Spirit convicts us of our deep need, and if we will acknowledge that need, He brings grace and supplication.

The Spirit of grace and supplication. I want Him today. Do you?

The Thorn in the Flesh

And lest I should be exalted above measure by the abundance of the revelations, a thorn in the flesh was given to me, a messenger of Satan to buffet me, lest I be exalted above measure. 2 Cor. 12:7, NKJV.

My late dear friend Tom Blincoe, with whom I worked closely at the seminary, used to recount an amusing experience when he began his ministry. Assigned as an intern to a little church in Detroit, Michigan, Tom began to preach his first sermon during prayer meeting. He hadn't gotten far along when a man interrupted him. "Sit down! You don't know what you're talking about!" Startled, Tom gulped, paused, then scrambled to complete the address.

He soon learned that the same man made a point of interrupting the preacher. The bane of any pastor who tried to help the little congregation, he stated that God had appointed him to be "a thorn in the flesh of the ministers." And he intended to fulfill his calling!

Incredibly, this truculent individual held an office in the local church. So overpowering was his presence that the nominating committee, intimidated, returned him to the responsibility year after year. But Tom, young though he was, determined to face the man down. He insisted that his behavior disqualified him from holding office. The committee members were nervous, the man fumed and threatened, but Tom held his ground—and the man was not returned to office. Whereupon he transferred his membership elsewhere; another congregation now had the "blessing" of his thorn-in-the-flesh gift!

The gospel indeed gathers in all types of fish. Some people we encounter in church try our patience. Maybe God lets them be there to help us develop that character trait. Some people seem a bit strange. But I remind myself of the old saying that everyone else is a bit strange "except thee and me—and even thee's a little strange."

Paul had his thorn in the flesh, and so do we. Paul's may have been a physical infirmity, very likely bad eyesight; ours may be any of a raft of persistent, nagging difficulties. Like Paul, we wish it were not so. Like Paul, we may ask God to remove it. But like Paul, God's answer may be "No." Instead, God supplies grace to live with the problem. "My grace is sufficient for you, for My strength is made perfect in weakness," He tells us (2 Cor. 12:9, NKJV).

That's His promise to you on this new day.

Swimming on Christmas Day

He measured off another thousand, but now it was a river that I could not cross, because the water had risen and was deep enough to swim in—a river that no one could cross. Eze. 47:5, NIV.

I went swimming on Christmas Day—in the ocean.

No; I'm not one of those hardy souls who takes a plunge year-round. The water I swam in was a pleasant 75° F or so, on the coast of Dubai in the Persian Gulf. With clean, white sand and clear water, it was a delicious experience.

To readers accustomed to white Christmases, it sounds bizarre to go swimming on Christmas Day. But not to those who live in the Southern Hemisphere or the tropics. I grew up in southern Australia, where the mercury sometimes rises to 100° F or more on December 25, and air-conditioning was yet to make its mark. We always had a large, hot meal, topped off with plum pudding—and ate it with sweat pouring down our faces. Then in the afternoon we'd head for the beach and get into the water as fast as we could.

From Australia Noelene and I went to India. For several Christmases we drove with friends to Goa, and stayed by the beach. One year we arrived just after midnight and, after unpacking the cars, plunged into the sea, which felt as warm as bathwater.

Come to think about it, swimming and Christmas Day fit rather well together. Not that December 25 carries any particular significance in itself (it almost certainly wasn't the date of Jesus' birth); the importance lies in what His coming to our world signifies.

Grace. Swimming and grace go hand in hand. To lie back and let His love hold you up, to lose the deadweight of your body, to feel aches and pains seep away—this is the experience of grace.

The book of Ezekiel, which contains many puzzling things, closes with a wonderful vision. When Ezekiel wrote, the Jews were in Babylonian exile, their Temple burned, their beloved Jerusalem destroyed. But through the prophet the Lord gave a series of messages of hope: the exile would end, the people would return, a new temple would be built.

Out of the new temple would flow a pure, healing stream—small at first, then a river deep enough to swim in. That river flows out and on, even to the whole world.

The river of God's grace.

Jillian's Choice

How can I give you up, Ephraim? How can I hand you over, Israel? Hosea 11:8, NIV.

When a massive wall of water shattered Jillian Searle's idyllic vacation, she was forced to make a horrific choice no parent should ever have to face: which of her two young sons to save.

Jillian was near her hotel pool with her sons Lachie, 5, and Blake, 2, on the Thai resort island of Phuket when the tsunami of December 26, 2004, struck without warning. "I just heard a terrible roaring, a loud roaring sound, and I turned around and I just saw masses, masses of water coming for us," she later told a television reporter in Perth, Australia. "I straightaway thought, *How am I going to keep my two children alive?*"

Realizing that she could not keep the three of them afloat, she was forced to choose which of her boys to hold on to and which one to let go. "I knew I had to let go of one of them, and I just thought I'd better let go of the one that's the oldest," she said.

Amid the churning water Jillian noticed a young woman clinging to a post. She begged the woman to take care of 5-year-old Lachie. As she pried his hand from hers, he pleaded, "Don't let go of me, Mummy." The raging currents wrenched them apart. She looked back at Lachie, who had not yet learned to swim, and thought that was probably the last time she would see him alive.

Meanwhile Jillian's husband, Brad, watched the terrifying scenario play out from a hotel balcony. He tried to rush to assist, but the rising water had blocked the doors.

When the water subsided, he found Jillian and Blake, and the family began a frantic search for Lachie. "You have to find him, because I let go of him," Jillian told her husband. "I gave him to somebody else, and I let go of him. . . . And there is no possible way I can live my life knowing that I took his hand off mine."

The story had a happy ending. Two hours later the Searles found Lachie with a Thai policeman. He had survived by clinging to a hotel door.

There is Another who longs after His children with inexpressible love. His heart breaks at the thought of separation—separation that not He, but we, choose.

Don't break His heart today.

Sanctified Work

But because God was so gracious, so very generous, here I am. And I'm not about to let his grace go to waste. Haven't I worked hard trying to do more than any of the others? Even then, my work didn't amount to all that much. It was God giving me the work to do, God giving me the energy to do it. 1 Cor. 15:10, Message.

Occasionally we learn with sadness of a minister who gets caught up in a fault that leads to their having to resign. Now and then it's an evangelist who, it comes to light, had been having an affair. Along with the shock and disappointment, a troubling question arises: How could this person's work have apparently been so successful when they were leading a double life? The evangelist, or minister, may have been winning people to Christ right up to the disclosure of his clandestine activities. God apparently blessed his efforts despite his sinful living.

The fact is that every one of us, whether a member of the clergy or not, is a flawed instrument. So God makes do with what He has; He uses agents far from the ideal. He grants success even to those whose secret lives deny the power of the gospel they proclaim.

Still, God calls every follower, ordained to ministry or not, to sanctified service. He challenges us to give Him our best, our all, to live lives of ever-deepening submission to His will and reliance on His strength.

Like Paul, we must not let grace go to waste. Having been treated so generously by a loving Father, we will be eager to do and to share. Effort and hard work are the appropriate response, but only so long as all that we do is sanctified by His presence and power.

"We need to look constantly to Jesus, realizing that it is His power that does the work. While we are to labor earnestly for the salvation of the lost, we must also take time for meditation, for prayer, and for the study of the Word of God. Only the work accomplished with much prayer, and sanctified by the merit of Christ, will in the end prove to have been efficient for good" (*The Desire of Ages,* p. 362).

In Paul's day there were those who preached Christ, but out of envy and selfish ambition (Phil. 1:15, 16). Some were no better than mere peddlers of the Word of God (2 Cor. 2:17). Some looked for letters of commendation (2 Cor. 3:1).

Not much has changed. But over against all such efforts, God calls us today to work motivated by grace and sanctified by the merits of Christ.

Good King Hezekiah

Be strong and courageous. Do not be afraid or discouraged because of the king of Assyria and the vast army with him, for there is a greater power with us than with him. 2 Chron. 32:7, NIV.

The speaker is Hezekiah, one of the last of the kings of Judah, and one of the best. The faith he exhibits here is remarkable on two counts.

First, the outlook could not be bleaker. The mighty Assyrian armies, a byword in the ancient world for their cruelty, are at the door. As they have swept south from the area we today call Iraq, they have devastated every king and kingdom in their path. Now tiny Judah lies exposed and helpless. Jerusalem stands besieged; what chance do the children of Israel have of surviving the onslaught?

To make matters even worse, the Assyrian king Sennacherib sends officers with a message for Hezekiah that they read aloud to weaken the will of the people. "Hear the words of the great king, the king of Assyria!" they call out in Hebrew. "This is what the king says: Do not let Hezekiah deceive you. He cannot deliver you! Do not let Hezekiah persuade you to trust in the Lord when he says, 'The Lord will surely deliver us; this city will not be given into the hand of the king of Assyria'" (Isa. 36:13-15, NIV). And in a mocking gesture they offer, "Come now, make a bargain with my master, the king of Assyria: I will give you two thousand horses—if you can put riders on them!" (verse 8, NIV).

Second, Hezekiah didn't grow up in an environment that nurtured faith. Anything but. His father, Ahaz, was noted for his wickedness. An idolater and Baal worshipper, he even sacrificed his sons in the fire (2 Chron. 28:2, 3). He closed the doors of the Temple, instead setting up altars at every street corner in Jerusalem (verses 24, 25).

Many people today believe that we have little or no control over what we do, that all our decisions are determined by factors outside our control. Some argue for nature (our genes), others for nurture (environment), but either way we end up pawns.

Hezekiah's life debunks this philosophy. Against all odds of heredity and family influences, he became a devout servant of Yahweh and spiritual reformer of his people. "In everything that he undertook . . . he sought his God and worked wholeheartedly" (2 Chron. 31:21, NIV).

And against all odds God delivered him and his people.

Man With a Mission

But they were scheming to harm me; so I sent messengers to them with this reply: "I am carrying on a great project and cannot go down. Why should the work stop while I leave it and go down to you?" Neh. 6:2, 3, NIV.

He rides by night among the ruins. Silently he traverses the circumference of the city, past heaps of debris, broken walls, shattered gates. As he rides he thinks. The night is a good time to get the big picture, to weigh possibilities. He begins to see clearly what must be done, and his role in the work, if it is to be brought to completion.

The rider is Nehemiah, man with a mission, and one of my favorite Bible personalities. He has left a post of comfort and honor in the palace of the Persian king Artaxerxes to try to help his people, the remnant who have returned to Israel. They are in a sorry state: Jerusalem's walls are broken down, its gates burned, the people disheartened.

Nehemiah's plan: rebuild Jerusalem. It won't be easy. Their numbers are few. The surrounding inhabitants of the land oppose the project. Some of the Jews themselves have married the people of the land and are in league with them.

But Nehemiah is a person of prayer. His book is interlaced with prayer. He records the silent petitions he offered up to God as he faced key decisions. He is also a person of deep faith. "The God of heaven will give us success," he replied to those who opposed the rebuilding project (Neh. 2:20, NIV). Out of this life of prayer and faith was born a vision. Nehemiah saw clearly what needed to be done and set about to make it happen. He rallied the people to the work—priests, artisans, merchants. All pitched in (chapter 3 lists their names).

The enemies didn't like it. They mocked and ridiculed: "What they are building—if even a fox climbed up on it, he would break down their wall of stones!" (Neh. 4:3, NIV). They used their sympathizers among the Jews to sow doubts and rumors. They plotted to attack; Nehemiah posted guards at the vulnerable places.

They tried to unnerve Nehemiah. "Come, let us meet together," they said (Neh. 6:2, NIV). But Nehemiah responded, "I am carrying on a great project and cannot go down" (verse 3, NIV).

What a man! A man with a mission! Unstoppable. And still true today, for men and women of God.

Brass Shields

He took everything, including all the gold shields Solomon had made. So King Rehoboam made bronze shields to replace them and assigned these to the commanders of the guard on duty at the entrance to the royal palace. 1 Kings 14:26, 27, NIV.

King Solomon had made 200 large shields, each with about 15 pounds of hammered gold. He had also made 300 small shields, each with about 3¾ pounds of hammered gold. The total amount of gold in Solomon's shields alone weighed more than 4,000 pounds, a fortune in today's currency (1 Kings 10:16, 17).

Solomon's son Rehoboam succeeded him, and in all respects proved to be an inferior monarch. Because of his rashness he lost the full kingdom; 10 tribes split off, leaving only Judah and Benjamin. Rot set in, spiritually and politically. In the fifth year of his reign Shishak, king of Egypt, attacked Jerusalem. He carried off all the treasures of the Temple and the royal palace, including the gold shields that Solomon had made. Rehoboam made bronze shields to replace them. The change epitomized the decline of the kingdom overall. The glory had departed.

Let's take inventory of our spiritual storehouse. "Examine yourselves to see whether you are in the faith; test yourselves," says the apostle Paul (2 Cor. 13:5, NIV). Could we have somehow abandoned the glory of Jesus, full of grace and truth, for substitutes?

Because grace is totally unlike the world around us—the way that God accepts and treats is altogether different from the way people relate to others—we easily lose it. Having begun with grace (like the Galatians), we slip away to a mix of grace and works that is not grace.

In our spiritual experience we substitute the brass shields of formal observance, predictable worship and habit, for living, vital, daily communion. We polish the brass until it shines brightly, but it's still brass, not gold.

We heap up books, sermons, tapes, videos, and DVDs about God and think we have a pantry stocked with food for the soul. But we neglect the gold, which is found only in personal, prayerful study of the Word of God. The reproach of Christianity today is that so much that is said and done in the name of the lowly Teacher from Nazareth denies who He was and what He stood for. Brass shields instead of gold.

Let it not be so with me, dear Lord!

Called to the Kingdom

For if you remain completely silent at this time, relief and deliverance will arise for the Jews from another place, but you and your father's house will perish. Yet who knows whether you have come to the kingdom for such a time as this? Esther 4:14, NKJV.

In the entire book of Esther we do not find even one mention of God's name. Nonetheless, the book glows with a sense of divine providence. In spite of the intrigues of Haman and the enemies of the Jews to annihilate the people of God, "behind the dim unknown standeth God within the shadow, keeping watch above his own" (James Russell Lowell).

The story reads stranger than fiction. A series of dramatic improbabilities and surprising coincidences lead first to a sense of impending doom but ultimately to turning of the tables on "the bad guys" as God's people are delivered.

Queen Vashti defies the king's order to come into the banquet he has prepared for his drunken officials. From a moral standpoint, Vashti did right—she refused to be exploited as a sex object. It was an act of extraordinary courage, and it cost her the kingdom.

Out of the confusion caused by Vashti's deposition, a Hebrew maiden—poor, without immediate family but beautiful—is catapulted to the palace. She goes from obscurity to empire. Will she stand true to the principles she learned as a child from her cousin Mordecai?

In another twist, bitter rivalry develops between Mordecai and Haman the Agagite. The king elevates Haman to high office, but Mordecai refuses to bow or pay homage. Furious, Haman devises a scheme to destroy not just Mordecai but the entire Jewish population.

It's a moment when history holds its breath. The stage is set. Who will come forward to turn the wheel on the side of right? Mordecai trusts God; God will provide deliverance. But the immediate source Mordecai can see is his own foster daughter, placed in a position of great influence for this very time. The course is risky; Esther may lose her life by going to see the king without an invitation. "If I perish, I perish," she says (Esther 4:16), and goes to her fate.

We too have a tryst with destiny. In matters high or low, small or great, God wants to use us today to work out His purposes.

The Promise of the Sunrise

Let us acknowledge the Lord; let us press on to acknowledge him. As surely as the sun rises, he will appear; he will come to us like the winter rains, like the spring rains that water the earth. Hosea 6:3, NIV.

Did you know that every sunrise embodies a precious promise from the God of grace? "As surely as the sun rises, he will appear," the scripture assures us.

This wonderful word from the Lord comes to us from the book of Hosea, the twofold love story of the prophet and Gomer, and God and Israel. For much of the book we read God's anguished heart cries as the people He loves drift ever further away from Him and into deeper and deeper sin:

"My people are destroyed from lack of knowledge" (Hosea 4:6, NIV).

"Ephraim is joined to idols; leave him alone" (verse 17, NIV).

"Your love is like the morning mist, like the early dew that disappears" (Hosea 6:4, NIV).

"His hair is sprinkled with gray, but he does not notice" (Hosea 7:9, NIV).

"They are like a faulty bow" (verse 16, NIV).

"They sow the wind and reap the whirlwind" (Hosea 8:7, NIV).

"Ephraim feeds on the wind . . . and multiplies lies and violence" (Hosea 12:1, NIV).

"Now they sin more and more" (Hosea 13:2, NIV).

In the midst of this litany of unfaithfulness we catch a note of hope. Erring, fickle Israel decides to turn back to God: "Come, let us return to the Lord. . . . After two days he will revive us; on the third day he will restore us, that we may live in his presence" (Hosea 6:1, 2, NIV).

If only the book had closed right there! If only God's people had continued on the road to repentance and restoration! However, God can still be counted upon. If we turn to Him, then "as surely as the sun rises, he will appear." He will come to us like the refreshing rains that cause the seed to sprout and the bud to swell.

That promise is for you and me today, dear friend. Claim it; claim it right now—the promise of the sunrise.

Seasons of the Soul

*Sow to yourselves righteousness, reap the fruit of unfailing love, and break up your un-
plowed ground; for it is time to seek the Lord, until he comes and showers righteousness
on you. Hosea 10:12, NIV.*

I n our Christian life we pass through spiritual seasons.

The springtime of the soul finds us full of energy and enthusiasm, glowing in our first love, the joy of discovery of the riches of grace.

In summer our spiritual powers strengthen and mature as the Lord leads us into new and exciting ventures for His glory.

The fruit of the Spirit ripens to full sweetness in autumn, as spiritual judgment and discernment enable us to see clearly and articulate readily the values of heaven.

In winter our lives are blanketed with the pure white of Christ's righteousness, smoothing out bumps, covering dirt and ugliness. And beneath that covering life is stirring and growing, ready in God's good time to burst out in a glorious spring showing.

There are other ways to view the seasons of the soul, of course. Winter may find us cold and lifeless, the spiritual life force seemingly buried beneath a weight of neglect and lost opportunities. In autumn we may act tired and listless. Even in summer we may spend seemingly boundless energies in doing the work of the Lord for our own ego stroking instead of putting the Lord and His kingdom first in everything.

We pass through seasons of the soul, sometimes progressing as the Lord would have us from spring, to summer, through autumn, to the beauty of a winter scene. Unfortunately, we also bounce around. The path of our spiritual life is a curve, a series of highs and troughs, instead of a straight line toward the fullness of life in Jesus. We start well but fall back. Our resolutions are like ropes of sand.

This is not the Lord's doing but ours. We are weak, flawed. But He is gracious and long-suffering. He notes the tenor of our lives, not just the occasional good deed or misdeed, and this is what counts. He is nurturing us, polishing us as jewels for eternal glory.

Today let's seek Him with all our hearts.

Gomer and God

I will betroth you to me forever; I will betroth you in righteousness and justice, in love and compassion. Hosea 2:19, NIV.

No book of the Bible reveals the passionate, yearning love of God like the book of Hosea. This short work, often overlooked, is the first of the "minor prophets," so named not because their material is less important, but because they are shorter than Isaiah, Jeremiah, Ezekiel, and Daniel.

The book of Hosea divides readily into two parts. Chapters 1-3 tell the love story of the prophet; his wife, Gomer; and their children. The last 11 chapters focus on Yahweh and His bride, Israel. Beyond this bare-bones outline the book defies further analysis. For the most part it consists of a series of anguished cries expressing sorrow for the descent into sin and degradation of an adulterous wife. And the speaker is God, despairing for His wayward people.

The book begins with a command from Yahweh that the prophet surely could scarcely comprehend: "Go, take to yourself an adulterous wife and children of unfaithfulness, because the land is guilty of the vilest adultery in departing from the Lord" (Hosea 1:3, NIV). They marry, and Gomer bears Hosea a son. She later bears a daughter, and then another son, but they aren't identified as having Hosea as their father. The account is terse, leaving us to read between the lines. Then in chapter 3 we hear the Lord telling Hosea to take Gomer back. "Go, show your love to your wife again, although she is loved by another and is an adulteress" (verse 1, NIV). Apparently she left him and has become a slave. Hosea buys her back (verse 2).

Did this really happen, or is it some sort of parable? The evidence of the Word is that it's a true story, an incredible love story of hope for an unfaithful spouse. And out of the prophet's gut-wrenching experiences—the elation of genuine love, the heartbreak of a marriage gone sour, the struggle to forgive and love again—he gains insight into an even more incredible love story, God's love for Israel.

Why did God love the Jews so much? But that's to ask Why does He love you and me so passionately? Why is He willing to betroth us to Himself, because we are unfaithful and unreliable? Why does He forgive us? Why does He take us back? Only because "God is love" (1 John 4:16). That's what Hosea learned. That's what Jesus showed us.

The Shepherd Prophet

But the Lord took me from tending the flock and said to me, "Go, prophesy to my people Israel." Amos 7:15, NIV.

Among that extraordinary roll call of individuals, the Hebrew prophets of the eighth and seventh centuries B.C., none is more arresting than Amos. We know only what he tells us about himself, and that is little; but it is enough for us to sketch a portrait of an amazing person.

The opening words of his book tell us that Amos was "one of the shepherds of Tekoa" (Amos 1:1, NIV). Later he tells us that he was "a shepherd, and I also took care of sycamore-fig trees" (Amos 7:14, NIV). By the latter work he could have meant either gathering sycamore figs for his own use or cultivating them for others. Sycamore figs, inferior to true figs, need to be punctured some time before harvesting in order to render them edible.

We get the picture. Amos came from a lowly background. He eked out a living. His occupations were basic, rooted in the land.

Nor could he claim family tree or education as setting him apart in any sense. "I was neither a prophet nor a prophet's son," he said of himself (verse 14, NIV). In those days there were schools of the prophets, plus a class of professional prophets who served the interests of the monarch, rather than the Lord.

Lacking though Amos may have been in the credentials that his contemporaries sought, he had the greatest qualification of all to be a prophet, the single characteristic without which all others were useless: the Lord put His hand on him. "The Lord took me from tending the flock and said to me, 'Go, prophesy to my people Israel'" (verse 15, NIV).

So Amos leaves the flock and journeys to the northern kingdom of Israel, where he pronounces impending doom because of the sins of the king and people. Here he runs afoul of Amaziah, the priest of the shrine at Bethel. Amaziah tries to get the king, Jeroboam II, to expel Amos. "Get out, you seer!" he orders. "Go back to the land of Judah. Earn your bread there and do your prophesying there" (verse 12, NIV).

Amaziah was a paid puppet, and he evaluated Amos by himself. But he was wrong.

The Lord still puts His hand on men and women. He calls them from their daily round of activities and says, "Go, speak for Me." And the Lord provides grace for the mission.

Their Finest Hour

Arise, shine, for your light has come, and the glory of the Lord rises upon you. Isa. 60:1, NIV.

With the fate of France hanging in the balance in 1940, a massive evacuation of British and Allied troops took place from Dunkirk. Nearly 350,000 armed forces escaped to England. Outnumbered and outgunned, they fled on anything that could float.

The British celebrated as if they had won a great victory. But Prime Minister Winston Churchill brought them back to reality. On June 4 he told the House of Commons, "Wars are not won by evacuations."

Then Churchill delivered a magnificent address, what some have called the greatest speech in a thousand years. "We shall not flag or fail. We shall go on to the end. We shall fight in France, we shall fight on the seas and oceans, we shall fight with growing confidence and growing strength in the air, we shall defend our island, whatever the cost may be, we shall fight on the beaches, we shall fight on the landing grounds, we shall fight in the fields and in the streets, we shall fight in the hills; we shall never surrender."

Exactly two weeks later, on June 18, 1940, England braced for the invasion by air. Churchill stood up and addressed Parliament again. "Upon this battle depends the survival of Christian civilization. . . . The whole fury and might of the enemy must very soon be turned on us. . . . Let us therefore brace ourselves to our duties, and so bear ourselves that, if the British Empire and its Commonwealth last for a thousand years, men will say, 'This was their finest hour.'"

As followers of Jesus Christ, we have come to the climax of history. The forces of evil are marshaling for the earth's final battle. What sort of men and women will we be at such a time as this?

"The greatest want of the world is the want of men—men who will not be bought or sold, men who in their inmost souls are true and honest, men who do not fear to call sin by its right name, men whose conscience is as true to duty as the needle to the pole, men who will stand for the right though the heavens fall" (*Education*, p. 57).

Armed with the grace of God, we can indeed rise and shine. "The Lord will rise upon us and His glory appear over us" (see Isa. 60:2). This will be our finest hour.

He Tasted Death

But we see Jesus, who was made a little lower than the angels, crowned with glory and honor because he suffered death, so that by the grace of God he might taste death for everyone. Heb. 2:9, NIV.

What does the apostle mean when he says that Jesus "tasted" death?

Chrysostom, the golden-tongued, famous preacher from the early centuries of Christianity, put an interesting spin on these words. He likened Jesus to a physician who, in order to encourage his patient to swallow bitter medicine, put his lips to the glass and sipped a little. So, argued Chrysostom, Jesus experienced just enough of death's bitterness to know what it is like.

Chrysostom was a great preacher, but he badly misinterpreted this text. Jesus didn't merely sip the cup of death; He drank it to the dregs. By "tasting" the apostle is trying to tell us that He really died, really experienced death. See Him in the Garden of Gethsemane as He shrinks from the rejection, spitting, and flogging that lie just ahead, and especially the hiding from the Father's face when He hangs on Calvary. See Him agonizing in prayer, pleading for another way. Hear His plaintive cry, thrice uttered, "My Father, if it is possible, may this cup be taken from me. Yet not as I will, but as you will" (Matt. 26:39, NIV). But it wasn't possible, not if He were to win the world back to God. So He went to the cross, dying alone, dying for everyone. He tasted death—not just physical death, but the horror of separation from God, which the Bible calls "the second death" (Rev. 20:6).

The apostle tells us that Jesus tasted death "by the grace of God." I find that a strange expression—that God's favor should lead Jesus to death. Although the majority of ancient manuscripts read this way, a few of the very earliest have a startling variant. Instead of "by the grace of God," they read "without God."

The change involves just two letters of the Greek alphabet. It looks as if some scribe, probably in the second century, changed a couple letters as he copied the text. Maybe he found the thought of Jesus dying "without God" too hard to comprehend and made the change to "by the grace of God."

But Jesus *did* die feeling utterly alone, utterly forsaken. "My God, my God, why have you forsaken me?" He cried out (Matt. 27:46, NIV).

Oh, what a Savior, to go to such lengths for us!

The View From on High

The Lord is in His holy temple, the Lord's throne is in heaven; His eyes behold, His eyelids test the sons of men. Ps. 11:4, NKJV.

I wonder how life on earth must appear from God's perspective, from the throne room of the universe, where, as the poet Milton wrote,

> "Thousands at his bidding speed
> And post o'er land and ocean without rest."

How strange and twisted and distorted and broken must our actions seem.

Recently I came across an item in the news that seemed so far out I thought it had to be a joke. But it wasn't, and I can hardly share it without dissolving into mirth. It seems the legislature in the state of Oklahoma outlawed cock fighting in 2002. And so they should have; it's a barbarous activity in which roosters slash and peck each other to death, as human spectators bet on the outcome. The shutting down of the "sport" wiped out a $100 million business, according to a senator and longtime defender of the bloody game. He had a plan to revive it.

He proposed that roosters wear little boxing gloves attached to their spurs (I am not making this up) so that the birds could "punch" each other instead of slashing! What the senator planned to do with their beaks, or if he had a plan, the news item failed to mention. Would he put little covers on them, also?

But there's more. The roosters would wear lightweight chicken vests, configured with electronic sensors, which would record hits and help keep score to determine the winner. Can you imagine the scene—roosters in chicken vests and boxing gloves, going at each other? It's hilarious.

What isn't hilarious are the people in the state of Oklahoma, and every state and every country, who are struggling to make it through each day and each night. Single parents, anxious about kids. Worries about making the rent, or the next mortgage payment. People fighting sickness. Fears about crime. So many people burdened down with cares, so many looking for a way out or even a ray of hope. So much to do, so much that needs fixing.

And the legislature debates putting vests and boxing gloves on roosters. *Even so, come, Lord Jesus, and fix this mess!*

The Power of Reading

And that from childhood you have known the Holy Scriptures, which are able to make you wise for salvation through faith which is in Christ Jesus. 2 Tim. 3:15, NKJV.

One day a strange figure showed up on the campus of Bethel College, a small Presbyterian school in western Tennessee. He stood six feet tall, with unkempt red hair, and his tattered sweater was held together by safety pins. There were holes in his shoes, and his front teeth were gone. He came from the tiny hamlet of Rosser, consisting of only three homes, where he lived in a ramshackle farmhouse without indoor plumbing. He had never ridden a bicycle or been inside a movie theater or out on a date. And he had never been to school.

Robert Howard Allen, 32, was applying for college.

When administrators gave him the college placement test, they were astounded. He "blew the lid off" it. His head was filled with history and classical literature. The scope of his learning was far greater than that of any professor at Bethel. They invited him to skip most of his freshman courses.

Ten years later Robert Allen completed his formal education, graduating from prestigious Vanderbilt University in Nashville with a Ph.D. in English. He began to teach English to college students.

This man's story inspires me. It shows the power of the human spirit to rise up and succeed in the face of overwhelming odds. Overwhelming odds indeed! Allen's parents divorced when he was very young, and he was raised by elderly relatives who managed to arrange with the local school board to have him taught at home. A teacher did make occasional visits at first, but soon Allen was lost track of.

Still, by age 12 he had taught himself to read, and soon he began to read the King James Bible to his blind aunt Ida, going through it twice from cover to cover.

Soon he was reading everything he could find, from Shakespeare to Will Durant. He read through the county library, taught himself to read Greek and French. He began to write poetry. It's a story stranger than fiction—and more wonderful. And it all began with reading the Bible.

Learning From Mistakes

Though a righteous man falls seven times, he rises again, but the wicked are brought down by calamity. Prov. 24:16, NIV.

The person who has never made a mistake has never made anything. Thomas Edison, the famous inventor, was often called a genius, but he said of himself, "Genius, nothing! Sticking to it is the genius. I've failed my way to success."

If we have the right frame of mind, a mistake may turn out to be a valuable accident. Such as Christopher Columbus, who set out for Asia and discovered America.

Or innkeeper Ruth Wakefield, who was baking Butter Drop Do cookies one day in the 1930s, using a recipe that dated back hundreds of years. She cut up a Nestlé chocolate bar and put the chunks in the batter, expecting them to melt. When she pulled the tray out of the oven, instead of chocolate-flavored cookies she had butter cookies studded with chocolate chips. From that mistake came one of the all-time favorite cookies.

Yellow sticky notes, known as Post-it notes, came about from a researcher at the 3M Company who was trying to improve adhesive tape. Another 3M scientist was attempting to make synthetic rubber to be used in airplane fuel lines. One day some of the new substance spilled on her assistant's canvas shoe, and they couldn't get it off. As the tennis shoe got older, it grew dingy—except where the substance had spilled. That "mistake" eventually became Scotchgard, used today to help prevent dirt from staining fabric.

The list goes on. Alexander Fleming finding penicillin, Charles Goodyear learning how to stabilize rubber. Wilson Greatbatch figuring out an improved implantable pacemaker for the heart. All these discoveries came about through "mistakes" at one level or another.

It's similar in the Christian life. Because God wants us to grow by His grace, we haven't arrived, don't have everything figured out. We fall, and fall again.

Sometimes we beat ourselves up mentally after we fall. But God promises that even though we fall seven times (or 77), we will get up again. His grace takes us by the hand, lifts us up, and sends us on our way more mature. He wants us to learn from our mistakes.

Crooks and Christians

The master commended the dishonest manager because he had acted shrewdly. For the people of this world are more shrewd in dealing with their own kind than are the people of the light. Luke 16:8, NIV.

As I write from the United States, two aspects of the current scene amaze me. I have never seen so much political posturing alongside the Stars and Stripes and quoting the Bible; and I have never seen such blatant displays of greed.

An executive of a leading company works for three months and decides to quit. He walks away with a cool $32 million. In other companies CEOs, who presided over a period of sharp decline in share value, move on to other pastures—along with a golden parachute. And hardly a week passes without some new revelation of financial manipulation or crookedness.

I have singled out the wealthy, but greed is an equal-opportunity enticer. People in all walks of life seem obsessed with getting more money. It was ever thus, but in today's world money-grubbing has reached a new low. That's why we find Jesus, whose audiences consisted mainly of ordinary people, frequently talking about money. The fact is, how we relate to money is the clearest evidence of our relation to the kingdom of heaven. Or, to put it another way, what we do about money reveals the impact that grace has (or has not) made in our lives.

In Luke 16:1-9 we find what at first seems to be a puzzling parable. A rich man's manager has been cooking the books, and the boss finds out. He fires the manager and calls for a complete audit. The manager now resorts to a clever ruse to ensure his future: he calls in various debtors and alters their accounts—in their favor! He lets them know he's taking care of them so that they'll take care of him. But here's a surprise: the rich man praises the crooked manager. Why? Because of his shrewdness. Sounds as if the boss himself had used slippery business practices—one crook commending another!

Many of Jesus' parables begin "The kingdom of heaven is like . . ." But not this one. In the kingdom God's people aren't money-grubbers. They're generous givers, because God has given to them generously.

It's true; you can be outwardly religious but inwardly covetous. The Pharisees were like this (Luke 16:14); so we may become. Only as grace floods and controls our lives will we be delivered from greed.

Day of Grace

There remains, then, a Sabbath-rest for the people of God. Heb. 4:9, NIV.

The Sabbath is a day of grace. It is God's loving gift to us in this hectic, pressure-cooker age. In His loving wisdom He who knows what is best for us, what we need to be made whole again, set aside this 24-hour period from the Creation. Today we need this day of grace more than ever.

An interesting development in recent years has been the rediscovery of the Sabbath by many people. Jews brought up in a secular environment, whose families long ago abandoned Sabbath observance, have found that this forgotten treasure is just what they need to keep marriages and families together, and to find peace of mind. Many Christians, some individually, others as congregations, have switched to Sabbath as their day of worship.

Over the years Sunday has lost its significance. For the great majority of those who attend church on that day it is in no sense holy time. After church they customarily go to a restaurant, and then watch baseball or football.

But God's plan from the beginning was that the Sabbath—which He designated as the *seventh* day of the week, not just any day, not a seventh part of time—would be "remembered" (Ex. 20:8) as holy time. That means all 24 hours of it. That is what God specified; that is what our bodies and minds crave.

Setting aside this 24-hour period—from sunset to sunset, according to the biblical reckoning—also orders our priorities. It says nothing is more important than God—not work, pleasure, business, or travel. This time is special. It is consecrated time, time set apart by God that we, in turn, set apart *for* God.

In the book of Hebrews the author plays on the word "rest," surely a term with highly desirable connotations for modern people. He first applies "rest" to the 12 Hebrew tribes wandering in the wilderness: "rest" would be Canaan, when they would reach their home and wander no more (Heb. 3:11, 18). Then he moves on to the Christian believers to whom he is writing, and applies "rest" to the experience of salvation in Jesus—grace (Heb. 4:3). He coins a word, calling it a *sabbatismos,* a Sabbath-rest.

What a high value to put on the Sabbath! The Sabbath rest exemplifies our rest in Jesus our Savior. Day of grace indeed!

AUGUST

What's in a Name?

Therefore God exalted him to the highest place and gave him the name that is above every name, that at the name of Jesus every knee should bow, in heaven and on earth and under the earth. Phil. 2:9, 10.

When Jackie Ordelheide Smith and her husband, Bob, moved back from New Mexico for Jackie to take up a position at the *Adventist Review,* they searched high and low for affordable housing in the Washington, D.C., area. It was discouraging; everything was out of their price range, and they wondered how they could avoid a long commute from farther out, where prices were lower.

Then, seemingly providentially, they found just the house they wanted at a marked-down price. Snapping it up, they moved in. But there was just one problem—the street name: Satan Wood Drive!

For a couple years they lived with that name but never felt comfortable. They grew tired of coping with others' reactions when they heard their address—the shocked looks, the jokes, the comments.

The Smiths discovered that others on Satan Wood Drive were uncomfortable with the name also. One man disguised it by trying a French pronunciation. Another simply called it S Street. Some deliberately misspelled their address as Satinwood Drive. A priest who lived on the street sprinkled holy water around his house each year.

At last someone researched the old records and found that the street was supposed to be named Satin Wood Drive, based on an obscure poem by a whimsical poet. Some clerk way back either couldn't spell straight or made a careless copy error. (I wonder if it might have been deliberate.) But to get the street name changed would require going through all sorts of red tape, signatures from 19 of the street's 21 homeowners, and a couple thousand dollars.

The community rallied to get the signatures and raise the money. A local paper picked up the story, then the TV news, and the Baltimore *Sun* put it on page 1. No longer would Jackie, Bob, and their neighbors live on Satan Wood!

What's in a name? Plenty. Especially our name. And most of all, in one name—the name of Jesus, full of grace. His name is above every name in heaven and earth, anytime, anywhere.

Love Message in Blood

In Him we have redemption through His blood, the forgiveness of sins, according to the riches of His grace. Eph. 1:7, NKJV.

Early in 2005 a terrible train wreck occurred in Los Angeles. A man, planning a bizarre suicide, parked his sports utility vehicle on the tracks. He changed his mind at the last minute, however, abandoning the vehicle before a rushing Metrolink commuter train plowed into it, derailed, and struck another Metrolink train. Eleven people died and some 200 were hurt in the carnage that resulted.

John Phipps worked at an aerospace plant in Burbank. Normally he would not have been on that train, but he had been called to work early. He found a seat upstairs in the double-decker and went to sleep. Then he was jerked awake, feeling mist falling on his face and seeing smashed bits of the train all around. He touched the back of his head, and his hands came away covered in blood. He called for help, but no one answered. Trapped under debris, he began to sing, "Why me, Lord?" and waited for rescuers. Then he reached out and felt a chair, leaving a bloody handprint on it. The realization hit him: he was going to die. He would leave a message for his wife, Leslie, and his children. On the upended train seat he scrawled, in his own blood, "I ❤ my kids. I ❤ Leslie."

Fire captain Robert Rosario was the first to reach Phipps and discovered the message in blood. "I've seen some gruesome things on this job," he said later, "but that moved me. My only thought at that point was *I have to get this sent to his wife and kids.*"

John Phipps survived. At a news conference several days later he appeared on crutches and identified himself as the writer of the love note. "I don't know why I did it," he told the press. "I didn't think they would see it." Which to me makes his act even more wonderful—expecting to die, he left a message that simply expressed the love he felt.

Two thousand years ago Another left a message in blood—His own blood. Jesus of Nazareth hung on a wooden cross outside the gate of Jerusalem. He had left the safest place in the universe, heaven itself, to identify Himself with the victims of a terrible global train wreck, and by dying to give us redemption, forgiveness, and life.

Jesus' love message in blood reads, "I ❤ you." And then He writes in your name and mine.

Signs of the Times

You know how to interpret the appearance of the sky, but you cannot interpret the signs of the times. Matt. 16:3, NIV.

When the deadly tsunami hit Phuket in Thailand on the day after Christmas 2004, on one beach no one was killed or seriously hurt, all because of a British schoolgirl who recognized the signs and gave warning.

Two weeks before, Tilly Smith, 10, had studied about tsunamis at her school in Oxshott, just south of London. When she saw the tide suddenly rush out, she knew that the tidal wave driven by the massive earthquake off the coast of Sumatra was only minutes away. She warned her mother that they were in danger. So her family and some 100 other tourists at the Thai beach were saved.

Jesus tells us to be alert to the signs of the times. Just as in the days of the Pharisees and Sadducees, to whom He addressed the remarks in today's passage, people today still comment on the weather: Is it going to rain? What will be the temperature? Do I need to take a coat with me because of a sudden change? It's the most common topic of conversation, used to break the ice between strangers, or when acquaintances meet.

But Jesus tells us as He told the religious leaders of His day, "You show interest in the weather; you need to show as much interest in the bigger and more important signs around you." They had come to Him asking that He show them a sign from heaven. In fact, all around them were signs of the times—Jesus' miracles, His teachings, the witness of His noble life. These signs shouted out that although Jesus came from humble circumstances, He was not just one more wandering teacher; that although no pomp or show attended His ministry, it was attested by something far greater—the blessing of God. This was no ordinary man. This was indeed the Messiah!

We who love and follow Jesus today, we whose lives have been touched, saved, and blessed by His salvation, must open our eyes to the signs of the times today. Like Tilly Smith, who studied and saw the danger coming, we must tell those around us that they stand in the face of far greater danger. This world is in its death throes. Get out of the water! Flee to safety!

Which means flee to Jesus, who is full of grace and truth.

The World's
Most Amazing Hotel

*For you know the grace of our Lord Jesus Christ, that though he was rich, yet for your
sakes he became poor, so that you through his poverty might become rich. 2 Cor. 8:9, NIV.*

On the shores of the Persian Gulf rises one of the world's most
striking buildings. The Burj al-Arab, at 1,053 feet (321 meters) is the tallest hotel on the planet. More notable than its
height, however, is the design, which resembles a sail. The
Burj, opened in 1999, quickly established itself as the icon of the emirate
of Dubai and placed it among the distinctive buildings on the planet, in
the company of the Eiffel Tower, Big Ben, and the Sydney Opera House.

The Burj is set on its own island just off the coast from Jumeirah
Beach. International recognition stops at five stars, but the Burj, lacking
nothing in pretentiousness, rates itself as seven stars. Guests are picked up
at the airport in one of the fleet of 12 white Rolls-Royces. They are driven
across a bridge that shoots jets of flame to acknowledge the arrival of a
VIP. The standard room, a duplex suite, costs about US$1,000 for a night;
the most expensive suite costs a cool US$28,000 for the night.

The Burj doesn't permit gawkers and casual tourists to get on its island. Friends, however, invited Noelene and me to a brunch on the top
floor of the hotel. Inside, the Burj is even more outrageously extravagant
than the daring exterior design suggests. A large waterfall greets the eye in
the lobby, which is flanked by floor-to-ceiling aquariums so vast that the
staff has to don scuba gear to clean them. Gold leaf covers almost every
surface. The view from the top is spectacular, while the buffet, a huge variety of hot and cold dishes, salads, and sweets from various cultures, offers everything the palate might crave (at US$100 per head).

I enjoyed the experience—just once. When the appetite is satisfied,
the dozens of unsampled dishes hold no attraction. And if you have a
comfortable, familiar bed for a good rest, what do you really gain from
paying $1,000, or more, for the night?

We are followers of Jesus of Nazareth. He laid aside the riches of
heaven and identified with the poor of earth. And He bids us, "Follow Me."

No, that doesn't mean we should live like monks. But it does mean
that we should give careful thought to how we spend the means God has
entrusted to us—both $100 and $1,000 can feed a lot of hungry people.

The Angry Christ

And when He had looked around at them with anger, being grieved by the hardness of their hearts, He said to the man, "Stretch out your hand," and he stretched it out, and his hand was restored as whole as the other. Mark 3:5, NKJV.

Over the years the myth has circulated that religion is for weak people, a crutch; that Jesus takes away the sparkle from life. Strong people, teach many psychologists, can make it on their own; and red-blooded men and women certainly don't need the insipid Jesus as model.

The nineteenth-century poet Swinburne summed up this attitude in bitter words:

"Thou has conquered, O pale Galilean;
The world has grown gray from thy breath."

This caricature of Jesus contradicts the portrait of Him we find in the Gospel accounts. What sort of person would drive the sheep and oxen out of the Temple, overturn the tables of the merchants, and send the money changers packing? Certainly no weak doormat of a character!

And have you ever considered why the religious establishment wanted to get rid of Him, and eventually did so? Because He posed a threat to their position and authority. Jesus was controversial, a big political problem for them.

In the text for today we find Jesus becoming angry. Does that surprise you? Are grace and anger opposites? There is anger, and there is anger. Most times we get angry because someone has wounded our ego. We react in defense of our pride. Our anger is self-centered and self-protective.

Jesus got angry at times, but in a different way. When He saw the merchants and money changers turning the house of prayer into a place for business and profiteering, He burned with righteous zeal. And when one Sabbath He went to the synagogue where there was a man with a withered hand and realized that the religious leaders were watching Him closely to see if He would heal the man, His moral indignation rose again. Hypocrites!

Friend of mine, follower of Jesus, I hope you get angry also. When you read of children abused and exploited, I hope you burn with righteous rage. When you learn of the weak and powerless denied justice and fairness, I hope you get angry, not for yourself but for them.

Grace makes us angry.

The Amazing Story of Catherine Lawes

And the King will answer and say to them, "Assuredly, I say to you, inasmuch as you did it to one of the least of these My brethren, you did it to Me." Matt. 25:40, NKJV.

Catherine was the wife of Lewis Lawes, who was warden at the notorious Sing Sing Prison in New York State from 1920 to 1941. The prison had a reputation for destroying wardens: their average tenure before Lewis Lawes was only two years. Lawes once joked, "The easiest way to get out of Sing Sing is to go in as warden."

But Lawes lasted 21 years. He instituted many reforms. Behind this successful man was, as is often the case, a woman. His wife, Catherine, was a key figure in the changes that came to the grim prison environment. Catherine believed that all the prisoners were worthy of attention and respect. She regularly visited within the walls of the penitentiary, encouraging the prisoners, listening to them, running errands for them. She cared for them, and they in term cared deeply for her.

One night in October 1937 Catherine was killed in an auto accident. As the news spread from cell to cell, the prisoners petitioned the warden to permit them to visit her home, where her casket lay. He granted their request. A few days later the south gate of Sing Sing swung slowly open. Hundreds of men—murderers, thieves, many of them lifers—marched slowly from the prison gate to the home, nearly a mile away, and returned to their cells. There were so many that the whole event took place unguarded. But not one tried to escape.

In the famous parable of the sheep and the goats, from which today's text is taken, Jesus spoke about visiting the prisoners. He also talked about feeding the hungry, clothing the naked, comforting the sick. By this vivid parable He was telling us about the life that counts for time and eternity, what the poet called "that best portion of a good man's life, his little, nameless, unremembered acts of kindness and of love."

"If the heart were indeed transformed by divine grace, an external change would be seen in true kindness, sympathy, and courteousness. Jesus was never cold and unapproachable," wrote Ellen White (*Testimonies for the Church,* vol. 4, p. 488).

Kindness is a language that even those who cannot hear or speak can understand. It's a fruit of grace.

An Atheist's Prayer

In the same way, the Spirit helps us in our weakness. We do not know what we ought to pray for, but the Spirit himself intercedes for us with groans that words cannot express. Rom. 8:26, NIV.

Victoria and Orestes met at a party in Havana, Cuba. Children of loyal Communist Party workers, she was 16, he 18. Two years later they married. Almost immediately Orestes was sent to the Soviet Union for two years of military training. Victoria stayed in Cuba and studied to become a dentist.

In the 1980s they went to Russia as a family (they now had two children), where Orestes was to get advanced flight training. Because Vicky's Cuban dentistry license wasn't accepted in Russia, she found work in a bottling plant. One day a machine ripped her hand open, and at the hospital she suffered a severe adverse reaction to a vaccine. As she lay at the point of death, her husband asked her a question he had never brought up before.

"Do you believe in God, Vicky?"

"Yes," she replied.

"You never told me!" That night Orestes went home and prayed for the first time in his life. "God, I don't believe in You, but Vicky has so much faith. Why don't You help her so she won't die?"

A strange prayer indeed! But God understands; He reads the heart. The Holy Spirit makes up for our deficiencies, interceding for us "with groans that words cannot express" (Rom. 8:26, NIV).

The Lord granted the plea of an atheist crying out for help. Vicky recovered. Nothing was the same for Orestes and Vicky after that. As political openness swept across the Soviet Union, Orestes began visiting the libraries and devouring newspapers. He learned a new version of history, found out that much of what he had been taught in school was lies.

The next few years would bring suspense, grave danger, and the pangs of separation in an adventure that is too wonderful to be cut short in the telling. Tomorrow we shall take up the rest of the story.

Rescue From the Sky

And if I go and prepare a place for you, I will come back and take you to be with me that you also may be where I am. John 14:3, NIV.

Orestes Lorenzo had found God. A hardened atheist, he had cried out in desperation for God, if God existed, to save his beloved wife, Victoria, who was at the point of death. God heard and answered—Vicky recovered. And their lives changed forever.

A few years later Orestes, a major in the Cuban Air Force, conceived a dangerous plan. One day he took off in his Russian-built MiG-23 from the naval base at Santa Clara. Wave-hopping as low as 12 feet above the water to elude American radar, he startled the Naval Air Station in Key West, Florida, by arriving unannounced. Seeing no way to smuggle his wife and two children aboard, he left them behind. He also realized that he might not survive the perilous mission, but if he made it to the Untied States, he would find a way to retrieve them.

Various dignitaries came to his aid. President George Bush, Mikhail Gorbachev, Coretta Scott King, senators, congressmen—all wrote on his behalf. But the Cuban authorities refused to release the family of one whom they considered a traitor. As the months passed, Orestes grew desperate. He decided to take matters into his own hands.

Through messages conveyed by trusted friends, Orestes instructed Vicky to be ready on an appointed day. Wear an orange blouse to stand out in the dying light, he said. At 5:00 p.m. that evening Orestes took off from Key West in an ancient borrowed six-passenger Cessna. Hovering low above the Straits of Florida, after 43 minutes he saw the bridge at Matanzas. Then he saw a flash of orange on the side of the road, just where it was supposed to be. He pulled the plane down on the highway, right in front of an astonished truck driver. Vicky and the children ran to the plane, and in moments the Cessna's wheels were spinning.

But now Orestes was running out of highway. "It was humanly impossible to take off," he said later. The asphalt ran out, and at that moment the plane lifted. Orestes credits the God whom he did not believe in at all five years before.

Two thousand years ago a heavenly Pilot embarked on a dangerous rescue mission. In spite of fierce struggle, He succeeded. And that victory guarantees that one day soon He will drop down again from the sky, pluck us up from this earth, and take us to our eternal home.

Hurting Together, Rejoicing Together

If one part hurts, every other part is involved in the hurt, and in the healing. If one part flourishes, every other part enters into the exuberance. 1 Cor. 12:26, Message.

The apostle Paul uses many metaphors to describe God's people, the church. One that speaks to us tenderly is the family; the church is the family of grace. But Paul seems to have been intrigued by the image of the church as the body of Christ. In his first letter to the Corinthians he develops the idea at length, devoting most of a long chapter to it (1 Cor. 12:12-30). He returns to the idea in his letters to the Romans (Rom. 12:4, 5), Ephesians (Eph. 1:22; 4:15, 16), and Colossians (Col. 1:18-24).

"The way God designed our bodies is a model for understanding our lives together as a church," he wrote to the believers in Corinth, "every part dependent on every other part, the parts we mention and the parts we don't, the parts we see and the parts we don't" (1 Cor. 12:24-26, Message).

No hierarchy here. No division into "priesthood" and laity. No exalting of paid workers over unpaid ones. We depend on each other, support each other, enter into each other's pain and joy.

From the South Pole comes a remarkable story of interdependence. Here in the most extreme place on the planet, the healer had to depend on her patients. Dr. Jerri Nielsen spied an ad in a medical journal seeking doctors to work at a research base in Antarctica. Newly divorced, Dr. Nielsen, an emergency room physician, was ready for a change. On November 21, 1998, she arrived at the Amundsen-Scott South Pole Station as the summer was beginning. Before the onset of winter most of the "Polies" departed, leaving Nielsen with 40 scientists, construction workers, and support staff. The last flight out left February 15. With temperatures dropping to −100°F, jet fuel turned to Jell-O. No passenger flights possible until November. And in early March Dr. Nielsen discovered a lump in her right breast.

As the doctor battled for survival, the drama taking place at the South Pole gripped the world. Her patients now gave her a chance to live. One repeatedly inserted a needle into the mass in an attempt to withdraw fluid. A welder helped perform a biopsy. Others administered the chemotherapy provided in a relief drop. She survived.

When we support each other, great things happen.

The Reversal of Grace

But many who are first will be last, and many who are last will be first. Matt. 19:30, NIV.

Grace turns the world upside down. By His life and His teachings Jesus showed us that. He was the king of heaven, but He became a servant. He ruled the universe, but He became a poor man without a place to lay His head. He died the worst of deaths, executed as a felon, but by dying He won back the world.

The first became the last, and the last became the first.

Jesus used this expression many times. Often it came at the beginning of a parable, or at its close. Sometimes He introduced the parable with "The kingdom of heaven is like . . ."

His parables, so simple in wording and apparently simple in ideas, have enormous depth. Their easy accessibility masks the profound ideas they convey. Compare them with Aesop's fables, and you immediately see the difference. Or better yet, try writing a parable of your own. Jesus' parables are about grace, and grace is radical. Grace is literally out of this world—it comes from another world, a better one. The parables aren't about the world we know; they're about the kingdom of heaven. And in that kingdom the first are last and the last are first.

Grace reverses expectations. Grace reverses the scheme of rewards. Grace reverses priorities. Grace reverses everything.

Christianity has been around a long time. For most people it's a conservative, ritual-bound, predictable system. Long, long ago the radical nature of Jesus' life and message leaked away in religious formalism.

It can leak away in our lives also. What most concerns me about my own walk with Jesus is that it will stagnate into predictable patterns. Oh yes, I may still take the time for daily devotions, but they become routine, and prayer becomes rote.

I want my life as a Christian to glow with the reversal of grace—the reversal of routine, the reversal of predictable patterns, the reversal of taking God's gift for granted.

But here's the marvel: God can make it happen. Grace itself can keep us in grace.

When the apostles went out preaching everywhere, their opponents called them "these who have turned the world upside down" (Acts 17:6, NKJV). So they had, because they had a message, one that still does just that.

A Puzzling Parable

So when those came who were hired first, they expected to receive more. But each one of them also received a denarius. Matt. 20:10, NIV.

J esus' parable of the workers in the vineyard is strange almost any way you look at it. The behavior of the landowner runs counter to our experience. More important, on the surface the parable offends our sense of fairness.

Remember the story? This man goes out early in the morning and hires men for the day. They agree on the going rate for day laborers—a denarius (maybe about $50 in today's marketplace). A couple hours later the landowner finds other men standing around. "You want to work?" he asks. When they say yes, he sends them to the vineyard also. There's no bargaining about compensation; the man simply says, "I will pay you whatever is right" (Matt. 20:4, NIV), and they go off to work. He does the same for more men at 12:00 and others at 3:00 p.m.

Late in the day, the "eleventh hour," or 5:00 p.m., the landowner sees some men standing around on the street corner. He hires them also, even though it's only one hour to sundown.

So far, no surprises. But now comes the twist in the story, when the workers lay down tools at the end of the day and line up to receive their pay. First strange thing: those hired last get paid first. Just the opposite of what they (and we) expect. Second, something very strange indeed: the men hired on at 5:00 p.m. receive a denarius, a full day's wages! Third, another shocker: those who worked the full day receive a denarius. That is what they hired on for, but after the one-hour fellows got a denarius each, they feel it's unfair. "You have made them equal to us who have borne the burden of the work and the heat of the day," they grumble (verse 12, NIV).

You won't find a boss today like the landowner. He'd probably run afoul of labor regulations if he acted like that. But remember how the parable starts: "For the kingdom of heaven is like . . ." (verse 1, NIV). And how it ends: "So the last will be first, and the first last" (verse 16, NIV).

Grace reverses everything. When the love of Jesus wins our hearts, we no longer work for rewards. We simply trust Him to do "whatever is right"—and He does. In His kingdom we all receive the same incredible "denarius"—eternal life, no longer jealous of one another, no longer comparing and complaining.

What a parable! A shaft of light on grace.

The Bishop and the Bag Lady

God, be merciful to me a sinner. Luke 18:13, NKJV.

re you familiar with Jesus' parable of the bishop and the bag lady? Of course you are! You know it better as the Pharisee and the tax collector ("publican" in the King James Version). In our telling of the parable of the Pharisee and the tax collector we usually fail to grasp the strong contrast Jesus made between the two individuals in the story. We note that one man is a religious person, while the other makes no profession of religion, and leave it at that. But Jesus was saying much more by His choice of the two characters.

In Jesus' day the Pharisees considered themselves the most pious, most scrupulous, of the nation. They weren't involved in the high priesthood. Another group, the Sadducees, controlled that and had made it as much a political power base. The Sadducees didn't believe in angels or in the resurrection of the dead, and accepted only the first five books of the Bible, the Torah, as inspired. In sharp contrast, the Pharisees strictly obeyed the law, both written and in the form of oral traditions.

For the people of Jesus' day, if anyone would be saved it would be the Pharisee first of all. So Jesus selected His first character from the top rung of the religious ladder. And the last would be the tax collector. He was hated and despised as a collaborator with the Romans, a traitor. The Romans didn't collect the taxes directly; they farmed out the work to Jewish agents. These agents often were unscrupulous; they'd collect all they could squeeze out of the people.

Catch the radical nature of this parable now? The two characters represent the people who appeared to be the ones with the best chance of gaining eternal life, and those with the least chance.

But at the end of the day the tables had been turned. The least likely candidate went home "justified," which means counted righteous in God's eyes. And the other went home just the same as he had arrived at the Temple, which was a sinner in need of salvation.

What made the difference? One, only one, saw his true condition. One, only one, cast himself upon God's mercy. And he alone found salvation.

Grace flows full and free to the soul that feels its need and cries out to God.

Grace for Lefties

His disciples asked him, "Rabbi, who sinned, this man or his parents, that he was born blind?" John 9:2, NIV.

Thirty-one years ago today August 13 was declared International Lefthanders' Day. The date was selected because it was not yet a holiday, and in 1976 it happened to occur on Friday the thirteenth.

Left-handed people make up 10 percent of the population. They find themselves forever battling the cultural biases of the right-handed majority. From way back the notion has prevailed that left equals bad. The French word *gauche* means left, and also awkward, clumsy, or lacking in grace. In the Bible, the right-hand side is the place of honor (Ps. 110:1-5).

Lefties have to cope with a host of inconveniences, from computer keyboards (even though Bill Gates is left-handed!) to can openers to chain saws to toilet paper dispensers to classroom desks. They can't even tackle a crossword puzzle without continually lifting their writing hand.

No wonder someone got the bright idea for a special day to campaign for lefties' rights. But the plan fizzled—the organization that started the movement is now defunct. Lefties are left with the consoling thought that because the right side of the brain controls the left side of the body, lefties are the only people in their right minds.

But they can boast of many famous people in their ranks: Henry Ford, Albert Einstein, Gandhi, Winston Churchill, Queen Elizabeth II, and seven U.S. presidents, including Ronald Reagan, George H. W. Bush, and Bill Cliinton.

The Gospels don't mention any left-handed people among Jesus' followers, but of course they were there. The Savior made it abundantly clear that the accidents of our makeup, over which we have no control (our height, coloring, gender, race), mean nothing to Him. When the disciples asked Him about the man who had been born blind, He replied, "Neither this man nor his parents has sinned, but this happened so that the work of God might be displayed in his life" (see John 9:3, NIV).

As they always have, people today single out minorities because they are different. But grace changes everything. Whether we're short or tall, Black or White, left-handed or right-handed, it's all so that the work of God may be displayed in our lives.

The First Christians

So for a whole year Barnabas and Saul met with the church and taught great numbers of people. The disciples were called Christians first at Antioch. Acts 11:26, NIV.

The Christian church began in Jerusalem, but the first Christians by name came along only several years later and many hundreds of miles removed. And probably the designation "Christian" originated as a taunt by unbelievers.

During Jesus' lifetime those who accepted Him were simply called followers, which is what "disciple" means. Jesus avoided applying "Christ" (Greek for the Hebrew "Messiah") to Himself, probably because popular expectation associated it with a political leader who would set the nation free of Roman bondage.

After Jesus' resurrection those who participated in the burgeoning movement seem to have been most commonly called followers of "the Way" (Acts 9:2, NIV; see also Acts 19:9, 23; 22:4; 24:14, 22). Presumably this term derived from the words of Jesus, who said: "I am the way" (John 14:6). They were also known as the Nazarene sect (Acts 24:5, NIV).

The designation "Christian" comes by joining the Greek *Christos* ("Christ") with a Latin ending. Almost certainly the followers of Jesus did not coin the word "Christian"; rather, it was probably a term of ridicule heaped on them by the Gentiles. The Jews would not have employed it, because it literally means "followers of the Messiah," and they rejected Jesus as Messiah.

There in the pagan city of Antioch the new religion took strong root. Apparently the name of Jesus as the Christ was constantly on the lips of believers, and their unbelieving neighbors coined a word to mock them. "The name was given them because Christ was the main theme of their preaching, their teaching, and their conversation," notes Ellen White. "Well might the heathen call them Christians, since they preached Christ and addressed their prayers to God through Him" (*The Acts of the Apostles,* p. 157).

And then she adds this insight: "It was God who gave to them the name of Christian. This is a royal name, given to all who join themselves to Christ" (*ibid.*). So what the pagans considered a taunt had in reality a divine dignity and purpose.

So much has happened since Antioch. So many wars by "Christians". So much bloodshed. So sad the degrading of that royal name. Then, and now. Am *I* a Christian?

Continuing in Grace

When the congregation was dismissed, many of the Jews and devout converts to Judaism followed Paul and Barnabas, who talked with them and urged them to continue in the grace of God. Acts 13:43, NIV.

Yes, we can be *in* grace, but we can also fall *out* of grace. The idea that once you accept Jesus as Savior you can never be lost runs contrary to the teachings of Scripture. "You who are trying to be justified by law have been alienated from Christ; you have fallen away from grace," writes Paul to the Galatians (Gal. 5:4).

It is one thing to begin a race, altogether another to complete it. "You were running a good race. Who cut in on you and kept you from obeying the truth?" (verse 7). Many set out on the road to heaven, but far fewer make it to the pearly gates: "But small is the gate and narrow the road that leads to life, and only a few find it," said the Lord Himself (Matt. 7:14).

Many years ago a vision of the Christian life came to a young woman, Ellen Harmon. In it she saw a trail leading upward, becoming steeper and narrower as it progressed. A large company started out, but many, burdened down by possessions or cares, fell along the way. Some became discouraged and gave up. But others kept their eyes fixed on Jesus and made it through to the heavenly home. (See *Early Writings*, pp. 14, 15.)

Probably everyone who reads this page can think of someone who started but quit. Maybe a sibling, maybe a spouse, maybe a child, maybe a friend. Quitters and finishers—what makes the difference? Continuing in grace, as Paul and Barnabas told the new believers in the Pisidian city of Antioch (in modern Turkey).

Grace, God's unmerited gift of love and salvation, brings us into close relationship with Him. We hear, the Spirit speaks to our heart, we say yes, and we become a child of God, a child of grace. Now, for the rest of our days, we must continue in that relationship.

Anytime we begin to take a relationship for granted, it begins to die. Anytime we begin to take grace for granted, we begin to lose it. Continuing can sound dull, even boring. But continuing lies at the heart of the best and the most beautiful experiences in life: continuing in a love relationship with someone more precious than life itself continuing in a noble endeavor, continuing in integrity "as true to duty as the needle to the pole" (*Education*, p. 57).

Today, Lord, keep me continuing in grace.

The Message of Grace

Paul and Barnabas spent considerable time there, speaking boldly for the Lord, who confirmed the message of his grace by enabling them to do miraculous signs and wonders. Acts 14:3, NIV.

Here in a nutshell we find the secret of the power of the apostles' preaching: they preached God's unmerited favor, and the Lord confirmed that message with demonstrations of His presence.

As a minister of the gospel for more than 40 years, I know from my own experience how easy and tempting it is to put the emphasis elsewhere. Books of sermons and even many classes in homiletics can start you on the wrong track. You get the idea that a sermon is an art form of which you, the preacher, are the primary architect. You select a passage of Scripture and carefully study and analyze it. You break it down into three or four parts, you explain each part in relation to an overall theme, and then you look for illustrations that will drive home the points to hearers today.

All this is well and good—up to a point. It is certainly preferable to the course more and more preachers seem to be following, that is, to base their remarks around a story, or series of stories, with a text thrown in here and there. The object too often seems to be to interest, even entertain, and when that is the case, the human channel, not the Lord, receives the praise.

Quite a few years ago (I can't pinpoint the time) I began to change my speaking and writing. No single event or reading led to the change, which was gradual. Perhaps it was immersion in the reading of the Bible that resulted in a shift. I think all along I had incorporated grace as an element in my work; the change was to make grace the focus. Slowly, slowly, I came to the point of seeking to ensure that every presentation was a message *of* grace, not just incorporating grace but embodying grace.

I have been wonderfully blessed ever since, blessed in new and abundant ways. I have preached the message of grace (not the same sermon, but always the same message) across the face of the globe. I have preached it to audiences small and very large, to sophisticated groups and to unsophisticated ones. And *always* the Lord has confirmed it by His presence.

One big change is that the message now isn't about me—it's about Him. That makes all the difference.

Committed to Grace

From Attalia they sailed back to Antioch, where they had been committed to the grace of God for the work they had now completed. Acts 14:26, NIV.

The New King James Version translates the passage thus: "They had been commended to the grace of God." With its freer approach *The Message* reads, "Finally, they made it to Attalia and caught a ship back to Antioch, where it had all started—launched by God's grace and now safely home by God's grace. A good piece of work."

Paul and Barnabas came home. They'd been away for two or three years, pioneering the gospel in Cyprus and Asia Minor (modern-day Turkey). In some places they had been well received, but elsewhere they encountered opposition sometimes so fierce that they had to flee for their lives. In one city, Iconium, Paul had been stoned, dragged outside the gates, and left for dead. Small wonder that their young companion, John Mark, soon quit and went back home.

Now Paul and Barnabas were home again. Not as quitters, but with the satisfaction of a job well done. They had preached Jesus without fear or hesitation, and had raised up companies of believers in the major centers. To help keep the young churches intact, they ordained elders.

Back at Antioch in Syria, "they gathered the church together and reported all that God had done through them and how he had opened the door of faith to the Gentiles" (Acts 14:27, NIV). What stories they had to tell! What marvels of providence and deliverance! What testimony to the power of the living Christ! The believers in Antioch must have been thrilled at the report, bursting into song and praise to God.

Antioch was where it all began—the missionary thrust of Christianity that would spread west through Paul's labors; east, south, and north through the work of others; and that still goes forward in our days, reaching to earth's remotest bounds. The believers in Antioch had recognized the call of the Holy Spirit to set aside Paul and Barnabas for this great endeavor. In obedience to the divine mandate, they fasted and prayed, then ordained them and sent them out.

Paul and Barnabas went out not just committed to a mission, but committed to grace. The church had given them over to the grace of God for guidance, protection, and coping power in their labors. And this grace did not fail them. As we go out into our new day, we too have the inestimable privilege of being committed to the same grace. Let's launch the day by grace and come safely home by grace.

The Grace of Sleep

In vain you rise early and stay up late, toiling for food to eat—for he grants sleep to those he loves. Ps. 127:2, NIV.

Imagine what it would be like never to have a dream, never to be able to fall asleep, always to lie in bed exhausted but with eyes wide open. That would be a nightmare indeed.

A real but very rare disease called fatal insomnia has recently come to light. We might never have heard of it without the medical detective work of an Italian family who, we now know, was stalked for centuries by a terrifying fate.

Ignazio Roiter is a country doctor. His wife, Elisabetta, comes from a prominent Italian family with roots in Venice since the 1600s. Roiter's medical training hadn't prepared him for the puzzling symptoms that Elisabetta's aunt, a woman in her 40s, began to show. She appeared to be sleeping all the time but claimed she had insomnia. Sleeping pills didn't help. In a few months she couldn't walk, then had difficulty in speaking. One year after the onset of this mysterious sleepless condition the aunt was dead.

Then another aunt suddenly became sleepless. The symptoms were exactly the same. She also died a year after the onset of the mysterious ailment. Desperate to find a diagnosis and a cure, Dr. Roiter turned to the dusty records of births and deaths in the local church. As he traced Elisabetta's family tree, a pattern began to emerge. His search led him further afield to San Servolo, an island off Venice and site of Europe's first mental asylum. The yellowed records showed it: Elisabetta's relatives had been dying of sleeplessness for centuries.

Then Uncle Silvano arrived for a visit. He seemed depressed, anxious, a different person. The sleep disease had struck him also. Determined to help find a cure, Silvano consented to clinical studies by sleep experts. But he too succumbed, dying exhausted at only 52. Silvano's brain was removed and examined, and it was found to be full of small holes caused by a rogue protein disorder. Now scientists are working on a cure for this hideous hereditary disease.

Sleep! It's a gift, a grace built into our system by a wise and loving Father. We take it for granted until we lose it. What's worse than feeling desperately tired but not being able to drop off to sleep?

The best things in life are free—including sleep.

A Tale of Two Runners

Do you not know that those who run in a race all run, but one receives the prize? Run in such a way that you may obtain it. 1 Cor. 9:24, NKJV.

Several times Paul referred to the Christian life as a race. So, fellow believer, you and I are runners in the race of life. But the big question is *Why* do we run? And with it another searching query: *How* do we run?

The 1924 Olympic Games, held in Paris, France, featured two amazing runners, both from England. They were driven men; their story, stranger than any novel, provided the framework of the classic movie *Chariots of Fire*.

One runner, Harold Abrahams, had a chip on his shoulder. Although his father, a financier, was a very wealthy man, and although Abrahams had been admitted to Cambridge University, a school for the elite, he still felt that he had much to prove, both to the world and to himself. Abrahams was Jewish and painfully sensitive to every slight, real or imagined—to any hint or suggestion that indicated that he was not fully an Englishman. Instead of bowing to social pressures or merely enduring slights, Abrahams would take the battle to the critics. He would become England's finest runner and win an Olympic gold.

To the north, in the Scottish Highlands, a runner of a vastly different stripe also prepared himself to be the fastest runner in the world. Eric Liddell, born of missionary parents in China, had come back to his parents' native land. A devout Christian, he committed himself to returning to the mission in China—but only after he had witnessed to his faith on the track.

Both men were selected for Britain's Olympic team and sailed for France with high hopes. Abrahams' years of punishing training paid off: he won the 100-meter sprint, married a beautiful actress, and lived out a long life, respected and admired.

But for Eric Liddell the Olympic dream turned into a nightmare. He learned that the qualifying heats for the 100 meters would be run on a Sunday. For him that would mean desecrating the day he regarded as the Sabbath. He came under enormous pressure to run, but he stood fast. His hope for an Olympic gold was gone. But then a door of hope opened— not for the 100 meters, but in the 400 meters. Liddell hadn't prepared for this distance, but he entered the race and won, to universal acclamation.

Friend, *why* do you run? And *how?* Make sure it's *because of* grace and *by* grace. •

Shaped by the Word, or Shaped by the World

And do not be conformed to this world, but be transformed by the renewing of your mind, that you may prove what is that good and acceptable and perfect will of God. Rom. 12:2, NKJV.

U nless we are shaped by the Word we will be shaped by the world. The prevailing culture will gradually squeeze us into its mold. Imperceptibly, its attitudes and values will become ours. Our only safeguard is to let the Word transform daily into the pattern God desires for us. The Bible is His gift to us, a gift of grace, to light our pathway. If, under the influence of the Holy Spirit who first called forth the Word, we permit it to leaven our whole being, it will make us "complete, thoroughly equipped for every good work" (2 Tim: 3:17, NKJV).

The sad part is that although many Christians today have access to the Bible in various translations, they are letting the Word die out in their experience. America, for instance, is a land of Bibles, but Americans have become biblical illiterates. A survey of 1,156 high school students showed that only one in every 39 students could name three books written by Paul. Only one in 38 could name three Old Testament prophets.

For Americans generally, 84 percent say they believe that the Ten Commandments are still valid, but more than half of them can't identify even five of the commandments! The Barna Research Group polled people who called themselves Christians. They found that 22 percent thought there actually was a book of Thomas in the Bible, while 13 percent didn't know whether Thomas was a book of the Bible or not. And 42 percent thought that the expression "God helps those who help themselves" came from the Bible.

Why this appalling ignorance? Because the Bible isn't being read. Almost all Americans own at least one Bible, and most own more than one; but the Bibles gather dust on the shelves. On average, Jews spend 325 hours in Bible study each year and Roman Catholics about 200 hours, but Protestants only 25 hours. The Bible cannot help us if we neglect it.

We have to choose, individually, to be shaped by the Word. That means that we need to make Bible reading a priority in our lives, setting aside quality time each day for quiet, prayerful listening as God speaks to us. We don't have to choose to be shaped by the world. Neglect the Word, and the world takes over.

Justified by Grace

For all have sinned and fall short of the glory of God, being justified freely by His grace through the redemption that is in Christ Jesus. Rom. 3:23, 24, NKJV.

This wonderful passage presents in cameo the story of our salvation. It summarizes the human dilemma, then God's marvelous initiative to rescue us, and finally the means by which deliverance was made possible.

All have sinned; all fall short of the glory of God. We have messed up, blown it. We are in big, big trouble. That's where the story starts, where it must always start, because this is the truth about us. Before the good news about God comes the bad news about us.

That little word "sin"—how powerful it is! So filled with failure, guilt, shame, and despair. The Bible employs a variety of words to express the one basic idea of our desperate need of help from outside us. Sin is a missing of the mark, as when one shoots an arrow at a target. Sin is a "falling short." Sin is an act of disobedience. Sin is a perversion, a twisting of the straight and the good. Sin is a rebellion. And sin is also an omission, a failure to do the right.

God made humanity perfect, in His own image. But we chose to go our own way and spoiled everything. Now we are lost, without hope. We fall far short of God's glory. And anyone who thinks otherwise simply doesn't grasp the holiness of the One who made us.

Now comes good news. God "justifies" us freely. The image here comes from a scene familiar (perhaps painfully so) to every one of us. It's a court of law, and we are on trial. The verdict comes down: "We find the accused guilty as charged!" Guilty of messing up, blowing it, falling short of God's glory. But now the Judge speaks up. "Let John Doe go free! His slate is wiped clean, the record expunged. In My eyes he has never sinned!"

This is grace. Incredible gift. Set free!

How can God *do* this? Isn't He a God of justice, after all?

Yes, indeed. He justifies us freely "through the redemption that is in Christ Jesus." He so loved the world that He gave His only Son, that whoever believes in Him should not die but have eternal life.

Jesus took our place. He who never sinned stands up for us. He takes upon Himself our sin and woe—all our brokenness and lostness—and gives to us His perfect life.

What an exchange! This is grace, grace incredible and free. Praise His name!

Persona Non Grata

Therefore, since we have been justified through faith, we have peace with God through our Lord Jesus Christ, through whom we have gained access by faith into this grace in which we now stand. Rom. 5:1, 2, NIV.

T he phrase persona non grata literally means "a person without grace." It indicates that someone is not acceptable or welcome. And I know it keenly from an embarrassing experience several years ago.

The church publishing house in São Paulo, Brazil, was celebrating its centenary. Along with others, I was invited to attend the festivities and given a speaking assignment to preach at the 11:00 service at Brazil Adventist University, also located in São Paulo. Thursday evening of the week of celebration found me with others from the world church headquarters on our way to Reagan National Airport in Washington, D.C., to board the flight to Brazil. But that's as far as I got.

As we were checking in for the flight I wondered why the clerk was taking so long with my papers. He kept thumbing through my passport, going back and forth. Then he said, "Mr. Johnsson, I don't find a current visa for Brazil in your passport."

My heart sank. A visa? In all my preparations for the trip that was one element I had forgotten about. "Well, can't I get a visa after I arrive in São Paulo?" I asked.

"No. The government does not permit that. If we allow you on our airplane, you will be refused access. You will be sent back to the United States, and we will be fined $10,000."

My mind raced. "Then maybe I can get on a flight to Buenos Aires, get a visa there, and fly back to Brazil. Please see if that is possible."

His fingers flew across the keyboard. "I am sorry, but all flights are full. Your only hope is to go to the Brazilian embassy in Washington tomorrow, get a visa, and travel tomorrow night—if you can get on a flight."

Doing that, I realized, would have me arriving too late for much of the celebration and too late to meet my speaking appointment. Disappointed and feeling foolish, I bade my colleagues goodbye, hailed a taxi, went back home, and sent an e-mail, apologizing for my failure.

Thank God, I have a stamp in my heavenly passport! Through Jesus Christ I have access—access into grace. I can get in! I am welcome!

Enriched by Grace

I always thank God for you because of his grace given you in Christ Jesus. For in him you have been enriched in every way—in all your speaking and in all your knowledge. 1 Cor. 1:4, 5, NIV.

Grace is more than God's unmerited favor extended to us, bringing us from lostness and death to salvation and life. When we accept the divine gift, we pass into the realm of grace. We enter a *state* of grace, and *stand* in grace. (See Rom. 5:2; 1 Peter 5:12.)

As we live in grace the Lord, who delights to give, pours upon us spiritual blessings. We are enriched in Him in all our speaking and in all our knowledge. He imparts to us abilities for His service. "We have different gifts, according to the grace given us" (Rom. 12:6, NIV).

O, how wonderful is the church! Although it appears enfeebled and defective, "it is the theater of His grace, in which He delights to reveal His power to transform hearts" (*The Acts of the Apostles,* p. 12). In this fellowship of those called out of the world by God, you don't find many famous or brilliant people as the world calls brilliant. For God chooses "the foolish things of the world to shame the wise," "the weak things of the world to shame the strong," "the lowly things of this world and the despised things . . . to nullify the things that are, so that no one may boast before him" (1 Cor. 1:27-29, NIV).

I know a man of whom it can truly be said that he has been enriched in every way, "in all speaking and in all knowledge." His doctoral degree was conferred by a world-famous university. He speaks to audiences numbering in the thousands in many lands and serves in a position of heavy responsibility. Yet when as a teenager he felt God's tug at his heart and responded to the call to ministry, many who knew him doubted. The young man stammered; how could he ever function effectively?

But God's Spirit can overcome natural deficiencies. Moses also had a problem in speaking (Ex. 4:10), but he became the greatest leader in the Old Testament.

I understand well the feelings of Moses and the young man I referred to above. As a teenager I was very shy. I used to sit in the back row of the meeting for young people and slip away at the close. One day when they asked me to help take up the offering I almost died!

Enriched by grace. That is my story also. And if you let God work out His plan for your life, His grace will equip you for service that you cannot imagine right now.

50

Overflowing Grace

But the gift is not like the trespass. For if the many died by the trespass of the one man, how much more did God's grace and the gift that came by the grace of the one man, Jesus Christ, overflow to the many! Rom. 5:15, NIV.

In a marvelous passage in the marvelous Book of Romans, the book that sparked the Reformation, the apostle Paul contrasts Adam and Jesus Christ. From this basic juxtaposition a series of other stark contrasts emerge: sin and righteousness, death and life, condemnation and gift. And the word that Paul comes back to again and again is *charis,* grace.

This passage, Romans 5:12-21, unfortunately has engendered endless controversy for centuries. The argument stems from Paul's opening sentence (verse 12), in which he begins the contrast of Adam and Christ but gets carried away by the power of the ideas he is presenting. He starts, "Therefore, just as sin entered the world through one man" (NIV), but doesn't wrap up the idea with "so righteousness came to all through one man, Jesus Christ." Out of the silence of that gap, that unfinished sentence, theologians have injected an idea that I think was foreign to Paul— "original sin," the idea that we all bear the guilt of Adam's transgression.

We don't need to get involved in that controversy. Paul's theme throughout the passage is abundantly clear. And what a theme it is! No wonder it swept Paul away, so that, dictating, he left the opening sentence incomplete.

In our text for today Paul contrasts "the gift" with "the trespass." "The gift" is eternal life, salvation, offered to every person who has ever lived. "The trespass" is Adam's first sin, his disobedience to the explicit word of the Lord. Because of Adam's trespass, "the many" died. Not because Adam's guilt was laid upon them, but because, as Paul stated in verse 12, "death came to all men, because all sinned" (NIV).

One man sins and dies. As a result of that transgression, sin passes down the line, generation after generation. All sin—none is exempt, "no, not one" (Rom. 3:10)—and so death comes to all.

But grace enters the picture. Grace overflows. As far as sin spreads, grace spreads further. As far as death extends its domain, grace extends further! Through Jesus Christ all that was lost because of Adam is made up—and more, much more!

Grace Is a Flock of Robins

If death got the upper hand through one man's wrongdoing, can you imagine the breath-taking recovery life makes, sovereign life, in those who grasp with both hands this wildly extravagant life-gift, this grand setting-everything-right, that the one man Jesus Christ provides? Rom. 5:17, Message.

On the last day of February I opened the front door of our home to go out for the morning paper. Across the front lawn I saw a flock of robins busy at work in the gray and yellow post-winter grass. Not one, or five, or a dozen, but scores of robins.

As I walked down the driveway, the birds flew back and forth, almost brushing me. They seemed lively, animated, as if they wanted to say, "We're glad to be back! Isn't spring wonderful?"

As it turned out, spring hadn't quite arrived. A snowstorm roared up from the south later that day, closing schools and shutting down much of the Washington, D.C., area. And that isn't unusual; the robins invariably come early, harbingers of the spring, anticipating the spring, pulling the spring behind them on their wings.

I love the spring. I look for the first crocuses that come out a couple weeks ahead of the robins. And especially for the first robin, the sure herald of warmer days and nest building. Usually the first robins come widely scattered. Often we see just one bird. That's why the scene on February 28 so amazed me. One robin would have sufficed to make me happy, but God sent a whole flock. Talk about abundance!

Just like grace; grace is a flock of robins.

In the excellent paraphrase of Romans 5:17, our text for today, Eugene H. Peterson doesn't use the word "abundant" or "abundance," but Paul did in the original letter. The Revised Standard Version of this text has "those receive the *abundance of grace*," and the New International Version "those who receive God's *abundant provision of grace*."

Earlier in this wonderful passage Paul wrote about *overflowing* grace (verse 15, NIV). Now he describes *abundant* grace. And, as we shall see, he isn't finished. As he continues the passage, in emphasizing grace he moves up the ladder of superlatives, higher and higher, until he exhausts the limits of vocabulary.

Grace overflows. Grace is abundant. Grace is wonderful. Grace is Jesus.

Grace Wins Hands Down

All that passing laws against sin did was produce more lawbreakers. But sin didn't, and doesn't, have a chance in competition with the aggressive forgiveness we call grace. Rom. 5:20, Message.

The apostle Paul is running out of superlatives. In Romans 5 he has already described grace as *overflowing* (verse 15, NIV), then, going up the ladder one step, as *abounding* (verse 17, NIV). When he comes to verse 20 and wants to raise the ante even higher, he pulls in a rare compound word. He says that grace "superabounds." The only other place we find this word is in 2 Corinthians 7:4, where Paul again is the writer: "I am *overwhelmed* with joy despite all our troubles" (Message).

Paul here is comparing and contrasting sin and grace. "But where sin abounded, grace did much more abound," as the King James Version translates. So he puts forth two realities: abounding sin, and superabounding grace. And that assertion leaves us with a big question. That sin abounds is obvious, but how can Paul say the grace abounds even more so; or, as *The Message* renders, "grace wins hands down" (Rom. 5:20)?

I could fill the rest of the page in describing how sin abounds, and at the end would have scarcely begun. Everywhere, on all sides, in all aspects of life we see the surge of evil and its baleful effects. The world is rushing headlong to its date with destiny, and it isn't getting better. The more we learn, the more knowledge and technology is devoted to ever new manifestations of wickedness and corruption. As it was in the days before the Flood, every inclination of people's heart is only evil (Gen. 6:5). War, murder, rape, sexual abuse, incest, lies, pornography, malice, hate, deception, pride, arrogance—sin indeed abounds, seemingly unchecked. No problem to accept Paul's statement here.

But what about his other part: grace *superabounds?* Is not this a "cognitive dissonance," meaning that the evidence belies the assertion? To outward appearances, yes. But not to the eye of faith. Not to the soul that lives in grace. Not to the man or woman who breathes the life-giving air of heaven, who knows that the atmosphere of grace surrounds this earth just as surely as nitrogen and oxygen are all around us. Not to the person who *knows,* not just by the head but by the heart, that Jesus Christ is alive. Not to the Christian who has personally experienced and experiences the battle between sin and grace and can witness that grace wins hands down.

Grace Reigns

So that, just as sin reigned in death, so also grace might reign through righteousness to bring eternal life through Jesus Christ our Lord. Rom. 5:21, NIV.

Paul's ladder of superlatives in Romans 5 now reaches the top rung:

Grace overflows (verse 15)
Grace abounds (verse 17)
Grace superabounds (verse 20)
Grace reigns (verse 21)

The reign of grace is set over against the reign of sin. And Paul, guided by the Holy Spirit, has said it right: sin reigns. Sin is a taskmaster, a cruel lord, bringing us into subjection, stifling our noblest impulses and dragging us down individually and corporately.

And Paul is right again: sin reigns *in death*. Death, the great leveler, the great inevitable, holds sway. Bill Gates may be the wealthiest person on the planet, but all his money cannot hold back the floodgates of death. Michael Jordan can turn the basketball court into an athletic wonder world, but all his ability cannot stop the inexorable footsteps of the Grim Reaper. Lady Diana—so beautiful, so admired, so unhappy, so fragile— perished in a terrible car wreck, leaving only tears and regrets.

Sin reigns. Sin reigns in death. No question. But sin and death don't have the last word. *Once* sin and death reigned, but *now* grace and life reign! Jesus Christ, God's Son, has come to earth and banished sin and death. He met the devil on his own turf and bested him. On Calvary Jesus took our place, dying a despairing death, the death that rightly was ours, that we might receive the life that rightly is His.

But early Sunday morning Jesus' tomb was empty. The body had disappeared; only the graveclothes, neatly folded in separate piles, remained. And then Jesus appeared to Mary Magdalene, and to some other women, to Cleopas and his friend on the road to Emmaus, to Peter, to the 11, to more than 500 all at once. Over a period of 40 days He spoke to His disciples, even at times sitting down to a meal with them (Acts 1:4). And later He appeared to Saul, who became the apostle Paul.

My friend, do you believe that grace and life *reign* even now? Open your heart to Jesus; let Him reign there.

Grace Is a Diamond

And God is able to make all grace abound to you, so that in all things at all times, having all that you need, you will abound in every good work. 2 Cor. 9:8, NIV.

L
ike a diamond sparkling as it turns in the light, grace has many facets. Surprising facets, facets new to us, unexpected facets—but every one beautiful. Our text for the day shines the spotlight on five features of grace.

God is able to make all grace abound to us. God doesn't just give; He lavishes. He doesn't save us by the skin of our teeth; He provides abundant entry into His kingdom. And He doesn't supply just enough grace for our needs; He pours out *all* grace, grace *abounding*.

This day let us go forth confidently, joyfully, serenely. God's promise goes before us, like the star that led the Magi to Bethlehem. Let us walk in its light, knowing that something more precious than gold—yes, more valuable than the Hope Diamond—is ours. Grace.

In all things. Not just when life smiles upon us. Not just when we feel we have the world at our fingertips. But in *all* things: when life smashes us in the face, when we feel ill-used, abandoned by friends, dealt an unfair hand.

Hear Paul again: "For I am convinced that neither death nor life, neither angels nor demons, neither the present nor the future, nor any powers, neither height nor depth, nor anything else in all creation, will be able to separate us from the love of God that is in Christ Jesus our Lord" (Rom. 8:38, 39, NIV). And that means today. The promise goes before us in all things.

At all times. A diamond, says the advertisement, is forever. And so is grace. Noonday's warm brightness and darkest midnight. Youth's steady stride and old age's tottering step. In love and in loneliness. In elation and in bereavement. Today the promise goes on before God will be with us every moment, come what may.

Having all that you need. Not what we want, not even what we pray for, but what we need. Not the treasures of earthly value but eternal treasures, unfailing in heaven above. All that we need to live for God, all that we need to meet the enemy, all that we need to overcome, all that we need. Today, in Jesus, we already have all that we need.

You will abound in every good work. Abounding grace must abound for God's glory. What a promise! What a day lies ahead for us!

Grace Is a Fountain

And now, brothers, we want you to know about the grace that God has given the Macedonian churches. Out of the most severe trial, their overflowing joy and their extreme poverty welled up in rich generosity. 2 Cor. 8:1, 2, NIV.

Late one fall Noelene dumped a pile of fresh garden mulch alongside the path in our backyard. She raked some of the mulch into the nearby azalea bed, but didn't have time to remove the heap completely before winter set in. When the snow came and covered everything with four inches of new carpet, you could still detect a rise by the side of the path, as though a giant mushroom was getting ready to pop out.

No mushroom, but something better lay under that heap of mulch—daffodils, crocuses, and hostas. As I walked to and fro on the way to the woodshed, I wondered if they would survive being dumped on. So did Noelene.

When the snow melted in the early days of March, we had our answer. Out of the newly thawed mulch heap new life emerged like a fountain, a yellow fountain. The plants came out yellow from their long trip upward in darkness. Within a day or two the sun worked its magical chlorophyll formula, and the leaves took on their normal color.

Ever feel like those plants under the mulch heap, that you've been dumped on? Maybe you feel that way right now. Grace is for you, my friend. Grace is like a fountain, welling up with sparkling, refreshing, life-giving water. And grace will make you like a fountain. Its divine power can enable you to fight your way upward to the light until you emerge, maybe a bit the worse for wear, but ready to enjoy the spring.

When Paul wrote the letter we call Second Corinthians, he was on his way to Jerusalem. The Christians in that city needed help, physical help, and Paul was gathering up a love offering from the churches along the way to take to the church at headquarters. He writes at some length to the Corinthians about it, and tells them about the churches of Macadonia as an incentive. Those churches, he writes, had undergone a "most severe trial." They also suffered "extreme poverty." Nevertheless, grace so touched their hearts that, in spite of their own needs, they overflowed with joy and generosity.

Grace is a fountain. And it makes us a fountain.

Going Where No One Has Gone Before

It has always been my ambition to preach the gospel where Christ was not known, so that I would not be building on someone else's foundation. Rom. 15:20, NIV.

What do James Cook and the apostle Paul have in common? On October 27, 1728, a boy was born to James and Grace Cook in a mud-and-thatch hovel, a structure known as a "biggin," in Yorkshire, England. Farm animals wandered in and out of the hut's two small rooms. Sacking spread on the dirt floor kept down the damp and odor.

The prospects for the baby, James, were bleak. Four siblings had perished by the age of 5; a brother died at 23. Cook's father was a day laborer, close to the bottom rung of the social strata. Public education didn't exist. James Cook seemed destined to a tightly confined life of a day's walk in radius, and the well-trod loop of home, field, church, and, finally, family grave plot.

But James Cook exploded the cycle. Escaping to sea as a teenager, he worked his way to the upper reaches of the naval hierarchy and won election to the Royal Society, the pinnacle of London's intellectual establishment. His greatest feat, however, was the three epic voyages of discovery he made in his 40s.

When Cook embarked on his first voyage in 1768, about a third of the world's map remained blank. Cook sailed into this void and returned three years later with charts so accurate that some of them were still used in the 1990s. On the two later voyages Cook explored from the Arctic to the Antarctic and from the northwest shore of America to the far northeast coast of Siberia. By the time he died, stabbed to death in Hawaii, Cook had sailed more than 200,000 miles, all in a small wooden ship.

"Ambition leads me not only farther than any other man has been before me, but as far as I think it possible for man to go," Cook wrote in his journal. And thereby he was like the apostle Paul, who wrote, "It has always been my ambition to preach the gospel where Christ was not known, so that I would not be building on someone else's foundation."

There are few, exceedingly few, Captain James Cooks. There are exceedingly few apostle Pauls. Most of us follow in the trail they blazed. But God still calls men and women, and young people, to go where no one has gone before, to take the gospel to "every nation, and kindred, and tongue, and people" (Rev. 14:6). To think new thoughts, to explore, to sail blue horizons—all for His glory.

Embrace Grace

As God's fellow workers we urge you not to receive God's grace in vain. 2 Cor. 6:1, NIV.

The word here translated "receive" has the meaning "to receive favorably," "to approve," "to embrace." God doesn't want us merely to give mental assent to grace; He wants us to live in grace and share in its manifold benefits. He wants us to embrace grace.

Paul makes plain that it is possible to receive God's grace in vain. Like the seed in Jesus' parable (Matt. 13:5-7) that fell on stony ground or among thorns, we may accept Jesus as our Savior but never grow into the fullness that He offers us. He offers us *life,* not just deliverance from a death sentence. The Christian life has only just begun when we are reconciled to God and enter upon a relationship with Him. God intends that we shall be transformed into His likeness through the power of the indwelling Holy Spirit (2 Cor. 3:18).

Let's *embrace* grace. Grace at the beginning of our Christian journey. Grace at every stage of the way. Grace new every morning. Grace that brings us safe to glory at last.

How might we receive God's grace in vain?

By neglect. God speaks, and speaks again; but we may refuse to hear. We may let the things of this world—its noise and bedlam—drown out the voice of God. Each time He speaks His voice will seem softer and more distant, until we no longer hear Him. He does not cease speaking, but our ears have become closed to Him (Isa. 6:9, 10).

By using grace as an excuse for sin. God calls us to obedience—not the obedience of human effort but the obedience of grace. The Lord hasn't changed: what He abhorred in Bible times He still abhors. He calls His people to shine as lights in a dark place, in the midst of "a crooked and depraved generation" (Phil. 2:15, NIV).

By adding human ideas and works to grace. Whenever we seek to earn credit with God, whenever we would add to grace's all-sufficiency, we adulterate grace. That lay at the root of the heresy among the Galatian Christians.

When we fail to take grace into our lives. It's possible to study about grace in the Hebrew and the Greek, to memorize passages and to marshal theological arguments—and not to know grace as a living power in personal experience.

Today let's not receive grace in vain. Let's *embrace* it.

SEPTEMBER

The Dreamers

And it shall come to pass afterward that I will pour out My Spirit on all flesh; your sons and your daughters shall prophesy, your old men shall dream dreams, your young men shall see visions. Joel 2:28, NKJV.

One of the characteristics I look for in people is their dreams. Does a person imagine blue horizons, new ventures to be conquered?

Dreams, I believe, are part of the image of God in which God made our first parents, and that we still retain even in our broken state. For God is the heavenly dreamer, who sees unlimited possibilities. We sell ourselves too short, and thereby we disappoint Him.

Over the years I've spoken to many groups of young people. My first work in the ministry was hostel dean at a boarding school. I enjoy speaking to youth more than to any other group, and it has been a delight to find that even though the age differential has stretched to put me in a "grandfather" relationship, young people still listen with interest.

Maybe that's because I see my role as dream planter. In a verse celebrating the coming of spring Robert Frost wrote:

"Come with rain, O loud Southwester!
Bring the singer, bring the nester;
Give the buried flower a dream."

That's what I'm about—to give the buried flower a dream. What sort of dreams? Dreams of personal advance. Dreams of service to God and to humanity. Dreams of impacting the world for lasting good.

Listen to the counsels of Ellen White as she addresses young people: "Are you ambitious for education that you may have a name and position in the world? Have you thoughts that you dare not express, that you may one day stand upon the summit of intellectual greatness; that you may sit in deliberative and legislative councils, and help to enact laws for the nation? There is nothing wrong in these aspirations. You may every one of you make your mark. You should be content with no mean attainments. Aim high, and spare no pains to reach the standard" (*Messages to Young People*, p. 36).

Grace sets us free to dream.

The Excellencies of Grace

But may the God of all grace, who called us to His eternal glory by Christ Jesus, after you have suffered a while, perfect, establish, strengthen, and settle you. 1 Peter 5:10, NKJV.

R ecently I took down from the shelf in my home library a book that had influenced me greatly as a young man. I couldn't find a single page without something underlined, and some pages were almost totally underscored. Here and there I found asterisks and occasional notes to myself, such as "This is a beautiful section!"

In the flyleaf of the book I had written out a quotation: "The precious graces of the Holy Spirit are not developed in a moment. . . . By a life of holy endeavor and firm adherence to the right the children of God are to seal their destiny."

I look at that flyleaf and study the handwriting. Yes, once I received an elementary school award for penmanship. Almost impossible to believe that now; after millions of words, today I spit out words in a barely legible scrawl. The flyleaf shows me that the penmanship award isn't a figment of the imagination.

But these words in the flyleaf—why these? They must have summed up my aspirations, my earnest desire as a young person who had experienced the miracle of salvation. How far these words shaped my life—how closely I may have approached the holy ideal, and how far I have fallen short again and again—I leave with the Lord, who is gracious and merciful.

Ah, that book? Here's something I wonder at. This same book that blessed and shaped the life of this young man has come under heavy fire during the past 20 years or so. It's been criticized as an unfortunate book, a bad book, a discouraging book. Some people have not found it helpful at all in their Christian walk. Just the opposite, in fact.

I was blessed by it. Does that make me any better than someone who wasn't? Not at all. The book spoke to me at a critical time I my life. It lifted my sights to aim high and seek the best. It was a message tailor-made for me. For some others it came across as directive, even legalistic. I can see now how that could happen.

I would wish for every Christian the blessing that I found, finding it by whatever means—the excellencies of grace.

Oh, the book? *Messages to Young People,* by Ellen G. White. And the quote in the flyleaf? *Testimonies for the Church,* volume 8, page 314.

His Poverty, Our Riches

For you know the grace of our Lord Jesus Christ, that though he was rich, yet for your sakes he became poor, so that you through his poverty might become rich. 2 Cor. 8:9, NIV.

I t's the greatest story ever told, the story of Jesus. The story of the great condescension, from heaven's summit to earth's lowest point. From the realms of glory, where myriads of angels sing "Holy! Holy! Holy!" and bow down in worship to a manger in a stinking stable.

Rich? The wealth of the universe was His. He made all things, He sustained all things. "He's got the whole world in His hands." As Commander of the heavenly hosts.

"Thousands at his bidding speed
And post o'er land and ocean without rest."

All this was, and is, His—His by right, His by virtue of who and what He is and always will be.

But He turned His back on it all. He set it aside, didn't consider it a right or privilege to be grasped tight. He emptied Himself, taking on the form of a servant. He humbled Himself, became obedient even unto death—even death on a cross.

Have you ever thought of it this way? Jesus Christ became the heavenly borrower. They borrowed a manger for Him in which to lay His baby head. He borrowed a boat to teach from. He borrowed five barley loaves and two fishes to feed the multitude. He borrowed a donkey for the triumphal ride into Jerusalem. And, at last, His dead body was laid to rest in a borrowed tomb.

"The King of glory stooped low to take humanity. Rude and forbidding were His earthly surroundings. His glory was veiled, that the majesty of His outward form might not become an object of attraction. He shunned all outward display. Riches, worldly honor, and human greatness can never save a soul from death; Jesus purposed that no attraction of an earthly nature should call men to His side. Only the beauty of heavenly truth must draw those who would follow Him" (*The Desire of Ages*, p. 43).

Through His poverty we become rich. The riches of eternity are ours—as a gift! We are rich, my friends, rich in hope, rich in life, rich in salvation, rich in *Him*.

This is grace.

The Throne of Grace

Let us then approach the throne of grace with confidence, so that we may receive mercy and find grace to help us in our time of need. Heb. 4:16, NIV.

All the many grace texts of Scripture ring with gladness, but none more than this one. We find here grace mentioned twice: the throne of grace, and grace for timely help. We might say, "From the Center of grace in the universe grace comes to us when we need it most."

The prophet Micah enquired, "With what shall I come before the Lord and bow down before the exalted God?" (Micah 6:6, NIV).

That has been the heart plea of spiritual men and women throughout the ages. They have tortured their bodies, fasted, denied themselves sleep. They have made pilgrimages and done penance, following, like the monk Martin Luther, every course of action prescribed by the church structure. And still, like him, they have been left with a feeling of emptiness and uncertainty.

Only in and through Jesus Christ do our religious aspirations find a home. Only as we open our eyes, by the Spirit, to the wonder of the story of His coming to us and dying the death that was rightfully ours do we find the peace and assurance that our heart yearns for.

Now, because of Him, we can *know* that heaven is a welcome place. We belong, as every son and daughter belongs. God's presence, holy as it is, no longer strikes terror in our hearts. The throne of grace stands at the center of the universe.

Because it's a throne of grace, the Lord, as it were, holds out the scepter of entry. We come before Him confidently, not with servile cringing, but like a child running into the open arms of a loving parent.

That throne of grace extends mercy to us—and grace to help us. The thought is similar to an earlier text in Hebrews: "Because he [Jesus] himself suffered when he was tempted, he is able to help those who are being tempted" (Heb. 2:18, NIV). In this context the grace He supplies is overcoming grace, grace just right for our needs and right on time.

> "From every stormy wind that blows,
> From every swelling tide of woes,
> There is a calm, a sure retreat;
> 'Tis found beneath the mercy seat."
>   —Hugh Stowell

The Voice From the Mercy Seat

And there I will meet with you, and I will speak with you from above the mercy seat, from between the two cherubim which are on the ark of the Testimony, about everything which I will give you in commandment to the children of Israel. Ex. 25:22, NKJV.

God gave Moses detailed instructions concerning the construction of the wilderness sanctuary. It consisted of three main parts: an outer court, which contained the bronze altar and to which the children of Israel brought their various offerings; the first tent, or apartment, called the holy place, where the priests served; and the innermost, most sacred, area called the Most Holy, where only the high priest entered but once a year, on the Day of Atonement.

The Most Holy Place, cubic in dimensions, was simplicity itself. Its only furnishing was the ark of the covenant, a box made of acacia wood overlaid with gold. Inside the ark was the Testimony, the two stone tablets with the Ten Commandments written by the finger of God. And covering the ark of the covenant was a sheet of solid gold, with an angel at either side beaten out from the same piece of metal, their wings stretching to touch each side of the Most Holy and each other.

This simple, beautiful structure represented the heart of heaven. In the throne room of the universe myriads of celestial beings surround the King of kings and Lord of lords, singing ceaseless songs of adoration and worship. Here Jesus, our great high priest, intercedes on our behalf—not that the Father is reluctant to accept us, but that every benefit that flows to fallen men and women comes by virtue of the blood spilled on Calvary.

The earthly Most Holy contained no representation of the Majesty of heaven, for one can never be imagined or devised. But while we cannot know the form of God, He has made clear that He is a God of law. The tablets of stone in the Most Holy tell us that heaven, the universe, are divinely established on divine principles.

If we had only the law—if the Most Holy had only the ark of the covenant and the tablets of stone—we would be without hope. We have all gone astray, fallen short, transgressed. The law condemns us with a severity harder than the stone of its tablets.

But there is a mercy seat! God speaks to us from the mercy seat! He speaks, not in the severity of Sinai, but with the salvation of Calvary.

Praise Him for the mercy seat!

Gourmands and Grace

Do not be carried about with various and strange doctrines. For it is good that the heart be established by grace, not with foods which have not profited those who have been occupied with them. Heb. 13:9, NKJV.

During my college days in Australia I shared a room for a while with an interesting character. As a hobby Roy made violins, and pretty fine ones at that. His other defining trait was his dining room etiquette.

The college was coed, which in itself seemed a questionable philosophy, since the multiple rules of conduct seemed designed to keep the sexes apart. For instance, the only legal place for a boy to talk to a girl was on "the lawn," a notorious square of grass with benches outside the window of the college president's office. One day I received a sharp rebuke from a professor who caught me in the act of giving my sweetheart (later to be my wife) a rose from the college garden. We were standing on the path alongside the lawn, but he called me to account with "There is a place for doing that sort of thing, you know!"

Mealtimes were exercises designed by the watchdog faculty to develop (they hoped) fine manners without encouraging intimacy. Boys entered through one door, girls another. Hosts directed us to tables of four—two and two—vigilantly thwarting any plan for prearranged seating.

When the girls saw Roy coming to their table, they groaned. Roy took lots of food—sometimes two trays of it—and, health nut that he was, insisted on chewing every mouthful 33 times. Roy's table would always be the last out of the dining room.

I could always get a rise out of Roy by asking him what he thought about white bread. "White bread!" he'd explode. "Not fit for pigs to eat!"

I happen to agree that humans, at least, can do much better than white bread. I'm a bread lover, but make it from stone-ground wheat flour or multigrains if you wish to please me. And I also happen to agree (also with Roy) that what we eat affects us physically, mentally, and spiritually. I like to exercise and run marathons; and you have to eat right to run. You have to eat right to think right. And it's much, much harder to be gracious to others when you have a sour stomach.

Some people, anciently and still today, want to turn food into faith, diet into devotion. They're related, but poles apart. Hearts are established by grace alone.

Hero

You therefore, my son, be strong in the grace that is in Christ Jesus. 2 Tim. 2:1, NKJV.

Heroes come in all shapes and sizes and ages—regardless of gender. Like Ashley Smith, thrust into the media limelight by a spectacular act of bravery. Smith had moved into a suburban apartment complex in Atlanta, Georgia, only a few days before. Early one Saturday morning, when she returned from a store, a man accosted her in the parking lot. Sticking a gun in her side, he ordered her into her apartment, saying, "I'm not going to hurt you if you just do what I say. I don't want to hurt you. I don't want to hurt anybody else."

Ashley Smith at first was not aware of the identity of her assailant. She didn't realize that the man who proceeded to tie her up with masking tape, a curtain, and an extension cord was the object of the largest manhunt in Atlanta's history.

The day before, Brian Nichols, facing a rape charge, had seized the weapon of the officer escorting him to the court, then shot and killed the presiding judge and a court reporter, and killed a deputy who tried to prevent his escape. Later he killed a federal agent and took his gun, badge, and pickup truck.

Now Ashley Smith was tied up alone in her apartment with this desperate individual. "I thought he was going to strangle me," she said later. Through the early-morning hours she kept talking to him, trying to win his trust. She told him that her husband had died four years before, and that if he hurt her, her little girl wouldn't have a mother or father. She told him that she was supposed to see her daughter at 10:00 that morning, but Nichols refused to let her leave.

Eventually Nichols untied her. He said he felt as though "he was already dead," but Smith urged him to consider the fact that he was still alive a "miracle." "You're here in my apartment for some reason," she told him. Perhaps the Lord wanted him to spread the Word of God to fellow prisoners.

Nichols put down his weapons. Smith made him pancakes. Then he let her go. She called 911 and, when a small army of police arrived, he surrendered peacefully.

What incredible strength! What bravery! I would like to know much more about Ashley Smith and the source of her heroism.

I think I do know—not source, but Source.

The Grace of Generosity

But just as you excel in everything—in faith, in speech, in knowledge, in complete earnestness and in your love for us—see that you also excel in this grace of giving. 2 Cor. 8:7, NIV.

The love of money has given Christianity a bad name. Many people today see themselves as post-Christian. They were brought up in a Christian framework but abandoned it because they found it wanting. Sometimes these post-Christians, still hungry for God, turn to New Age, Buddhism, or Hinduism. Again and again those who feel they have left Christianity behind associate it with an organization concerned primarily with grabbing money from people.

How the church in general and each of us as individual Christians relate to money is of vital importance. To get the picture right, we have to start with Jesus of Nazareth, the heavenly borrower. Although He owned the wealth of the universe, He emptied Himself. Born into poverty, He spent His time on earth as a poor man. Those (and they are many) who associate Christianity with raking in money have a problem, not with Jesus, but with so-called followers of the Man of Galilee.

And the problem is huge. Just as the medieval popes lived in luxury on the backs of the peasants, so televangelists (not all, but some prominent ones) live in opulence from their appeals for funds. They build mansions, fly around in private jet planes, breaking their journeys to take the presidential suite in expensive hotels. What an affront to the life and message of Jesus Christ! What a turnoff to people who have their eyes open!

The other side of the coin is that the life and message of Jesus touches every aspect of our lives, including the very private area of our pocketbook. Grace, which is Jesus, is lavish, abundant, overflowing, surpassing expectations, generous beyond surprise. Viewed in crassly business terms, the price paid for our salvation was incredibly reckless. But that is grace—reckless love.

As grace takes root in our lives, as we yield to its influence day by day, it changes us into those with the same reckless, loving behavior. We give because we delight to give, because we have to give—not by demand but by an inner compulsion. This is the grace of which Paul wrote to the Corinthians—the grace of generosity. A stingy Christian is an oxymoron.

Lord, today grant me the grace of generosity.

A Letter of Grace

I am sending him—who is my very heart—back to you. Philemon 12, NIV.

The shortest of the letters of Paul that have survived is perhaps the most beautiful of all. In the letter to Philemon we see grace shining in every verse. It is a very personal piece of writing, this letter, hardly more than a note. Over the years some people have questioned why it should have a place among the works of Scripture, because it contains no theological argumentation or development.

But how wrong such critics are! This short letter is rich in content and even richer in feeling. Today one hardly ever hears a sermon based on it, and that is a loss to Christian reflection and experience. We shall spend several days with this letter, mining its treasures, and I am confident that by the close you will agree with me that it is a rare jewel.

The letter begins with grace and ends with grace. "Grace to you and peace from God our Father and the Lord Jesus Christ," writes Paul in his customary introduction (verse 3, NIV). And he closes with this benediction: "The grace of the Lord Jesus Christ be with your spirit" (verse 25, NIV).

Bookends of grace! What a way to write! What a way to live! And what a prayer for our day that before and behind, first and last, we might be encompassed by grace. Paul doesn't refer to grace specifically, apart from these references at the beginning and the close. But what he does is *demonstrate* grace—how grace works, what grace is like. Elsewhere in his letters, especially Romans and Galatians, Paul sets forth the theology of grace; here, he lives graces. So if we would understand what he means by grace, we had better take note of his practice in this personal note.

A word, almost untranslatable in English, that Paul uses three times as he writes to Philemon opens a window into his deep feelings. We find it in verse 7: "You, brother, have refreshed the hearts of the saints" (NIV); in verse 12: "I am sending him—who is my very *heart*—back to you" (NIV); and in verse 20: "refresh my *heart* in Christ" (NIV).

The word isn't "heart" but literally "viscera," "guts," to put it bluntly. And when do we feel deep emotions, especially negative ones? In our bellies, in our guts. Grace is about deep emotion—guts. Anyone who wants to restrict grace to theology, debate, and argument needs to read Paul's letter to Philemon. Until grace gets in their guts, they don't know what it is.

Paul's Son in Prison

I appeal to you for my son Onesimus, who became my son while I was in chains.
Philemon 10, NIV.

Paul was single, but he had sons. He called Timothy "my true son in the faith" (1 Tim. 1:2, NIV) and "my dear son" (2 Tim. 1:2, NIV). And writing to Titus, he began, "To Titus, my true son in our common faith" (Titus 1:4, NIV).

Timothy and Titus were Paul's coworkers in the gospel cause. They traveled together, labored together, suffered together. The great mission into which they poured their hearts and lives bonded them together in ties closer than those of flesh and blood.

But Paul had a son of a different sort. No coworker he, no compatriot in trials and triumphs of the gospel. Onesimus was his name, and he became Paul's son while Paul was in prison, probably in Rome.

We know very little about this young man. We don't know anything about him before he met Paul, or even how he came to meet Paul. We don't know what happened to him afterward. The letter of Philemon gives us a slice of his life and leaves most of the story blank. But it tells us enough to leave us intrigued by possibilities. Most important of all, the story—brief and fragmentary as it is—opens a window on grace.

This we know for sure: Onesimus was a slave. Paul says so directly in verse 16: "no longer as a slave" (NIV). Another clue: Onesimus may have come from Colossae, a city in what we call Turkey today, because in writing to the Colossians Paul mentions a certain Onesimus, "who is one of you" (Col. 4:9).

When Paul writes to Philemon, Onesimus is a runaway slave. He has taken his life in his hands and seized his freedom from Philemon, who owns him. Onesimus runs and runs, as fast and far as he can. Where better to escape capture than in the big city, the biggest city of the day, in Rome itself?

Onesimus has done a very dangerous thing. If caught, he can be thrown to lampreys, voracious fish that tear the flesh from his bones. He can be branded with a hot iron, designated for life a slave who tried to run away.

The old man Paul is rotting in chains. Onesimus is on the lam. God brings them together, and Paul begets another son—a miracle of grace.

The Christian Slave Owner

Perhaps the reason he was separated from you for a little while was that you might have him back for good—no longer as a slave, but better than a slave, as a dear brother. Philemon 15, 16, NIV.

Philemon, to whom Paul wrote as "our dear friend and fellow worker" (verse 1, NIV) and whose home provided a place for a church to meet (verse 2, NIV), was a slave owner. He owned at least one slave, the young man Onesimus, who ran away and found Paul in prison, where he became a Christian. How could it be? Is not this a contradiction in terms, an oxymoron?

Abraham Lincoln said that he would not wish to be either a slave or a slave owner. Both are debased by the relationship.

Some years ago I turned on the evening news and caught a segment that both amazed and appalled. The camera captured pictures from an exhibition of scenes from that dastardly chapter in American history that ran from the late nineteenth century into the early twentieth century, the era of lynchings. The photographs revolted me, and one in particular still clings to my brain calls. Here is a group of men and a few boys leaning on the railing of a bridge, looking foursquare into the camera's lens. Their faces show no trace of shame or remorse. Behind them, a charred body swings from a rope tied to a tree. Next we see a picture of a postcard mailed the next day bearing the caption "We had a barbeque last night."

What about slavery in Paul's day? Perhaps it was different. Yes and no. The Roman Empire ran on slavery. A large percentage of the population were slaves. Unlike the American institution, slavery in Paul's time did not have an ethnic basis. People became slaves through birth or piracy, or by falling into debt. Their status varied greatly. Some slaves were highly educated, tutors, philosophers, or musicians. They ran shops or factories and managed estates.

But the slave owner held absolute power over them. Slaves could own no property, could not legally marry, could be separated from wife and children at the master's whim. They had no appeal for justice, no place to flee for asylum. Slavery was a school for cowardice, flattery, dishonesty, and basest immorality.

Philemon, Paul's dear friend, was a slave owner. How could it be? Because his practice lagged behind his knowledge. The gospel of grace had yet to have its full sway in his life.

Am I any better?

Paul's Strangest Conduct

Therefore, although in Christ I could be bold and order you to do what you ought to do, yet I appeal to you on the basis of love. Philemon 8, NIV.

Well may we ask how Philemon, Paul's good friend, could own slaves, when slavery dehumanizes both master and subject. But what about Paul himself? How do we explain his own conduct?

Paul had a runaway slave on his hands. Somehow Onesimus had found Paul in prison, had heard the good news from him, and had become a Christian. Now Paul writes to Philemon, who owned Onesimus, body and soul. Then what does he do? *He sends Onesimus back!*

Whatever is Paul thinking? Why doesn't he write Philemon and rebuke him for his denial of Creation and the gospel by taking another person to be his slave? Why doesn't he keep the young man with him to make his wretched prison existence a little easier?

In sending Onesimus back to Philemon, Paul subjected him to grave risk. Roman law provided for severe penalties for runaway slaves: Onesimus could legally be crucified, thrown to voracious lampreys, or at best branded with a permanent, visible scar to prevent future escapes.

Slavery was widespread across the Roman Empire, and Philemon wasn't the only professed follower of Jesus Christ to own slaves. In his letters Paul refers to relationships between masters and subjects several times. To the Corinthians he wrote: "Were you a slave when you were called? Don't let it trouble you—although if you can gain your freedom, do so" (1 Cor. 7:21, NIV). Elsewhere he advised slaves to serve their lords with honesty and faithfulness, and slave owners to treat slaves fairly and justly (Eph. 6:5-9; Col. 3:22; 1 Tim. 6:1, 2; Titus 2:9, 10).

Paul nowhere told slave owners to set their slaves free, nor did he counsel slaves to try to revolt. What happened to Paul's moral compass?

It was right where the Lord placed it. With slavery institutionalized within the society of his day and Christians a tiny minority without legal standing, it would have been folly to call for a change in the social order. But Paul in fact was involved in changing the social order. His message, the gospel of grace, planted ideas that were time bombs, ticking, to eventually blow slavery away. Time bombs such as "There is neither . . . slave nor free, . . . for you are all one in Christ Jesus" (Gal. 3:28, NIV) and "There is no . . . slave or free, but Christ is all, and is in all" (Col. 3:11, NIV).

Grace is still a time bomb—do you believe that?

From Useless to Useful

Formerly he was useless to you, but now he has become useful both to you and to me.
Philemon 11, NIV.

We do not know how the story of Onesimus began, nor do we know what happened after Paul sent this runaway slave back to his master, Philemon, presumably bearing Paul's personal letter. But we can reasonably conjecture as to the former, and a fascinating item from early church history gives us a window into the latter.

It seems clear that Onesimus, fleeing for his freedom (even though that entailed high risk under Roman law), became a Christian after meeting Paul in prison. If that occurred, as is probable, in Rome the odds of such a meeting occurring have to have been long. Rome was a city of about 1 million people. What might bring Onesimus into contact with the apostle? A divine Hand, of course. Maybe Paul had met the young man when he visited Philemon's home (if he did). Maybe before the slave went on the lam he already knew that Paul was in prison. Maybe, touched by the warmth of the previous encounter, he sought Paul out in jail.

We are on firmer ground as we consider the rest of the story. Paul sent Onesimus back to his master, asking Philemon to welcome him, no longer as a slave but as a brother (verses 16, 17). If Onesimus owed Philemon anything, Paul guaranteed to pay it back (verse 19). And then Paul penned: "I write to you, knowing that you will do even more than I ask" (verse 21, NIV).

What could this "even more" entail? Surely just one thing: give Onesimus his freedom.

Philemon got the point and acted on it. If he hadn't, Paul's letter wouldn't have survived—Philemon would have thrown it away.

The lad, apparently born into slavery, was given a name common to slaves: Onesimus means "useful." But instead he became *useless*, as Paul notes. However, "now he has become useful both to you and to me" (verse 11, NIV).

Perhaps we can know what happened to Onesimus. About 50 years after Paul wrote to Philemon, a character by the name of Ignatius wrote to the leader of the church in Ephesus. That letter has survived, and from it we can be sure that Ignatius was aware of Paul's letter to Philemon. He plays on the meanings of "useful" and "useless," as Paul did. And the name of the person to whom he addresses the letter, the bishop of the church in Ephesus: Onesimus!

What a story of forgiving, transforming grace!

Wisdom of the Moken

Therefore do not worry about tomorrow, for tomorrow will worry about itself. Each day has enough trouble of its own. Matt. 6:34, NIV.

On the islands off the coast of Burma and Thailand live a people almost untouched by modern civilization. They call themselves the Moken. The Moken are born on the sea, live on the sea, and die on the sea. They are nomads, constantly moving from island to island, living more than six months a year on their boats.

The Moken don't know how old they are. Their view of time is altogether different from ours. The word "when" doesn't exist in their language. Nor do they have a word for "want." They want very little; they have no desire to accumulate anything. When you are a nomad, goods only get in your way.

Ancient wisdom is not so different from Jesus' counsel to His followers: "Do not worry about your life, what you will eat or drink; or about your body, what you will wear," He said. "Is not life more important than food, and the body more important than clothes?" (Matt. 6:25, NIV).

And there is more wisdom from the Moken. They share an intimacy with the sea. They know its moods and motions better than any marine biologist. They have a legend, passed on from generation to generation, the legend of the Laboon, the "wave that eats people." Before it comes, the sea recedes.

On December 26, 2004, the Moken saw the sea recede—and knew what was coming. They fled toward higher ground before the first wave struck. Some of the Moken were at sea when the water receded. They knew what to do—they made at once for deeper water. Like the Moken on the land, they were spared when the tsunami struck.

All around them others lost their lives. Some fishermen collecting squid saw nothing unusual. Suddenly the sea rose up, throwing their boats in the air.

A skilled Moken spear fisherman, Kalathalay, read the signs in nature and ran around warning everyone. But the young people called him a liar, said he was drunk. He grabbed his daughter by the hand and climbed to higher ground.

Hear the word of the Lord: "While people are saying, 'Peace and safety,' destruction will come on them suddenly" (1 Thess. 5:3, NIV).

National Forgiveness Day

Get rid of all bitterness, rage and anger, brawling and slander, along with every form of malice. Be kind and compassionate to one another, forgiving each other, just as in Christ God forgave you. Eph. 4:31, 32, NIV.

S ome time ago a man I have never met wrote me with an idea. "I believe that we need to have a National Forgiveness Day (or week), where every pastor of every church would write a letter to every former member, asking that person to forgive the church for whatever we have done to hurt or harm them emotionally or spiritually," he suggested. "There are thousands of persons who used to be part of our family and who have left for reasons that maybe the church needs to apologize for.

"I don't believe that our churches can grow while we have angry, bitter people, both inside and outside the church. Many members have been emotionally damaged by harsh words, or even well-intentioned words, poorly spoken or spoken at the wrong time. I would suggest that each church make a concerted effort to locate every person's address, and on a certain day mail out a letter, asking for their forgiveness for whatever the church has done to harm them."

I share this brother's concern for former members. While realizing that we should keep our focus on Jesus, and that ultimately each is responsible for their own actions, I also agree that many former members feel bitter and resentful over real or perceived hurts they suffered in church. Forgiveness is a wonderful healer. It's one of the sweetest words in the language. It's God's way to peace and wholeness.

God built forgiveness into the very fiber of our beings. Anger, bitterness, and resentment corrode our bodies, not only sapping our strength but breaking down our immune system. Anger is now listed as one of the causes of high blood pressure, and research has shown that as we find relief from our anger by learning to forgive, the elevated blood pressure caused by that anger is lowered.

The way of grace is the way of forgiveness, and thereby the way to a life freed of malice, bitterness, rage, and anger. Instead of bitterness, compassion. Instead of resentment, kindness. Instead of anger, forgiveness. This is the way to fullness of life on this earth and life everlasting in God's presence. Let's make today a Personal Forgiveness Day.

Apostle of the Bleeding Feet

John was a lamp that burned and gave light, and you chose for a time to enjoy his light.
John 5:35, NIV.

Every now and then grace touches a follower of Jesus with such focused intensity that he or she burns with a light that melts others for Christ. And, it seems, the light burns so brightly that it doesn't burn long.

John the Baptist was one of these persons. Jesus called him "a lamp that burned and gave light," but the lamp burned only a few years. Another was one whom most Christians in the West have never heard of—Sadhu Sundar Singh, variously called "the Apostle of the Twentieth Century" and "the Apostle of the Bleeding Feet."

Sundar Singh was born into a devout Sikh family in the Punjab, India. An intense young man, he at first was strongly opposed to Christianity. Once he publicly tore up a Bible and burned it. One morning he rose at 3:00 and prayed that if there were a God, He would reveal Himself and show him the way of salvation. If the prayer wasn't answered, Sundar Singh determined to lie on the tracks and die under the wheels of an approaching train.

He prayed and waited, expecting to see Krishna, Buddha, or some other Hindu deity. Instead, a light shone in the room, increasing in intensity until he saw not the form he expected but the living Christ. "To all eternity I shall never forget His glorious and loving face or the few words which He spoke: 'Why do you persecute Me? See, I have died on the cross for you and for the whole world,'" he later recalled.

From that moment Sundar Singh became a new person. "My heart was filled with inexpressible joy and peace, and my whole life was entirely changed." He was baptized on his sixteenth birthday.

Filled with a passion to proclaim the message of Jesus, he adopted the simple garb of an Indian holy man. Eventually the influence of his life and writings touched Christians everywhere. He spoke in London, Paris, Germany, America, and Australia. But the greatest burden on his heart was for the unentered country of Tibet. He made many journeys into its mountain fastnesses, and from his final one he never returned. No one knows what befell him. He was only 39 when he disappeared, a lamp burning with the light of grace.

Stinky the Robot

Then David said to the Philistine, "You come to me with a sword, with a spear, and with a javelin. But I come to you in the name of the Lord of hosts, the God of the armies of Israel, whom you have defied." 1 Sam. 17:45, NKJV.

Ever hear about Stinky the Robot? Stinky is a really ugly robot, a ragtag contraption constructed of crudely painted, cheap pipes pasted together. The glue used to hold Stinky together smells foul, hence the name.

The United States Office of Naval Research and NASA ran an underwater robotics contest, the Marine Advanced Technology Remotely Operated Vehicle Competition. Stinky was entered—and was greeted with barely suppressed snickers. Stinky had to go head to head with the entry from Massachusetts Institute of Technology, a handsome machine created by 12 elite engineering and computer science students.

Stinky cost all of $800, donated from local businesses. Its creators were four teenage guys in baggy pants and sneakers, students at Carl Hayden High School in Phoenix, Arizona. All four were illegal Mexican immigrants. They saw a flyer put up by a couple of Hayden science teachers who offered to coach a team in the contest, and they signed up. They built Stinky out of PVC pipes and off-the-shelf computer parts, then headed for Santa Barbara, California, where the contest would be held.

The competition requires the construction of a robot that can explore a sunken mockup of a submarine. When the Hayden four saw the entry from MIT, American's most prestigious engineering school, they felt intimidated. But a funny thing happened on the way to the contest. Stinky won the grand prize. It performed a task the MIT robot couldn't: sucking fluid from a tiny container 12 feet under water.

Why do I love this story, every bit of which is true? Because I love tales of underdogs who battle against long odds and come out on top. Which is one of the reasons the story of David and Goliath appeals to people of all ages. It has all the elements of high drama: a callow youth, going out to battle without armor or weapon, against the giant, clad in iron mail and wielding a huge sword. David's story is maybe the best underdog story in the Bible, but the Good Book is full of them. That's because the Bible is about grace, which makes heroes out of ordinary men and women.

Beethoven's Hair

We're not all going to die—but we are all going to be changed. You hear a blast to end all blasts from a trumpet, and in the time you look up and blink your eyes—it's over. 1 Cor. 15:51, 52, Message.

Recently I read an interesting book, *Beethoven's Hair,* by Russell Martin. Part history, part mystery, part forensic science, it traces the travels of a lock of hair snipped from the great composer's head in the days after his death.

In his time Ludwig van Beethoven towered over the musical world like a colossus. So great was the influence and power of his compositions that some fellow composers stated that he could not be a mere human, that there was something divine about him.

Yet this man who created such incredible sound and who was hailed so widely suffered terribly during the last 30 years of his life. He seemed to be in constant pain, inflicted with gastroenteritis, jaundice, internal bleeding, and headaches. Worst and most tragic of all, he gradually lost his hearing until he was stone deaf. He composed perhaps his greatest works when the music was totally internal. One of the most poignant scenes imaginable came at the close of the premiere performance of his monumental Ninth Symphony, which he conducted. The audience was on its feet, shouting and applauding, but Beethoven knew nothing of it until someone turned him around.

As Beethoven lay dying in 1827, a young Jewish man named Ferdinand Hiller, later to become a composer and musician of note, came to pay his respects. Along with others, he later cut a lock of hair as a keepsake. The relic was passed down for more than a century through Hiller's family until during World War II it made its way into the hands of a doctor in Denmark, who was helping Jews to escape the Nazis.

Eventually the keepsake was bought by two American Beethoven enthusiasts. A few years ago, when the hair was examined, using the most advanced methods, it was found to have an extremely high concentration of lead. Thus, a longstanding mystery was apparently solved. The great man's infirmities apparently were caused by lead poisoning.

A fascinating link with the past. But when Jesus calls forth His people, He won't need a lock of hair, or any molecules carried over from this life. His word—the word of the Creator—will be enough. We shall be changed!

The Spiritual Athlete

Exercise daily in God—no spiritual flabbiness, please! Workouts in the gymnasium are useful, but a disciplined life in God is far more so, making you fit both today and forever. 1 Tim. 4:8, Message.

I f you think running a marathon is the ultimate test of human endurance (or craziness), consider the people who run five marathons in a row. Called ultramarathoners, they keep slogging away for 20 nonstop hours.

In the world of these superathletes, the toughest race is the Badwater Ultramarathon. The 135-mile course winds through Death Valley, a stretch of the Mojave Desert that is considered the hottest place on earth. Temperatures can reach more than 130° F, and the asphalt gets so hot (up to 200° F) that runners stay on the white line to keep their shoes from melting. The race starts below sea level and ascends 8,400 feet to the finish line halfway up Mount Whitney, the tallest peak in the lower 48 of the United States.

During a recent summer 72 runners from 11 countries qualified for the race. Seven were women, including Pam Reed, 46, a mother of three, who had won the event the previous two years. Reed, five feet four inches tall, weighs only 100 pounds. Her approach is unorthodox. With no coach, no nutritionist, and no training schedule, she simply runs as much as she can, up to five times a day.

Another competitor, Dean Karnazes, 43, runs as much as 30 miles on weekdays and 100 miles on weekends. He has probably run farther than any living person—350 miles in 81 hours. That's three days without sleep. For Karnazes and others who engage in extreme sports, the goal is to see how far they can push their bodies. They compete not for a reward (the winner at Badwater receives only a belt buckle and a pat on the back) but for the personal satisfaction the super effort brings them.

How much more important to throw ourselves into the race of life, to discipline ourselves to be spiritual athletes fit for the Master's service, to strive to be and to do our very best for His glory, and to making this world a better place! A new day stretches before us. We know not where its course may take us, but this we know: One has gone on before us. His feet were blistered, His brow sweaty and bloodied. And in His conquering strength we too shall conquer.

Fakes and Faith

Now faith is the substance of things hoped for, the evidence of things not seen. Heb. 11:1, NKJV.

Several years ago a stone box was discovered in Israel. It was an ossuary, an object used to hold the bones of the dead in the time of Jesus. Nothing special about that—many such boxes have been unearthed by the archaeologists. But this one had an engraving on its side. The writing, in ancient Aramaic, read: "James, son of Joseph, brother of Jesus."

The box caused a sensation. More than 100,000 people turned out to see it when it was first exhibited. It made the New York *Times* and the *Biblical Archaeology Review*. It seemed to provide the first firm archaeological evidence that Jesus once lived.

But some scholars doubted. The box wasn't dug up at an authorized excavation; it just turned up in the shop of an antique dealer. And script experts noted that the two halves of the inscription didn't match: "James, son of Joseph" is straight, but "brother of Jesus" is uneven, with different letters. Eventually the box was traced to the Tel Aviv apartment of an Israeli entrepreneur, Oded Golan. He claimed to have bought it from an Arab dealer in the 1970s.

Shortly after the ossuary was exhibited in Toronto, a second major find came to light—a tablet that supposedly was a remnant from King Solomon's Temple. And when that tablet was traced back, the trail led to—Oded Golan's apartment! Israeli detectives searched the building and found a workshop containing drills, half-completed seals, soils, and charcoal. They called it a factory of fakes and charged him with forgery.

Anciently and today, many people look for tangible pegs on which to hang their religion. But true faith doesn't require such props. Faith is "the hand by which we lay hold upon Christ, and appropriate His merits, the remedy for sin" (*The Desire of Ages,* p. 175). The original word rendered "substance" in Hebrews 11:1 can mean "title deed." Faith means that we hold in our hands the title to heaven; we've never been there, never seen it, but it's ours just as truly as if we had been there.

Faith plays a key role in the Christian experience. "Through faith we receive the grace of God; but faith is not our Savior. It earns nothing" (*ibid.*).

Today, let's put our hand into the hand of Jesus and go forward in simple, perfect trust.

The Unforced Rhythms of Grace

Walk with me and work with me—watch how I do it. Learn the unforced rhythms of grace. I won't lay anything heavy or ill-fitting on you. Keep company with me and you'll learn to live freely and lightly. Matt. 11:29, 30, Message.

There is something beautiful in the unforced rhythms of the athlete: the baseball player putting bat to ball, or arcing the ball to the shortstop for a double play. He makes difficult plays seem routine, effortless.

Likewise, there is something beautiful in the unforced rhythms of the musician: the violinist drawing flawless sounds from her instrument as she makes the violin concerto vibrate in the air. She seems transported, lost in a world of excellence.

The well-hit baseball and the well-played violin—both call for discipline and concentration. Both come only after hour upon hour of training and practice. Yet they emerge from a state in which excellence flows without apparent labor.

When baseball players fall into a slump, often it's because the unforced rhythm has been broken for some reason. As soon as they start thinking too hard about what they want to do, become too conscious of mechanics, the ease and the fluidity they desire disappear. And so long as the musician is too conscious of the score, concentrating on not making a mistake, her playing will lack the transcendent quality that soars above "getting it right."

The Christian life is like baseball, like playing a violin concerto. It calls for discipline and concentration. We each must cultivate spiritual exercises—prayer, study of the Word, reflection. But God would have us go beyond concentrating on the mechanics of hitting the ball and following the score; He wants us to reach the state of the unforced rhythms of grace. "Walk with me and work with me—watch how I do it," He invites us. "I won't lay anything heavy or ill-fitting on you. Keep company with me and you'll learn to live freely and lightly."

I wish that for you today, my friend, to live freely and lightly. To live in the innocent trust of God's child, safe, protected, affirmed. To be obedient, but not to be law-bound. To be zealous for the highest, noblest, and best, but in tranquillity of spirit, not in restless striving.

Dear Master, teach me this day Your enforced rhythms of grace.

Paul's Happiest Letter

Rejoice in the Lord always. I will say it again: Rejoice! Phil. 4:4, NIV.

hilippians is Paul's happiest letter. His exuberance spills over and begins to lift us up almost from the first lines. Notice how "joy" and "rejoice" flow out from beginning to close: "I thank my God upon every remembrance of you" (Phil. 1:3); "request for you all with joy" (verse 4, NKJV); "in this I rejoice" (verse 18, NKJV); "joy of faith" (verse 25, NKJV); "your rejoicing for me" (verse 26, NKJV); "fulfill my joy" (Phil. 2:2, NKJV); "I may rejoice" (verse 16, NKJV); "I am glad and rejoice" (verse 17, NKJV); "you also be glad and rejoice" (verse 18, NKJV); "you may rejoice" (verse 28, NKJV); "rejoice in Christ Jesus" (Phil. 3:3); "my joy and crown" (Phil. 4:1); "rejoice . . . always . . . rejoice!" (verse 4, NKJV); "I rejoiced in the Lord" (verse 10, NKJV).

What makes this overflowing happiness all the more remarkable is that Paul was writing from a jail cell. His work was under attack from competitors; some who professed to preach Christ actually sought to do Paul harm. And after many years of ceaseless travel on behalf of the gospel, surviving hardships, shipwreck, lashings, and stonings, Paul surely was growing weary in body.

But not in spirit. He *knew* the One whom He proclaimed. The risen Lord renewed his inner being day by day so that regardless of where and how he found himself, he could be happy. And not just happy—an *overflowing* happiness that was infectious.

"But circumstances are incidental compared to the life of Jesus, the Messiah, that Paul experiences from the inside," writes Eugene H. Peterson in his introduction to Philippians in *The Message.* "For it is a life that not only happened at a certain point in history, but continues to happen, spilling out into the lives of those who receive him, and then continues to spill out all over the place. Christ is, among much else, the revelation that God cannot be contained or hoarded. It is this 'spilling out' quality of Christ's life that accounts for the happiness of Christians, for joy is life in excess, the overflow of what cannot be contained within any one person."

Today, my friend, we know not what shadows may fall across our path. But this we know: no matter how our day may turn out, the new life in Jesus is ours, gushing out and spilling over.

The Tower of Silence

Think of it! All sins forgiven, the slate wiped clean, that old arrest warrant canceled and nailed to Christ's Cross. He stripped all the spiritual tyrants in the universe of their sham authority at the Cross and marched them naked through the streets. Col. 2:14, 15, Message.

In the western coastal region of India, clustered around Bombay as center, live the the Parsis, remnants of a once-mighty people. They fled from Persia (Iran) some 1,400 years ago when invading Arabs overran their country and brought Islam.

The Parsis represent only a speck among the 1 billion population of India, numbering fewer than 100,000, and are declining; but their influence on the country is huge. Within their community you find some of the captains of industry, leading physicians, and other professionals and artists.

Their religion, for which they fled to refuge, once flourished as Persia dominated the world scene. Harking to the founder Zoroaster, it is a moral religion that teaches that earth, water, and fire are sacred. The Parsis' temples feature an eternally burning flame.

These beliefs have led to a unique practice for disposing of the dead. Because earth is sacred, a dead body (considered highly defiling) cannot be buried. Nor can it be cremated or thrown into a river, since fire and water are sacred.

The tower of silence is a round tower where the dead are exposed to the sky. Vultures pick clean the skeleton; the bones fall below. Today in India the vulture population is reduced because of insecticide poisoning. The dead bodies simply rot away under the influence of sun and air.

What a contrast to Jesus' death! Yes, He was laid in the stone-cold tomb. Yes, His followers wept. But He rose again, a mighty victor. He smashed the power of sin. He wiped our slate clean. He canceled the arrest warranty, nailing it to His cross. He disarmed the powers of darkness, stripped them, and marched them naked through the streets.

No tower of silence here! Rejoicing and hallelujahs! Hail to the Chief! The Lord Jesus reigns! Creator of heaven and earth, Savior of humanity, and Conqueror of death! All heaven resounded with the triumphant shout:

> "Lift up your heads, O you gates!
> Lift up, you everlasting doors!
> And the King of glory shall come in" (Ps. 24:7, NKJV).

Manasseh

And when he prayed to him, the Lord was moved by his entreaty and listened to his plea; so he brought him back to Jerusalem and to his kingdom. Then Manasseh knew that the Lord is God. 2 Chron. 33:13, NIV.

Every now and then we hear someone tell the story of the dramatic change in their life after they met Jesus, from drugs and gangs to the Christian walk, and so on. Or we read a book that perhaps goes into lurid detail of the years before Jesus became the writer's Savior and Lord. None of these stories, however, comes even close to matching the experience of Manasseh.

Manasseh, king of Judah in the seventh century B.C., was one of the worst monarchs to rule anywhere, let alone over the people of God. Only 12 years old when he ascended the throne, he reigned for 55 years. We find his story told in 2 Kings 21 and 2 Chronicles 33. The accounts are very similar in describing the king's wickedness, but Chronicles adds intriguing details.

This king followed the idolatrous practices of the surrounding nations, so that the people "did more evil than the nations the Lord had destroyed before the Israelites" (2 Chron. 33:9, NIV). He erected altars to the Baals and made Asherah poles; he worshipped the starry hosts, even building altars to them in the Temple of the Lord. He sacrificed his son in the fire (an abominable practice associated with the worship of the god Molech). He practiced sorcery, divination, and witchcraft. He consulted mediums. "Moreover, Manasseh also shed so much innocent blood that he filled Jerusalem from end to end" (2 Kings 21:16, NIV).

Did you ever hear of such revolting behavior? Surely here was an individual for whom all hope of salvation had long since perished.

Not so fast. Never discount the power of grace. Never give up on a sinner as lost beyond recall. God permitted the Assyrians to overrun the land. They took Manasseh prisoner, put a hook in his nose (bas-reliefs show the Assyrians doing just this), bound him with bronze shackles, and took him to Babylon. And there, wonder of wonders, this sorry excuse for a leader of God's people had a change of heart. "He . . . humbled himself greatly before the God of his fathers" (2 Chron. 33:12, NIV). He prayed—and God heard him.

God always hears us. He turned Manasseh around, and He can turn us around also. Never give up on a sinner, because God never does.

Grace in the Night

On my bed I remember you; I think of you through the watches of the night. Ps. 63:6, NIV.

The great Reformer Martin Luther made it a practice to spend more time in prayer the busier he was. When cares and duties crowded in upon him, he would rise earlier. In the hours before dawn he would spend the watches of the night in communion with the Source of wisdom and strength.

A seeming contradiction here, something that makes no sense to the unspiritual person: the less time he had for prayer, the more time he took for prayer. It's the same apparent paradox represented by the title of Bill Hybels' book *Too Busy Not to Pray*.

The "contradiction" lays bare the essence of the Christian life, which is, at heart, a big contradiction. Paul captures the paradox in 2 Corinthians 12:7-10, where he talks about his "thorn in the flesh" and concludes with "When I am weak, then I am strong." The Source of our wisdom and power lies outside of ourselves. Only as we connect with that Source (which takes time, quiet time) can we live and serve as God would have us.

I am no Martin Luther, but I have come to understand the power of his paradoxical prayer life. As more and heavier responsibilities were laid upon me in Christian service, I too learned that the secret of bearing them is found in the watches of the night. God gives grace in the night—grace for the moment, and grace for the day ahead.

So facing a challenging situation, and waking at 3:00 a.m. (or earlier) with my mind already at work on the day ahead, I learned that instead of tossing around, trying to extract a couple of hours more sleep, it is infinitely better to get up. To spend time with the Word. To take as long as necessary in communion with God, petitioning and listening. To work through what lies ahead in unhurried fashion, letting the Lord sort through the agenda.

Again and again the tangled skein unravels effortlessly. Again and again priorities suddenly crystallize in blinding clarity.

Very often I combine this most precious time with the Lord with a walk. It's dark; the streets are empty, the only vehicle an occasional police cruiser; but the walk is delicious in the cool, serene vigor of the day that is aborning. The whole experience is bathed in communion with a loving Father, with grace. I commend it to you.

The Greedy Mind

There is no one greater in this house than I, nor has he kept back anything from me but you, because you are his wife. How then can I do this great wickedness, and sin against God? Gen. 39:9, NKJV.

Joseph's reply to Potiphar's wife is a classic. The scenario is one that fits a soap opera: the young man and the older woman; the slave and the master's wife, who plots his seduction, waits for the opportune moment, and then strikes. But with the odds stacked against Joseph (the desires of the flesh, the manipulation, the power play), he doesn't act as the script dictates. Joseph turns and flees.

We don't know what Potiphar's wife looked like, whether she was attractive or not. Being the wife of a government official, chances are she was attractive. No doubt she decked herself out in her most alluring clothes and jewels as she moved in to snare the young man she had marked out for conquest. But she may not have been attractive at all. Temptation often works through very ordinary means. Temptation works principally through the mind, whispering that forbidden pleasures are the greatest, stolen waters the sweetest. (Compare Proverbs 7:21.)

A great work from yesteryear, Izaak Walton's *The Compleat Angler,* is ostensibly about fishing. It is; but it is more a meditation on life itself. In one wise saying Walton observes "how poor a thing" will captivate "a greedy mind."

The greedy mind of the fish leads it to bite on a miserable piece of bait dangling in the water. And the greedy mind of the human leads it to bite on the less-than-attractive willing flesh dangling before it.

We see them throughout Scripture, people selling themselves for so "poor a thing." Esau letting his birthright, the privileges of the firstborn, slip away for a bowl of lentil stew. Achan selling his soul for a wretched garment and a wedge of gold. And the ultimate: Judas, one of the twelve, selling his Lord for 30 miserable pieces of silver. Again and again the pattern's the same: the person focuses on the forbidden bait, becomes infatuated, and takes the hook.

But not Joseph, thank God! How did he emerge unscathed from such powerful temptation? Because he knew and loved God and would do nothing—nothing—to dishonor Him.

By His grace, let's live like that today.

Hold On to the Good

Test everything. Hold on to the good. 1 Thess. 5:21, NIV.

I was on my way home from a visit to India. My flight plan coming and going put me through Frankfurt, Germany, so before I left home I rummaged through the travel folder in my drawer and put in my wallet a 10-euro note, adding it to the 100-rupee bill I found there.

The flight into Mumbai (previously known as Bombay) arrived at 1:30 a.m. The departing time was another unearthly hour—2:50 a.m. (The plane simply refueled and went back each night.) So there I was, checking in about 11:00 p.m., in plenty of time to clear security, immigration, and customs. I hardly needed help with my bags, but to give a porter some work I let him carry them and get them cleared in the security area.

By now I had 30 rupees left in my billfold, a fair return for his efforts. But, not uncommonly, he began to complain that he should be given more.

"Give me a 100-rupee note, sahib," he urged.

I tried to shoo him off, but he clung to me like a leech. It was late, and I was tired. I just wanted to get checked in and find a place where I could get my feet up and my head down. Maybe a dollar (worth about 40 rupees) would get him off my back. I pulled out my wallet and—surprise! There was a 10-rupee note that I had apparently overlooked. *It's worth a try,* I thought. I handed it to him. He took it without a word and vanished with a pace that surprised me.

The next morning I understood why. When I went for a little shopping trip at the Frankfurt airport, the 10-euro note was gone from my wallet. Of course. The 10-rupee note is a similar color to the 10-euro bill and about the same size. That porter was handsomely paid indeed—a week's earnings or more!

In the Christian life we need to test everything. Change is good and necessary, both individually and for the church corporately. But not all change is good. We need to be *conservative;* that is, hold on firmly to what really counts.

That's true for the fundamental teachings of Scripture; grace doesn't change them. True, also, for the principles of life that the Bible teaches— integrity, faithfulness, honesty, purity, truthfulness. And true for worship: with reverence and decorum.

Let's hold on to the good.

God of a Second Chance

Only Luke is with me. Get Mark and bring him with you, because he is helpful to me in my ministry. 2 Tim. 4:11, NIV.

Note who is writing: it is the apostle Paul. Many years earlier he didn't want to have John Mark associated with his ministry because Mark had let him down on the first missionary journey. When the going got tough in Pamphylia (a coastal territory in Asia Minor), Mark quit and went home. So later, when Barnabas wanted to invite Mark along on their second tour, Paul would have none of it. The two leaders had such a sharp disagreement that they split; Paul chose Silas and went one direction, while Barnabas took Mark and went elsewhere.

But now Paul, old and a prisoner, with death looming close, has changed his mind. He wants John Mark at his side. He asks Timothy to get him and bring him with him "because," says Paul, "he is helpful to me in my ministry."

When anyone, man or woman, fails in their assignment, we feel disappointed. When a young person fails, I feel doubly sad. Young people have enough critics ready to find fault and waiting for them to fail without giving them grist for their mill.

When a minister fails, the pain is even greater. The saints can abide a person making all manner of mistakes before they come to Christ (at times they glory in lurid details), but watch out after you are baptized. Especially watch out if you are a minister. The saints' willingness to forgive dries up before your eyes.

But John Mark made good. He failed, and failed so badly that Paul didn't want him on the team. But Barnabas gave him a second chance. And he made good! Thank God for the Barnabases in the church—the men and women who don't drag up our failures, and instead give us a second chance.

Not only did John Mark make it in the ministry; so highly respected did he become that his account of the story of Jesus, one of the earliest to be written down, found its place in the canon of Scripture. Think of it: dropout to Gospel writer, quitter to revered leader.

I love stories about second chances, of quitters who become stalwarts, of failures who write Gospels. For they are living demonstrations of what grace is all about.

Grace is all about second chances. And third. And fourth. And fifth. And sixth. And seventh.

The Blessing of Asher

Asher, best blessed of the sons! May he be the favorite of his brothers, his feet massaged in oil. Safe behind iron-clad doors and gates, your strength like iron as long as you live. Deut. 33:24, 25, Message.

A fervent evangelical Christian has set up a company to drill for oil in Israel in the territory occupied by the tribe of Asher. He is sure the promise to Asher—"let him dip his foot in oil" (Deut. 33:24, KJV)—guarantees that oil lies beneath the surface.

I'm not rushing to buy shares in that company. The "oil" that Moses, who pronounced the blessing, referred to certainly wasn't mineral oil. It was more likely olive oil, or oil used for blessing people. Eugene Peterson in *The Message* is closer to the mark with "his feet massaged in oil."

So forget about commercial schemes and focus on the blessing itself. And what wonderful ideas it contains. Look at them—a fivefold outpouring of good things.

First, Asher is "best blessed" of the 12 sons of Jacob. How this was realized we can only speculate. Among the 12 tribes, the two that appear most prominent in Israelite history are Judah, which led to a line of monarchs over the southern kingdom; and Ephraim, which established a dynasty in the north. Reuben, though the firstborn, never rose to leadership. Levi, however, became the priest tribe. But Asher? We don't know of any leader who was an Asherite.

So "best blessed" Asher must have excelled in other areas. And life is more than power and authority. Asher was to be "the favorite of his brothers." I like that! Not the leader, not the clever one, but the one most loved. I would prefer that blessing.

For Asher's feet will be massaged in oil. Ever had a foot massage that goes on and on, pulling every pain out of your body, draining out all the weariness and stress? I have (it was in Romania), and I can identify closely with this blessing. Asher was a fortunate son indeed.

Asher also would be kept safe, as though ironclad doors and gates shut out evil. Does that sound inviting in these troubled times?

Last and best: Asher's strength would be "like iron" as long as he lived. I like the King James Version: "As thy days, so shall thy strength be" (verse 25).

Now, *that's* a blessing to take into this new day.

The Grace of Healing

God said, "If you listen, listen obediently to how God tells you to live in his presence, obeying his commandments and keeping all his laws, then I won't strike you with all the diseases that I inflicted on the Egyptians; I am God your healer." Ex. 15:26, Message.

God desires for us fullness of life, wholeness in body, mind, and spirit. It has been a great error of the church over the centuries to focus on the inner life to the neglect of the physical. Indeed, in the early centuries ideas rooted in Greek philosophy took over in Christianity, ideas that denigrated the body. Out of this aberration developed the monastic ideal, celibacy and mortification of the body. What a far cry from the Genesis account of Creation, where the Lord Himself is the Maker of the human body.

When the Son of God came to earth to show us what God is like and to restore all that was lost by sin, He devoted much of His time to the healing ministry, bringing sight to those who were blind, hearing to those who were deaf, speech to those who could not speak, movement to those with disabilities, and sound mind to the mentally afflicted. Jesus was constantly on the move, and an aura of wholeness trailed behind Him. After He passed through a village, not one sick person remained.

What grace flowed from Jesus, the grace of healing! Think of life in a community in which pain had been vanquished, in which there were no aches and anxieties—and no funerals! Jesus broke up every funeral He attended. Before Him death fled away, because He was the Life-giver.

Indeed, we may say that Jesus' entire work was healing. He made people whole, no matter what their problem. It's interesting that the same Greek word, *sozo*, is used for saving and for healing the body. For instance, when Jairus sends messages imploring Jesus to come and heal his daughter (Mark 5:23), the word for heal is *sozo*, identical with what we find in the passage "The Son of man is come to seek and to save that which was lost" (Luke 19:10).

"I am God your healer," God told the Israelites. And He still is. The most skilled physician cannot heal us; he or she is an agent or minister of the healing God alone effects.

Jesus spent His days mending broken people. He still mends broken people. His grace alone can turn days of darkness into songs of hope and new life. And we who profess to follow Jesus today must also be agents of healing. Whether or not we are involved in medical ministry, our mission is to help broken people find wholeness.

OCTOBER

God of the Unexpected

Before they call, I will answer. Isa. 65:24.

Slowly, slowly over the years I have come to wait upon God. To know, not just in the head (because that's the easier part) but in the heart, that nothing, absolutely nothing, takes God by surprise. What catches us off guard, throwing us into perplexity and consternation, doesn't faze Him. He's the God of the unexpected.

Several years ago I flew into Seattle, Washington, to give a series of talks at a camp meeting. I checked into a motel nearby and commuted back and forth in a rented car. Friends from Seattle heard I was coming and contacted me so we could get together after my duties were completed. After my final sermon Sabbath morning, we would have a picnic lunch, drive to Mount Rainier for hiking, then return to Seattle for supper.

When my secretary made the motel reservation, there had been some uncertainty about room availability for part of my stay, so before the weekend I checked with the desk clerk. She assured me everything was fine.

That Saturday, my last day of the visit, turned out to be unforgettable with the blessing of worship, the blessing of the mountains, the blessing of friends. I arrived back at the motel tired but happy—a perfect day.

Not so perfect. I unlocked the door to my room and experienced total shock. The bed was made up, but everything of mine—computer, clothes, pajamas, toiletries—was gone. Not one thing left. Head reeling, I hurried to the desk. Instead of apologies I got an angry earful. "You were supposed to check out this morning! Another party is waiting to get into that room!"

My response was equally angry; but they showed me that my reservation had ended that morning. And my things? In a cardboard box!

Eventually I realized that it was an honest mistake on their part, and they realized that I wasn't lying. Then they pulled out all stops to find me another room. But every motel within driving distance was booked solid. As I contemplated spending the night in the airport lounge, they came up with an idea—their own trailer at the back of the parking lot. It didn't have light, but I would have a bed for the night. And I did.

The God of the unexpected came through again.

The Still, Sad
Music of Humanity

For He knows our frame; He remembers that we are dust. Ps. 103:14, NKJV.

With all our progress and knowledge, we humans are still very frail. The biggest, burliest football player gets sick, gets hurt, dies. We are dust.

To realize and accept this frailty is a sign of mature thinking. It's simply a realistic assessment of who and what we are. Thus, in "Tintern Abbey" the poet William Wordsworth reflected:

> "For I have learned
> To look on nature, not as in the hour
> Of thoughtless youth; but hearing oftentimes
> The still, sad music of humanity,
> Nor harsh nor grating, though of ample power
> To chasten and subdue."

And another poet, Percy Bysshe Shelley, observed in "To a Skylark":

> "We look before and after,
> And pine for what is not:
> Our sincerest laughter
> With some pain is fraught;
> Our sweetest songs are those
>   that tell of saddest thought."

If we dwelt too long on our frailty, we could be burdened to the point of despair. Except for one saving element—grace. God remembers that we are dust. That this life, infinitely beautiful, is infinitely sad. Grace brings hope. It supplies strength and determination.

Open your Bible anywhere, and you find God acting on behalf of erring humanity. Here is a passage from the days of the kings of Israel: "God was fully aware of the trouble in Israel, its bitterly hard times. No one was exempt, whether slave or citizen, and no hope of help anywhere was in sight" (2 Kings 14:26, Message). This is humanity; this is us.

But read on: "God wasn't yet ready to blot out the name of Israel from history, so he used Jeroboam son of Jehoash to save them" (verse 27, Message). This is deliverance; this is grace.

And God is still the same today. *This* day.

Day of Destiny

But instead he sacrificed himself once and for all, summing up all the other sacrifices in this sacrifice of himself, the final solution of sin. Heb. 9:26, Message.

Some events burn themselves into our memories. For an earlier generation, it was the death of John F. Kennedy. People could tell you where they were and what they were doing when they heard the news of his assassination. For people today, September 11 has become the day of destiny.

It was a Tuesday morning, which meant that the Administrative Committee of the General Conference would meet at 9:00. As I joined the other committee members a few minutes before the appointed hour, someone reported that a plane had crashed into one of the twin towers of the New York World Trade Center. We didn't pay attention to the news—probably a small aircraft had hit the building on a foggy morning.

We started the committee. Fifteen minutes later another piece of news: the other tower had been hit by a second plane. And the events were not accidental; they were part of a terrorist attack.

We tried to focus on business, but then a third report: the Pentagon, only miles from where the General Conference is located, had been hit by yet another plane. And still one other terrorist plane was unaccounted for. Rumor had it that the State Department had been struck.

The committee adjourned—it was impossible to concentrate on the agenda. Members rushed to TV screens and watched in horror as first one tower collapsed and then the other.

Shortly afterward church president Jan Paulsen called a general meeting for all staff. He updated them on events, urged everyone to stay calm, and shared words of assurance from the Scriptures.

September 11. The date itself has become a compound noun standing for the events of that terrible day. It was a day of destiny, a turning point. We sensed in our innermost being that life would never be the same again. For the United States and the world the future would be different, forebodingly different.

When Jesus died on Calvary, that was the ultimate Day of Destiny. History turned on that day—and for the better. For that day Jesus paid the ultimate price for our sins and assured our salvation.

Heaven Is a Local Call

Cast all your anxiety on him because he cares for you. 1 Peter 5:7, NIV.

A story on the Internet tells about a man who travels the world trying to find a way to talk to God. He comes to this big church and sees a telephone on the wall marked "Hotline to God."

"Can I make a call?" he asks.

"It will cost you $4,000."

No way can he afford to make the call. He goes to other churches, other countries. He finds more big churches with hotlines to God. They all charge $4,000 for the call.

At last he comes to Australia and sees a church with a hotline telephone on the wall.

"How much does a call cost here?" he asks.

"Forty cents."

"Forty cents! Everywhere else it's $4,000!"

"Yes. But it's a local call from here."

As you guessed, that story came from Australia. It's a good one, but I hasten to correct it. Heaven is a local call from anywhere in the world.

By His cross Jesus has linked heaven and earth with a fabulous communication network. The network never goes down. It's totally free of interference. You never get put on hold. The line is never busy. Your call always goes straight through. And it's person-to-person.

What a network!

"Prayer," notes Ellen White, "is the opening of the heart to God as to a friend" (*Steps to Christ,* p. 93). She goes on to describe how inviting the call can be. We can lay out all our cares, all our concerns, all our anxieties. Nothing is too small or too big for God to deal with. We can speak to Him just as if He were sitting in the chair next to us, telling Him all that is on our hearts.

> "I tell Him all my sorrows,
> I tell Him all my joys,
> I tell Him all that pleases me,
> I tell Him what annoys."
> —Mary Ann Shorey

Yes, heaven is a local call—anytime, anywhere. Pick up the telephone right now and speak to the Friend who cares so much for you.

Embrace What God Does for You

So here's what I want you to do, God helping you: Take your everyday, ordinary life—your sleeping, eating, going-to-work, and walking-around life—and place it before God as an offering. Embracing what God does for you is the best thing you can do for him. Rom. 12:1, Message.

It's easy to get fixated on the trees and never see the forest. The details of life can become an end in themselves. Then our Christianity deteriorates into rule-bound observances that lack freedom, spontaneity, and joy.

I remember a brief conversation I had with a 94-year-old at a convention. When I complimented her on how well she looked (for indeed she did), I got back a lecture on the evils of ice cream. "I haven't touched that stuff in 63 years!" she exclaimed triumphantly.

I can think of a lot of things more evil than ice cream. And I wonder what the Lord thinks of a religion that focuses on a checklist of do's and don'ts.

But there's the other side of the coin to consider. While we shouldn't get hung up on details, life does consist of details, not just the big picture. That's what Paul emphasizes in the passage for today—our ordinary, everyday life of sleeping, eating, going to work, and walking around. This is our life outside of church, outside of a religious front we may put on to impress the saints.

One definition of religion states that it's what we do when we are alone. That's true—but only part of the picture. Religion, at least in the Pauline model, is also what we do when we are in public. Christianity embraces all of life, our total being in all we do consecrated to the glory of the Lord of grace.

And the way we live as we present ourselves as an offering to God isn't a matter of checking a list; it's embracing what God does for us. From one point of view, we are the ones doing; but the true Actor is God. He works in us to will and to do according to His good pleasure (Phil. 2:13).

Today, let's embrace what God does for us. That means our eyes will be focused not on ourselves but on Him. Eagerly we receive the guidance of His Spirit, joyfully we note evidences of His opening providence, willingly we yield to His Lordship.

Lord Jesus, live out Your life in me today.

The Call to Holiness

God spoke to Moses: "Speak to the congregation of Israel. Tell them: Be holy because I, God, your God, am holy." Lev. 19:1, 2, Message.

L ast century the German theologian Rudolf Otto, in reflecting on the various manifestations of religious experience, wrote a small book that became a classic—in the German, *Das Heilige;* translated into English, *The Idea of the Holy.*

Otto argued (rightly, I think) that the most basic idea of religion is a sense of the sacred. He coined an expression that, in the very sound of the words, evokes the impact of the Holy on us: *mysterium tremendum et fascinans.* Mysterious. Tremendous (powerful). But withal fascinating, attracting us.

Everywhere, in any place and every age, men and women lift their hearts in worship to a superior being. Often their adoration is benighted and, from the standpoint of Christianity, infantile and flawed. Yet Jesus, the Light of the world, shines into their hearts and they reach out, even in faulty ways, after Him.

Throughout the Bible God declares His holiness and calls His followers to holiness. Three times in Leviticus He tells us to be holy because He is holy (Lev. 11:44, 45; 19:2; 20:7). The New Testament picks up the same challenge (1 Peter 1:16).

We must never lose our sense of the holiness of God. True, God wants to be our friend, but He can never be a buddy whom we address as an equal. That is an error into which some Christians, who like to talk a lot about grace, sometimes fall. And one of the saddest spectacles I have witnessed is a preacher who, caught up in the modern entertainment craze, turns his hour in the pulpit into a stand-up comedy act. A minister who doesn't distinguish between the sacred and the profane . . . What a travesty!

The Holy One calls us to holiness. "Be holy," He says. That is both an invitation and an incentive. And the book of Hebrews tells us, "Be holy; without holiness no one will see the Lord" (Heb. 12:14, NIV).

God is forming His people, His people whom He saved by grace, after His image. Day by day—this day—and moment by moment He is fashioning us after the divine likeness, into the burning purity of heart and life that is Himself.

May the Holy One have His way in us today.

The Rocks of Leviticus

In fact, the law requires that nearly everything be cleansed with blood, and without the shedding of blood there is no forgiveness. Heb. 9:22, NIV.

Many Christians, fired up with a New Year's resolution to read through the Bible, see their plans crash and burn on the rocks of Leviticus. The seemingly endless details about offerings and sacrifices, the clean and unclean, and purification rituals wear down the reader, and weariness sets in.

Why all these regulations about sacrifices? Why all this shedding of blood?

Eugene H. Peterson in his introduction to Leviticus in *The Message* suggests an answer: "The first thing that strikes us as we read Leviticus . . . is that this holy God is actually present with us and virtually every detail of our lives is affected by the presence of this holy God; nothing in us, our relationships, or environment is left out. The second thing is that God provides a way (the sacrifices and feasts and Sabbaths) to bring everything in and about us into his holy presence, transformed in the fiery blaze of the holy. It is an awesome thing to come into his presence and we, like ancient Israel, stand in his presence at every moment (Psalm 139)."

So much shedding of blood seems repulsive. The priests were, in essential respects, religious butchers. But through these rituals, which, let us not forget, came from God, God was teaching vital lessons to His people.

First, that sin costs. Sin isn't a light matter, something God dismisses with a wave of His hand. Only those whose moral sensitivities have been dulled can dismiss sin easily.

That's still a lesson for modern people, for us. Sin costs. A lot of people today, especially in the media, try to attract an audience by shocking them. They make light of God, sin, sex; they scorn taboos and taboo topics. But sin still costs.

Second, the way of cleansing from sin requires shedding of blood. No, the blood of bulls and goats, calves and lambs, couldn't purify humanity; sin involves a moral quality, not to be removed by mechanical means. All the sacrifices of Leviticus pointed toward the one great Sacrifice, He who, both high priest and sacrifice, would take our sins with Him to the cross.

Thus, Leviticus taught salvation by faith to the Israelites. God prescribed what the sinner should do to find forgiveness, and the person who accepted God's way obeyed. Yes, the bedrock of Leviticus is grace.

Jubilee!

Sanctify the fiftieth year; make it a holy year. Proclaim freedom all over the land to everyone who lives in it—a Jubilee for you: Each person will go back to his family's property and reunite with his extended family. Lev. 25:10, Message.

Land is a precious commodity. In an agricultural society it provides the basis for livelihood. To lose one's land means to become a nothing, with slavery the only option.

God set up a gracious provision for His people, the children of Israel, as they came to Canaan after centuries in Egypt. They would be farmers, tied to the land; but they must not be severed permanently from owning land. Inevitably, some would lose their land. Because of sickness, tragedy, death, or poor management they would have to sell all they owned, land included. But the land sale would not be forever.

Every fiftieth year all debts were canceled. Every fiftieth year land that had been sold would revert to the original family. Every fiftieth year freedom would ring out. Time to return to family property; time to reunite with family.

This meant that all land transactions had a temporary factor attached. Israel's real estate business was governed by a 50-year cycle. If the jubilee was a long way off, the land would command a high price; if the cycle had almost run its course, a low price.

Think of what the jubilee provision would mean to a family living in poverty, bereft of its land, toiling as slaves. They had hope. The years of grinding labor were sure to come to an end. The jubilee would arrive, and on the tenth day of the seventh month (the Day of Atonement), the trumpet blast would sound, proclaiming freedom.

The principles of the jubilee—release, freedom, return, reunion—are the essence of the gospel. The jubilee is suffused with grace. It was a wonderful idea, a divine idea, the jubilee. Unfortunately, we have no indication that the Jews put it into practice. We can imagine how reluctant wealthy landowners would be to let go of land, to simply turn it over without a penny to its traditional owners. We can imagine how the powerful banded together to deprive the poor. It happens, then and now. Those out of power have a hard time, and true religion is trampled by greed.

But in God's gracious provision, One would come proclaiming freedom, release, return, reunion. He was Jesus, the jubilee incarnate.

King Without a Crown

After Jesus was born in Bethlehem in Judea, during the time of King Herod, Magi from the east came to Jerusalem and asked, "Where is the one who has been born king of the Jews? We saw his star in the east and have come to worship him." Matt. 2:1, 2, NIV.

He sits on a mountainside, a grassy knoll His throne, this king without a crown. Crowds gather around Him—simple folk, poor people, fishermen, and farmers. And He begins to speak—surprising words, startling words, words that set out the principles of the kingdom He has come to establish.

Appearances to the contrary, King He is indeed! Matthew, who paints the scene and hands on to us His words, makes that point clear. The opening line of his Gospel tells us, "A record of the genealogy of Jesus Christ the son of David" (Matt. 1:1, NIV), and he traces Jesus' descent through Israel's famous monarch, David. And Matthew alone records that at Jesus' birth Wise Men came from the east, inquiring, "Where is the one who has been born king of the Jews?" (Matt. 2:2, NIV), which, of course, got the attention of another king, Herod the Great.

The King of the Jews was born not in a palace but in a stable. He was laid not in a royal crib but in a manger. He was attended not by courtiers but by animals. Supreme irony: never did a king enter this world seeming so contrary to expectations.

He was a king without a crown. The only crown ever placed on His head would be one plaited from thorns and thrust there by taunting, hate-filled Roman soldiers. Yet He wore a crown, not of gold and jewels but of infinitely greater worth. He was crowned with love, crowned with grace.

Those who looked for a king who wore a conventional crown looked on this son of David and saw only a peasant. They refused to take seriously His words, his wonderful words of life, refused to be moved by His compassion and miracles. No way could He be a king—He didn't fit the pattern.

But those with eyes to see, those open to God's Spirit, saw in Jesus someone altogether lovely, someone winsomely attractive. They didn't at once call Him king (that seemed too big a stretch), but they knew that in Him they had found someone they wanted to be around, someone they wanted to get to know.

Jesus, be king in my life today!

Christ, All and in All

He set it all out before us in Christ, a long-range plan in which everything would be brought together and summed up in him, everything in deepest heaven, everything on planet earth. Eph. 1:10, Message.

From the flyleaf of a godly woman's Bible comes the following outpouring of love for Jesus, whom she called "Christ, All and in All."

He is my *resurrection* and *life* (John 11:25).
He is my *truth* to cleanse me (John 14:6).
He is my *way* in which to walk (John 14:6).
He is my *Lord* to rule (John 20:28).
He is my *teacher* to instruct (Rev. 3:2).
He is the *root* on which I grow (Rev. 22:16).
He is my *shepherd* to lead (1 Peter 5:4).
He is the *living water* to quench my thirst (John 7:37).
He is the *heavenly bread* to satisfy my soul (John 6:48).
He has a pure white *robe* to cover me (Isa. 61:10).
He has *"meat"* to strengthen me (John 4:32).
He has *medicine* to restore me (Jer. 30:17).
He is my *light* to guide (John 1:9).
He has *gold* to enrich me (Rev. 3:18).
He has *wine* to cheer me (Ps. 104:15).
He has *righteousness* to justify me (Rom. 5:17).
He has *mercy* to save me (Luke 1:22).
He has *grace* to sustain me (Heb. 4:16).
He has *happiness* to crown me (Ps. 146:5).
He is my *song* to cheer (Ps. 40:3).
He is my *solace* in affliction (Ps. 34:19).
He is my sure *refuge* from the enemy (Heb. 6:18).
He is my *prophet* pointing to the future (Acts 3:22).
He is the sum total of all things (Eph. 1:10).

October 11

Man Without a Tux

But when the king came in to see the guests, he noticed a man there who was not wear- ing wedding clothes. "Friend," he asked, "how did you get in here without wedding clothes?" The man was speechless. Matt. 22:11, 12, NIV.

Have you noticed how weddings, no matter how meticulously planned and rehearsed, often fall prey to a last-minute glitch? We were sitting around swapping wedding stories with friends (and what an entertaining hour it was) when someone came up with the following incident that she witnessed. You might say it takes the (wedding) cake.

Everything was ready for the BIG EVENT—bridesmaids' dresses, hon- eymoon plans, reception, and on and on. The groomsmen had been mea- sured for their tuxedos, which had been picked up and brought to the church. Nothing had been left to chance.

But Murphy's Law kicked in. When the groomsmen came to change into their tuxes, they came up one tux short. In collecting the tuxes, some- how one had been left at the store. And it was now Sunday, and the store was closed.

What to do? Someone looked around, especially at the sizes of the groomsmen, and did some fast figuring. And so the wedding started on time, with two groomsmen escorting parents and grandparents of the bride and groom to their places. The groomsmen did their job and slipped out back. After a short pause the wedding processional started, and the cere- mony proceeded. After it was over, again there was a slight pause, and then the two groomsmen reappeared to usher the guests out of the church.

My friend said that throughout the entire event you would have found one man—but not the same one—sitting in his underwear at the back of the church!

Jesus' parable of the wedding banquet also has an element of surprise. In fact, there are a series of surprises. The king throws this big event, but those who are invited turn up their noses. Outraged, the king then tells his servants to go out to the town and round up everyone, good or bad, that they can lay their eyes on. Then the king enters and looks over the scene. One man stands out: he isn't wearing the tux the king provided. And they throw him out.

We're all invited to the big wedding. We really don't belong, but we're invited. We don't know what to wear, but the King provides a tux or a gown—a perfect fit!

Better Righteousness

Unless you do far better than the Pharisees in the matters of right living, you won't know the first thing about entering the kingdom. Matt. 5:20, Message.

When a new president of the United States is elected, he immediately begins the process of selecting those who will help him form the government. Secretary of the treasury, secretary of state, homeland security, and so on—there are many portfolios to be filled, and urgently.

So when the King of heaven comes to earth and commences His rule, what does He do? He sits down on a hillside overlooking the Lake of Galilee and begins to speak to His subjects. Instead of announcing the members of His cabinet ("For foreign affairs, I have selected Peter; for secretary of the treasury, Matthew"), He begins to describe what His kingdom will be like. And He focuses not on what the people under His rule *do* but on what they *are.*

"Blessed *are* the poor in spirit . . ."

"Blessed *are* those who mourn . . ."

"Blessed *are* the meek . . ."

"Blessed *are* those who hunger and thirst for righteousness . . ."

"Blessed *are* the merciful . . ."

"Blessed *are* the pure in heart . . ."

"Blessed *are* the peacemakers . . ."

"Blessed *are* those who are persecuted . . ."

And He goes on to say, "Unless you do far better than the Pharisees in the matters of right living, you won't know the first thing about entering the kingdom" (Matt. 5:20, Message). If the earlier ideas surprised Jesus' hearers, these must have astounded them.

More righteous than the Pharisees—whoever could live up to that? The Pharisees meticulously ordered their lives in strict obedience to the written and unwritten rules of their religion, and Jesus is telling us we have to do better? Impossible!

The Sermon on the Mount isn't a formula for governing a city or a state. It's not about the kingdoms of this world but about *God's* rule, as Jesus' first words make clear: "Theirs is the kingdom of heaven." This is a real kingdom, right now. Jesus rules here, in hearts and lives. He turns everything upside down. Because grace, not power, is the basis.

Tell Someone: "Go Free!"

This is God's year to act. Luke 4:19, Message.

Each of the Gospel writers, following a divinely inspired but separate plan, focuses on a different incident at the start of Jesus' ministry. That incident sets the tone for the particular emphasis the writer will develop.

Thus, Matthew commences the ministry with the Sermon on the Mount, reminding us of Moses on Mount Sinai. In this Gospel, built around five discourses of Jesus that also echo the five books of the Pentateuch, Jesus emerges as the great teacher, the king who goes beyond Moses as He says, "You have heard that it was said . . . but *I* say to you . . ." (Matt. 5:21-44, NKJV).

Mark, on the other hand, begins his account of the ministry with Jesus healing a demon-possessed man in the synagogue during a Sabbath service (Mark 1:21-28). Jesus' actions are powerful and dramatic, leaving the onlookers amazed. This portrayal of Jesus will recur throughout Mark's Gospel. Jesus here is preeminently a man of decisive action who evokes surprise and wonder at every turn.

John's Gospel has yet a different emphasis at the outset. We find Jesus in conversation not with a crowd of people, as in Matthew, but one on one with His first disciples, and especially with Nathanael (John 1:35-51). This pattern persists throughout John's presentation as He builds his Gospel around encounters between Jesus and a series of disparate individuals: His mother, the Pharisee Nicodemus, the woman by the well, the nobleman, the man by the Pool of Bethesda, and so on.

What about Luke? Like Mark, Luke selects an incident in the synagogue on Sabbath morning, but in Nazareth rather than Capernaum. And instead of a miracle, Jesus reads a scripture and delivers remarks that infuriate people rather than amaze them (Luke 4:16-30).

The passage Jesus selected was Isaiah 61:1, 2, where the prophet foretold One who, anointed by God's Spirit, would proclaim good news to the poor, freedom to the prisoners, and recovery of sight to the blind. He, Messiah, would announce, "This is God's year to act."

The people of Nazareth didn't appreciate Jesus; they knew Him, and He was no Messiah! But He was. And His jubilee message still rings out across the land: "This is God's year to act. Go free!" Today, my friend, tell someone, "Go free!"

The Kingdom of the Gentle

"The wolf and the lamb will feed together, and the lion will eat straw like the ox, but dust will be the serpent's food. They will neither harm nor destroy on all my holy mountain," says the Lord. Isa. 65:25, NIV.

On a visit to my hometown of Adelaide in the state of South Australia, I caught a glimpse of God's ideal society, the kingdom of the gentle. Adelaide lies on a plane between a range of low mountains to the east and the seashore. As a boy I roamed those hills with my brothers. We'd see rabbits, foxes, and an occasional kangaroo. I had no conception of the life that once frequented the area.

A professor of mathematics set out to restore a portion of the hills to the way it was some 200 years ago. (The first settlers came to the state in 1836.) He bought out a dairy and began to refresh the land with native trees and plants. Around the whole area he constructed a stout fence to keep out the predators—foxes, feral cats, and dogs. And then he introduced species that had once inhabited the environment but had almost become extinct. He didn't provide food for the animals, merely a safe place to live and multiply.

The guided tour of the sanctuary starts just before dark because most of the animals we would see are nocturnal. As the light faded, flashlights marked the path. And soon the land came alive with such a variety of creatures, large and small, as I had never imagined. Caught in the flashlight beams, startled into sudden movement, were a range of hopping creatures, some as small as rats, others—wallabies—the size of small kangaroos. They looked surreal, something out of a Steven Spielberg movie, toy creatures to wind up and they hop away.

Here I encountered a host of new names of kangaroo-like animals: pademelons, potoroos, euros, woylies, bilbys, bettongs, and so on. Delightful creatures. Fun creatures. And defenseless creatures, easy prey for the foxes, cats, and dogs introduced to the continent by the settlers.

The kingdom of this world is violent. Violence surrounds us; movies and TV feed the appetite for still more. And given the nature of society, many argue that the organized violence that is war and the legal violence that is execution are both inevitable and necessary.

Maybe so. But the kingdom of heaven, where the gentle Jesus rules (even now), is altogether other. Grace and violence have nothing in common.

October 15

Not Just Happy—Blessed!

You're blessed when you're at the end of your rope. With less of you there is more of God and his rule. Matt. 5:3, Message.

Our text for today graphically illustrates the seeming contradictions of the life of the believer, the life of grace. According to usual thinking, to be at the end of one's rope is the last place we'd want to be. It means distress, perplexity, and fear. But the kingdom of heaven, where Jesus rules in love, turns everything upside down. It reverses expectations; it surprises; it shocks.

Grace shocks.

Happiness is the sought-after by people in the kingdom of this world, an elusive goal. But as Jesus, sitting on the hillside by the lake, lays out the Magna Carta of His kingdom, He doesn't talk about happiness. He offers something far greater—blessedness.

Happiness comes from the verb "to hap." When the sun shines bright and the birds sing, our spirits soar. But when the dark clouds roll in and the cold wind blows and we start to shiver, our feelings take a nosedive. Happiness comes and goes. Happiness is fleeting.

But nine times Jesus says "You're *blessed*" as He delivers the Sermon on the Mount. The word He uses, *makarios,* has an ancient history. Long before the New Testament was written, way back in the time of Homer, it designated the life of the gods, who lived in ease and sport atop Mount Olympus. Later it was broadened to include the happy dead, those who had left the cares of this life. And then *makarios* developed further. It described the fortunate among the living, those who, being wealthy, did not need to toil with their hands and who had resources to protect them when sickness or loss should strike.

But Jesus says to the farmers, fishermen, and artisans; to the housewife, the child: "You are blessed." Not shall be blessed in the future life—you even now are blessed.

Jesus doesn't promise us a rose garden; He offers something better. Jesus doesn't dangle the elusive goal of happiness before us; He has far more for us.

Jesus offers us Himself. He invites us to come to Him and to take upon ourselves His yoke. It's easy; it's light. As we take Him into our lives as Savior and Lord, His words become reality. They're not a gigantic hoax. We are blessed with the transcendent joy of His grace.

The Poor in Spirit

Blessed are the poor in spirit, for theirs is the kingdom of heaven. Matt. 5:3, NIV.

The Sermon on the Mount is all about grace, as the opening words of Jesus make clear. Grace is the operative principle in the kingdom of heaven. However much politicians and leaders laud the Sermon on the Mount, don't hold your breath to see them put it into practice. Any president who counsels the country to turn the other cheek when the foe is at the door is heading for impeachment; and any candidate for office who renounces pride and power will be fortunate if even his own family members vote for him.

But in the kingdom of heaven grace, not power, rules. The citizens of this kingdom are happy to be "poor in spirit"—poor in the spirit of self-seeking and self-aggrandizement that characterizes life in the world. But not poor in God; in Him they are rich. They are poor in themselves but rich in Christ, in whom all the treasures of earth and heaven reach their pinnacle.

It has ever been thus. Those who feel they have everything—who are full, who sense no need—don't "get" grace. Grace begins in human experience with a deep realization of our hunger, our thirst, our insufficiency, our lostness, our need of help outside of ourselves. Only when a person realizes they can never make it on their own are they ready to receive grace.

But then grace *does* flow to them. Forgiving grace. Transforming grace. Grace all-sufficient. Amazing grace. Theirs *is* the kingdom of heaven. Even now. In their lives Jesus reigns as Lord.

During Jesus' ministry on this earth the common people heard Him gladly (Mark 12:37). Harlots and tax collectors went into the kingdom ahead of priests and Pharisees (Matt. 21:31). That has been the pattern throughout the centuries. As Christianity has spread, it has been welcomed by the slaves, the outcasts, the marginalized—the poor in spirit.

Celsus, a famous critic of Christianity, mocked Jesus and His followers. "What a singular teacher the Christians have," he sneered. "All other religious leaders say, 'Come to me, you who are worthy,' but *this* man says, 'Come to me, you who are beaten and broken by life.' And so, being taken at his word, he is followed by the rag, tag, and bobtail of humanity, trailing behind him."

And the Christian Origen replied, "Yes; but He does not leave them the rag, tag, and bobtail of humanity. Out of material you would discard as worthless, He fashions men!"

Grace for the Mourners

Blessed are those who mourn, for they will be comforted. Matt. 5:4, NIV.

This simple saying, the second of the Beatitudes, speaks powerfully to both Christian and non-Christian alike. In it we hear comfort for those in sorrow, but also rebuke for much of what passes as entertainment today, and the promise of a new world order that will reverse the priorities of the present one.

God cares for those whose hearts are breaking. This is the most basic meaning of the text. Jesus Himself became "a man of sorrows, and familiar with suffering" (Isa. 53:3, NIV). He who wept with Mary and Martha at the tomb of their dead brother Lazarus weeps with us in our grief. He is our great high priest who knows and understands how we feel (Heb. 4:14-16).

If we but permit Him, He will turn our mourning into a blessing. Suffering never leaves a person the same; it either draws us closer to the Lord or drives us from Him. Some of the saintliest men and women of past ages (and still today) are those who, yielding their all to Christ, have experienced the power of the second beatitude. And in the ranks of the unbelievers are those who point to the sufferings or death of loved ones as reason for their rejection of faith.

Eugene H. Peterson renders Jesus' words thus: "You're blessed when you feel you've lost what is most dear to you. Only then can you be embraced by the One most dear to you" (Matt. 5:4, Message). How true! As dear as a loved one is to us, Jesus is even dearer.

Ellen White's comment also is too good to pass by: "The trials of life are God's workmen, to remove the impurities and roughness from our character. Their hewing, squaring, and chiseling, their burnishing and polishing, is a painful process; it is hard to be pressed down to the grinding wheel. But the stone is brought forth prepared to fill its place in the heavenly temple. Upon no useless material does the Master bestow such careful, thorough work. Only His precious stones are polished after the similitude of a palace" (*Thoughts From the Mount of Blessing*, p. 10).

Jesus' words also rebuke much of the so-called comedy of our times. Irreverent, coarse, and savage, it trades on shock value—get a laugh at any cost. "Change your laughter to mourning and your joy to gloom," the Scriptures counsel those caught up in such "entertainment" (James 4:9, NIV). For the day is coming that will reverse everything: when those who mourn now shall laugh, and those who laugh now will mourn (Luke 6:21, 25).

Owners of Everything That Can't Be Bought

You're blessed when you're content with just who you are—no more, no less. That's the moment you find yourselves proud owners of everything that can't be bought. Matt. 5:5, Message.

The usual translation of this text, "Blessed are the meek, for they shall inherit the earth," has led to jokes and mocking. In the world we know the meek don't inherit anything; they get trampled on. People value assertiveness and aggressiveness. Meekness they despise because it is weak.

But from the biblical worldview, the worldview of grace, meekness isn't weakness. The most outstanding person in the Old Testament was Moses, who was said to be the meekest person on earth (Num. 12:3). And the New Testament centers on the person and work of Jesus Christ, who did not grasp at divine status but condescended to become a human being, and "became obedient to death—even death on a cross!" (Phil. 2:8, NIV).

The thinking that meekness means becoming a doormat totally misses the mark. Rather than being a nobody, the meek man or woman is a *strong* person who accomplishes much, as did Moses, who led his people to freedom, or Jesus, who saved the entire human race. The more a person is emptied of self, of pride, ambition, and grasping for fame and personal glory, the more God can use him or her to do great things. That is to say, the meeker the greater.

"Human nature is ever struggling for expression, ready for contest; but he who learns of Christ is emptied of self, of pride, of love of supremacy, and there is silence in the soul. Self is yielded to the disposal of the Holy Spirit. Then we are not anxious to have the highest place. We have no ambition to crowd and elbow ourselves into notice; but we feel that our highest place is at the feet of our Savior. We look to Jesus, waiting for His hand to lead, listening for His voice to guide" (*Thoughts From the Mount of Blessing*, p. 15).

This means having a realistic sense of our strengths and weaknesses, of being content with just who we are. Our self-worth no longer depends on what we do but on who we are, for we are sons and daughters of God. We are of infinite value to God.

And the meek do inherit the earth after all. Not only the better land to which we're headed, but even now the riches of the kingdom of grace— "everything that can't be bought."

The Community of the Hungry

Blessed are those who hunger and thirst for righteousness, for they will be filled. Matt. 5:6, NIV.

My father, born near Stockholm, Sweden, went to sea in his youth. He sailed the world, first on sailing ships, later on steam. Twice he went around Cape Horn. He used to tell exciting and amazing stories about his years before the mast. On one dreadful voyage the corrupt ship's purser, in cahoots with the captain, did not take on enough supplies. They pocketed the unspent money.

The ship left the port of Hamburg, Germany, sailed west in the Mediterranean, through the Strait of Gibraltar, and into the Atlantic. As they made their way south, they encountered the doldrums, where the sails hung limp, waiting for a puff of wind. Days passed into weeks and weeks into months for the desperate crew trapped in the ship, hungry day and night. When scraps of leftover food and rotten potatoes were emptied onto the deck, they flew upon them.

Hunger, and thirst even more so, become the focus of their beings. The most basic existence comes down to finding something to put into our aching bellies and water to quench thirst.

Hungry people dream about food. The Bible mentions it: "A hungry man dreams that he is eating, but he awakens, and his hunger remains" (Isa. 29:8, NIV). Rarely in my fortunate life have I gone to bed hungry; but when I have, I have dreamed about food, and awakened with food on my mind.

I wonder: how hungry are we for God? And if we were hungry for Him, would we dream about Him and wake up with Him on our minds?

Notice that this fourth beatitude, like all the others, is addressed in the plural. Jesus speaks to His followers as community, not as individuals. His people, the citizens of the kingdom of heaven, are the community of the hungry—hungry for God.

Most of the people on the hillside that day were common folks. They ate only two meals each day, and very simple ones at that. The mention of food would have released their salivary juices. But Jesus spoke of food more precious than bread and fishes. He offered the bread of heaven, the true manna, the food of the kingdom.

Himself.

The Merciful

Blessed are the merciful, for they will be shown mercy. Matt. 5:7, NIV.

The Beatitudes show a development in conception. In the first four—the poor in spirit, the mourners, the meek, the hungry and thirsty—the emphasis falls on *attitudes*. Although from the world's standpoint these people are nobodies, broken, losers, and not worth a second glance, God calls them "blessed." He blesses them because they are open to Him.

In the next three beatitudes we see a movement away from attitude toward *action*, from being to doing. Whereas the first four describe the sort of people who can receive Messiah's blessing, these three begin to describe how such people will live in the world.

First of all, the citizens of Jesus' kingdom are merciful. The word, a powerful one, connotes acts of kindness and graciousness, as in the good Samaritan's deed of caring (Luke 10:25-37). To be merciful means more than having a forgiving nature; it means going where the people are—people in need, people who are hurting, people in despair. It means going to them and bringing hope and kindness. The merciful are merciful because they *do* mercy.

We cannot be citizens of Jesus' kingdom and live as hermits or monks, fleeing the world and its needs. I once visited the rock-carved temples of an ancient religion. Into these recesses men retreated from the world to spend their days contemplating the enigma of human existence. They lived lives of celibacy, prayer, and self-denial in cells hewn from the rock. But inside the meeting halls were frescoes, worked in color. Although moisture and smoke had destroyed much of the work, after 20 centuries the voluptuous scenes—dancing, drinking, scantily clad women—were still evident.

"How is it," I asked the guide, "that these monks decorated the walls with such pictures?"

His reply: "Since they were shielded from temptation in the world, they had to have scenes like these to develop character!"

How unlike the way of Jesus! We who follow Him do not contemplate mercy—we practice it. We do not meditate on purity of heart—we live it in everyday relations. We do not talk about peace—we seek to bring peace, from God and among men and women.

"To the appeal of the erring, the tempted, the wretched victims of want and sin, the Christian does not ask, Are they worthy? but, How can I benefit them?" (*Thoughts From the Mount of Blessing*, p. 22).

The Pure in Heart

Blessed are the pure in heart, for they shall see God. Matt. 5:8, NKJV.

O f all the Beatitudes, this one is my favorite. It soars to the ultimate blessing—to see God. "They shall see His face, and His name shall be on their foreheads," promises the Book of Revelation in its final chapter (Rev. 22:4, NKJV). And so the ancient prayer of Moses, "Please, show me Your glory" (Ex. 33:18, NKJV), will be fulfilled, not for just one person but for all God's people.

In the sixth beatitude Jesus links this ultimate blessing to an ultimate trait of character: "Blessed are the pure in heart." His words are an invitation and a challenge. They startle us because they rebuke the way people all around us live, and the way we tend to live. They call us higher, Godward, reminding us that "godliness—godlikeness—is the goal to be reached" (*Education*, p. 18).

Jesus is concerned with the fountain of our life, our heart. The world looks on appearances; He looks at our heart. And as the world is full of filth in deed, word, and imagination, He calls for purity in the fountain.

Purity of heart extends beyond moral purity, although it includes that. Purity of heart denotes a life that puts God first, that is focused on Him, devoted to Him and His glory, a heart for which Charles Wesley prayed:

"O for a heart to praise my God!
A heart from sin set free,
A heart that always feels Thy blood,
So freely shed for me.
A heart resigned, submissive, meek,
My dear Redeemer's throne,
Where only Christ is heard to speak,
Where Jesus reigns alone.
A heart in every thought renewed,
And full of love divine,
Perfect, and right, and pure, and good,
A copy, Lord, of Thine."

God of grace, give me such a heart today!

Blessed Are the Peacemakers

Blessed are the peacemakers, for they shall be called sons of God. Matt. 5:9, NKJV.

Blessed are the peacemakers, for warmongers are proliferating. Angry voices and violent actions surround us. Some of the harshest words come from people of religion, Christians included. They condemn those who see issues (and God) in a different light than they do. They call for exclusion, excommunication, elimination.

Blessed are the peacemakers, for they pour oil on troubled waters in the church. They discern the difference between the eternal, the unchanging, and the temporary, the changeable. They stand for the right but are ready to flex in other matters. When opposing parties dig in their heels and clench tight their jaw, they gently lead to the middle position. They restore harmony.

Blessed are the peacemakers, for they follow in the steps of Jesus, the Prince of Peace. "He Himself is our peace" (Eph. 2:14, NKJV). He has reconciled us to God and broken down the dividing wall of hostility, the enmity that separates White from Black, Asian from European, Hutu from Tutsi, male from female. "Peace I leave with you, My peace I give to you; not as the world gives do I give to you" (John 14:27, NKJV) was His parting promise to His followers.

Blessed are the peacemakers, for they shall be called the children of God. "You're blessed when you can show people how to cooperate instead of compete or fight. That's when you discover who you really are, and your place in God's family" (Matt. 5:9, Message). Because the peacemakers are children of God, they do the works of their heavenly Parent. They're like Him; they bring peace, they spread peace, they live peace.

What has this beatitude to do with grace? Much, in every way. Peace is the fruit of grace. "Grace to you and peace from God our Father and the Lord Jesus Christ" is Paul's customary greeting in his letters (e.g., Rom. 1:7). Grace the root, peace the fruit.

"The grace of Christ received into the heart subdues enmity; it allays strife and fills the soul with love. He who is at peace with God and his fellow men cannot be made miserable. Envy will not be in his heart; evil surmisings will find no room there; hatred cannot exist. The heart that is in harmony with God is a partaker of the peace of heaven and will diffuse its blessed influence on all around" (*Thoughts From the Mount of Blessing*, pp. 27, 28).

The Blessing
We Shouldn't Seek

Blessed are those who are persecuted because of righteousness, for theirs is the kingdom of heaven. Matt. 5:10, NIV.

The eighth and final beatitude echoes the first one: "Blessed are the poor in spirit, for theirs is the kingdom of heaven" (Matt. 5:3, NIV). "Blessed are those who are persecuted because of righteousness, for theirs is the kingdom of heaven."

These eight blessings summarize the Sermon on the Mount. They range from what the citizens of the kingdom of heaven *are* (the first four—poor in spirit, mourners, meek, hungry), to how they *live* (the next three—show mercy, wholly devoted to God, make peace). And how does the world relate to people who differ so radically? It persecutes them. It puts them down or throws them out or speaks lies about them to discredit them.

But there's something that sets this eighth beatitude apart from the others. We shouldn't seek it. The persecution comes of itself—it's inevitable because truth and error, light and darkness, good and evil, cannot be reconciled. It's shocking to contemplate but true: the first son born on earth became the world's first murderer. "And why did he [Cain] murder him [Abel]? Because his own actions were evil and his brother's were righteous" (1 John 3:12, NIV).

In the early centuries of the Christian church some people sought persecution. One was a leader named Ignatius, who was taken to Rome to be thrown to the lions. Along the way he wrote letters in which he anticipated his fate and reveled in imagining it. If the wild beasts refused to attack him, he said, he would incite them to anger so they would leap upon him.

Ideas like those aren't bravery but twisted thinking. Persecution *comes*; it should not be invited. But when it comes—for come it surely will to all who live godly lives (2 Tim. 3:12)—the Master's promised blessing will come too. "Rejoice, and be exceeding glad, for great is your reward in heaven" (Matt. 5:12).

On a trip abroad I talked in private with the leader of a church in which followers of Jesus have suffered much for their faith. In a secluded garden, away from listening devices, he told me, "I fear for the day when we will be free. Under the present conditions our people are earnest and faithful. I fear the materialism that will come with freedom."

He understood the truth of the eighth beatitude.

The Color of Money

For the love of money is a root of all kinds of evil. 1 Tim. 6:10, NIV.

What would you do if you stumbled onto a fortune and no one was looking? Say, $200 million? Would you keep it, or turn it in?

A pair of United States Army sergeants faced this situation on April 18, 2003, during the invasion of Iraq. In the chaos after the fall of Baghdad they found two sheds, filled with metal boxes. And inside each box was US$4 million in cash, US$230 million in all. The soldiers turned the money in. "These guys are absolute heroes," said their commander.

But other soldiers caught the money fever. They ran through the bushes, looked in old buildings, turned over garbage dumps. And they found a building, just like the one they'd heard about. They broke in and discovered 50 more metal boxes, like the ones from earlier that day. The boxes were jammed tightly together. Inside them was another $200 million, in $100 bills.

And then the power of the money took over. "There was a moment that everything turned . . . evil. The air was thick. . . . The looks had changed. You could see that everyone was just out for themselves," recalled a sergeant, who was later kicked out of the Army because of his role in the looting.

Soldiers stuffed wads of cash in their pockets. Two men dumped boxes of money into a nearby canal, intending to retrieve the $8 million later. Others stashed another $600,000 in loose bills inside a palm tree.

Then an officer, fresh from locking up the money from the previous find, showed up. He knew immediately that something was wrong. Right in front of him, 20 feet away, was a wad of cash stuck in the fork of a tree, in plain view. He recovered the money from the tree and began an investigation. Three boxes that had been hidden were recovered, one no longer full. All told, $780 million came to light from four different finds. The money was flown out of Iraq, but not before a military driver tried to take $300,000 on the way to the airport.

An old song used to intone, "Money is the root of all evil." But the problem lies not with money per se, but with the *love of money.* The color of money reveals our true colors.

We who follow the Lord Jesus, He who came to give, not grasp, know that the only riches we will retain are those we impart to others.

I Shall Not Want

The Lord is my shepherd; I shall not want. Ps. 23:1.

Everyone has their favorite psalm, but there is one universally acclaimed for its appeal: Psalm 23, the shepherd's psalm. Among the many meditations and reflections on it, a writer of a previous generation, G. Henderson, wrote: "What is it I shall not want? The finger of faith runs over the keyboard, brings out 11 distinct notes. Listen to them."

Updating Henderson's language and elaborating his points, we get the following:

I shall not want *rest,* for God makes me lie down in green pastures. The grass is lush and cool. I lay down my head and relax, become like a rag doll.

I shall not want *refreshment,* for He leads me by still waters. A long draught of cool, clear water—what better to quench my thirst and revive me.

I shall not want *guidance,* for He leads me. For my relationships, my family, my future—I need help outside myself. Praise God, He is my guide!

I shall not want *peace,* for I fear no evil. Dark is the night, powerful the forces of darkness, but He is more powerful. Hand in His, I go forward boldly, confidently, into each new day.

I shall not want *friendship,* for God is with me. He promises: "I will never leave you nor forsake you" (Heb. 13:5, NKJV). Dearer than any human companion is my Lord, closer than any fleshly tie His love.

I shall not want *comfort,* for God's rod and staff sustain me. He bids me grasp His hand for support. In every place, at every moment, He is there for me.

I shall not want *nourishment,* for He prepares a table for me. He invites me into His banquet hall, and His banner over me is love.

I shall not want *joy;* for He anoints my head with oil. Like the sacred oil that ran down Aaron's beard, His blessings flow over me, never failing.

I shall not want *anything,* for my cup runs over. Jesus is all I need, now and forever.

I shall not want *happiness,* for goodness and mercy follow me. What more could I ask?

I shall not want *glory* hereafter, for I shall dwell in the house of the Lord forever. Just to be there, just to see Jesus—that will be glory.

Graeme's Witness

Do not let your hearts be troubled. Trust in God; trust also in me. John 14:1, NIV.

I have a longstanding friend in Australia whose life has been vastly different from mine. Because of a physical affliction he is restricted to the limited life afforded by a group home. During a recent visit I looked him up. He expressed disappointment that his Christian witness is so limited. "I share materials with the other people here," he said, "and try to talk to them about spiritual things. But no one seems to be interested."

Graeme distributes little messages of faith to those around him. During this visit he shared several with me:

> Absolutely loving,
> Infinitely true.
> Understanding all things,
> Understanding you.
> Absolutely tender,
> Exquisitely near,
> This is God our Father—
> What have we to fear?

And also this:

> Make a little fence
> Of trust around today.
> Fill the space with loving work
> And therein stay.
> Look not through
> The sheltering bars upon tomorrow;
> God will help thee bear
> What comes of joy or sorrow.

I think of Graeme in the confines of his group home. His pleasures are few, his opportunities limited. But he keeps the faith. He trusts. And so he does witness. His faithful life and these words of trust go onward and out to God's glory.

Prisoners and Pizzas

The Spirit of the Lord is on me, because he has anointed me to preach good news to the poor. He has sent me to proclaim freedom for the prisoners and recovery of sight for the blind. Luke 4:18, NIV.

Some time ago an Australian prison siege ended in an unusual manner. A group of inmates seized control of the reception area of the maximum-security prison in Hobart, capital of the southern island state of Tasmania. Demanding better treatment and improvements to the jail, the prisoners compiled a list of 24 items. They took a guard and held him hostage until their demands were met.

But after two days the siege ended quietly. No rush by an assault team brandishing shields and heavy firepower. No tear gas. No shooting. A negotiator secured the release of the guard unharmed for the delivery of 15 pizzas. Apparently none of the 24 earlier demands eventually proved to be as pressing as the need for a take-out meal!

Desperate people, people who think they have nothing to lose, do desperate acts. But the calm patience of a mediator (and the prospect of pizza after two days without food) can turn even desperate men around.

In several places in the Bible we find God's followers in prison, not because of wrongdoing but for obeying conscience. The young man Joseph, falsely accused by Potiphar's wife, was incarcerated. Many centuries later the prophet Jeremiah was placed under house arrest because he predicted Jerusalem would fall to the Babylonians. In the New Testament John the Baptist was put behind bars and eventually executed after he denounced King Herod Antipas' marriage to the monarch's sister-in-law. The apostle Paul was jailed several times. He wrote many of his letters while in chains. In the book of Hebrews we read of unnamed Christians imprisoned for their faith (Heb. 10:34; 13:3). And the Bible closes with the Apocalypse, given by the Lord to John, exiled to the island of Patmos (Rev. 1:9).

Among all these Bible characters, not one ever rioted, took hostages, or demanded better treatment. They trusted in God; they endured as seeing Him who is invisible. In fact, we all are prisoners, believers and nonbelievers alike. Our warden is harsh and cruel; Satan is his name. But Jesus proclaims freedom to the prisoners: release from sin's shackles, a new beginning. And one day the cruel jailer himself will be locked up (Rev. 20:1-3).

The Case of the Jaywalking Chicken

O Jerusalem, Jerusalem, you who kill the prophets and stone those sent to you, how often I have longed to gather your children together, as a hen gathers her chicks under her wings, but you were not willing! Luke 13:34, NIV.

The lowly chicken, whether floundering in flight or waddling on the ground, lacks grace. No lover's sonnets will ever invoke it; no artist will make it the subject of an oil painting. It seems to exist for strictly utilitarian purposes—laying eggs and providing food for carnivores. Pity the poor chicken! It will never be lauded like the bluebird, the robin, or the lark; it will never soar like the eagle. All it gets is scorn, as in the inane question "Why did the chicken cross the road?"

Now the joke has gone one step beyond. A chicken has been ticketed (I am not making this up) for jaywalking! The ticket was issued by a sheriff's deputy in Kern County, California. Actually, the chicken didn't get the ticket, presumably because it refused to accept it, but the chicken's owners did. The offender was charged with impeding traffic in Johannesburg, a rural mining community near Ridgecrest, some 220 miles northeast of Los Angeles.

So now we know why the chicken crossed the road: it didn't know that jaywalking is illegal. But that's not all. The community where the chicken broke the law has a population of only 50 residents! With crowds of people like that, a jaywalking chicken obviously would create traffic jams.

The chicken's owners say they were cited because they complained that sheriff's deputies weren't doing their job in controlling off-road-vehicle riders. No, replied the guardians of the law; chickens on the roadway were the problem,

Jesus once likened His ministry to that of a mother hen. Addressing the Jewish people, He wept that His desires and efforts to gather them under His care were rejected. He still weeps. He weeps over the world. He weeps over us.

We truly are stupid. Stupid as chicks that wander away from the mother hen, refuse to heed her warning clucks of impending danger, her call to return to the safety of her sheltering wings. Stupid as jaywalking chickens. But grace is for stupid people like you and me.

The Song From Eternity

In the beginning was the Word, and the Word was with God, and the Word was God.
John 1:1.

Mysterious, intriguing, profound, the opening lines of John's Gospel captivate our attention. The language itself is simple, both in English and in the original Greek text, but it sweeps us off our feet. It is a song that echoes from eternity.

"In the beginning . . ." Our minds race back to the first words of the Bible. "In the beginning God created the heaven and the earth" (Gen. 1:1). The beginning in the Gospel, however, stretches back beyond the birth of earth, of our solar system. Before the world was, before the universe existed, before time, before all things—this is the beginning before all beginnings that we can imagine.

We are creatures of time and space, we human beings. Even if we reach the biblical fourscore mark, even if we attain a century of years, the span of our days is but a speck against the span of eternity. Look at the universe itself, incomprehensible in its vast reaches, with stars so distant that their light, traveling at 186,000 miles per second, takes millions of years to reach our planet; so distant that eons ago they burned out but their light that we see kept on its long, long journey until it came into view.

And the beginning that the apostle John writes of is even further back, before all this. Let's be sure of this point John is hammering home. The Word is no newcomer on the scene of the ages. Go back as far as you can stretch your minds, and you will find the Word.

The Word entered time and space. He pitched His tent among us, took on human flesh. John will shortly talk about this and spend the rest of his Gospel describing the glory of the incarnate Word, who was "full of grace and truth" (John 1:14). This Word made flesh, whom people called Jesus, looked just like any other person. But He wasn't. He came from way, way back, from eternity.

In any consideration of Jesus of Nazareth, the ultimate—the critical—question is: Was Jesus only a man, or was He *more?* John informs us from the get-go that He was more, much, much more! He is from eternity. He is God.

Throughout history people have wondered if God or gods existed, have sought to make contact with them, to appease them, to placate them. John says, Yes, God exists. From all eternity. And God became flesh. He left eternity and entered our time and space. He came to save us.

Jesus.

318

Creator of All

Through him all things were made; without him nothing was made that has been made.
John 1:3, NIV.

The eternal Word, He who is the great communicator of the Godhead, is also the agent of creation. We are used to thinking of Jesus, the Word made flesh, as our Savior. Less commonly do we live in realization that He is our Creator also. Yet He is. John affirms that "without him nothing was made that has been made." Paul goes further: "For by him all things were created: things in heaven and on earth, visible and invisible, whether thrones or powers or rulers or authorities; all things were created by him and for him" (Col. 1:16, NIV).

Such a view transforms the way we look at the world around us. The natural word with its dazzling array of trees, plants, flowers, and herbs; with its amazing variety of animal life, from amoebas to elephants, from hummingbirds to whales—He made it all. It didn't just happen; it's His creation. So let us respect it and handle it as stewards entrusted with its care.

And especially people: they are the summit of His creative activity. He made us a little lower than the angels, in His image, Godlike. By His act of creation He conferred a dignity upon every man and woman born into this world. True, the image of God has been well-nigh obliterated by sin, but traces remain. The person who scorns another human scorns the Creator; the person who harms another human one day will have to give account to the Creator.

And the bottom line of this great truth that the Word created everything is this: He made *me* also. I am special. I have value. I have a divine origin, no matter how lowly the circumstances of my birth. I have a divine destiny, for He wants me to live forever in His presence.

Because we bear the stamp of the divine image, we possess the will and ability to "create" also, albeit on a much lower level. Some people make wonderful music; I cannot. Some people make furniture, build houses; I cannot. The closest my efforts approach creativity is through writing. For me, writing has been a lifelong hobby. It gives me much satisfaction. And I have noticed an interesting phenomenon: what I write takes on a life of its own. Every reader interprets my article or book according to their lives. They find meaning there that I did not consciously include. If I protest, "But I didn't *mean* that!" they reply, "Well, that's how *I* read it!"

In a small way, like God and us. He made us, but He lets us go our own way.

The Triumph of the Light

The Life-Light blazed out of the darkness; the darkness couldn't put it out. John 1:5,
Message.

Never has, never will—the darkness can't put out the Light. At
times the dark feels so dense that you think you can touch it.
It's impenetrable, seemingly totally beyond the Light; but the
Light comes and dispels it.

I am an optimist. Every now and then I meet or hear from people terribly concerned about the state of the world. Everything has gone to pot,
they say; never have things been so bad. They can see only worse times
ahead. Sometimes their negative outlook is applied to the church. The
church has become corrupt and is getting worse; even worse times loom
on the horizon.

But the darkness can't put out the Light. Never has, never will.
Throughout the ages, in the midst of evil and ignorance as dark as midnight, God has always had those who love and serve Him, people who
shine like candles, dispelling the gloom.

So it was at the time before Jesus began His ministry. The people lived
in darkness, note the Scriptures (Matt. 4:16). But on those who dwelt in the
shadow of death a bright light arose. First, John the Baptist, whom Jesus
called a "burning and shining lamp" (John 5:34, NKJV). Then Jesus Himself.
He was, and is, the Light of the world. And so the period of gross ignorance
and bondage, to sin and the devil, gave way to the era of unsurpassed light.

The deepest darkness still comes just before the dawn. When all hope
seems gone, help is just around the corner.

In the nineteenth century a party led by the explorers Robert Burke
and William Wills set out from Melbourne to attempt to make the first
crossing of Australia, south to north. Eventually they reached Cooper's
Creek, deep in the outback. Here the party stayed put, as Burke and Wills
went on, attempting to reach the sea. Those left behind waited and
waited—but their leaders did not return. At last, concluding that Burke
and Wills had perished, they broke camp, first burying a cache of food beneath a tree that they emblazoned with one word: "DIG."

Just after they left, Burke and Wills showed up and found the supplies. But the leaders and the rest of the party never did find each other,
and Burke and Wills eventually perished. So near, and yet so far!

Never forget it: the Light still shines and always will.

NOVEMBER

The Man From the Desert

There was a man sent from God, whose name was John. John 1:6, NKJV.

He stood tall, the man from the desert. Bronzed by the glare of the Judean wilderness, his eyes keen and piercing, he was used to living alone, to speaking alone—a lone voice.

God sent him. Born of parents advanced in years, Zechariah and Elizabeth, who had long since given up hope of a child. He was a miracle child. God brought him into being; God had a message for the times, and he would be the person to deliver it.

His life, like the One greater whom he was raised up to proclaim, was cut off at high noon. But short though it was, it burned like a Roman candle, lighting the darkness of first-century Palestine. "He was the burning and shining lamp, and you were willing for a time to rejoice in his light," said Jesus of John the Baptist (John 5:35, NKJV).

For a while John was hugely popular. Crowds came out to hear him from Jerusalem, from all Judea, from the region around the Jordan—and to be baptized for the forgiveness of their sins (Matt. 3:5). Even Pharisees, scrupulous in religious observance, and Sadducees came out to the happening in the desert. Even soldiers and tax collectors (Luke 3:12, 14).

So great was the popular enthusiasm that some people wondered if the Baptist were the long-awaited Messiah. The religious hierarchy in Jerusalem took notice and sent a delegation, asking, "Who are you?" (John 1:19, NKJV).

But John, light though he was, was not the Light. He "came for a witness, to bear witness of the Light, that all through him might believe" (verse 7, NKJV). John knew his role; he never claimed more for himself than what God intended. Some of his disciples grew resentful when Jesus came on the scene and the crowds around John dwindled. But not John. "He must increase, but I must decrease," he nobly told them (John 3:30, NKJV).

That can be a bitter pill to swallow, to see your popularity ebb away. An even harder situation to handle gracefully is to find yourself the target of official wrath because you tell the truth. That happened to John. He found himself incarcerated for speaking out against King Herod Antipas' adulterous liaison with his brother Philip's wife.

This lone figure from the desert died alone in Herod's dungeon. A wasted life? Not in God's eyes! "There was a man sent from God, whose name was John."

A Man for the Century

That was the true Light which gives light to every man coming into the world. John 1:9, NKJV.

Among the luminaries of the twentieth century none shines brighter in my estimation than Albert Schweitzer. Winner of the Nobel Peace Prize, this gifted individual earned doctorates in three totally different fields—theology, music, and medicine. But I salute him not for his towering academic achievements, but for his life. Schweitzer gave up a brilliant career to found a mission hospital in French Equatorial Africa.

In theology Schweitzer is known for his classic that appeared in Germany in 1906 and later in English under the title *The Quest of the Historical Jesus*. For about 150 years the best minds of Germany had poured intense energy and speculation into finding an answer to the question What was Jesus, the Jesus of first-century Palestine, *really* like? Schweitzer's masterpiece critically examined 91 "lives" of Jesus from this period. With devastating insight he showed how writer after writer, claiming to recover the "real" Jesus, painted a portrait created in his own image. In effect, Schweitzer's book pronounced "Ichabod" on the whole endeavor.

In music Schweitzer brought to prominence the works of Johann Sebastian Bach. We can scarcely comprehend it today, so revered is Bach, but without Schweitzer he might be lost amid the dust of the eighteenth century.

Yet at the height of his fame Schweitzer left it all—the acclaim, the security of academia, the comforts of his native Germany. Left it all to start a hospital in the steaming jungles of Africa. Why?

The final paragraph of his massive *Quest* gives the clue. "He comes to us as one unknown, without a name, as of old, by the lakeside, he came to those men who knew him not. He speaks to us the same words, "Follow thou me!" and sets us to the tasks which He has to fulfill for our time. He commands. And to those who obey him, whether they be wise or simple, he will reveal himself in the toils, the conflicts, the sufferings which they shall pass through in his fellowship, and, as an ineffable mystery, they shall learn in their own experience who he is."

If you want to know Jesus, take Him at His word. Obey Him. Follow Him—wherever He leads you. Yes, even today.

Drifting

Therefore we must give the more earnest heed to the things we have heard, lest we drift away. Heb. 2:1, NKJV.

On a blustery April day two boys, ages 17 and 15, went sailing off Sullivan's Island, South Carolina. The United States National Weather Service warned small boats to stay off the water, but Josh and Troy nevertheless set out in a 14-foot sailboat.

Very soon they realized they were in trouble. They tried to swim to shore, pulling the boat behind them. People on the beach did not hear their shouts. The current steadily drew them away from the shore, and within hours they were out to sea. Without food or fresh water, at the mercy of wind and water, they knew their plight was desperate. Hours lapsed into days. The sun scorched them relentlessly. Sharks circled the sailboat, waiting to strike.

The pair quenched their thirst with seawater and slipped into the ocean to cool off, but sharks chased them back onto the boat. At night they used a single wetsuit to keep warm. All alone in the vast Atlantic Ocean, at one point the teens thought they had drifted clear across and were nearing the coast of Africa. Instead, they were about 100 miles north. By the sixth day their last hope was waning. Fifteen-year-old Troy asked God to "take him."

Then, just hours later, fishermen spotted the boys and plucked them from the water. Sunburned, dehydrated, and exhausted, they were transferred to a Coast Guard vessel where they received medical attention—and made the phone call to anxious parents.

"We were praying for a miracle, and we got one," said the Coast Guard commander. And when Troy's father received the call from his son, he started screaming, "It's my boy; it's my boy! He's been found; he's been found!"

Miraculous deliverance. Plucked from the waters of death when all hope seemed gone. A story of grace.

Also a story about drifting. Like Troy and Josh, at times we set off on our own, heedless of the warnings of bad weather. Before long we are way out to sea, far from land. And the sharks circle, waiting to strike.

Sometimes we're drifting—and don't know it! The only safe course? Treasure the Message; hold it close.

Saved by a Stray Dog

Can a woman forget her nursing child, and not have compassion on the son of her womb? Surely they may forget, yet I will not forget you. Isa. 49:15, NKJV.

C an a woman forget her nursing child?" the Lord asked through the prophet Isaiah. It's a rhetorical question, the implied answer being "No!" For a mother to abandon the fruit of her womb seems impossible, incomprehensible.

Yet the impossible, the incomprehensible, is happening more and more in our time. In many countries, including "advanced" ones such as the Untied States, infants are turning up on doorsteps, outside hospitals, and even in dumpsters.

What terrible circumstances would lead a woman to do such a thing? What desperation, what sense of hopelessness, would drive a mother to such an unnatural act? Only God, who knows and understands, can plumb the depths to which these poor women descended.

Sometimes these tragic stories have a happy ending; often they do not. From Nairobi, Kenya, however, comes a tale with a difference. A stray dog found a newborn baby abandoned in a forest. The dog apparently carried the baby across a busy road and through some barbed wire to her litter of puppies. The infant, clad in tattered clothing, had been left in a plastic bag. Weighing seven pounds three ounces, she was taken to a hospital and put on antibiotics. At last report she was stable and responding to treatment. Health workers called the infant Angel. No one came forward to claim her, but as word of the wonderful rescue got out to the public, donations of diapers and baby clothes began to arrive.

After the Lord asked the question "Can a woman forget her nursing child?" He went on: "Surely they may forget, yet I will never forget you." More faithful than mother love, stronger than father love, is His love for us.

"What stronger or more tender language could have been employed than He has chosen in which to express His love toward us? He declares, 'Can a woman forget her sucking child, that she should not have compassion on the son of her womb? yea, they may forget, yet will I not forget thee' (Isa. 49:15).

"Look up, you that are doubting and trembling; for Jesus lives to make intercession for us" (*Steps to Christ*, pp. 54, 55).

The World Didn't Even Notice

He was in the world, the world was there through him, and yet the world didn't even notice. John 1:10, Message.

Across the face of the globe, one name is uttered every day far more than any other. Only the Lord can count how many millions, or billions, of times it falls from people's lips. Jesus Christ.

But sad to say, most often His name is used carelessly. People drop it as a swearword, even in lewd contexts. Could it be that while the world tries to forget Jesus, tries to erase Him from its uneasy conscience by making His name a byword, He is never far away? that every effort to drown out His appealing voice succeeds only in making it louder?

The Word became flesh. He who made the world came into the world. And, most astonishing, the world didn't even notice. Such is the mystery of sin, the power of evil to blind.

The world didn't notice because it didn't want to notice. It chose not to notice.

Just like today.

G. A. Studdert Kennedy captured the poignancy of Jesus' rejection, anciently and today, in his poem "Indifference."

"When Jesus came to Golgotha they hanged Him on a tree,
    They drave great nails through hands and feet, and made a Calvary;
    They crowned Him with a crown of thorns, red were His wounds
        and deep,
    For those were crude and cruel days, and human flesh was cheap.
    When Jesus came to Birmingham they simply passed Him by,
    They never hurt a hair of Him, they only let Him die;
    For men had grown more tender, and they would not give Him pain,
    They only just passed down the street, and left Him in the rain.
    Still Jesus cried, 'Forgive them, for they know not what they do,'
    And still it rained the wintry rain that drenched Him through and
        through;
    The crowds went home and left the streets without a soul to see,
    And Jesus crouched against a wall and cried for Calvary."

How to Become a Christian

Yet to all who received him, to those who believed in his name, he gave the right to become children of God. John 1:12, NIV.

Here we find the simplest formula for becoming a Christian: receive Jesus. Just open your life to Him, let Him be your Savior. Let Him be Lord of your life. Receive Him in His love. Receive Him in His forgiveness. Receive Him in His transforming power. Receive Him in His abiding presence. Receive Him in His all-sufficient grace.

Many people, especially those who oppose Christianity or who were brought up to attend church and abandoned it when they became adults, see Christianity in negative terms. Jesus, to them, gets in the way—in the way of fun, having a good time, being yourself and all you can be. Christianity means giving up. It's a series of "don'ts" and guilt trips and stern-looking people who criticize and condemn.

No, says John the Beloved. No way! Christianity isn't a losing but a getting. Not a giving up but a receiving. It's true that when we receive Jesus our lives undergo a change. Not because He orders us to conform to His set of rules, but because our attitudes, desires, and motives change. We *want* to be like Him; we *want* to live like Him. Receiving Him means that He fills our life.

Receiving Jesus is like falling in love. How often do you notice some young fellow who, smitten by a young woman, seeks to be in her presence at every opportunity. See how habits change. Maybe he was always late for everything, but now he is on time—even early—to meet her. He was careless about how he looked. Now he shaves first thing in the day, keeps his clothes pressed and neat, always wants to be at his best.

Many years ago a famous preacher gave a sermon titled "The Expulsive Power of a New Affection." In terms of today's headlines the title sounds pretty heavy, but the chief idea of the sermon comes through: a new love drives out old ways. We're chugging along through life, reasonably content with where we're going. But then the "new affection" comes into our lives—a new person, a vision of what might be, of a life much richer and grander, more beautiful. And the new expels the old. That's the way it is when we receive Jesus.

Pixie in the Store

But when the chief priests and scribes saw the wonderful things that He did, and the children crying out in the temple and saying, "Hosanna to the Son of David!" they were indignant. Matt. 21:15, NKJV.

Intent on Friday afternoon grocery shopping, I turned into the fruit aisle of the supermarket. It was empty except for a little girl, a pixie pushing her miniature shopping cart. She was going down the aisle, very serious and focused in her work.

I headed for the shelf with golden Delicious apples; she ended up right next to me where the red Delicious apples were displayed. Barely able to see into the bins, she had to stretch her little hand to pull out fruit for careful inspection and stowing in the plastic bag she'd nonchalantly plucked from the roller.

As I was placing another apple in my plastic bag, the bag slipped and went *bump* against the edge of the shelf. "Careful!" she admonished. It was incongruous, a pixie giving orders to a man at least 10 times her age.

Swallowing the laughter rolling inside me, I replied, "That was close! Almost lost it."

Now the ice had been broken. "Do you do the shopping in your house?"

"Yes; my wife is actually in the supermarket today, but usually I do the shopping."

Big smile. "Usually guys don't like to shop."

"I know. I used to hate it. I do it to help my wife, who works full-time. And now I like it."

"So do I. I think it's *fun*."

From nearby a voice called out "Tracy!" and she responded. Flashing me a smile, she said goodbye and slipped away. Just then Noelene came along and asked what it was all about. I told her about the encounter that, it was obvious to her, had elated me.

Jesus too was elated that last Sunday of His life when He heard the children crying out "Hosanna to the Son of David!" in the Temple. The religious leaders weren't happy, not with His taking charge in the Temple. This was *their* territory, after all!

They tried to vent their anger against the weakest element—the children. "Do you hear what these are saying?" they demanded to Jesus. But Jesus simply said, "Yes. Have you never read, 'Out of the mouth of babes and nursing infants You have perfected praise'?" (Matt. 21:16, 17, NKJV).

Jesus defended the children. He still does.

Conspiracy of Kindness

Give away your life; you'll find life given back, but not merely given back—given back with bonus and blessing. Giving, not getting, is the way. Generosity begets generosity. Luke 6:38, Message.

During the dark days of 1940, as Hitler's forces overran Europe with seemingly unstoppable power, a light of grace shone bright and brave. It was held by a Japanese diplomat who found himself at a moment of destiny, with the fate of thousands of lives in his hands.

Chiune Sugihara's father had mapped out a career in medicine for him, but Chiune didn't want to be a doctor. When he went in to write the entrance examination for medical school, he deliberately failed the test. His father found out why he had failed, and, furious, refused to help the young man get an education.

So Chiune made his own way. He worked to gather funds, enrolled in university, and majored in English. Seeing an advertisement for diplomatic service, he won a scholarship over a large number of others, and began to train to serve his country. Fluent in several languages, this handsome, polished diplomat began a career that seemed marked for distinguished achievements. In Manchuria he negotiated an important deal with Russia. Then, as war broke out, he was sent to the Baltic state of Lithuania to gather intelligence on troop movements.

By 1940 Hitler had singled out the Jews for extermination. With the Nazi forces cutting off escape to the west and Russian armies closing in from the east, time was running out. The Jews looked for a place of refuge and found the Dutch possession of Curaçao in the Caribbean, where no visa was needed. But first they would have to reach Japan—which meant they needed a Japanese transit visa to cross Russia.

Hundreds of desperate Jews pleaded with Sugihara. Without permission from Tokyo and by working 18-hour days, he issued more than 2,000 visas, writing them up to the last minute as the train took him away to a new assignment.

At the close of the war, when Sugihara returned to Tokyo, he was removed from the diplomatic corps. This learned, gifted man, this man of kindness and bravery, was forced to work at menial jobs to support his wife and family. For many years Sugihara refused to talk about his actions. At last, pressed to explain why he had disobeyed orders at no benefit to himself, he struggled to understand the question. He simply said, "You do what is right because it is right."

The God-begotten

These are the God-begotten, not blood-begotten, not flesh-begotten, not sex-begotten.
John 1:13, Message.

The Light came into the world, but the world turned its back on the Light. Instead of coming to the Light, its response was "Put out the Light!"

But not everyone; not the whole world. Some turned to the Light. And something marvelous happened: the Light, which indeed exposed their flaws, also covered their flaws. The Light had a wonderful, regenerating, making-over effect.

"But whoever did want him, who believed he was who he claimed and would do what he said, he made to be their true selves, their child-of-God selves" (John 1:12, Message).

True then, true now. The majority of people go their own way, even many who profess to be Christians. But some still come to the Light. Some still discover their true selves, their child-of-God selves.

God is our home. Only when we come home do we become whole persons. These are the God-begotten, those who come home. God made man at the Creation; God makes man again at the new creation. Male and female He made them, in His image; men and women He makes them again, in His image. "But we all, with unveiled face, beholding as in a mirror the glory of the lord, are being transformed into the same image from glory to glory, just as by the Spirit of the Lord" (2 Cor. 3:18, NKJV).

Christians are a new race. We are separate and distinct. Our race, however, doesn't depend on genes. This new race doesn't define itself by "blood." In fact, the "blood" of all the races on earth mixes in the blood of this new race. What constitutes this race is just one factor: we are the God-begotten.

Not blood nor "flesh." Not human will—not its ambition, its striving, its fierce demand—gives entry into this race. "That which is born of the flesh is flesh, and that which is born of the Spirit is spirit" (John 3:6, NKJV). Not the desire for progeny, not sexual activity or fertility clinics. Only one way.

The God-begotten.

Healing Leaves

On each side of the river stood the tree of life, bearing twelve crops of fruit, yielding its fruit every month. And the leaves of the tree are for the healing of the nations. Rev. 22:2, NIV.

I have been raking leaves. Every fall brings this activity to our yard, where a stand of tall oak trees produces an abundant harvest. I look forward to this time; I love the musty smell of this carpet of red and yellow, black and orange. And I am always glad when the last of the 37,492,187 (est.) leaves has been laid to its rest.

American poet Robert Frost wrote about gathering leaves in his native New England:

> "Spades take up leaves
> No better than spoons,
> And bags full of leaves
> Are light as balloons....
> But the mountains I raise
> Elude my embrace,
> Flowing over my arms
> And into my face."

This man had been there. This is the real stuff. You have to try to gather in this ocean of lightness to appreciate his words.

The leaf job at the Johnssons, on average, takes about 20 hours. A year of great abundance requires more work, longer time. Noelene and I handle it all, working together, or separately if travels take us away from home. We gather the leaves into piles, haul the piles away to a corner of our lot, and bring out the mulcher. Usually the cutting and shredding takes 10 to 12 hours and covers us in the grime of leaf dust.

But that mulch pile—it's the secret of our garden. Wetted down, soil mixed in, it goes to work in the midst of winter. By spring that mulch will nourish and nurture the entire yard. The leaves of autumn come back in brilliant colors, vibrant shrubs, and trees.

And, the Lord assures us, in the earth made new He will provide healing leaves.

Christ is the tree of life. His grace heals the nations, heals the people, heals us. He sets us free from our spiritual diseases.

Jesus, Exegete of God

No one has ever seen God, but God the only Son, who is at the Father's side, has made him known. John 1:18, margin, NIV.

In describing how Jesus the Son reveals God the Father, John uses an interesting verb. Translated as "has made him known," the verb is *exegeomai*, which means "to lead forth," "to unfold [in teaching]," "to reveal," "to interpret." It's the word from which we get exegesis (the interpretation of Scripture), to exegete (verb—to interpret) and exegete (noun—the interpreter of Scripture).

The Son, says the beloved John, is the Exegete of God. He interprets God for us, not only by showing the meaning of the sacred writings, given through the Holy Spirit, but by revealing God in Himself. Seeing Jesus, we see God; knowing Jesus, we know God.

Jesus made the same claim for Himself. When Philip asked Him, "Lord, show us the Father and that will be enough for us," He replied, "Don't you know me, Philip, even after I have been among you such a long time? Anyone who has seen me has seen the Father" (John 14:9, NIV). On another occasion He told the disciples, "No one knows the Son except the Father, and no one knows the Father except the Son and those to whom the Son chooses to reveal him" (Matt. 11:27, NIV).

Want to know what God is *really* like? There's only one Interpreter who will give you a true picture: Jesus, the Exegete of God. People may say this or that, trundle out their long arguments and convoluted reasoning; but forget all about that and just go to Jesus. Let Him reveal the Father to you.

There are thousands of exegetes of Scripture, millions of exegetes of God. Almost everyone believes in God or "god"; all interpret Him in their own way.

But only one exegesis counts: that of the Son, Exegete of God. Read what He tells us about God in the four Gospels. And better yet, study and meditate on His life—and death! There we find God revealed.

And what a God! A God tenderhearted and loving, gracious and compassionate. A God we can trust, who is on our side, who will never let us down.

Full of grace and truth.

God of the Pieces

God made my life complete when I placed all the pieces before him. When I cleaned up my act, he gave me a fresh start. 2 Sam. 22:21, Message.

Second Samuel 22 is a long psalm that was written, according to the opening verse, by David after the Lord delivered him from the hand of Saul and from all his enemies. The song rings with thanksgiving and gratitude as it exalts Yahweh as "my rock, my fortress and my deliverer" (verse 2, NIV).

David had come through stormy waters. His career had blossomed early. His dramatic victory over the giant Goliath propelled him to the national stage and made him the object of popular songs. He quickly advanced to a key post in the king's army; then Saul gave his daughter's hand in marriage. The young man became a celebrity. Everyone began to talk of him as the future king of Israel.

Then the bubble burst. Saul, jealous of his popularity and success, turned against him. In a mad fit he attempted to kill him. David had to flee for his life. In a short time he went from dining at the king's table to holing up with a bunch of malcontents in the cave of Adullam, the leader of 400 men "in distress or in debt or discontented" (1 Sam. 22:2, NIV). What a ragtag army! What a comedown!

David's life was in pieces. He had lost everything—but not God. God was his rock, his fortress, his deliverer. He placed all the pieces before Him, and God made his life complete.

Friend, do you feel like your life is in shreds? Place all the pieces before God. He can put them together; He can make you whole. The day that stretches ahead may seem daunting. You wonder how you can just get through it. Right now, turn your day over to God.

A couple verses further along, David sings, "God rewrote the text of my life when I opened the book of my life to his eyes" (2 Sam. 22:25, Message).

God the Mender, the one who puts us back together, is also God the Author. He can rewrite the script. Maybe all you see for the story of your life is a bad ending. You don't want to think about it. Open the book to God. Let Him change the text. He loves happy endings.

Saving Righteousness

For in the gospel a righteousness from God is revealed, a righteousness that is by faith from first to last, just as it is written: "The righteous will live by faith." Rom 1:17, NIV.

A long while ago an earnest young man tried everything the church of his day had to offer, and nothing worked. A new religion was born.

Martin Luther, gifted intellectually but troubled in spirit, renounced the world and its pleasures to follow the sheltered life of the cloister. A monk of the Franciscan order, he tortured his body as he tried to find peace with God. Prayers, fastings, penances, vigils—he was unrelenting in his quest.

"I was a good monk, and I kept the rule of my order so strictly that I may say that if ever a monk got to heaven by his monkery it was I," he later wrote. "If I had kept on any longer, I should have killed myself with vigils, prayers, readings, and other work."

Then he got the chance to visit Rome. Elated, he contemplated all the sacred sites and relics deposited there that could confer merit to a seeking soul. But they failed to bring the comfort he longed for. Later he said that he went to Rome with onions and brought back garlic.

The church prescribed confession, and confess he did. For hours on end, wearing out the patience of his confessor. But in the still of night he'd remember something he hadn't confessed; or worse, what if there were other misdeeds that he couldn't recall?

The church also prescribed the mystic way: cast yourself into the ocean of God's love. But when Luther contemplated Christ coming in judgment, he could not love Him. "Love God? I hated him!" was his despairing response.

Then he was assigned to teach Scripture at the University of Wittenberg. Starting with the Psalms, he encountered the cry of dereliction that Jesus uttered on the cross: "My God, my God, why have you forsaken me?" (Ps. 22:1, NIV). That was the cry of Luther's heart! He finished Psalms and moved on to Romans, then Galatians. Wrestling to understand Paul's meaning of "righteousness," he at length discovered that "the justice of God is that righteousness by which, through grace and sheer mercy, God justifies us through faith."

Luther was delivered, and the Reformation was born.

Wedding in the Sky

Let us rejoice and be glad and give him glory! For the wedding of the Lamb has come, and his bride has made herself ready. Rev. 19:7, NIV.

Every now and then the media carries stories of people getting married in exotic places, such as under water. But no wedding that I have heard of was more surprising than the one that took place on Monday, May 30, 2005—atop Mount Everest!

At 29,035 feet (8,850 meters), Everest if the highest point on Planet Earth. Even in summer the thin air is bitingly cold, and fierce winds rake the summit. The mountain is a killer; hundreds have lost their lives trying to conquer it. But two young Nepalese climbers conquered Mount Everest: Moni Mulepati, 24, and her fiancé, Pem Dorjee, 23. With the weather turning treacherous, they briefly took off their oxygen masks and donned plastic garlands as they exchanged vows.

No organ, no procession, no attendants for this wedding. Only a white carpet of snow and a breathtaking view. But there were guests— some friends who climbed with them and took pictures. Because of the perilous conditions, the ceremony was kept brief, only 10 minutes. Then the newlyweds and their friends headed down the mountain and back to Kathmandu, surprising their parents with the news.

The wedding was unconventional, not just for its locale. The bride is from the Newar community, and the groom is a Sherpa, an unusual pairing in a country where most marriages are arranged by parents and people tend to stick to their castes. "With our interracial marriage we also wanted to give the message that caste and race have no barriers when it comes to marriage," said Dorjee, the groom.

What a couple! What pluck! What a wedding—a wedding in the sky!

But the grandest wedding is soon to take place. It will be at a locale far beyond this earth; it will be at the most desired place in the universe. No dangers there; no need for a quick ceremony and a hasty retreat.

Soon and very soon Jesus will take His bride, His beautiful bride. She will wear white, pure white, the fine cloth of His righteousness (Rev. 19:7, 8). What a day! Let's plan to be there.

Jesus the Pearl

Again, the kingdom of heaven is like a merchant looking for fine pearls. When he found one of great value, he went away and sold everything he had and bought it. Matt. 13:45, 46, NIV.

The merchant was a seeker. He bought and sold pearls; he traded only in the best. And one day he found the most beautiful pearl he had ever seen—big, perfect in form, lustrous. It was incredible, almost too wonderful to be real.

He wanted to own that pearl! But a pearl like that didn't come cheap—the price was huge, out of his reach. But oh, how he wanted that pearl! He wracked his brains. He went through his books. He figured and figured. And at last he had a way to make it happen. If he sold off this asset and that, cashed in all his bonds, put his shares on the market, scraped together every last penny—yes, he could just do it! All his other pearls would have to go, his home, his boat, his SUV—everything!

But he would have *the* pearl. And that was all that mattered.

Do you know value when you see it? Have you found Jesus, the pearl of supreme worth? Will you give up anything and everything to have Him?

"Christ Himself is the pearl of great price. In Him is gathered all the glory of the Father, the fullness of the Godhead. He is the brightness of the Father's glory and the express image of His person. The glory of the attributes of God is expressed in His character. Every page of the Holy Scriptures shines with His light. The righteousness of Christ, as a pure, white pearl, has no defect, no stain. No work of man can improve the great and precious gift of God. It is without a flaw. In Christ are 'hid all the treasures of wisdom and knowledge' (Col. 2:3). He is 'made unto us wisdom, and righteousness, and sanctification, and redemption' (1 Cor. 1:30). All that can satisfy the needs and longings of the human soul, for this world and for the world to come, is found in Christ. Our Redeemer is the pearl so precious that in comparison all things else may be accounted loss" (*Christ's Object Lessons*, p. 115).

But notice the paradox of grace. Grace comes to us as a gift, altogether underserved, absolutely unearned. And yet, as in the case of the merchant, it claims our all. So grace isn't "free," after all? Yes—and no. Grace is for all, without money and without price. But only those who receive it, receive Jesus, find it. And when Jesus takes over, He possesses us wholly. He is our Lord!

The Preacher
Who Can't Say "Jesus"

Not that I speak in regard to need, for I have learned in whatever state I am, to be content. Phil. 4:11, NKJV.

By any measure David Ring is a successful minister of the gospel. This nondenominational evangelist has spoken in more than 6,000 churches and on national television. Every year he receives some 400 invitations from congregations who have heard of the inspiration his messages bring.

Yet this preacher says of himself, "I can't even say 'Jesus' properly." His words are slurred, and he walks with a limp. When he eats, his hand shakes violently. David developed cerebral palsy when his brain was cut off from oxygen for 18 minutes at birth. He grew up feeling rejected, enduring the taunts of other kids about his funny speech and funny walk.

But he knew one person loved him. With one person he could always find a place of acceptance and security. With her, his mother, he was safe.

Then tragedy struck. His mother contracted cancer and died. Fourteen-year-old David Ring wanted to die too. Life seemed too hard to endure. He was an orphan (his father had died earlier) and desperately alone in the world. But God sent a beam of grace into this sad, lonely life. One day David went to church and discovered Jesus. Previously he was sure God didn't love him, because he'd been born with cerebral palsy. Now he learned that he was precious to Jesus, just as he was.

His attitude changed; his life changed. From that point he went on to do a series of "impossible" things: finish college, get married, and father children (four of them). And, perhaps most remarkable of all, fulfill the divine calling to be a minister of the gospel.

"Look at me," he says. "I have cerebral palsy. What's your problem?" He challenges people to quit whining and start sharing, to count their blessings and let the Lord lead them to new and deeper levels of service.

He likes to quote Paul's words about being content (Phil. 4:11), following immediately with verse 13: "I can do all things through Christ who strengthens me" (NKJV). That's the story of David's life. As he says, every one of us limps into the kingdom. But when we get inside, we will *run!*

The Dragnet

Again, the kingdom of heaven is like unto a net, that was cast into the sea, and gathered of every kind. Matt. 13:47.

When I was a boy, I spent many hours by the seashore. A relative owned a dragnet, and often my brothers, all older than I, would organize a netting trip to the ocean. We would carry the net out to sea in a rowboat, feed it into the water, and then wade ashore, hauling in the net by each end. Dragging the net up on the beach, we would stoop over the harvest of the sea.

As more and more of the net came from the water and only a few yards were left, excitement would mount. What strange sights, dredged from the ocean bed, would meet our eyes? We found a marvelous conglomeration of animal and vegetable life. Crabs and fish, shrimps and octopuses, slimy creatures and oozy leaflike streamers, along with sand, seaweed, and mundane objects—the dragnet gathered them all in.

For many years now I have been "catching" people instead of fish, but how like the harvest from the sea is the church of the living God. Christians come off no production line; they bear no common stamp to set them apart from the rest of humanity. They are Black, Brown, and White; they are rich, poor, and middle-class; they are laborers, professionals, and businesspeople; they are young, middle-aged, and old; they are female and male. And they come from every continent.

We must jealously preserve this individuality. We are strong collectively as we are strong separately. Some members emphasize one aspect of healthful living; some stress a particular facet of doctrine. This variety is good, as long as we refrain from a spirit of judgmentalism and pull together in the task God has assigned us. My brothers and I used to sort out the good fish from the bad by the sea, but in the church that work is assigned to the angels, not to us (see Matt. 13:49, 50).

In Revelation we read that waters are a symbol of "peoples, multitudes, nations and languages" (Rev. 17:15, NIV). The net of God's last message is dredging these waters. From them will emerge at last the people of God who will dwell with Him forever. That will be the glorious harvest of the sea.

Ordinary Grace

But without a parable He did not speak to them. And when they were alone, He explained all things to His disciples. Mark 4:34, NKJV.

The parables of Jesus have a distinctive character. Scholars have combed through Jewish and other writings, but they have never found teachings that match Jesus' teachings. Similarities, yes; but Jesus' parables stand apart.

His parables aren't teaching aids any more than they are quaint tales with a moral. Although couched in simple language and easy to grasp on the surface, they have an existential quality, an immediacy that still strikes us today. We find ourselves drawn into these stories; they speak to *us* and challenge us to decision.

The first and most obvious point to notice about the parables is how *ordinary* they are. A number of them draw on the natural world: the seed that falls in different types of soil; weeds that grow along with the wheat; the tiny seed that grows into a large bush; and the stages in the growth of a plant. Others take everyday happenings and weave a simple story around them: the fishermen dragging their net to shore and sorting the good from the bad; the traveler mugged on the road to Jericho; the son who leaves home and "blows" his fortune; weddings; two people who go up to the Temple to worship; day laborers; a lost sheep; a crooked manager; a lost piece of silver; a corrupt judge; heart attacks; and so on.

Nothing fanciful here. No talking animals, monsters, or bizarre happenings. Everything is predictable. Except that the parables aren't predictable. The conclusion defies our expectations. The first become last, and the last first. Because the parables, seemingly so ordinary, are about the kingdom. The ordinary conceals the extraordinary.

The parables are all about grace, because that's the essence of Jesus' life—and death. That's what the kingdom of God is all about—God's rule in the hearts and lives of men and women who accept His offer of new life, here and now.

And the parables teach that God works through the ordinary, the everyday. He works through nature; He works in human hearts. He works through commonplace occurrences at work, at school, at home, at church. No need to go somewhere else to find God. He's right here with us, now, anywhere we open ourselves to Him.

The General Store

He said, "Then you see how every student well-trained in God's kingdom is like the owner of a general store who can put his hands on everything you need, old or new, exactly when you need it." Matt. 13:52, Message.

By chance I came across an old general store in a little town in mid-America. It was no longer used as a store (it sold quick food), but you could still see where the soda fountain had been and the shelves that had once been stocked with food items.

It reminded me of Hamer's, on Mahatma Gandhi Road, Poona, where we shopped for groceries when we lived at Spicer College in India. Hamer's was incredibly cluttered, but it had everything. You didn't try to find an item yourself: you put in your order, and the clerks scurried off to fill it, climbing ladders, disappearing into recesses, moving items, but always presenting your with a box of good things, just as you hoped for.

I was back in India recently, and walked down Mahatma Gandhi Road and sought out Hamer's. Only after I'd gone the length of the street and back did I find it. Less grand than I'd remembered it, it seemed even more cluttered than in the old days and out of step with the new, booming economy, where supermarkets are taking over.

The general store! It flourished on service. And, said Jesus, the student, well-trained in God's kingdom, is like the owner of a general store. Service is his or her hallmark. They know just where every item that a customer might need is located. They bring out familiar goods but also new ones.

The grace of Christ makes us like this, if only we will permit God to fulfill His plan for our lives. We will continually grow in knowledge of Him and of His Word; and to share what we have with others will be our delight.

"The truth as it is in Jesus can be experienced, but never explained. Its height and breadth and depth pass our knowledge. We may task our imagination to the utmost, and then we shall see only dimly the outlines of a love that is unexplainable, that is as high as heaven, but that stooped to the earth to stamp the image of God on all mankind" (*Christ's Object Lessons*, p. 129).

Lord, make me the manager of Your general store.

A Song of the Night Shift

He who dwells in the shelter of the Most High will rest in the shadow of the Almighty. Ps. 91:1, NIV.

One day Bill Longard, who worked for years in the pressroom of the Review and Herald Publishing Association, stopped by my office. He pulled out an old time card and showed me something he wrote during the night shift. He had taken one of the most loved psalms, Psalm 91, and put it into English verse form:

O how precious is His promise that we all may safely dwell
in the safe and secret hiding place with Him we love so well.
He's our refuge and our fortress. We can trust Him with our cares,
for He's promised us deliverance from all ills and fowler's snares.
With what comfort we are sheltered 'neath His wings so widely spread,
armored with the shield and buckler of His truth which we have read.
There's no terror for the night or for the missiles on their way,
nor for pestilence in darkness, or destruction at noonday.
When a thousand at our side shall fall, ten thousand at our hand,
we shall watch the wicked get their due as by His side we stand.
And because we chose the Lord most high to be our dwelling place,
there'll no evil plague befall us while abiding in His grace.
That His angels will protect us is a blest assurance sweet;
we shall fear not lion nor adder, but them trample underfeet.
O how wonderful His promise that we'll sit with Him above,
And by Him will be delivered, since on Him we've set our love.
When we call Him He will answer, He will always with us be,
And with long life He will honor us through all eternity.
Can we then neglect salvation that our blessed Lord doth give?
Let us turn unto Him gladly, with repentance true, and live.

That's our Lord! He lights up the darkness; He turns a wearisome task into a time of communion with our Eternal Refuge. He's the God of the noontide—and the night shift.

The Evidence of Grace

When he arrived and saw the evidence of the grace of God, he was glad and encouraged them all to remain true to the Lord with all their hearts. Acts 11:23, NIV

For the first several years of the Christian church, the apostles and other believers, who were all Jews, preached the good news only to other Jews. Light hadn't dawned that Jesus came to save the *world*, not just the children of Israel scattered throughout it.

It took a vision from the Lord to open Peter's eyes. Only then was he ready to accept the truth that he should not call any man impure or unclean (Acts 10:28). Even so the door of salvation opened only slowly to the Gentiles. In Acts 11, however, we read of a major thrust forward, as "men from Cyprus and Cyrene . . . went to Antioch and began to speak to Greeks also, telling them the good news about the Lord Jesus" (verse 20, NIV). And large numbers believed and turned to the Lord.

Antioch (in Syria, in contradistinction to Antioch farther west in Pisidia) quickly became an important center for "followers of the Way," as Christians were then called. The church, headquartered in Jerusalem, heard about what was happening and decided to send the beloved Barnabas to check out matters. Very quickly he "saw the evidence of the grace of God" (verse 22, NIV), was glad, and encouraged the new believers to be faithful to the Lord.

What was "the evidence" of grace that Barnabas saw and caused him to rejoice? Surely, lives changed by the power of the gospel. Whenever grace finds lodging in the heart, it transforms the whole being. Perhaps slowly and imperceptibly but ultimately dramatically, men and women become new people; they are born again. "Christ gave His life to make it possible for man to be restored to the image of God. It is the power of His grace that draws men together in obedience to the truth" (*Counsels to Parents, Teachers, and Students,* p. 149).

With delight I have observed the evidence of grace in the lives of others. I have seen it iin India; I have seen it in developed societies. I believe passionately in the ability of people to change, regardless of what they are like and what their circumstances are. With delight I observe the evidence of grace in people I know and love dearly. As I see them generous and thoughtful, concerned about others, I know this is grace at work.

But do *I* show the evidence of grace?

The Intruder

When the wheat sprouted and formed heads, then the weeds also appeared. Matt. 13:26, NIV.

One spring I decided to replace some of the perennials in the large front flower bed. Looking through the gardening books, my eye fell on pictures of *Rudbeckia,* commonly known as coneflower, which was recommended for the Washington, D.C., area. So off to my favorite nursery, and in with several plants of this flower that was new to me.

I left on an overseas trip shortly after planting the coneflowers. I returned with anticipation to the garden. How were the coneflowers doing? All were fine. Maybe too fine. One of them was growing tall, flourishing. It was bigger than the others; in fact, it looked different from the others.

I watched and waited. The big plant got bigger and bushier. Its leaves definitely weren't the same shape as the other coneflowers, which soon began to put out buds. Now doubts assailed me. How many coneflowers did I buy? Did I really plant that flourishing growth at the edge of the bed? It was all show—no buds, no flowers.

At last I was convinced—it was an intruder in the garden. I rooted it out.

Jesus told a parable about weeds in the garden. A farmer sowed wheat, but one night his enemy came and sowed weeds among the wheat. When the wheat sprouted, the weeds also came up. For a while it was hard to tell the difference, and wheat and weeds grew side by side. But the passage of time brought the picture into sharp focus. The wheat formed heads; the weeds did not. Some of the farmer's hired hands wanted to root out the weeds. "Not yet," he told them. "While you are pulling the weeds, you may root up some wheat with them. Let both grow together until the harvest; then we'll collect the weeds and burn them."

Sin is an intruder in God's garden. God didn't cause it to appear; the devil is its author. But God foresaw sin's coming and made provision to meet it. Long before we were born, before ever the world came into being, the divine covenant—the covenant of grace—was formed in heaven. The Son would come, take our guilt and woes upon Himself, and win back all that was lost to the intruder.

The intruder took all; the Savior took back all.

The Mystery of Grace

Then Jesus said, "God's kingdom is like seed thrown on a field by a man who then goes to bed and forgets about it. The seed sprouts and grows—he has no idea how it happens." Mark 4:26, 27, Message.

Here's a suggestion for anyone who wants to understand grace: grow a garden. If you have land to develop a plot, so much the better. If you live in a townhouse or apartment, you can still have a window box, or potted plants inside the home.

If you're starting out, don't attempt too much. You might be wise to buy young plants from a nursery until you gain confidence in your agricultural skills. But I hope that sooner or later (and sooner rather than later) you'll go back to basics and plant seeds, bulbs, or tubers. That way, windows on the mystery of life—and the mystery of grace—will be open to you.

In the comparatively few years of my gardening experience, I continue to be astounded at the rhythms of life that the Lord built into the natural world. You can plant a variety of bulbs in the soil any November—plant them side by side, in identical soil—and they will amaze you with their different cycles. Depending on where you live (in the Northern Hemisphere), you will see crocuses breaking through the ground and maybe snow cover, with yellow, white, or purple blooms, as early as January or into March. Close behind come daffodils, then hyacinths, then tulips in April and May. By now lilies of the valley are up and scenting the air. As summer moves in, dahlias, lilies, and gladioli take over.

What wonder! Every seed, bulb, and tuber has its own time clock. Who can fathom the mystery of life contained in a seed?

Nor can I explain the mystery of grace. How the seed of the gospel— a seemingly passing word, a message read long ago on a scrap of paper, a "chance" encounter with a stranger—lies hidden in the heart for days, months, years, or decades until the divine alarm wakens it to life. I cannot explain it, but I have seen it happen.

Ellen White once advised that agriculture is the ABCs of education. Exactly. As kids work the soil, plant the seed, and see the miracle of life unfold, their minds open to the miracle of life in Jesus.

Hidden Treasure

Again, the kingdom of heaven is like treasure hidden in a field, which a man found and hid; and for joy over it he goes and sells all that he has and buys that field. Matt. 13:44, NKJV.

People who went through the Great Depression of the 1930s came to have a lasting distrust of banks. Some lost most or all of their savings when the financial institutions of America collapsed, and ever after salted their money away in places they thought would be safe. Trouble was, often these people would go to their graves with their private treasures hidden away where no one else knew. Then years later someone would discover a trunk in the attic filled with valuables, or an old padded chair would divulge a roll of banknotes inside the fabric.

Much like Jesus' parable of the hidden treasure. Here's a man who has rented a field to grow a crop. As he is plowing he hits something hard. A large rock, perhaps? No; it turns out to be a metal box. Immediately the man knows he has stumbled onto a fortune. He drops the plow and rushes home, where he begs, borrows, and scrapes to put together the price of the field. It costs him his shirt, but he is happy—oh, is he happy!—because the treasure will now be his.

Jesus told this parable right next to the story of the pearl buyer who seeks—and finds—a magnificent pearl. In several respects the two parables cover the same ground, but there is an important difference: the merchant was looking for the fine pearl, while the man in the field came upon the treasure seemingly by chance.

Some people find salvation because they are seekers; others encounter grace out of the blue, as it were. During my years of ministry I have noticed both types.

I remember the morning Henry showed up at the school where I was teaching a "Saturday seminar" on early church history. Henry was interested in history, not in my nearby church. He attended the seminar to the end; then he began to come to church just for the music. He got connected with a ham radio club run by one of the members. For years he'd be around the church—but had no thought of joining it. But something eventually happened: Henry decided to join. Later his wife also made the switch. And then later Henry took an early retirement from his job with NASA, went back to school, and became a Seventh-day Adventist minister.

Henry showed up that first morning seeking knowledge. But the Lord led him to hidden treasure.

The Hippo and the Tortoise

For he himself is our peace, who has made the two one and has destroyed the barrier, the dividing wall of hostility. Eph. 2:14, NIV.

From Kenya comes a strange and beautiful story about the unlikeliest of friendships. Who would think that a hippopotamus would bond with a tortoise?

The hippo, nicknamed Owen by wildlife rangers, is only a baby but weighs about 650 pounds (300 kilograms). Owen was swept down the Sabaki River and into the Indian Ocean, then forced back to shore when tsunami waves struck the Kenyan coast on December 26, 2004, the day of the great underwater earthquake.

Hippos are social animals by nature and like to stay with their mothers for four years. Owen, less than a year old, lost his mother when she was swept away. Traumatized, Owen looked for a surrogate mother and found one in a giant male tortoise in an animal facility in the port city of Mombassa. And the tortoise, aged about 100, seems to be very happy with being a "mother."

The hippo follows the tortoise exactly the way he followed his mother. If somebody approaches, Owen becomes aggressive, as if protecting his biological mother. Hippo and tortoise, the oddest imaginable couple, swim, eat, and sleep together.

I would have had difficulty believing this story except for the photographs that accompanied it. But this unusual bonding caused me to think of other friendships, biblical friendships, that defied expectations.

Ruth and Naomi. There's one that turns all those mother-in-law-jokes on their heads.

David and Jonathan. Another unlikely bonding. The prince and the shepherd boy; one born to be king, the other called to be king. They should have been archrivals, not bosom pals.

Ruth and Boaz. Who could predict the association that led to marriage? Ruth is homeless, destitute, a widow, a foreigner. Boaz is older, well off, respected. But they got together (meaning the Lord brought them together).

From that union, three generations later, came Israel's greatest king, whose reign stamped the years indelibly and evoked nostalgic memories. And after many more generations, "Jesus Christ, the son of David, the son of Abraham" (Matt. 1:1) was born. With Him the ancient barriers—the prejudice, the pride of race, the hostility—crumbled away. He Himself became our peace, making us one in Him.

The Silence of Grace

He told them still another parable: "The kingdom of heaven is like yeast that a woman took and mixed into a large amount of flour until it worked all through the dough." Matt. 13:33, NIV.

Our world has become very noisy. On talk shows (a modern abomination) guests try to outmuscle each other by interrupting rudely, raising their voices, and speaking nonstop so that no one else can get a word in. On television the volume jumps when commercials begin to air. And the space around us is jammed with sounds of music of varied qualities, cell-phone chatter, and people hawking opinions and products.

God works in an utterly different manner. He doesn't shout; He sends the "still small voice" (1 Kings 19:12). When God came to earth (we call Him Jesus), it wasn't with megaphones, banners in the sky, or first-class sound systems. "He will not shout or cry out, or raise his voice in the streets," the prophet predicted of Him (Isa. 42:2, NIV).

Grace works silently. Grace is like yeast, said Jesus, yeast that a woman mixes in with flour to bake bread. Today we have leaven that acts rapidly, cutting breadmaking by hours. But whether fast or slow, yeast acts silently, permeating the whole lump of dough, making it rise.

The yeast in the parable "illustrates the quickening, assimilating power of the grace of God," wrote Ellen White. She continues with encouraging words:

"None are so vile, none have fallen so low, as to be beyond the working of this power. In all who will submit themselves to the Holy Spirit a new principle of life is to be implanted; the lost image of God is to be restored in humanity" (*Christ's Object Lessons*, p. 96).

I believe passionately that everyone can change. That regardless of age or circumstances, we don't have to traipse along in the same rut of life. I believe that we can grow, advance, stretch our wings, and soar. I believe that dreams can become reality. But the secret lies outside ourselves. It's outside ourselves, but can become part of ourselves. Like yeast that a woman takes and mixes with flour, silently, mysteriously the grace of Christ can change people—can change *you and me.*

We don't have to muddle along with a bad temper and sour disposition. We can change! Let's pray today for life-changing grace.

A Thanksgiving Hymn

He has shown kindness by giving you rain from heaven and crops in their season; he provides you with plenty of food and fills your hearts with joy. Acts 14:17, NIV.

"Have you cut the wheat in the blowing fields,
The barley, the oats and rye,
The golden corn and the pearly rice?
For the winter days are nigh."
    "We have reaped them all from shore to shore,
    And the grain is safe on the threshing floor."

"Have you gathered the berries from the vine
And the fruits from the orchard trees,
The dew and the scent from the roses and thyme
In the hive of the honey-bees?"
    "The peach and the plum and the apple are ours,
    And the honey-comb from the scented flowers." . . .

Then lift up the head with a song!
And lift up the hands with a gift!
To the ancient giver of all
The spirit of gratitude lift!
For the joy and promise of Spring,
For the hay and clover sweet,
The barley, the rye, and the oats,
The rice and the corn and the wheat, . . .

"Thanksgiving! Thanksgiving! Thanksgiving!"
 Joyfully, gratefully call,
"To God, the preserver of men,
 The bountiful Father of all."
      —Anonymous, from the 1894 *Agricultural Almanac*

Forgiving as Christ Forgave

Bear with each other and forgive whatever grievances you may have against one another. Forgive as the Lord forgave you. Col. 3:13, NIV.

In the early 1980s a wave of terror swept over the residents of King County in the state of Washington in America. Young women began disappearing. Then bodies began to show up in the Green River, in the woods. Autopsies showed that the women had been raped and then murdered. Other women simply disappeared without a trace.

As the toll continued to mount, the police poured all their resources into tracking down and apprehending the serial murderer, whom they dubbed the Green River killer. Several leads connected victims with a young man who worked spraying trucks. But when the police searched his home, they found nothing to link him to any of the deaths.

As suddenly as it had begun, the surge of killings ceased. The investigation grew cold; the task force was cut in size until only one detective remained on the case, and at last he too went on to other duties. Nearly 20 years rolled by.

But those years brought dramatic advances in forensic science—in particular, the use of DNA to identify individuals. The Green River killer case was reopened, with powerful results. DNA tests matched three of the victims with the car painter whom police had suspected. Microscopic examination of spray paint particles linked him to four other murders. Arrested and faced with the evidence of his guilt, the painter confessed.

At length his day in court arrived. As the judge read the list, name by name, he pleaded guilty to each. The tally climbed higher and higher. Each someone had been special to a parent, sibling, or friend, and special to God. On and on he read, until the list stopped at the numbing figure of 48.

Throughout, the killer sat expressionless, showing no emotion, no remorse or regret. Nothing, it seemed, could touch him. Then came the moment the judge gave time for relatives of the victims to express themselves. A gentleman with a white beard rose and told the killer he forgave him. He said that his Lord had taught us to forgive, regardless of how large the matter, and so, hard as it was, he forgave him.

And the killer, seemingly made of stone, broke down and wept.

Forgiveness melts ice. Forgiveness shatters stones. Which is what Jesus did with our cold, hard hearts.

A Race Between Life and Death

We are therefore Christ's ambassadors, as though God were making his appeal through us. We implore you on Christ's behalf: Be reconciled to God. 2 Cor. 5:20, NIV.

Susan Torres was in perfect health when she found out one February that she was pregnant. She and her husband, Jason, accepted the news of a second child with the usual mixture of joy and apprehension. Susan was 26. When she was 17, doctors had removed a malformed freckle on her arm, and the biopsy showed melanoma. But the doctors had given her the all clear.

Now, in late April, she began to complain of feeling mildly ill with nausea. She experienced gradually worsening headaches. When the symptoms persisted, Jason took her to the emergency room, where doctors said she was simply dehydrated. They went home.

On May 7 her husband prepared a meal for her and propped her up in bed for dinner. She apologized for being too much trouble. "Ah, that's all right," her husband replied. Moments later Susan stopped breathing. Jason called for an ambulance and administered CPR. At the hospital, doctors did a CT scan and found no brain function. She had a cancerous growth at the back of her head that had metastasized and bled, causing pressure on her brain.

At age 26 Susan Torres was brain-dead—and five months pregnant.

After a conference with Susan's parents and the doctors, a bold choice was made: they would try to keep Susan's body alive on a ventilator and provide nutrition and hydration in the hope that the fetus might make it to 25 weeks (about mid-July), when it would have a chance of surviving outside the womb. It would also be a race against the deadly melanoma that was steadily moving through her body, and had the ability to penetrate the placenta and attack the baby.

The toll on Jason Torres, trying to care for his wife and 2-year-old son, was enormous.

The medical bill was enormous: more than $1 million.

Why did he do it? Why did the medical staff do it? To give a child a chance for life.

And why did the apostle Paul throw himself into the gospel work, not sparing himself? To give a child of God a chance of eternal life.

Life—that's what it's about. Eternal life. It's worth all we are, all we have, to give a child a chance for life.

The Lion Guard

Then one of the elders said to me, "Do not weep! See, the Lion of the tribe of Judah, the Root of David, has triumphed. He is able to open the scroll and its seven seals." Rev. 5:5, NIV.

The scene described in Revelation 5 is one of the most powerful in all of Scripture. John, weeping because no one is worthy to open the book of destiny, hears a comforting word: The Lion of the tribe of Judah will open the book! So John waits expectantly for the Lion to appear. Instead, he sees a Lamb, looking as if it had been slain.

We customarily think of lions as ferocious animals that threaten our safety and very life. But the Bible here presents another side. Jesus as lion is our strong protector who wards off all who seek to harm us.

The Associated Press ran a remarkable story about lion protection. A 12-year-old girl in Ethiopia was taken by seven men who wanted to force her to marry one of them. They abducted her and beat her repeatedly. After she had been missing for a week, police and relatives found her on the outskirts of Bita Genet, a provincial capital about 350 miles southwest of Addis Ababa, the nation's capital.

When found, the girl was being guarded by three lions that had apparently chased off her captors. When the rescue party arrived, the lions "just left her like a gift and went back into the forest," according to a police sergeant. "If the lions had not come to her rescue, then it could have been much worse," he said. "Everyone thinks this is some kind of miracle, because normally the lions would attack people."

The girl, youngest of four siblings, was "shocked and terrified" after her abduction, and had to be treated for the cuts from her beatings.

Ethiopia's lions, famous for their large black manes, are the country's national symbol. They adorn statues and the local currency. But in spite of a government crackdown, hunters kill the animals for their skins, which can fetch $1,000. Only about 1,000 Ethiopian lions remain in the world.

We too have been abducted and badly beaten. Our adversary is strong and diabolically clever. He prowls around like a roaring lion, looking for someone to devour.

But don't be afraid of him. Don't dwell on his wiles or his power. One far stronger stands guard over us to protect us. Before Him the devil and his hosts flee with tails between their legs.

DECEMBER

A Gift of Life

This is how we know what love is: Jesus Christ laid down his life for us. And we ought to lay down our lives for our brothers. 1 John 3:16, NIV.

Of all the wonderful stories that came into the *Adventist Review* office over the years, none illustrated grace to me better than Geri Kennedy's gift of life to her brother Craig. I had heard snatches of the story, but Geri was reluctant to share something so personal. At last she permitted managing editor Myrna Tetz to write it up for publication.

Craig was in a desperate condition with acute renal failure. He needed someone to donate a kidney. Geri wrestled with what she might do to help him. If the tests came out positive, would she be healthy enough to give one of her kidneys? How would her husband, daughters, and her parents relate to her doing this for someone who drank alcohol and smoked? And would Craig forever feel an obligation?

After much prayer and discussion, Geri decided to go forward. Craig begged her not to do it. She told him that she believed that God would lead, and that it was all in His control. "The feelings of love, awe, and tears are beyond my skills to put into words," she remembers. "His question was 'What will I ever do to repay you?'" She answered with a grin, "Don't worry; I'll have a list." Then she added, "This kidney of mine doesn't drink or smoke, and it goes to church every Sabbath, so please try not to change its lifestyle."

In the operating room the staff put Geri's and Craig's gurneys side by side. They looked at each other and held hands. Then Craig asked seriously, "Where is it?"

"Where's what?"

With tears flowing down his face, he said, "The list."

Now Geri's tears were flowing also. "Craig, there is no list—this is a gift. I love you, and God loves you. He will see us through."

A thousand words couldn't describe the look on Craig's face, Geri remembers. All he could do was squeeze her hand even harder, smile through his tears, and shake his head.

After the surgery there were more tears of happiness as the rest of the family learned that Craig was doing fine. During the following days his body twice started to reject Geri's kidney, but each time God heard their pleas for his complete recovery.

Living Graciously

So all bore witness to Him, and marveled at the gracious words which proceeded out of His mouth. And they said, "Is this not Joseph's son?" Luke 4:22, NKJV.

This passage is my model for daily living. Jesus, full of grace, lived graciously.

To talk about grace is one thing; to live grace is a different story. How well I know that! Over the years, with increasing frequency and intensity, my preaching and writing have focused on grace. And with every telling, every sharing, the blessing has come back to me, grace upon grace. But I have to tell you that all too often my practice falls woefully short of my proclamation. Whereas Jesus' words were always full of grace, mine easily become tinged with sharpness and negativity. Whereas Jesus' life was always encouraging and affirming of others, mine comes in a mixed bag, positive qualities mixed with self-seeking and pride.

Of all the areas of life, I suppose that our speech best reveals who and what we are. "Out of the abundance of the heart the mouth speaks," said Jesus (Matt. 12:34, NKJV). He followed it up with a strong statement indeed: "For by your words you will be justified, and by your words you will be condemned" (verse 37, NKJV). And James noted, "If anyone does not stumble in word, he is a perfect man, able also to bridle the whole body" (James 3:2, NKJV).

In my work I receive thousands of letters and many telephone calls. I read all the mail, even letters so "hot" I need asbestos gloves to handle them. (Actually, my mail runs mainly positive, with just enough of the others to keep my feet on the ground.) Early in my tenure as editor of the *Adventist Review* I'd frequently reply to the correspondent, point by point. Which meant that they'd get back to me with another volley!

I learned after a while not to argue, not to debate. To reply softly and briefly, thanking the person for taking the time to write, and telling them that they might be right. And what a difference! Now those who had sent an angry letter got back to me, sometimes apologizing, sometimes requesting that I tear up their letter.

Telephone calls are more difficult. An accusing voice on the other end invites a knee-jerk response in kind. But that conversation goes nowhere. How much better are words of patience—grace words.

Living graciously: that's my goal. Easy to say, harder to do.

Cricket and All That

Let us fix our eyes on Jesus, the author and perfecter of our faith, who for the joy set before him endured the cross, scorning its shame, and sat down at the right hand of the throne of God. Heb. 12:2, NIV.

Because I grew up in Australia, I grew up playing cricket. Many hours of my boyhood passed by tranquilly (cricket moves slow) under the warm antipodean sun.

From Australia to India, and thence to Spicer College for a 12-year stint. And more cricket—India imbibed British traditions. Sunday afternoons under the tropical sun I joined with students who (many of them) lived close to sudden exit from the college but who never gave a hint of a problem in my classes. I meet them everywhere I go, students from those Spicer days. And they invariably bring up two things: the Life and Teachings of Jesus class that I taught for all students (I wrote the book) and cricket.

To the uninitiated (meaning those who didn't grow up with the game), cricket seems incomprehensible. In what other sport can two teams play for five, or even six, days (an international contest called a "test match"), and at the end of it all declare it a tie? The language of cricket is arcane: silly leg, the slips, silly point, no-ball, wrong 'un, googly, and so on. Did Shakespeare father language such as this? And where else in the world do you have to ask the umpire before he will raise his forefinger, signaling that the batsman (batter) is out? You've knocked down his wicket (the three upright wooden pegs)—they're lying flat—but you still have to enquire of the man in dark pants, tie, white coat, and hat (in the broiling sun), "How's that?" (Delivered with a shout, more like "Owzaaat!")

For those who love it, nothing comes close to cricket. Grown men—and boys—stay up through the night watching test matches in other parts of the world. It's been a long time since I played cricket, longer since I saw a test match. But one thing sticks out in memory: keep your eyes fixed on the field. The batsman has been out there for hours. He's put on more than 100 runs, and it seems as though he'll be there until "stumps" (end of the day). You look away—and there's a jubilant "Owzaaat?" and the batsman is walking away, bowled out.

And for Christians in the game of life, only one thing matters: keep your eyes fixed on Jesus.

Jesus' Final Teaching

Then those "sheep" are going to say, "Master, what are you talking about? When did we ever see you hungry and feed you, thirsty and give you a drink? And when did we ever see you sick or in prison and come to you?" Matt. 25:37, 38, Message.

For Jesus' final teaching before He went to the cross He chose His most familiar mode—the parable. In chapter 24 of Matthew's Gospel He outlines the course of sacred history, from the time of the disciples up to the Second Coming. Then in chapter 25 He speaks about preparation for that event, closing with a judgment scene wherein the righteous are separated from the wicked.

The parable of the sheep and the goats seems disarmingly simple. A shepherd sorts out sheep from goats, putting sheep to his right and goats to his left. And that, says Jesus, is the way it will be at the end, in the day of final dispositions.

Jesus identifies Himself as the one who will do the final sorting. "The Son of Man will take his place on his glorious throne. Then all the nations will be arranged before him and he will sort the people out" (Matt. 25:31, 32, Message). It is surely a reassuring thought that He who came to save us, giving His life for us on Calvary, is the one who sits as our judge.

But what about the sorting? On what basis are sheep and goats separated?

The criteria surprises us; first, because we *don't* find any specification of faith in Jesus as the only hope and Savior. Second, because the separation seems to be wholly on the basis of works—what has been done, or what has not been done.

What happened to the gospel? Where is grace?

Look a little closer. Sometimes the obvious is so close that we look right past it.

Jesus separates the *sheep* from the *goats*. He doesn't declare some to be sheep and others goats; they already are what they are. The judgment simply reveals their identity.

And the works, or lack thereof? Did you catch the note of surprise? The "sheep" are surprised (happily) to be commended for what they have done. Their lives reflected the transforming power of grace, but they didn't realize it. They didn't do good to *earn* salvation, but because they *were* saved.

No salvation by works, but also none apart from works.

Inventive Grace

Let's see how inventive we can be in encouraging love and helping out. Heb. 10:24, Message.

Ours is a world in which more and more people turn their God-given abilities to inventing evil. From weapons of mass destruction to the media, ingenuity and creativity are being used for harmful and, at times, diabolically wicked ends. At such a time as this, God calls us who follow Him to be creative in encouragement. He challenges us to show inventive grace.

I like to observe the way people leave church. When they slouch out, hardly saying a word, and leave as fast as they can, I say to myself, "They didn't hear the good news today." But when they sing the closing hymn with spirit, walk out standing tall, and maybe seem loath to leave the place of blessing, I reflect, "Today they heard a message of hope and courage."

We don't come to church to be beaten up by the preacher. Life already is hard enough. We don't need someone to tell us what we already know, that we've messed up, fallen short of God's ideal for us. We come to church not because we're perfect, but because we're far from perfect. We want to see Jesus, our Savior, our Healer, our Living Hope.

One of my favorite preachers is Seventh-day Adventist pastor James Gilley. Always interesting, his sermons are laced with illustrations, many of them out of his own life. He never puffs himself up; he simply shares his own struggles, interspersing his remarks with self-deprecating humor.

Pastor Gilley has written several books, one of which is *Keep On Keeping On*. Not surprisingly, he preaches a sermon with the same title. In it he tells of a diabetic man who for many years disciplined his eating rigidly. But at last he said to his family, "I'm going to eat what I like, even if it kills me." So he did, and it did. Just two weeks after his death injectable insulin was invented. He gave up too soon.

During his college days Jim Gilley reached a low, low point and decided to quit. When he went to the college president for the signature for dropping all his classes, the president quickly divined Jim's problem—he'd broken up with his girlfriend. The president told Jim to leave the campus for a few days and that he'd sign the "drop" forms when Jim returned. So Jim went away, drove and drove, and thought and thought. By the time he came back, he'd decided he wouldn't quit. So he stayed on, being as mean as he could be to his ex-girlfriend.

But grace is a funny, wonderfully inventive thing. A year later they married, and lived happily ever after.

December 6

The Compassionate Christ

When he looked out over the crowds, his heart broke. So confused and aimless they were, like sheep with no shepherd. Matt. 9:36, Message.

When you walk the streets of the big city, when you look out at the crowds massed for a sporting event or festival, what happens to your heart? We can look at them with jaundiced eye, see only their bad habits that keep them from achieving their full potential, or our hearts can go out to them, longing for their eternal betterment.

The familiar King James Version renders Matthew 9:36 like this: "But when he saw the multitudes, he was moved with compassion for them, because they fainted, and were scattered abroad." Jesus didn't think of their mistakes and abuses of freedom; He saw only their brokenness. And He was moved with compassion. An overwhelming concern gripped Him, a powerful, impelling force that wouldn't permit Him merely to look. He *had* to do something.

Jesus was moved with compassion when He saw the crowds. He was moved with compassion over every case of need that came His way. With the leper who fell at His feet and begged, "Master, if you want to, you can heal my body" (Matt. 8:2, Message). Jesus, disregarding the laws of ceremonial purity that forbade touching anyone or anything unclean (Lev. 5:3), reached out and touched him, saying, "I want to. Be clean" (verse 3, Message). Jesus' word would have sufficed, but His compassion moved Him to the highest expression of love a leper could know—the touch of a human hand.

With the widow, weeping by the casket of her only son, "his heart broke. He said to her, 'Don't cry.' Then he went over and touched the coffin" (Luke 7:13, 14, Message). He called the young man back from the sleep of death and presented him to his mother.

And with Peter, so bold and full of bluster when the sun shone bright, so craven when the storm clouds arose, the Master turned and looked at him after the rooster crowed. Not in anger, not in disappointment; only with sorrow and compassion. And Peter "went out and cried and cried and cried" (Luke 22:62, Message).

The whole ministry of Jesus falls under this rubric: "He was moved with compassion."

What we condemn in others, we overlook in ourselves. But Jesus reached beyond censure. Full of grace and truth, He extended grace to high and low, rich and poor, Jew and Gentile, male and female. His compassion knew no boundary or limit.

The Grace Life

For to me to live is Christ, and to die is gain. Phil. 1:21.

A man once wrote me about how unfair the church is. It isn't what you know, but whom you know, he said. Unless you have the right connections and the right name, you'll never get anywhere.

Not so, I replied. Maybe true in some cases, but definitely not in mine. The church entrusted me with high responsibilities, but in terms of connections and name I'm a nobody. Like Amos, who reminded his accuser that he was neither a prophet nor the son of a prophet (Amos 7:14), I was neither a leader nor the son of a leader. The Lord simply put His hand on me—on me, one who, as it were, came out of nowhere—and gave me a job to do.

I have been—*am*—the most blessed of individuals. Whatever I have accomplished for good has been only by the grace of Christ. Whatever influence I have cast for the glory of my Lord has come only as His grace has permeated my life and work.

The responsibilities with which I was entrusted have given me a place in the sun beyond that of others far more accomplished than I. For years people have been coming up to me in airports and other public places and telling me they recognized me from some photograph they saw associated with my writings or a television program. I'm no "star"—Jesus Christ is the only "star"—but my work has led to a measure of recognition beyond that of Christians whose life and deeds reflect Christ's far more than do mine.

We live in a strange age. The media has given rise to something altogether new in human history: the cult of celebrity. People hang on the images of men and women in the spotlight. They dwell on them; they idolize them. They're ready to do almost anything—even to exposing themselves to ridicule and gross conduct—in order to get on TV or in the movies.

For me, to live is Christ. It's all about Him; it's not about me. It's not a matter of the success of my plans; it's about His glory. It's not about stroking my ego, winning the argument to prove something to someone else or, especially, to myself.

I don't have to prove anything. Jesus loves me, accepts me, saves me. That's all I need on earth or in heaven.

This I Believe

I know whom I have believed and am persuaded that He is able to keep what I have committed to Him until that Day. 2 Tim. 1:12, NKJV.

I believe that God loves us with a love that is stronger than death, a love that will never let go, a love that will see us through the deepest of waters. I believe that God plans only what is best for us, that in His long-range vision He has a plan for our lives on this earth and into eternity. I believe that God never gives up on sinners, that He continues to woo and to draw us back to Himself, that He gives us a second chance, and a third, and a seventeenth, and a seven hundredth.

I believe that, in spite of all appearances to the contrary, the cup of human existence is half full, not half empty. I believe that people can change—everyone, all of us, myself; that we don't have to plow the same furrow year after year, but that at any age and in any circumstances, we can grow and improve intellectually, morally, socially, and spiritually.

I believe that grace is the greatest agent for change in the world, able to change individuals, congregations, and societies.

I believe that in the midst of overwhelming evil one solitary life, empowered by the grace of Christ, can exert a profound influence for good.

I believe that a smile or a laugh will accomplish more than an hour of preachment that points out faults.

I believe that we are not creatures of chance, that an all-wise and all-beneficent Creator brought the universe into being.

I believe that the One who made the worlds out of nothing, according to His purpose, also will bring all things to a glorious finale, according to His purpose.

I believe that we humans, finite, frail, and broken, can know the Creator of the universe in a personal relationship, and to enter into this relationship gives the meaning and fulfillment that we crave.

I believe.

I believe because of Jesus Christ, full of grace and truth. Not in what I believe, but in whom.

Buckets of Salvation

Joyfully you'll pull up buckets of water from the wells of salvation. And as you do it, you'll say, "Give thanks to God, call out his name." Isa. 12:3, 4, Message.

Isaiah 12, only six verses in all, overflows with joy. The chapter is a song of praise for God's deliverance, and it bubbles up like a cool, crystalline spring.

To understand why this little passage is so ebullient, we need to go back to the previous chapter. There we read of the Branch that will spring from the stump of Jesse (verse 1), the blessed Deliverer whose reign will bring righteousness and justice, banishing oppression and hate, and restoring the whole creation to peace and harmony.

Who is this? Only one person fits the bill: Jesus Christ, our Savior and Lord. The prophet anciently sang His praise, and I sing it today. I praise Him for the *reality* of His saving grace, for the *abundance* of that grace, and for the *joy* that fills my heart because of it.

His salvation, says the prophet, is like water from a deep well. It's an image that we find frequently in the Scriptures. The Bible lands are dry lands; water (meaning wells, springs, and the occasional river) make life possible. In the book of Genesis we find Abraham and Isaac digging wells, with rejoicing when they find an abundant source. We also read of disputes over wells, and wells being stopped up. Wells mean water, wells mean life.

And when the Root of Jesse appeared, He likened His new life to water. "Anyone who drinks the water I give will never thirst—not ever," He told the Samaritan woman. "The water I give will be an artesian spring within, gushing fountains of endless life" (John 4:14, Message).

Water. So simple, so basic, so *necessary*. And today valued even in places of abundant rain. Who could have predicted the huge market for bottled water?

Grace. So simple, so basic, so necessary. And so *abundant*. God offers us salvation by the bucketful. He doesn't dole out grace in thimbles.

This morning on our walk in the park Noelene and I saw a patch of cornflowers, brilliant in their summer dress. And then a bluebird flew by, the brilliance of its feathers exactly reflecting the blue of the cornflowers. A double blessing—one more evidence of the abundance of grace.

And we went on our way rejoicing.

The Reunion

While he was still a long way off, his father saw him. His heart pounding, he ran out, embraced him, and kissed him. Luke 15:20, Message.

When Reese Hoffa was 4 years old, he burned down his family's house. For his mother, Diana Chism, an unmarried teenager, it was the last straw in a losing battle with her life. She took Reese and his brother, Lamont, to a large brick building with long corridors and lots of children, embraced them, got in her car, and drove away.

Reese kept waiting for her to return to the orphanage, but it never happened. Eventually separated from his brother and adopted by another family, he plunged kicking and screaming into a new life. At first he was reluctant and confused, but grew into a successful, hardworking adult with a sense of humor. At 6 feet and 253 pounds, Reese Hoffa today is one of the world's best and most entertaining shot putters.

For nearly 20 years Hoffa searched for the missing pieces in his broken history. Mental snapshots, his only possessions from his youngest days, flashed into his mind again and again. Driven by pain and curiosity, he yearned to know and understand who he was. When he traveled to sports competitions, he would comb through local telephone books, looking for his brother, Lamont. But he had no clue as to his birth mother. He didn't know her first name, only that her surname began with C-h-i.

Meanwhile, Diana, happily married and with her life together, was searching also. She contacted the social worker who had arranged the space at the orphanage, but the worker declined to open Reese's file. Diana pored through news clippings of schoolchildren and graduating classes, stared at reels of microfilm, searched Web sites, but all to no avail. "I had a conversation with God," she said. "I said, 'I can't go through this anymore.'" She decided to post information in a last attempt to find her missing son.

One night Reese Hoffa, a senior at the University of Georgia, started his ongoing search for Lamont. He found a new site, plugged in his date and state of birth, and up popped a message: "I am a mother looking for a son given up for adoption at age 4 in 1981 in Louisville, Kentucky."

It had been 19 years since she had left him at the orphanage. Diana Watts was shaking as she picked up the telephone and dialed Reese's cell phone. And his first words, blurted out, were "I'm so sorry about the fire."

The Sunlit Fields of Life

You pulled me from the brink of death, my feet from the cliff-edge of doom. Now I stroll at leisure with God in the sunlit fields of life. Ps. 56:13, Message.

Grace is a walk in a sunlit field.

I grew up in a home on the northward edge of the city sprawl. Right back of us the large fields of a dairy stretched out, inviting us to fly our homemade kites. Beyond the dairy was a road, and across that a large, flat expanse of land that was attached to a military supply center but open to the public. A solitary tree stood out from the landscape, and near it a 22-yard strip of concrete laid down as a cricket pitch. We'd haul our cricket gear across the dairy and out into the empty army field. If we went farther, eventually we'd hit a wheat field. I remember wading into it, the grain almost as tall as I, flattening out a square, and lying on my back, looking at the sky, totally hidden from the world, with the buzzing of insects the only sound.

The Australian sun shines bright and clear. Every time I return to the land of my birth, that's what first strikes me, how bright the light is. One other place in my travels I always associate with light is Ireland. Not the brilliant rays of the antipodes, but light of a gentler but startlingly beautiful character.

In those days I walked carefree—hatless, unprotected by sunblock. Today I still walk sunlit fields, but with a difference. I have learned "the still, sad music of humanity" (Wordsworth); I have felt the icy clutch of death; I have peered over the cliff-edge of doom. And the God of grace has given me the inexpressible joy and comfort of continuing strolls in sunlit fields.

When I was a student at Avondale College in Australia, the symphonic choir sang a haunting melody, "My God and I." It spoke of a person clasping the hands of God and going out to walk in the fields with Him. They talk like good friends; they laugh together. God tells of His plan for them—a plan made long before they were born—and then, the anthem moving to its climax, of what is yet to be, when this earth and its little day has passed away. "God and I" will still walk together, for ever and always.

Dear God, take my hand and walk with me today.

Grace and More Grace

Oh yes, people of Zion, citizens of Jerusalem, your time of tears is over. Cry for help and you'll find it's grace and more grace. The moment he hears, he'll answer. Isa. 30:19, Message.

Notes Ellen White, "As your soul yearns after God, you will find more and still more of the unsearchable riches of His grace. As you contemplate these riches you will come into possession of them and will reveal the merits of the Savior's sacrifice, the protection of His righteousness, the fullness of His wisdom, and His power to present you before the Father "without spot, and blameless" (2 Peter 3:14)" (*The Acts of the Apostles*, p. 567).

The night may bring weeping, but joy comes in the morning (Ps. 30:5). God promises not only to dry our tears when He makes all things new (Rev. 21:4), but to get us past the times of tears in this life.

Are you feeling heavyhearted, wondering if you will ever smile or laugh again? I have been through such times, times when for a little while I would be glad to have life simply end, so unbearable was the pain. But God brought me through them. In my sense of desolation I cried out silently to God, and I found that His answer was grace, and more grace.

I long for the psalmist's experience to be my experience:

"As the deer pants for streams of water, so my soul pants for you, O God. My soul thirsts for God, for the living God. When can I go and meet with God?" (Ps. 42:1, 2, NIV).

And again: "O God, you are my God, earnestly I seek you; my soul thirsts for you, my body longs for you, in a dry and weary land where there is no water" (Ps. 63:1, NIV).

I claim the promise of the Word, reinforced by Ellen White's statement above, that the soul that yearns for God will find more, and still more, of the unsearchable riches of His grace. I want to contemplate those riches, that is, Jesus Himself, and come into possession of them. I want to reveal in my life the merits of the Savior's sacrifice. I want His righteousness to protect me. I want to have the fullness of His wisdom. I want to know the certainty of His power to present me before the Father "without spot, and blameless."

My friend, go with me into this new day, our hand in Jesus' hand, our hearts turned toward Him, confident that the moment He hears, He'll answer.

Why I Believe in an Afterlife

Now we see but a poor reflection as in a mirror; then we shall see face to face. Now I know in part; then I shall know fully, even as I am fully known. 1 Cor. 13:12, NIV.

Here is why I believe—and strongly believe—in an afterlife.

1. Intimations of immortality. Although I am surrounded by the temporary, I dream of eternity. Enveloped in change and decay, I envisage the fadeless. Nothing in my experience is perfect, least of all myself; but I can imagine the perfect, and long for it.

These impressions (for that is all they are) fail the test of cold, scientific analysis and verification. But to deny them would be to set aside not only a part of my life but perhaps the noblest and finest part, the part that points me beyond myself to another and higher plane of existence.

2. Justice and inequality. All around me I see the weak beaten down and driven from justice. In every land those with wealth fare better in the courts; corruption abounds.

Life isn't fair. Life isn't just. But my heart cries out that it should be fair, that it should be just. That the weak should have their day in court, and the poor their loaf of bread.

The Bible tells me about God—God who burns with zeal on behalf of the weak and the poor, who will set matters right in His time when He intervenes as the judge.

3. Meaning. Without an afterlife, this existence would be a journey without a goal, a love that dies unconsummated. We see in part, we understand in part. But then, says Paul, we shall see and know face to face (1 Cor. 13:9-12).

4. Jesus. The three arguments above come from within myself, but this one is rooted in history; and it is the supreme evidence. Jesus of Nazareth rose from the dead! He was crucified on a Roman cross, His corpse placed in Joseph of Arimathea's new rock-cut tomb, a large stone rolled across the entrance, and a guard placed to prevent any monkey business. But the body disappeared. Sunday morning the stone had been rolled back, the soldiers had fled, and the tomb was empty.

I believe in an afterlife because Jesus, who rose from the dead, promises it to me. "I am the resurrection and the life," He says. "He who believes in me will live, even though he dies" (John 11:25, NIV).

December 14

Wired for Service

I will praise You, for I am fearfully and wonderfully made; marvelous are Your works, and that my soul knows very well. Ps. 139:14, NKJV.

Dan Timon was just shy of his forty-ninth birthday when he succumbed to cancer. During the yearlong losing battle he became fully resigned to God's will, happy to live on, happy to die if that was the Father's plan. The grace of Christ that had won and ruled his heart kept him in divine peace.

Dan loved sound. A quiet person himself, he delighted in tweaking audio systems so that musicians, speakers, and congregants received the greatest blessing. At the memorial service hundreds of people from different backgrounds gathered to pay tribute to the life of this unpretentious follower of Jesus. They heard a moving letter from Dan to family and friends:

"In the past few years I have learned that eternal joy comes from choosing to let Jesus be Lord of my life, and I can say with conviction that it comes from doing those things He uniquely wired me up to do, and doing them in His service. This gave me success, and work became a pleasure.

"Since then, I have learned some steps for keeping the proper perspective when seeking guidance from the Lord. First, pray until you mean 'Not my will, but Thine, be done.' You must absolutely submit to the Lord when you pray, and give Him permission to stop, or modify, your requests. Think of Jesus in the Garden of Gethsemane. Second, use biblical advice to analyze motives. If they aren't pure, you will ignore the little voice of warning, and serious consequences will occur. This is the natural result of attempting to manage your life without the Lord's guidance. And you'll have nobody to blame but yourself. Think of David, and the consequences of his actions. Third, wait upon the Lord. Don't force things to happen. Think of Moses, and how the Lord let him cool his jets for 40 years before he was ready for service. Fourth, keep your mind focused on what you love to do. Explore your passions. Find out how the Lord has wired you. Then look for ways to serve Him. Think of Paul, and how the Lord turned Paul's focus completely around to continue using the same passion and gifts in His service.

"When I began serving my Lord, using the passions and skills that He wired into me, I was blessed with joy and happiness only to be exceeded in the life to come. In the earth made new I look forward to hearing how the Lord used your unique skills and passions and created for you a joyous life on earth that prepared you for a joyous life eternal."

Living in Hope

Listen, Jacob. Listen, Israel. I'm the One who named you! I'm the One. I got things started and, yes, I'll wrap them up. Isa. 48:12, Message.

These are days of unprecedented uncertainty and foreboding. Terrorists strike without warning. Streets of many cities are covered in blood. Nuclear proliferation, with the possibility that basements and inner rooms of houses may already hide small atomic weapons, makes the blood run cold. Climate changes and earthquakes cause floods and devastation. AIDS stalks abroad, menacing the very existence of communities.

At such a time as this, we who know the Lord Jesus and the reality of His grace may live in hope and peace. Our future is built not on the shifting sands of earthly leaders and plans, but on the Solid Rock.

"I got all things started," He assures us, "and yes, I'll wrap them up." He, the Creator of everything, will bring the End—and it will be a glorious finale. Creation and Conclusion are bound tightly together in the hand of our Lord, the hand that was nailed to the cross for us.

A few years ago famous philosopher Anthony Flew shocked the academic world. Flew has spent a lifetime debunking faith in God, publishing articles and books that argue persuasively that there is no God. But Anthony Flew switched sides—he now argued that God must exist.

What led to Flew's about-face? He was won over by the evidence of irreducible complexity all around. Human DNA, like many other structures in our wonderfully constructed human body, contains mutually dependent parts that could not have appeared just by chance—the odds are astronomical. A Superb Mind alone can account for the data.

That Mind is Christ, "for by him all things were created: things in heaven and on earth, visible and invisible, whether thrones or powers or rulers or authorities; all things were created by him and for him" (Col. 1:16, NIV). And that same Mind promises, "I will come again" (John 14:3). He who created all things will return to restore all things.

For many people today the universe had no beginning at the hand of a Creator. And it has no beneficent end—only a whimper. In between, in this existence, no meaning can be found. I pity them.

But, praise God, we know where we came from, why we are here, and where we are going. The One who started all things is going to wrap them up—soon!

Count Your Blessings

O my soul, bless God. From head to toe, I'll bless his holy name! O my soul, bless God, don't forget a single blessing! Ps. 103:1, 2, Message.

I t seems that the more affluent we become, the less we give thanks. Do our lives get caught up in counting baubles instead of blessings? Years ago, when people were less well off, they used to sing a gospel song whose chorus went like this:

> "Count your blessings, name them one by one.
> Count your blessings, see what God hath done.
> Count your blessings, name them one by one,
> And it will surprise you what the Lord hath done."

I haven't heard that rollicking tune in many a day. What happened?

Noelene recalls her growing-up years, and how she and her brothers found ways to spin out the Christmas experience. They'd gather the presents they received, the gifts so long anticipated, then joyfully opened, into little heaps. The day after Christmas they'd go over them again, one by one, savoring the experience, remembering the first thrill of seeing them. Sometimes they would continue in this vein for several days. It was a child's way of counting blessings.

Perhaps you say, How can I count my blessings when I don't have any to count?

Look again at what David says:

> "He forgives your sins—every one.
> He heals your diseases—every one.
> He redeems you from hell—saves your life!
> He crowns you with love and mercy—a paradise crown.
> He wraps you in goodness—beauty eternal.
> He renews your youth—you're always
>   young in his presence" (verses 3-5, Message).

What has He done for you? Take a moment and *think*. Don't hurry over sins forgiven; that's the greatest blessing of all. Count your blessings. Verbalize them. Tell God how grateful you are for them. Write them down. Tell someone else.

And it will surprise you what the Lord has done.

Psalm 117

Praise the Lord, all you nations; extol him, all you peoples. For great is his love toward us, and the faithfulness of the Lord endures forever. Praise the Lord. Ps. 117, NIV.

Psalm 117 has only two verses, but its message commends it for our prayerful meditation, not the oddity of its size. The psalm contains three elements: praise, the greatness of Yahweh's love, and the constancy of His faithfulness. These same themes run all through the Psalms; thus, Psalm 117 is the entire Psalter in cameo.

All the psalms center in praise. They are songs that exult in Yahweh, Creator of heaven and earth, and Israel's God. With candor and honesty the psalms run the gamut of human experience—joy and despair, happiness and sorrow, pleasure and pain. Sometimes the psalmist feels almost ready to quit, and sometimes he is floating on cloud 9. Sometimes he skips and dances, and sometimes he's at his wits' end. But always, in the final analysis, he turns to God. He waits on God, He *expects* God to come to his aid.

So, whatever the occasion in life, the psalms praise God. Their "bottom line" resounds like this: There is life only in God; without God there is no life.

Psalm 117, short as it is, has an interesting twist on the theme of praise. It calls not on the people of God, but on the "nations," that is, the Gentiles. It invites them to join in the adoration and acclamation of Israel's God. First, because "great is his love toward us." Not His awesome power. Not His mighty acts in history. Not His righteousness. But His love. A foreglimmering of John's affirmation here, John summed it all up with "God is love" (1 John 4:16). It's the greatest, most wonderful truth in the universe.

Second, because "the faithfulness of the Lord endures forever." Indeed! "Great is Thy faithfulness." Let every man on earth be a liar, but God stay true. We can take to the bank every word from His mouth. All else changes—"change and decay in all around I see"—but not Yahweh.

Eugene Peterson puts it this way:

> "His love has taken over our lives;
> God's faithful ways are eternal
> Hallelujah!" (Ps. 117:2, Message).

Shaped by Love

Let your love, God, shape my life with salvation, exactly as you promised. Ps. 119:41, Message.

As the potter shapes the clay, molding it into an elegant vase, so the Lord shapes our lives with loving attention. If we let Him work His plan for us, we will emerge as something beautiful and useful to Him and to humanity.

We're used to receiving instruction books when we buy a new appliance. The manufacturers want us to get the best and longest service from their product. They know it—they designed it, tested it, put it together—and they want us to benefit from their knowledge. Very often, however, we don't even look at their instructions. We don't even open the book (we're so sure we don't need it), or we toss it in the trash.

God, who made us with loving hands, provided us with an instruction book on how to live. But often we don't even bother to read it, or we consider it outmoded. We can get along fine without it. Then, when our lives go all wrong because of our decisions, we turn on God and accuse Him: "Why are You doing this to me?"

Some time ago I met Dorothea, a wonderful German woman. A devoted follower of Jesus Christ, she gives much of her time to speaking to women's groups, pointing them to the One who eagerly waits to shape their lives in love. She especially enjoys addressing secular people. One day, traveling by train to an appointment, she prayed that God would bring many secular women to the meeting. And He did.

During a break in the meeting, a woman approached her, wanting to know the name of the book from which Dorothea had frequently quoted.

"Come with me," said Dorothea, taking the woman to the bookstore. She spoke to the attendant, and handed the book to the enquirer.

"This is the book," she said. "A Bible."

Amazing to us who love the Word, but true. Many people today are Bible illiterates. They grow up without it, they never read it, and they will never see it unless we bring it to them. This precious Word comes from the hands of a loving God. He uses it to shape our lives in love for salvation, just as He promised. It's our instruction manual from our Maker.

Grace Is Like the Snow

Purge me with hyssop, and I shall be clean; wash me, and I shall be whiter than snow.
Ps. 51:7, NKJV.

It took me quite a few years to realize how breathtakingly beautiful the snow can be. When I was growing up in Australia, a warm country, my favorites were beach and ocean. From Australia we went to India, a hot country, but where, paradoxically, I saw my first snow in the mountains.

After India we went to Andrews University in Michigan. Winters in Berrien Springs are dull and snowy, and each year I longed for their passing. But one December, as I gloomily looked out on a white landscape with large flakes filling the air, I encountered a student who saw the world very differently. "Isn't it wonderful!" she exclaimed. "I can hardly wait for the winter every year!"

Gradually I made peace with the Michigan winters. If you can't lick 'em, join 'em. I was about ready to buy a set of cross-country skis when we moved to the Washington, D.C., area. And here, where winters are much milder, I have at last begun to appreciate the marvels of the snow.

I love to walk, especially in the company of Noelene. Walking in the snow has a character and delight that no hiking to a mountain lake or scaling a peak can come close to. You bundle up, pull on thick socks and boots, and venture out into winter's wonderland. It's especially grand if the flakes are still flying to sting your cheeks. You crunch, crunch along, the snow making a distinctive squeaking sound. The air is crackling crystalline; any sound carries far. No need to follow paths or trails—the snow is a great leveler. Make straight for where you want to go. Chances are you'll hear little birds singing cheerily in the thickets as you pass.

Everything looks beautiful under the white blanket. The plainest evergreen calls for a photograph. Simple red berries, frosted white, glisten and gleam. The coarsest clump of grass, the ugliest bush, has been transformed. Any garbage, any junk, is covered, hidden. The world has been born anew.

How like grace! Grace is like the snow, covering, blanketing our imperfections, our coarseness, our roughness. The person least endowed with physical attractiveness becomes a princess or a prince when touched by the Master of the snow, who is the king of grace.

Grace makes everything beautiful. Grace makes everything new.

December 20

The Best Gift for Jesus

On coming to the house, they saw the child with his mother Mary, and they bowed down and worshiped him. Then they opened their treasures and presented him with gifts of gold and of incense and of myrrh. Matt. 2:11, NIV.

The Christmas season in the West has become a spending extravaganza. In the United States people spend more than $200 billion between Thanksgiving and New Year's Day. And many of the gifts go to people who already have more than they need.

By contrast, the total for foreign aid that the United States dispenses is some $10 billion, while giving for charitable causes totals about $25 billion. We splurge nearly 10 times as much on ourselves as we do on others, and more than 20 times as much as we do to help to less-fortunate countries. How did Christmas ever come to this?

Think about how it all began. Joseph and Mary, poor people. They can't even get a place in Bethlehem's inn. So they spend the night among the cattle, and Mary delivers her firstborn and places Him in a manger. Shepherds come to worship the child. Shepherds! A group on the margins of society, looked down upon.

The scriptural story of Christmas bespeaks poverty at every turn. But Christmas in the West has become an outpouring of extravagance, where the well-off give to the well-off, leaving millions in want.

What a turning of the tables on the Christmas story! No wonder we sanitize the manger scene in our Nativity plays. The hay smells sweet and fresh, and Joseph and Mary—and the shepherds—look well dressed.

But the Magi! They break the pattern of poverty in the biblical story. They bring costly gifts. Gold, frankincense, myrrh—they lay a treasure at the feet of the baby Jesus. And that treasure very soon would be put to good use, providing the means for Joseph, Mary, and Jesus to flee to Egypt and survive there until the death of Herod the Great.

So the spirit of Christmas is the spirit of giving; God's giving His Son shows us that. The Magi's gifts confirm it. They brought the best for Jesus. It's time to get back to the way the story began. This Christmas, when we buy presents for loved ones and friends, how about giving Jesus the best gift? How about giving *Him* an offering greater than any sum we spend on someone else?

The Secret of Overcoming

To him who overcomes, I will give the right to sit with me on my throne, just as I over-came and sat down with my Father on his throne. Rev. 3:21, NIV.

The theme of overcoming features strongly in the book of Revelation. Each of the messages to the seven churches closes with a promise to the one who overcomes (Rev. 2:7, 11, 17, 25; 3:5, 12, 21).

But how can we overcome? The spiritual forces arrayed against us seem so powerful and we so weak. How can we ever emerge victorious in this battle?

Listen: in our weakness lies the secret of overcoming. If we will cast ourselves on the Savior and rely totally on Him, all the forces of hell will be turned back.

Friend of mine, I want to share with you a promise that I know to be true. I have tested it again and again, and it has never failed.

"Nothing is apparently more helpless, yet really more invincible, than the soul that feels its nothingness and relies wholly on the merits of the Savior. By prayer, by the study of His Word, by faith in His abiding presence, the weak-est of human beings may live in contact with the living Christ, and He will hold them by a hand that will never let go" (*The Ministry of Healing*, p. 182).

Notice the threefold formula here:

Prayer: The life of the overcomer is a life of prayer. This is prayer that lives and breathes the presence of God, prayer uttered and unuttered, prayer in the midst of our daily tasks and cares.

Study of the Word. Feeding on God's Word and the life of victory go hand in hand. Daily prayerful reading of the Scriptures is able to make us strong in the Lord and His will. Sporadic reading leaves us weak and vac-illating; it sets us up to fail. And no reading means we will quickly fall prey to the enemy of souls.

Faith in His abiding presence. We live by faith. Faith is the essence of the Christian life: it is the ultimate quality. All around, the forces of secularism and materialism vaunt their power, enticing us to throw in our lot with them and "eat, drink, and be merry." But faith says no! There is more to life than what our eyes can see. There is another world, the realm of ultimate reality, the pres-ence of God. This little life is *not* all there is. God has made us for Himself!

Try it. Cast yourself on God. The weaker you feel, the greater His strength at work in you. And Jesus, the overcomer, will work in you over-coming power.

Of Wheelbarrows and Lawn Mowers

And he said: "I tell you the truth, unless you change and become like little children, you will never enter the kingdom of heaven." Matt. 18:3, NIV.

It's been one of those giddy, glorious times when our grandchildren come to visit, and now that they've left, I'm still glowing and reflecting on what they taught me.

Almost the first words to come from 6-year-old Jacqui, when we met them at the airport, were "Granddad, can we have wheelbarrow rides?"

Wheelbarrow rides! We had stumbled on the game by chance the year before, and they became the hit of the visit. First, one granddaughter in the wheelbarrow, then the other, then (puff! puff!) both together. We chugged up the slope in the backyard, paused to give appropriate sound effects, then, passengers screaming with delight, charged downhill on the stone path. After that it was around the curve and up the hill and a final dash to the starting station.

So we had wheelbarrow rides again, and the next evening when I came home from work I was expecting more of the same. I looked at the lawn, badly in need of a haircut, and said to the girls, "The grass is really long, but I can do that after you've left. Let's have wheelbarrow rides."

"Granddad," said 7-year-old Madi, "could we help you cut the lawn instead of wheelbarrow rides?"

"Sure," I replied through my surprise. I got out the mower and started filling it with gasoline. The girls ran inside, emerging with scissors and small bowls. They began to cut and to put the grass in the bowls.

I brought up the mower and instructed them on keeping a safe distance. Then I started the engine and began to mow. The girls ran to and fro behind me, scooping up clumps of cut grass, putting the grass in their bowls, and then emptying the bowls into a large recycling sack.

The evening was hot and humid, and the job took more than an hour. The younger girl eventually tired out and went inside, but Madi stayed by till the job was done.

For days Madi had been making our bed, at her request, for 25 cents per time. After all the work on the lawn, however, neither she nor her sister mentioned a word about getting paid.

So what did they teach me? That simplest pleasures are the best, and that when you love, you don't even think about getting paid.

Treasures in Jars of Clay

If you only look at us, you might well miss the brightness. We carry this precious Message around in the unadorned clay pots of our ordinary lives. That's to prevent anyone from confusing God's incomparable power with us. 2 Cor. 4:7, Message.

Christians are ordinary people doing extraordinary things. They look oh-so-human—and are—but God works through them to His glory. His grace takes unadorned clay pots and makes them repositories of divine power.

Did you ever meet Desmond Doss, subject of the award-winning documentary film *The Conscientious Objector*? This Seventh-day Adventist noncombatant soldier was awarded the Congressional Medal of Honor for extraordinary bravery during the battle for Okinawa in World War II. Doss was a hero, but, from a worldly standpoint, he didn't look or act like one. He was altogether ordinary—and humble to boot—giving God the glory for what he accomplished.

Likewise, with the church. From a human standpoint, the church is altogether human, subject to the same strengths and weaknesses, flaws and intrigues, of any other human grouping. Indeed, the church is human—but not altogether so. The church is divine as well as human, and God is working out a divine purpose through unadorned clay pots.

"From the beginning it has been God's plan that through His church shall be reflected to the world His fullness and His sufficiency. The members of the church, those whom He has called out of darkness into His marvelous light, are to show forth His glory. The church is the repository of the riches of the grace of Christ; and through the church will eventually be made manifest, even to 'the principalities and powers in heavenly places,' the final and full display of the love of God" (*The Acts of the Apostles*, p. 9).

So to everyone who professes the name of Jesus, this challenge comes: "Christ has given to the church a sacred charge. Every member should be a channel through which God can communicate to the world the treasures of His grace, the unsearchable riches of Christ" (*ibid.*, p. 600).

Today God wants to take my ordinary life and do something extraordinary with it. To the onlooking world it may seem altogether humdrum, but in heaven's eyes it will be beautiful.

Lord, take this clay pot that is me and use it today for Your glory.

When Grace Flew
Out the Window

Glory to God in the highest, and on earth peace, goodwill toward men! Luke 2:14, NKJV.

Sometimes we get so caught up in preparing for Christmas that we lose its spirit. We want everything to be just right and to go just right, and before we know it grace flies out the window.

After our first furlough from service in India, we brought back a fake Christmas tree. It was white, and Noelene decorated it with blue balls and multicolored lights. Everybody who saw it loved it; the local newspaper sent out a reporter and put a picture in print.

That year we splurged on gifts for our children, ages 5 and 3. And Christmas Eve we feasted on a special treat: grapes. The agricultural college just down the road had cultivated the Thompson's seedless variety, and the first grapes had come in. They were sweet and delicious, the finest grapes we had ever eaten.

And then to bed. But it would be anything but a silent, holy night. A Hindu wedding got under way in the village nearby, with music from loudspeakers booming in through our open bedroom windows. Then our son appeared, feeling very sick. He'd eaten too many grapes too fast, and they all came up again. At last he settled down, but the music did not. Noelene and I tossed through the wee hours until silence descended just before dawn, when we fell into a deep sleep.

The kids woke up, fresh and excited, waiting to unwrap their gifts. They waited and waited for Mom and Dad to appear, but we kept on sleeping. At last they couldn't contain themselves any longer and started in on the gifts.

Finally Noelene and I got up. We found the living room awash with wrapping paper and, in the middle of it all, two children, one with very heavy eyelids.

That was the year, Noelene says, that grace flew out the window. All the parental plans to have it just right and do it just right had gone down the tube. And we let the children know it!

And we were wrong. Our son and daughter were, and are, far more important than any Christmas plans or preparations. Christmas is about grace, not just read and preached about, but lived out.

So, my friend, if perchance your Christmas plans don't turn out just the way you hoped and worked for, chill out. Let your plans fly out the window, but not grace.

The Liberator

Call his name Jesus, for he will save his people from their sins. Matt. 1:21, RSV.

Call Him Liberator, this virgin's firstborn Son, plucked from the womb of eternity, flung into an alien land. "The Spirit of the Lord is upon me, because he has anointed me to preach good news to the poor. He has sent me to proclaim release to the captives and recovering of sight to the blind, to set at liberty those who are oppressed, to proclaim the acceptable year of the Lord" (Luke 4:18, 19, RSV).

The Baby, liberator of humanity, cries. He cries, just as my firstborn son, plucked from the womb of life and flung into an alien land, cried.

So the carol "Away in a Manger" is all wrong when it says "The cattle are lowing, the baby awakes, but little Lord Jesus no crying He makes." Jesus cried at birth. Jesus cried when He awoke. For the Liberator came in no alien flesh to set us free. Bone of our bone, He would walk our trails, suffer our heartaches, bear our pain. He would know the lure of temptation, brave the laser bolts of the ancient enemy.

And, at last, death itself, a lonely, despairing, godforsaken death, rending heaven asunder with the awful cry "My God, my God, why have you forsaken me?" (Matt. 27:46, NIV).

Where is the face of the little Boy in the manger; that face so smooth and innocent and full of mystery? Bethlehem's Babe hangs contorted in death, wracked by the woe of the world.

And thereby—liberation! Once temptation fled in defeat; now death itself falls, slain by the Liberator's death.

Every time we look into the face of a little child we see mystery—the mystery of being, of where we came from, of what we may be. Every babe is a song of hope in a silent world.

That is because of the virgin's firstborn Son, who cried, who is the liberator. He has set humanity free, free to be fully human, free to be sons and daughters of God.

The Babe's birth also guarantees our future. The Desire of Ages, He has Immanueled our living. The Desire of all nations, He will come again. The Liberator, victor over sin, victor over death, will come back to reign!

Look into the Babe's face—so soft, so peaceful, so full of mystery.

And with the Wise Men, fall down and adore Him, bring your gifts, offer Him all.

The Baby Grew Up

And Jesus grew in wisdom and stature, and in favor with God and men. Luke 2:52, NIV.

For too many Christians Jesus never grows up. They remain focused on the story of His birth—Bethlehem, the star, the shepherds, the magic, Herod's plot.

The Gospels in two accounts (Matthew and Luke) give us details concerning Jesus' birth and infancy. It is fitting, therefore, that we take time to tell the story annually and reflect on it, always keeping in mind, however, that we do not know the date of His birth. (December 25 certainly is incorrect, because the shepherds stayed out all night with their flocks, which wouldn't have been possible in midwinter.)

Because the Incarnation is wonderful and incredible—the eternal God coming to earth as a baby—many hymns have tried to express the sense of adoration and worship. Some have succeeded more than others; and occasionally the sentiments convey wrong ideas—a Jesus who is so divine that He isn't really like us. And it's a conception that many believers never relinquish.

We need to follow the Gospel story, which takes us far beyond Bethlehem to Galilee. Here Jesus grew up; here He spent most of His public ministry. He was known in Jerusalem as the Galilean (Matt. 21:11).

In Galilee Jesus faced the temptations of youth. In Galilee He chose the twelve, cast out demons, fed the multitudes, stilled the storm, and cleansed the lepers. The Babe of the manger labored, sweated, prayed all night, showed us the meaning of a life that counts.

At the end, Jesus left Galilee for the last journey to Jerusalem. There He suffered and died, taking upon Himself the death that was ours.

Not the Babe of Bethlehem but the Christ of Calvary demands, calls me to follow in His steps.

> "Love so amazing, so divine,
> Demands my soul, my life, my all."
> —Isaac Watts

The Universal Constant

God is love. 1 John 4:16.

T he constant behind the universe, more sure than the stars in their courses, is this truth: God is love.

We live in the midst of a cosmic conflict; our world has gone terribly astray. But when evil has run its full course and sin and sinners are no more, emblazoned in the sky and emblazoned on the hearts of all created beings will be the affirmation that God is love.

We look on nature today. Thorns and thistles spring up from the good earth. Earthquakes and hurricanes, droughts and floods, pests and pestilences, ravage the planet. But "'God is love' is written upon every opening bud, upon every spire of springing grass. The lovely birds making the air vocal with their happy songs, the delicately tinted flowers in their perfection perfuming the air, the lofty trees of the forest with their rich foliage of living green—all testify to the tender, fatherly care of our God and to His desire to make His children happy" (*Steps to Christ*, p. 10).

When Ellen White set out to write the story of our redemption, tracing its beginnings with the rise of evil in heaven itself through the victory won by Jesus Christ to the final restoration of all things, her first words were "'God is love.' 1 John 4:16. His nature, His law, is love. It ever has been; it ever will be. 'The high and lofty One that inhabiteth eternity,' whose 'ways are everlasting,' changeth not. With Him 'is no variableness, neither shadow of turning'" (*Patriarchs and Prophets*, p. 33).

Five books and some 3,600 printed pages later, she laid down her pen. And the final paragraph of the final volume in the Conflict of the Ages series reads: "The great controversy is ended. Sin and sinners are no more. The entire universe is clean. One pulse of harmony and gladness beats through the vast creation. From Him who created all, flow life and light and gladness, throughout the realms of illimitable space. From the minutest atom to the greatest world, all things, animate and inanimate, in their unshadowed beauty and perfect joy, declare that God is love" (*The Great Controversy*, p. 678).

I live by the universal constant: God is love. When my house comes tumbling, God is love. When all else fails, God is love.

I want to live by that constant today. Do you?

Until the Morning Light

If you wake me each morning with the sound of your loving voice, I'll go to sleep each night trusting in you. Ps. 143:8, Message.

Grace is a good night's sleep. Solomon said that the sleep of a laboring man is sweet (Eccl. 5:12). True; but even sweeter is that of the woman or man who sleeps with the expectation of His loving voice in the morning.

In 2004 C. Harry Causey, music director of the National Christian Choir in the United States, wrote and composed a beautiful lullaby, "When I Lay Me Down to Sleep." In part the words read:

> "Keep me in Your care, Lord,
> All through the night.
> Hold me in Your arms, dear Father,
> Till the morning light, until the morning light." *

Interesting, isn't it, how our attitudes toward sleep change over the course of a lifetime. As children, we want to stay up with the "big" people—we're sure we'll miss out on all sorts of good things when they make us go to bed while they stay up, talking and laughing together.

Noelene and I have two wonderful granddaughters, the pride and delight of our eyes. That's the good news; the bad news is that they live overseas. But we get to see them once or twice every year, and we talk often on the telephone.

One night when we called, the older girl answered the telephone. We chatted for maybe 20 minutes; then she said, "Would you like to talk to Jacqui?" So then her 7-year-old sister came on the line. She's a talker—is she a talker! She talked and talked. She got going on riddles. She went on and on, until at last Noelene stopped her with "Jacqui, it must be time for your bath." "Oh, Grandma," she replied, "I already had my bath. I'm in bed!" Beloved rascal, spinning out the conversation and stealing an extra 30 minutes of waking time!

We who are older see sleep differently. We welcome it. We know that a good night's sleep is a gift of grace. Unless Jesus comes back during my lifetime, I shall lie down to sleep for the last, long time. I pray that my eyes will close trusting in Him, my Savior and Lord. He will keep me until the morning light, when He will awaken me with the sound of His loving voice.

---

* Taken from the National Christian Choir's recording *The Heart of a Child*; www.nationalchristianchoir.org; 800-599-4710.

Heaven

Then I saw a new heaven and a new earth, for the first heaven and the first earth had passed away, and there was no longer any sea. Rev. 21:1, NIV.

Through the prophet Isaiah the Lord promised:

"Pay close attention now:
I'm creating new heavens and a new earth.
All the earlier troubles, chaos, and pain
are things of the past, to be forgotten" (Isa. 65:17, Message).

And on the isle of Patmos, John the Beloved, now an old man, the last remaining of the twelve, saw in vision the promise fulfilled:

"I saw Heaven and earth new-created. Gone the first Heaven, gone the first earth, gone the sea. . . . I heard a voice thunder from the Throne: 'Look! Look! God has moved into the neighborhood, making his home with men and women! They're his people, he's their God. He'll wipe every tear from their eyes. Death is gone for good—tears gone, crying gone, pain gone—all the first order of things gone" (Rev. 21:1-4, Message).

My being cries out for God's new order, for the day when grace will reach its grand finale in the divine extravaganza of love, when Eden blooms on earth again and righteousness reigns from pole to pole. I read Isaiah's promise, and my heart cries out *yes!* I read John's vision, and my soul responds *amen!*

Have you ever paused and thought long and hard about heaven? It's good to do so; it will help keep this little life in perspective. "Let your imagination picture the home of the saved," writes Ellen White, "and remember that it will be more glorious than your brightest imagination can portray. In the varied gifts of God in nature we see but the faintest gleaming of His glory" (*Steps to Christ*, pp. 86, 87).

Yet I have to confess that some aspects of heaven baffle me. Life on this earth marches to the drumbeat of time, but not life in the earth made new. There time merges into eternity. Here existence involves exertion and struggle, overcoming; but there? Will heaven be like an unending cruise? I don't think so. Only in the sense of relaxation and freedom from worries that a good cruise brings. But beyond that—*life!*

God is making a new order—the order of heaven. We can trust Him to make it right.

Writing for God

Write this down for the next generation so people not yet born will praise God.
Ps.102:18, Message.

By calling, I am a minister of the gospel; by creative outlet, I am a writer. It's my happy lot from God's gracious hand that often my work and my hobby flow together. For 25 years my ministry has taken a specialized turn in writing and editing. But I was writing long before that—since the seventh grade.

I'm a compulsive writer; I *have* to write. The constraint, the urge, arises not from deadlines (although they are part of my life) but from within. When I'm involved with a major article or paper, the ideas build up inside me—leads, titles, illustrations, changes in order of presentation, how to close—and I don't sleep well. I'll wake up early (that means really early) and get it down on paper. Only when the work is over does my mind settle back down.

Finishing any piece of writing, be it an editorial, something short (like one of the readings of this book), a full-length article, a research paper, or a book manuscript, always leaves me with conflicting feelings. I feel elated, and I feel spent. The creative process pumps me up, but it drains me. After a sustained effort my mind and body need several days, or longer, to return to equilibrium.

Long ago I determined that whatever I wrote would be for God. I'd intentionally abstain from trying to be clever or cute or to impress the reader. I want the Lord and His incredible goodness to be seen with as little of human filter and ego as can be accomplished.

Some of the personally most wonderful moments of my life have come in writing for Him. Articles, editorials, pieces that were just right for the occasion; material, written at breakneck pace that emerged just right with the first draft.

This book itself is a work of grace. I covenanted with the publisher to write the manuscript, then got so busy that I asked for a later deadline. What I didn't realize was that eventually the work would fall due during the most hectic period of my life, when unforeseen major projects fell to my responsibility. What I mean is this: this manuscript shouldn't have been possible. And yet here it is; and I bow my head in amazement and gratitude before God.

This book is about grace. It's more: it's a work that only grace brought into being.

Grace Be With You

The grace of the Lord Jesus be with God's people. Rev. 22:21, NIV.

The letters of the apostle Paul end in similar fashion, "The grace of our Lord Jesus Christ be with you" (Rom. 16:20; 1 Cor. 16:23; Phil. 4:23; 1 Thess. 5:28; 2 Thess. 3:18), with occasional variations such as "The grace of our Lord Jesus Christ be with your spirit" (Gal. 6:18; see also 2 Tim. 4:22) or "Grace be with you" (Col. 4:18; Titus 3:15; see also 1 Tim. 6:21).

And not only Paul; the book of Hebrews, which is Pauline in some sense, also has "grace be with you all" as its last words (Heb. 13:25). Peter's second letter echoes it: "But grow in grace, and in the knowledge of our Lord and Saviour Jesus Christ" (2 Peter 3:18). And the Scriptures close with the final, hopeful words "the grace of the Lord Jesus be with God's people" (Rev. 22:21, NIV).

In view of these last words, I think it likely that the benediction of grace was common among the early Christians. Paul may have coined the expression, but it spread much further.

"Grace be with you!" What a wonderful way for Christians to part. It's a prayer, a wish that the loving favor of God, comforting, but also strong to empower and to keep, will watch over each of us until we meet again. Since Jesus is the one "full of grace," it's almost a prayer that He will be with us.

In the Scriptures we read that believers are *under* grace (Rom. 6:14, 15). Here grace is a shield, a canopy. Once we were "under" law, under its condemnation, but no longer. Now we are under grace.

We also read that we are saved *by* grace (Eph. 2:8) or *through* grace (Acts 15:11). Here grace is an instrument to the accomplishment of God's purposes for us.

Grace is also a gift, something that comes *to* us (as in Rom. 1:7), even God's offer of eternal life, free and abundant, awaiting our taking. And grace is something we can be *in* (2 Tim. 2:1), and *from* which we may fall (Gal. 5:4).

So, my friend, may God's grace be with you, be over you, be in you, now and forever. Amen.

① Forget the past.

- Change
- R.I.P. - Renewed Investment Plan.
③ Face the Future with Faith and Confidence.
    - Keep moving.
    - Fear Not - (365 times in the Bible)
    - Don't let fear overtake you.
    - Faith is the opposite of fear.
    - Courage is not the opp. of fear.
    - Abraham believed God.
    -